Places of special virtue:
megaliths in the Neolithic landscapes of Wales

Vicki Cummings and Alasdair Whittle

Cardiff Studies in Archaeology
Oxbow Books 2004

Published by
Oxbow Books, Park End Place, Oxford OX1 1HN

© Oxbow Books and the individual authors, 2004

ISBN 1 84217 108 9

A CIP record for this book is available from the British Library

Cover image: Pentre Ifan, south-west Wales
Photograph: Vicki Cummings

This book is available direct from
Oxbow Books, Park End Place, Oxford, OX1 1HN
(Phone: 01865-241249; Fax: 01865-794449)

and

The David Brown Book Company
PO Box 511, Oakville, CT 06779, USA
(Phone: 860-945-9329; Fax: 860-945-9468)

and

via our website
www.oxbowbooks.com

Printed in Great Britain by
Information Press
Eynsham

for Frances Lynch

Contents

Preface vii

Acknowledgements ix

Summaries x

List of figures xiv

Chapter 1　The Neolithic in Wales: the context of diversity 1

Chapter 2　Places, monuments and landscapes: ways of seeing 8

Chapter 3　Methodology 17

Chapter 4　The monuments of south-west Wales and their landscape settings 24

Chapter 5　The monuments of north-west Wales and their landscape settings 41

Chapter 6　The monuments of south-east Wales and their landscape settings 56

Chapter 7　Stones that float to the sky: seeing place, myth and history 69

Bibliography 92

Inventory 102

Preface

Debate on the nature of virtually every aspect of the Neolithic period continues to be lively and wide-ranging. How people saw and perceived their landscapes, and how they thought about their worlds in general, have come to be part of that discussion, and this volume is a contribution to arguments being put forward by many colleagues. It is a moot point whether research on the Neolithic period in Wales has lagged behind that in other parts of Britain and Ireland, but it certainly seems to be the case that early Neolithic monuments in Wales, particularly those of west Wales, do not figure as highly as they could in detailed discussions of the beginning of the Neolithic, of the nature of Neolithic worldviews, or of the character of changes through the fourth millennium BC and later. The aim of this volume is to help to redress this balance. The volume works, we hope, at several different spatial and temporal scales, from local place to wider landscape, from region to region, and from specific event to the deep time of mythologies and histories. No single proposition is likely to cover all these perspectives, and we hope to have teased out some of the many dimensions in which Neolithic people may be said to have existed.

The volume is based, first, on the PhD research of Vicki Cummings, funded by the School of History and Archaeology, Cardiff University (Cummings 2001) and secondly, on a wider one-year project in 2001–2, funded by the Board of Celtic Studies of the University of Wales. Vicki has played a major role in designing and executing the one-year project, and the authorship of the chapters reflects our relative contributions to this work. She has visited and carefully recorded all the sites listed in the volume, some in the course of her PhD, which focused on south-west Wales (along with south-west Scotland), or as part of other projects (Cummings *et al.* 2002), and the rest in the course of 2001–2.

Many others have studied the Neolithic megalithic constructions of Wales before us, and this volume reflects their contributions. Prominent among them for over three decades has been Frances Lynch, from one of whose important papers (Lynch 1972, 77) our title is adapted, and to whom this work is respectfully dedicated.

Alasdair Whittle
School of History and Archaeology, Cardiff University

Acknowledgements

Our first and greatest debt is to the two institutions which have funded the research presented here: The Board of Celtic Studies of the University of Wales, and before that, the School of History and Archaeology, Cardiff University. We are very grateful to Professor Geraint Jenkins, Ruth ab Ieuan, Richard Bullen and Peter Lloyd, and to Professor Jonathan Osmond, for their support and help.

Niall Sharples shared the PhD supervision of Vicki Cummings, and has contributed also with subsequent discussion. Chris Fowler, Andy Jones, Hannah Sackett, Steve Trick, Aaron Watson and Howard Williams have helped with fieldwork. Elke Oerter, Anne Tresset and J. Gwynfor Jones kindly translated the summary into German, French and Welsh. All four Welsh Trusts provided information, and a particular debt is owed to George Smith of the Gwynedd Archaeological Trust. Robert Johnston of the University of Wales, Bangor, provided a tour of the Carneddau Hengwm area and information on north Wales.

We are grateful to help from Richard Avent, Sian Rees and Frank Olding in Cadw, and to Mark Lewis for information on Monmouthshire. Chris Barker kindly commented on the inventory. Others have contributed helpful information and discussion, including Richard Bradley, Nic Cook, Hella Eckardt, John Evans, Chris Fowler, Matt Leivers, Maisie Taylor, Colin Richards and Howard Williams. Aled Cooke has helped with all things technical. Our final debt is to Mark Gillings, who has advised and guided us (especially Vicki) through the GIS maze, above and beyond the call of duty.

Radiocarbon dates

All dates are given in calibrated form, using the OxCal 3.5 programme.

Summaries

The Welsh evidence is frequently on the periphery of discussions on the Neolithic. However, it has a rich record of megalithic chambered monuments. Set against a broader theoretical discussion on the significance of the landscape, this volume explores the landscape settings of the megalithic constructions of Wales.

The first chapter begins with a review of the Neolithic evidence from Wales. Instead of seeing Wales as an area which lacks many of the 'classic' components of the Neolithic, it is argued that Wales has its own unique and individual Neolithic which is simply different from the Neolithic found further to the east. It is suggested that this may relate to an essentially mobile existence, with strong links back to the Mesolithic and the Irish Sea sequence. These suggested connections with the west are revisited in the last chapter.

In the second chapter the range of theoretical approaches to landscape is outlined. We begin by exploring the visual nature of place and landscape, and the possibility of different ways of seeing. We review the increasing interest in the role of visual landscapes in prehistory and explore the meanings attached to the landscape, and the values and beliefs invested in it. It is suggested that the landscape can no longer be seen as a neutral backdrop or even just a physical environment. Instead the landscape can be considered a fundamental part of the experience of places. By examining the landscape settings of monuments we explore how people viewed and understood the world in which they lived.

Although there has been considerable debate on the meaning of landscape, so far very little has been written on the methodology for doing a landscape archaeology. In the third chapter a methodology for the investigation of the landscape is outlined, which incorporates a range of methods including GIS. We critically assess the usefulness of a range of techniques, suggesting that it is the combination of strict recording methods and the presentation of a range of different visual diagrams that is the most successful in presenting views and interpretations of the landscape.

This is followed by three detailed case studies, examining the settings of sites in south-west, north-west and south-east Wales, in order to show the regularities, continuities and main emphases in the placing of monuments in the landscape. In each chapter we outline the history of research including the previous classification of the monuments and any excavations. We then detail the specific landscape settings of the monuments, emphasising views of mountains, rivers and the sea, as well as more localised features. This in turn leads us to reassess previous classifications of these sites.

In the final chapter we begin by returning to the issue of the visual nature of landscape archaeology. We begin by tackling the question of visibility in the Neolithic. Using the environmental data from Wales we argue that one of the traditional criticisms of landscape archaeology, that trees would have obscured the view, is too simplistic. Trees would certainly have been present around some of these sites, but in many cases would not have obscured the view all year round, and may even have been used to enhance the views of particular landscape features. Therefore, we support the idea that the visual was a critical part of the experience of these sites and their surrounding landscapes. We also argue that the builders of the portal dolmens in particular may have been more concerned about displaying stones in a striking fashion than creating places for the deposition of the dead. We go on to assess the significance of a variety of landscape features which would have been visible from the monuments, in particular emphasising the mythological and symbolic significance of the sea, rivers and mountains. Finally, we suggest that there were two rather different traditions of monument construction in Wales in the Neolithic. The first is found to the west, represented by portal dolmens which are connected to a broader tradition of monument building found along the Irish Sea and Atlantic seaboard. In contrast, the east of Wales contains a series of long cairns which share significant similarities in setting and form with monuments found to the east. As such, there seem to be different Neolithic traditions to the east and west of Wales, which tie into different histories and origins of the Neolithic to the east and west of Britain.

Résumé *translated by Anne Tresset*

Les sources galloises sont souvent marginales dans les discussions sur le Néolithique. Elles comprennent pourtant un riche corpus de tombes mégalithiques. S'appuyant sur une discussion théorique plus générale sur la signification du paysage, le présent ouvrage explore l'environnement des constructions mégalithiques du Pays de Galles.

Le premier chapitre s'ouvre sur une recension des sources néolithiques galloises. Nous proposons de percevoir le Pays de Galles non pas comme une région ne possédant pas les composantes classiques néolithiques mais comme ayant son propre Néolithique, unique et individuel, en un mot différent de ce que l'on trouve plus à l'Est. Nous suggérons que cela soit lié à une existence essentiellement mobile, fortement enracinée dans le Mésolithique et la séquence de la Mer d'Irlande. Ces liens suggérés avec l'Ouest sont revisités dans le dernier chapitre.

La diversité des approches théoriques est abordée dans le second chapitre. Nous commençons par explorer les caractéristiques visuelles des lieux et du paysage et la possibilité qu'ils aient été vus de manières différentes dans le passé. Nous passons en revue l'intérêt croissant pour le rôle du paysage visuel durant la préhistoire et les significations qui lui sont attachées, ainsi que les valeurs et les croyances qui y sont investies. Il est suggéré que le paysage ne peut plus être considéré comme une toile de fond neutre, ni même comme un environnement seulement physique. Il doit au contraire être perçu comme une part fondamentale de l'expérience des lieux. En examinant la localisation des monuments nous explorons la manière dont les gens voyaient et comprenaient le monde dans lequel ils vivaient.

Bien qu'il y ait eu un débat considérable sur la signification du paysage, très peu a été écrit jusqu'à présent sur la méthodologie à mettre en œuvre pour son étude dans un cadre archéologique. Dans le troisième chapitre, une méthodologie destinée à l'analyse du paysage est exposée, incorporant diverses méthodes, dont le SIG. Nous effectuons une analyse critique d'un certain nombre de techniques, suggérant que c'est une combinaison d'enregistrements précis et de différentes présentations sous forme de diagrammes visuels qui est la plus pertinente pour restituer les vues et les interprétations du paysage.

Ceci est suivi de trois études de cas détaillées, examinant l'environnement de sites du sud-ouest, nord-ouest et sud-est du Pays de Galles, afin de montrer les régularités, les continuités et les principales mises en valeur dans la localisation des monuments au sein du paysage. Nous exposons dans chaque chapitre l'histoire de la recherche, incluant de manière exhaustive la classification antérieure des monuments et les fouilles archéologiques. Nous détaillons ensuite l'environnement des mégalithes, en insistant sur la visibilité des montagnes, rivières et de la mer, ainsi que sur celle de caractéristiques plus locales. Ceci nous amène à revoir la classification proposée antérieurement pour ces sites.

Dans le dernier chapitre, nous commençons par reprendre la question du caractère visuel de l'archéologie du paysage. Nous nous attaquons tout d'abord au problème de la visibilité durant le Néolithique. En utilisant les données environnementales du Pays de Galles, nous postulons que l'une des critiques traditionnelles de l'archéologie du paysage – que les arbres devaient obstruer la vue – est trop simpliste. Les arbres étaient sans aucun doute présents autour de certains de ces sites, mais n'ont dans bien des cas vraisemblablement pas gêné la vue tout au long de l'année, et ont même pu contribuer à mettre en valeur certaines caractéristiques du paysage. Nous défendons donc l'idée que le visuel était une part capitale de l'expérience de ces sites et du paysage qui les environne. Nous suggérons également que les constructeurs des « portal dolmens » en particulier ont pu être plus intéressés par le fait de disposer des pierres d'une manière frappante que par celui de construire un lieu pour y déposer les morts. Nous continuons en analysant la signification d'une variété de caractéristiques du paysage qui devaient être visibles des monuments, mettant particulièrement en valeur la signification mythologique et symbolique de la mer, des rivières et des montagnes. Pour finir, nous concluons qu'il existait deux traditions très différentes de construction de monuments au Pays de Galles durant le Néolithique. La première se trouve à l'Ouest, représentée par les « portal dolmens » qui sont reliés à une tradition plus vaste de construction monumentale, localisée le long de la mer d'Irlande et de la façade Atlantique. De manière tranchée avec ce qui précède, l'Est du pays de Galles possède une série de longs tumulus qui partagent un certain nombre de caractéristiques, dans leur localisation et leur forme, avec les monuments trouvés plus à l'Est. Ainsi, il semble y avoir deux traditions néolithiques différentes au pays de Galles, qui renvoient à deux histoires et deux origines distinctes du Néolithique, respectivement dans l'Est et l'Ouest de la Grande-Bretagne.

Zusammenfassung
translated by Elke Oerter

Das walisische Material wird in der Diskussion über das Neolithikum oft nur am Rande erwähnt, obwohl in Wales eine große Zahl von Megalith Gräbern belegt ist.

Das vorliegende Buch untersucht die Platzierung der walisischen Megalith Gräber innerhalb der Landschaft vor dem Hintergrund einer umfassenderen theoretischen Diskussion der Bedeutung der Landschaft.

Das erste Kapitel beginnt mit einem Überblick über das neolithische Material aus Wales. Anstatt Wales als ein Gebiet zu sehen, in dem viele der 'klassischen' Bestandteile des Neolithikums fehlen, wird hier die Ansicht vertreten, dass Wales sein eigenes und individuelles Neolithikum hat, das sich lediglich von dem weiter östlich zu findenden Neolithikum unterscheidet. Es wird die These aufgestellt, dass dies mit einer im Wesentlichen mobilen Lebensform im Zusammenhang stehen könnte, die enge Verbindungen zum Mesolithikum und zu den Entwicklungen entlang der irischen See hat. Die hier vorgeschlagenen Verbindungen mit dem Westen werden im letzten Kapitel erneut aufgegriffen.

Im zweiten Kapitel wird die Bandbreite der verschiedenen Theorieansätze zur Landschaft umrissen. Dabei werden zunächst die visuelle Beschaffenheit von Ort und Landschaft, sowie die verschiedenen Möglichkeiten, Einblicke in die Vergangenheit zu gewinnen, untersucht. Anschließend wird das zunehmende Interesse an der Rolle visueller Landschaften in der Vorgeschichte kritisch gewertet, und die Bedeutungen, die der Landschaft zugemessen werden, sowie die Werte und Glaubensüberzeugungen mit denen diese ausgestattet wird, werden untersucht.

Es wird die These aufgestellt, dass Landschaft nicht länger als neutrale Kulisse oder gar als rein physische Umgebung gesehen werden kann, sondern als grundlegender Teil der Erfahrung von Orten betrachtet werden sollte. Indem die Platzierung von Monumenten in der Landschaft untersucht wird, wird erforscht wie die Menschen die Welt, in der sie lebten, sahen und verstanden.

Trotz einer beachtlichen Debatte über die Bedeutung der Landschaft wurde bisher sehr wenig zu einer Methodologie der Landschaftsarchäologie geschrieben. Im dritten Kapitel wird eine Methodologie zur Untersuchung der Landschaft skizziert, die eine Vielzahl von Methoden, einschließlich GIS, verbindet.

Die Nützlichkeit einer Reihe von Techniken wird einer kritischen Prüfung unterzogen, wobei die These aufgestellt wird, dass die Kombination genauer Erfassungsmethoden mit der Präsentation einer Reihe verschiedener optischer Diagramme am geeignetsten ist, Sichtweisen und Interpretationen der Landschaft zu vermitteln.

Im Anschluss daran wird anhand von drei detaillierten Fallstudien die Platzierung von Megalith Gräbern im Südwesten, Nordwesten und Südosten von Wales untersucht, um Regelmäßigkeiten, Kontinuitäten und Hauptakzente bei der Platzierung von Monumenten in der Landschaft zu zeigen.

In jedem Kapitel wird ein Abriss der bisherigen Forschungsgeschichte einschließlich der vorherigen Klassifizierung der Monumente und der Grabungsgeschichte gegeben.

Danach wird im Einzelnen auf die besondere Platzierung des Monuments innerhalb der Landschaft eingegangen, wobei die Aussicht auf Berge, Flüsse und Meer, sowie örtlich begrenztere Merkmale besonders hervorgehoben werden.

Auf der Grundlage dieser Ergebnisse werden anschließend frühere Klassifizierungen dieser Stätten erneut überprüft.

Im Abschlusskapitel wird zunächst das Thema der visuellen Natur der Landschaftsarchäologie wieder aufgegriffen. Dabei wird zuerst die Frage nach der Sichtbarkeit im Neolithikum zu beantworten gesucht. Aufgrund der Umweltdaten von Wales lässt sich zeigen, dass einer der traditionellen Kritikpunkte gegenüber der Landschaftsarchäologie, dass Bäume die Sicht versperrt hätten, zu vereinfachend ist. Obwohl man sicherlich davon ausgehen kann, dass einige dieser Stätten von Bäumen umstanden waren, hätten in vielen Fällen die Bäume die Sicht nicht während des ganzen Jahres versperrt, sondern sie wären im Gegenteil möglicherweise sogar dazu eingesetzt worden, die Aussicht auf bestimmte Landschaftsmerkmale zu betonen. Deshalb wird hier die Auffassung unterstützt, dass das Visuelle ein entscheidender Bestandteil der Erfahrung dieser Stätten und der sie umgebenden Landschaften gewesen sei.

Es wird außerdem argumentiert, dass insbesondere beim Errichten von 'Portal Dolmen' das Hauptinteresse der Erbauer weniger darin bestanden haben könnte, Bestattungsstätten zu schaffen, als Steine auf auffällige Weise zur Schau zu stellen.

Im Anschluss daran wird die Bedeutung einer Vielzahl von Landschaftsmerkmalen untersucht, die von den Monumenten aus zu sehen gewesen wären, wobei besonders die mythologische und symbolische Bedeutung von Meer, Flüssen und Bergen hervorgehoben wird. Abschließend wird die These aufgestellt, dass in Wales während des Neolithikums zwei verschiedene Traditionen des Monumentalbaus existierten. Die eine ist im Westen in Form von 'Portal Dolmen' anzutreffen, die in Verbindung zu einer umfassenderen Tradition von Monumentalbauten entlang der an Atlantik und Irische See grenzenden Küste stehen. Im Gegensatz dazu finden sich im Osten von Wales 'long cairns', die was Platzierung und Form betrifft, bedeutende Ähnlichkeit mit Monumenten im Osten aufweisen. Im Grunde genommen scheinen im Osten und Westen von Wales unterschiedliche neolithische Traditionen zu bestehen, die sich in die unterschiedlichen geschichtlichen Entwicklungen und Ursprünge des Neolithikums im Osten und Westen Großbritanniens einfügen.

Crynodeb
Translated by J. Gwynfor Jones

Y mae'r dystiolaeth Gymreig yn aml ar ymylon trafodaethau ar y Neolithig. Sut bynnag, y mae ganddi gofnod cyfoethog o gofadeiladau cellog Megalithig. O'u gosod ar gefndir trafodaeth ddamcaniaethol ehangach ar arwyddocâd y tirwedd, y mae'r gyfrol hon yn archwilio gosodiadau tirweddol adeiladau Megalithig Cymru.

Y mae'r bennod gyntaf yn dechrau gydag arolwg o'r dystiolaeth Neolithig o Gymru. Yn lle gweld Cymru'n rhanbarth sydd heb lawer o gydrannau clasurol y Neolithig, dadleuir bod gan Gymru ei Neolithig unigryw ac unigol ei hun sydd, yn syml, yn wahanol i'r Neolithig a ganfyddir ymhellach i'r dwyrain. Fe awgrymir y gallai hyn ymwneud â bodolaeth sydd, yn ei hanfod, yn symudol a chysylltiadau cryf ganddo'n ymestyn yn ôl i'r Mesolithig a'r olyniaeth ym Môr Iwerddon. Ailymwelir yn y bennod olaf â'r cysylltiadau awgrymedig hyn â'r gorllewin.

Yn yr ail bennod amlinellir amrediad y dull damcaniaethol o fynd i'r afael â thirwedd. Dechreuwn trwy archwilio natur gweledol lle a thirwedd, a'r posibilrwydd fod yna ddulliau gwahanol o weld yn y gorffennol. Adolygwn y diddordeb cynyddol yn swyddogaeth tirweddau gweledol mewn cynhanes, ac archwiliwn yr ystyron a gysylltir â thirwedd, a'r gwerthoedd a'r credoau a fuddsoddwyd ynddo. Awgrymir na ellir gweld tirweddau mwyach fel cefnlen niwtral neu fel amgylchedd ffisegol hyd yn oed. Yn lle hynny, gellir ystyried y tirwedd yn rhan sylfaenol o'r profiad o leoedd. Trwy ymchwilio i osodiadau tirweddol cofadeiladau archwiliwn sut yr edrychodd pobl ar y byd yr oeddynt yn byw ynddo a sut oeddynt yn ei ddeall.

Er bod cryn dipyn o ddadlau wedi bod ar ystyr tirwedd, hyd yma ychydig sydd wedi ei ysgrifennu ar y fethodoleg o drin tirwedd archaeoleg. Yn y drydedd bennod amlinellir y fethodoleg ar gyfer ymchwilio i dirwedd sy'n ymgorffori amrediad o ddulliau yn cynnwys GIS. Yn feirniadol mesurwn werth defnyddioldeb amrediad o dechnegau, sy'n awgrymu mai cyfuniad o ddulliau cofnodi llym a chyflwyno amrediad o ddiagramau gweledol gwahanol sydd fwyaf llwyddiannus wrth gyflwyno safbwyntiau ar y tirwedd a deongliadau ohono.

Dilynir hyn gan dair astudiaeth enghreifftiol fanwl, yn ymchwilio i osodiadau safleoedd yn ne-orllewin, gogledd-orllewin a de-ddwyrain Cymru, er mwyn dangos rheoleidd-dra, parhad a'r prif bwyslais wrth leoli cofadeiladau yn y tirwedd. Ymhob pennod amlinellwn hanes ymchwil yn cynnwys y dosbarthiad blaenorol ar y cofadeiladau ac unrhyw gloddiadau. Yna manylwn ar osodiadau tirwedd arbennig y cofadeiladau, gan bwysleisio golygfeydd o fynyddoedd, afonydd a'r môr yn ogystal â nodweddion mwy lleol. Y mae hyn, yn ei dro, yn ein harwain i ailfesur gwerth dosbarthiadau blaenorol y safleoedd hyn.

Yn y bennod olaf dechreuwn trwy ddychwelyd at fater natur gweledol archaeoleg tirweddol. Dechreuwn trwy ymdrin â chwestiwn gweledigrwydd y Neolithig. Trwy ddefnyddio data amgylcheddol Cymru dadleuwn fod un o'r beirniadaethau traddodiadol ar archaeoleg tirweddol, y byddai coed wedi cuddio'r olygfa, yn rhy syml. Yn sicr, byddai coed wedi bod yn bresennol o gwmpas rhai o'r safleoedd, ond mewn llawer achos ni fyddent wedi cuddio'r olygfa drwy'r flwyddyn gyfan, ac efallai iddynt gael eu defnyddio i gyfoethogi golygfeydd o nodweddion tirweddol arbennig. Felly, cefnogwn y syniad fod y gweladwy yn rhan hanfodol o'r profiad o'r safleoedd hyn a'u tirweddau amgylchynol. Dadleuwn hefyd y gallai adeiladwyr y cromlechi porth yn arbennig ymwneud mwy ag arddangos meini mewn dull trawiadol na chreu mannau ar gyfer gosod y meirw. Awn ymlaen i fesur gwerth arwyddocâd amrywiaeth o nodweddion tirweddol a fyddai wedi bod yn weladwy o'r cofadeiladau, gan bwysleisio'n arbennig arwyddocâd mytholegol a sumbolaidd y môr, yr afonydd a'r mynyddoedd. Yn olaf, awgrymwn fod yna draddodiadau adeiladwaith cofadeiladol pur wahanol yn y Neolithig yng Nghymru. Canfyddir y cyntaf i'r gorllewin, wedi'i gynrychioli gan gromlechi porth a gysylltir â thraddodiad ehangach o adeiladu cofadeiladau a ganfyddir ar hyd môr Iwerddon ac arfordir Iwerydd. Mewn cyferbyniad, cynhwysa dwyrain Cymru gyfres o feini hir sy'n rhannu cyffelybiaethau mewn gosodiad a ffurf â chofadeiladau a ganfyddir i'r dwyrain. Fel y cyfryw, ymddengys fod gwahanol draddodiadau Neolithig i ddwyrain a gorllewin Cymru, sy'n clymu â hanesau a tharddiadau gwahanol y Neolithig i ddwyrain a gorllewin Prydain.

List of Figures

Figure 1.1 Map of Wales, showing sites mentioned in chapter 1. Small black dots with white centres are the chambered tombs.

Figure 1.2 Plan of Clegyr Boia (after Williams 1952).

Figure 1.3 The wooden structure underneath the cairn at Gwernvale (after Britnell and Savory 1984).

Figure 1.4 Distribution of southern Welsh axes (Groups VIII, XIII and XXIII) in Wales (after Clough and Cummins 1988).

Figure 1.5 Distribution of northern Welsh axes (Groups VII and XXI) in Wales (after Clough and Cummins 1988).

Figure 1.6 Distribution of axes from elsewhere (Groups I, VI and IX) in Wales (after Clough and Cummins 1988).

Figure 3.1 A schematic representation of the landscape setting around the King's Quoit, south-west Wales which represents how the landscape looks to all points of the compass when standing at the monument. This can be viewed next to a plan of the monument which can show the orientation of the landscape in relation to the monument.

Figure 3.2 A GIS viewshed of the King's Quoit, south-west Wales. The black area is the part of the landscape visible from the monument.

Figure 3.3 The DEM of Wales, with the monuments marked as black spots with white centres.

Figure 3.4 The landscape settings of a number of Bronze Age cairns in south-west Wales. These views contrast with the settings of the monuments.

Figure 3.5 Control samples taken around Carn Wnda. At the centre is the view from Carn Wnda itself, and to the north, south, east and west the views taken in those directions at 60 paces from the site (approx 50m).

Figure 3.6 The site of Llech y Dribedd with a series of control points around the monument.

Figure 3.7 The landscape setting around Pentre Ifan (left) and the landscape from the tail of the long cairn at Pentre Ifan (right). From the tail of the long cairn the Preselis are no longer visible.

Figure 3.8 The viewshed from Cist Cerrig, north-west Wales, suggests that the mountains around Ardudwy are visible from the site. However, a visit to the monument shows that this is not the case (see embedded landscape schematic).

Figure 4.1 Distribution map of the monuments in south-west Wales. Dark shading indicates land over 1000ft (304m).

Figure 4.2 The 'classic' portal at Pentre Ifan.

Figure 4.3 The early Neolithic pot from Carreg Samson (after Lynch 1975a).

Figure 4.4 The rock outcrops visible on the horizon from Pentre Ifan.

Figure 4.5 The Great Treffgarne rocks are visible on the skyline from Garn Turne.

Figure 4.6 Carn Wnda stands up against rocky outcrops.

Figure 4.7 Carn Ingli visible behind Llech y Dribedd.

Figure 4.8 GIS control samples from Llech y Dribedd. The top left image is the viewshed from the monument, with the schematic representation of this view top right. Bottom left is a viewshed taken 200m to the north of the monument. From here it is no longer possible to see the Preselis. Bottom right is the viewshed 200m to the west of the monument, and from here it is no longer possible to see the sea.

Figure 4.9 Schematic views of Pentre Ifan. Left is the view from the chamber, right is the view from the tail-end of the long cairn. The tail of the cairn is set downslope from the chamber and from this point the Preselis can no longer be seen on the horizon. Just beyond the tail the ground drops away quite steeply meaning that the monument as well as the outcrops of Carnedd Meibion Owen would no longer be visible when approaching from this direction.

Figure 4.10 The outcrops on the summit of Carn Meini.

Figure 4.11 The stone circle of Gors Fawr with Carn Meini in the background to the right.

Figure 4.12 Control samples from Garn Turne. From the site itself the Preseli mountains are not visible, but a few metres uphill of the façade and they are visible.

Figure 4.13 GIS control samples from White House. The top image is the viewshed from White House. From this

List of Figures

site one can clearly see the sea and the Preselis. However, 500m to the west (bottom left) or 500m to the south (bottom right) this view of the sea is lost, as is the view of the Preselis to the west.

Figure. 4.14 The King's Quoit overlooks the sea at Manorbier.

Figure 4.15 Coetan Arthur with Ramsey Island in the distance.

Figure 4.16 Dinas Head.

Figure 4.17 The landscape settings of the stone circles of Gors Fawr (left) and Meini Gwyr (right).

Figure 4.18 The distinctive capstones at Carreg Coetan and Llech y Dribedd (after Barker 1992).

Figure 4.19 Plans of Cerrig y Gof, Pembrokeshire (top), Mull Hill, Isle of Man (bottom left) and Cairnderry, south-west Scotland (bottom right) (after Barker 1992; Burrow 1997 and Henshall 1972).

Figure 5.1 Distribution map of the monuments in north-west Wales. Dark shading indicates land over 1000ft (304m).

Figure 5.2 The first phase chamber at Dyffryn Ardudwy.

Figure 5.3 From the site of Hen Drefor there is a clear view of Snowdonia.

Figure 5.4 Viewsheds from around Hen Drefor. The image to the left is 500m to the north from the monument. Most of the views of the mountains are lost as well as the view of the sea. The centre image is the view from the monument itself. The image to the right is 500m to the south. Here the view of the sea is maintained, but all views of mountains are lost.

Figure 5.5 Holyhead Mountain, visible behind the final phase chamber at Trefignath.

Figure 5.6 The mountains visible from Bachwen.

Figure 5.7 The peak of Moelfre, aligned on the lateral chambers at Carnedd Hengwm North.

Figure 5.8 The viewshed from Bryn Celli Ddu, showing the visibility of the sea.

Figure 5.9 Maen y Bardd, with clear views over the Afon Conwy.

Figure 5.10 The outcrops beneath and around Din Dryfol.

Figure 5.11 The restricted view at Penarth.

Figure 5.12 Capel Garmon, in the Conwy valley.

Figure 5.13 Control samples taken around Barclodiad y Gawres. Just 50m to the north (top), south (bottom), west (far left) or east (far right) radically changes the view of the surrounding landscape when compared with the view from the monument itself (centre).

Figure 6.1 Distribution map of the monuments in south-east Wales. Dark shading indicates land over 1000ft (304m).

Figure 6.2 The Black Mountains escarpment, as visible from Clyro.

Figure 6.3 The long mound at Penywyrlod Talgarth is aligned on the edge of Mynydd Troed.

Figure 6.4 From Ty Illtyd there are clear views of the Brecon Beacons.

Figure 6.5 The wide ranging views from Arthur's Stone on the Gower.

Figure 6.6 The view of the Severn from Heston Brake.

Figure 6.7 The skylined profile of Heston Brake, seen from the north.

Figure 6.8 The enclosed setting at Parc le Breos Cwm.

Figure 6.9 The viewshed from Little Lodge, showing intervisibility with Pipton. Parts of the landscape visible from the site are shown in white.

Figure 6.10 The chamber at St Lythans. The landscape around this site consists of gently rolling hills.

Figure. 7.1 The woodland setting of Gwal y Filiast, south-west Wales.

Figure. 7.2 Carreg Samson, south-west Wales.

Figure. 7.3 Four different views of the capstone at Llech y Dribedd, south-west Wales.

Figure. 7.4 Carreg Coetan in south-west Wales.

Figure. 7.5 The 'floating' capstone at Pentre Ifan, facing uphill.

Figure. 7.6 The dolmen of Maen y Bardd, north-west Wales.

Figure. 7.7 The viewshed from Ty Isaf, with parts of the landscape visible marked in white.

Figure. 7.8 The long cairn at Penywyrlod, Talgarth.

Figure. 7.9 The view of Table Mountain and the Black Mountains from Garn Goch.

Figure. 7.10 The passage grave of Bryn Celli Ddu.

Figure. 7.11 The view of Snowdonia from Bodowyr.

Figure. 7.12 The mountains on the Lleyn peninsula, from Mynydd Cefn Amwlch.

Figure. 7.13 Mountains emerge through the cloud.

Figure. 7.14 The wide-ranging views of the valley from the mountain.

Figure. 7.15 Mountains appearing and disappearing in cloud.

List of Figures

Colour plate 1 The summit of Carn Meini, Preselis, south-west Wales.

Colour plate 2 Carreg Coetan with the Afon Nyfer visible to the left.

Colour plate 3 One of the chambers at Mynydd Llangynderyn, Carmarthenshire, which stands against outcrops.

Colour plate 4 Carreg Samson, south-west Wales.

Colour plate 5 Pentre Ifan, south-west Wales.

Colour plate 6 The distinctive summit of Carn Llidi on St. David's peninsula, south-west Wales.

Colour plate 7 Snowdonia, as seen from Bodowyr.

Colour plate 8 Plas Newydd with Snowdonia in the distance.

Colour plate 9 Bryn Celli Ddu, with the large outcrop visible to the left of the monument.

Colour plate 10 The Black Mountain escarpment.

Colour plate 11 Parc le Breos Cwm, Gower.

Colour plate 12 St Lythans, near Cardiff.

Colour plate 13 The view of Carn Ingli through trees in the summer.

Colour plate 14 The view of Carn Ingli through trees in the winter.

Colour plate 15 The viewshed from the Devil's Quoit, south-west Wales, with the parts of the landscape visible from the site in green.

(All photographs and images by Vicki Cummings).

1 The Neolithic in Wales: the context of diversity

Vicki Cummings and Alasdair Whittle

Introduction

The aim of this chapter is to suggest a context for the monuments that are the principal focus of this volume. It is not necessary here to summarise again the detail of all the Neolithic evidence from Wales, as this has already been presented recently (Lynch 2000a; Peterson 1999). Instead, we can focus on the character of the Welsh Neolithic as it is understood in relation to the Neolithic in the rest of Britain and Ireland. Not long ago, it might have been sufficient to apply general models based on the evidence from Britain and Ireland as a whole, but it has become increasingly clear that as well as practices held in common there was considerable diversity across these areas from the beginning of the Neolithic onwards. For example, a greater number of structures, some perhaps residential, has been found in Ireland than elsewhere (Cooney 2000), as well as stone-walled field enclosures (Caulfield *et al.* 1998), while there are also stone-built houses in northern Scotland (Barclay 1996), which have led to strong suggestions of a more sedentary existence than has often been argued in recent years with respect to the southern British evidence (e.g. Thomas 1999). Differing views on the processes behind the beginnings of the Neolithic coincide to some extent with these positions, opinion in Ireland and to some extent in Scotland more strongly supporting the colonisation hypothesis (e.g. Barclay 2001; Cooney 2000; Schulting 1998; 2000; Schulting and Richards 2002b) than the consensus (at least until recently) in favour of acculturation in southern Britain and elsewhere (Thomas 1999; Whittle 1996). Even within a given region, there may also be diversity, evidenced for example in the varying patterns of isotopic values in recent studies of diet from samples across southern Britain (Richards 2000; Richards and Hedges 1999).

How then can the Neolithic in Wales, one part of western Britain, be characterised in order to set the scene for the study of monuments and their landscape settings which follows? We suggest as working hypotheses that there was much that was distinctive about the western part of Wales: that beginnings may have been largely to do with the reaction of indigenous communities to wider events and processes; that settlement may have been largely mobile or semi-mobile, or at least not based on long-term sedentism; and that practices of monument building owed most to regional rather than external traditions and belief systems. The Neolithic in Wales resembles that of Ireland, or perhaps south-west Scotland, far more than that of southern Britain, but it is far from being a pale imitation of what lay across or at the top of the Irish Sea, and significant differences in terms of beginnings and the character of settlement have already been mooted.

Some of these arguments will be developed in chapter 7, but here we set out the case for the working view that we have to deal with a distinctive set of practices on the eastern side of the Irish Sea. The information available is of mixed quality.

A brief history of research

It might seem legitimate to blame two factors for the present state of the evidence: the dominant research traditions in Wales, and a comparatively low level of activity in recent years. But this argument is unconvincing, and may serve only to obscure the emergent case for another set of regionally distinctive practices within the wider British and Irish setting.

It is certainly the case that for many years the Welsh Neolithic was considered the result of colonisation, invasion or settlement from elsewhere, but at least in earlier years this was only part of the broader trend of assigning the beginnings of the Neolithic to European sources (e.g. Childe 1940; Clark 1966; Daniel 1950; Hawkes 1940; Piggott 1954). There has been a great deal of debate concerning the precise origins of the Welsh Neolithic, with suggestions including southern Europe (Daniel 1941), the Cotswold-Severn region (Davies 1945) and Ireland (Daniel and Powell 1949; Grimes 1965; Lynch 1976). The notion that the Neolithic arrived in Wales as a result of settlers has persisted in what we could call the Welsh literature. In 1980, Savory still saw the Neolithic in Wales as the result of colonisers from Wessex and Ireland, and Frances Lynch (2000a, 43) continues to argue for the colonisation of Wales, particularly from the Irish Sea area, although she suggests that the indigenous populations of central and north-east Wales remained dominant. But it is hard to see how this dominant interpretive stance has affected the gathering of evidence; indeed there has been a distinguished record of investigation of megaliths, stone circles, stone axe sources and where available settlements, within this research tradition (summarised in Lynch 2000a).

Has the pace of fresh field investigations fallen behind

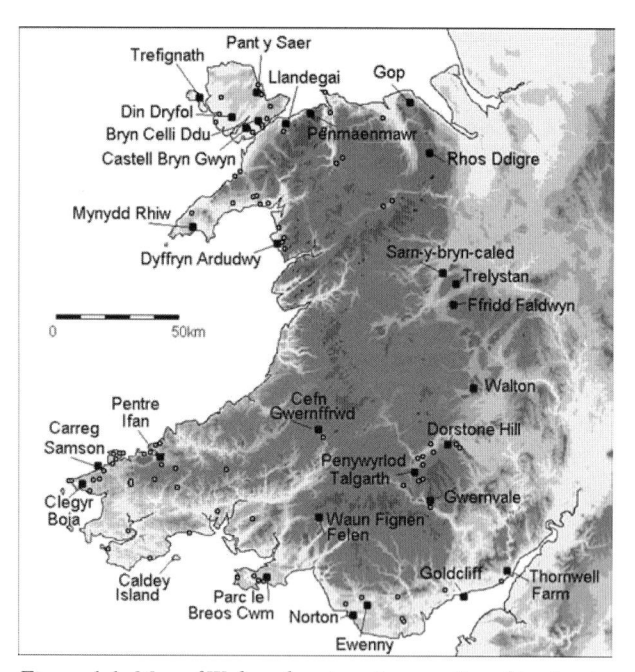

Figure 1.1 Map of Wales, showing sites mentioned in chapter 1. Small black dots with white centres are the chambered tombs. Reproduced by kind permission of Ordnance Survey. © Crown copyright NC/03/20516.

that set in recent times in southern and other parts of England, in parts of Scotland and in Ireland? It is certainly true that some parts of Britain have seen bursts of investigation, in southern England for example from the Somerset Levels to the monument complexes of Wessex, the Upper Thames valley and the western and southern fen edge of East Anglia; parts of northern Scotland, and parts of Ireland are further examples of recent concentrated research. But it is also the case that there are plenty of regions within England, Scotland and Ireland where there has not been quite the same level of research activity, or at least the same kind of prominent investigations.

The 1960s and 1970s saw a number of important excavations of Neolithic sites in Wales (Figure 1.1), including the monuments of Dyffryn Ardudwy (Powell 1973) and Carreg Samson (Lynch 1975a) and their results were important in debates about the Neolithic in Britain and Ireland as a whole (e.g. Corcoran 1969a; Powell *et al.* 1969). The 1980s saw the important publication of the excavations at Trefignath and Din Dryfol chambered tombs in north Wales (Smith and Lynch 1987) and Penywyrlod Talgarth and Gwernvale in south-east Wales (Britnell and Savory 1984), based on excavations undertaken in the 1970s. In the 1990s Gibson undertook significant excavations at the Sarn-y-bryn-caled complex and in the Walton Basin (Gibson 1994a; 1999a; 1999b), and Edmonds and Thomas investigated the setting of Bryn Celli Ddu on Anglesey, in the process discovering the ditched enclosure of Bryn Celli Wen (Thomas 2001). Among other research projects, Clegyr Boia has been reassessed (Vyner 2001). One of the authors is currently engaged, with Michael Wysocki, in a reassessment of the mortuary deposits in the monuments of south-east Wales (Wysocki and Whittle 2000) as well as obtaining a new set of radiocarbon dates for these sites (some of which are referred to in chapters 4 and 6). Research on the upper Severn foreshore has also provided fresh evidence for the Neolithic setting (Bell *et al.* 2000), as well as for the preceding late Mesolithic context. It is predominantly rescue work which produces new Neolithic sites at the present time, such as the chambered tomb at Thornwell Farm in Chepstow (Children and Nash 1996), and it is clear from the AHRB-funded project currently being conducted that the significance of small-scale investigations and evaluations has been undervalued across Britain as a whole (Richard Bradley, *pers. comm.*). Aerial photography has also produced results, from a possible causewayed enclosure at Norton at the west end of the Vale of Glamorgan (Burrow *et al.* 2001; Oswald *et al.* 2001) to the later inland complexes of the Walton basin and Sarn-y-bryn-caled in the Hafren valley (Gibson *et al.* 2001). Continued survey from the air may have most effect in lowland parts of eastern and southern Wales.

The state of play is clearly mixed. At the time of writing, Cadw is sponsoring both the creation of a research agenda for prehistory as a whole in Wales, as well as a review of funerary and ritual monuments (Richard Avent, *pers. comm.*; Sian Rees, *pers. comm.*), and further momentum may be predicted for the future. Two examples from recent fieldwork serve as a final example of what may lie ahead. A ditched and banked enclosure at Beech Court Farm, Ewenny, in the Vale of Glamorgan, was first seen from the air in 1989; it is some 150 by 200 m (Graves-Brown 1998). Recent rescue excavations have shown the ditches to be interrupted, with enhanced terminals; there is nothing diagnostic in primary fills (Yates 2000; Adam Yates, *pers. comm.*). The only certainly dateable context so far is a post-pit in the interior, from the early second millennium BC. It may be that the enclosure as a whole will be proved to be of this date or later, but at this stage an earlier date cannot perhaps be excluded. Likewise, the beginning of intensive survey of the area from Strumble Head to the Preselis, in the south-west, has already led to the recognition of a string of enclosures, possibly of Neolithic date, and if so, matching perhaps those of Carn Brea and Helman Tor in south-west England (Darvill and Wainwright 2002). In the case of Garn Fawr, 'eroded stone walls link natural rock outcrops to form an irregular polygonal enclosure 150x100m' (Darvill and Wainwright 2002, 623). If such irregularity has prevented recognition thus far, further fieldwork must surely produce more surprises.

The case for difference

From this perspective, we can look briefly at differing categories of evidence in support of our working hypotheses of indigenous beginnings, mobile settlement, and distinctive practices and traditions of monument building.

Beginnings

The wider setting of the late fifth and early fourth millennia BC will be considered in more detail in chapter 7. Here we simply note the lack of direct evidence in the western part of Wales in support of colonisation. The monuments themselves, which will be discussed throughout this volume, can be assigned to different traditions or groupings: portal dolmens; earth-fast monuments; passage graves; and so on. Apart from the passage graves, which presumably belong later than the very beginnings of the Neolithic, the western monuments do not have obvious direct continental counterparts. The portal dolmens must indeed be related to those in Ireland, but it is not immediately obvious that the relationship is explicable only in terms of a west-to-east colonisation.

Pottery traditions are mixed (see Peterson 1999). The vast majority of pottery comes from the chambered cairns, though the monuments of south-east and north-west Wales have produced considerably more pottery than the megaliths in the south-west, with 31 different vessels represented at Gwernvale in south-east Wales, for example, in contrast to only one from Carreg Samson, Pembrokeshire (Lynch 1976). The early Neolithic pottery from western Wales is often assigned to the 'Irish Sea Ware Group' which is a group of simple, frequently undecorated pots (Lynch 1976). This includes pottery from Pant y Saer, Trefignath and Pentre Ifan. One of the largest assemblages from Wales comes from Clegyr Boia. This assemblage is a series of early Neolithic bowls, some of which belong to the Irish Sea Ware tradition, while others are like Hembury pottery from south-west England (Lynch 1969a; Peterson 1999). There is no clear or dominant link in these assemblages of mixed style to the carinated Grimston bowl, which has been argued to recur in many other parts of Britain and Ireland in early Neolithic contexts (Herne 1988).

One category of evidence that perhaps sits less easily with a hypothesis of indigenous acculturation is isotopic analysis. Schulting (1998) has shown that human bones from coastal or near-coastal Neolithic sites in western Britain do not have a marine dietary signature, and this 'slighting of the sea' seems on the present, admittedly limited, evidence to extend to Wales, including Parc le Breos Cwm on the Gower (Richards in Whittle and Wysocki 1998), and Caldey Island (Schulting and Richards 2002a). We discuss the implications of this in chapter 7.

The monuments of south-east Wales have long been related to those of adjacent England, and the possible enclosure at Norton in the Vale of Glamorgan, already noted, seems to serve to underline that connection. It is not clear, once again, that such a relationship need imply colonisation, but at the very least the different orientation of affiliation and cultural memory is significant. Different pasts and different beginnings may be considered for western and south-east Wales.

Settlement

The evidence for permanent settlement in Wales remains ambiguous, despite the claim that people were living, for the most part, in houses (Lynch 2000a, 42). Clegyr Boia in south-west Wales is a good case in point (Figure 1.2). Excavations found traces of three huts, a firepit and midden, as well as ramparts surrounding the hilltop (Williams 1953; Vyner 2001). Some of these ramparts seem to be Neolithic in date (Vyner 2001, 82) although most of the defences probably date to the Iron Age. Clegyr Boia has been compared to Carn Brea (Mercer 1981) in Cornwall (Lynch 1976, 65; Vyner 2001, 84), although it is not on the same scale, and to Lough Gur in County Limerick (Lynch 2000a, 49). The evidence from Clegyr Boia, however, seems to suggest a short occupation phase, which ended with the burning of the site, and the recent

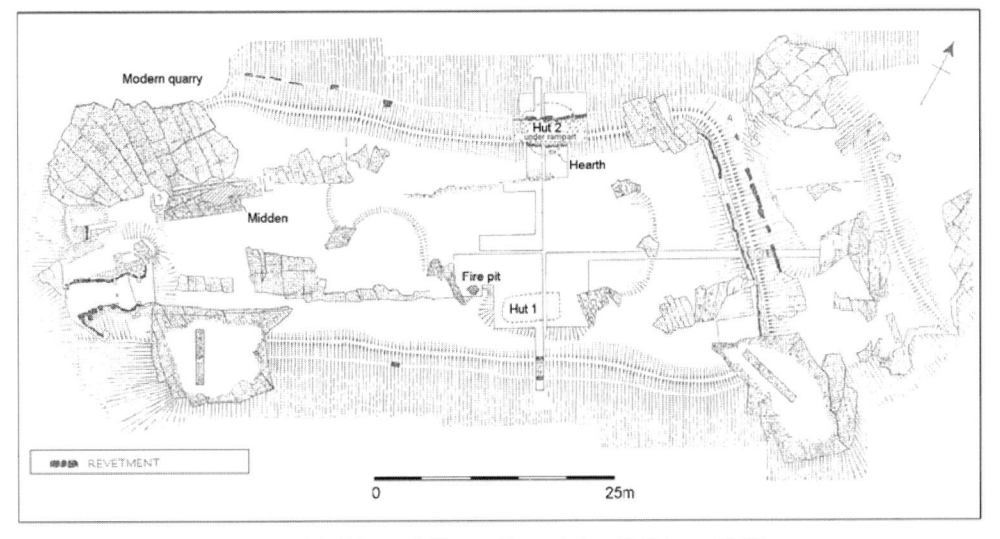

Figure 1.2 Plan of Clegyr Boia (after Williams 1952).

reconsideration of the site suggests only short-lived, episodic or seasonal occupation (Vyner 2001, 88).

A similar picture of small and possibly transient occupations may characterise settlement activity from other parts of Wales. In the upper Hafren valley in mid Wales the sites of Ffridd Faldwyn (O'Neil 1942), Y Breiddin (Musson *et al*. 1991; O'Neil 1937) and Trelystan (Britnell 1982) suggest short-lived, if not ephemeral occupations (see also Leivers 1999, chapter two). Dorstone Hill in the Black Mountains of south-east Wales is generally considered an occupation site (Olding 2000) as it has produced over 3000 flints, including leaf-shaped arrowheads and 54 axe fragments. However, the lack of any structures suggests that this site may have been used by mobile or transitory groups of people, returning time and again to a familiar spot in the landscape.

Houses, or at least structures, have indeed been found elsewhere in Wales. An array of postholes was found at Llandegai which the excavator suggested represented at least two buildings (Houlder 1968, 219) and a rectilinear wooden building 5m long by 2.5m wide was also found underneath the chambered cairn of Gwernvale in the Black Mountains (Britnell and Savory 1984). The context of that structure underneath a monument could suggest that its categorisation as a domestic building would be simplistic; alternative uses or functions can at least be envisaged, including something akin to wooden mortuary structures found elsewhere in the country (Kinnes 1992). At any rate, as in southern Britain as a whole, such evidence is generally rare, and such structures as have been found are normally on their own and have little evidence for repair or prolonged use.

The absence of permanent settlement or dwellings, then, so far contrasts strongly with the picture now emerging in eastern Ireland and northern Scotland. But instead of interpreting this lack of houses or permanent settlements as negative evidence, we could instead explore what this tells us about the nature of Neolithic settlement in Wales. This may have been an area where people did not create or use settlements of long duration, instead perhaps moving around the landscape in a structured way; tethered mobility has been one suggested label (Whittle 1997). There was probably considerable variation over time. However, lithic scatters seem to suggest an element of continuity from previous Mesolithic communities. Neolithic lithic scatters from south-west Wales, for example, are found in the same parts of the landscape as those dating to the Mesolithic, which supports the notion of considerable continuity between these two periods (Cummings 2001; Tilley 1994, 87). This is a pattern echoed in south-east Wales (Olding 2000, 9).

Many locations in Wales have provided environmental data (Caseldine 1990). In the south at Goldcliff in the Gwent Levels, there are three main phases of activity in the Neolithic, characterised by woodland clearance, the maintenance of grassland, and then forest regeneration (Bell *et al*. 2000; Smith and Morgan 1989). A similar pattern can be found at Waun Fignen Felen in inland Powys where there was a series of small-scale clearances from the Mesolithic to the Neolithic (Smith and Cloutman 1988). And from the site of Cefn Gwernffrwd in upland mid-Wales there is evidence of several episodes of interference with the vegetation marked by charcoal layers and peaks in grassland species (Chambers 1983). From this admittedly scattered evidence we could suggest that the Neolithic human impact on the vegetation in Wales was recurrently characterised by small-scale activity which created short-lived clearances (Caseldine 1990).

Within this possible pattern, people may have made use of many different parts of the landscape. There is some evidence for Neolithic activity in natural places, particularly caves and rock shelters. The use of natural places in the Neolithic is increasingly coming to light across Britain as a whole, particularly in relation to the use of these places for the disposal of human remains (Bradley 2000; Barnatt and Edmonds 2002; Tilley and Bennett 2001). The well-known site of Gop Cave in north Wales (Boyd Dawkins 1901) produced human remains, and elsewhere in north Wales, the Rhos Ddigre caves have also produced human remains mixed with animal bone, pottery and stone artefacts (Boyd Dawkins 1874; Leivers 1999). The record of the use of natural places is not restricted to north Wales. In south-west Wales, Neolithic human remains have been found in the Caldey Island caves (Lacaille and Grimes 1955) and Neolithic human bones were recovered from Ifton Quarries near Newport (Knowles 1909). The production of stone axes, noted below, is another form of activity in the landscape.

As already noted several times above, there need have been no uniformity of practice, even within quite small areas. In one limited study of human teeth from mortuary assemblages from the long cairns (and therefore possibly a not very representative sample) around the Black Mountains in south-east Wales, it was found that there was considerable variation in a small area (Wysocki and Whittle 2000). Rates of caries, enamel hypoplasia, tooth loss, crowding and eruption all seem to have varied. Though the sample is small, these variations can tentatively be connected with variations in subsistence, diet and food processing (Hillson 1996; Larsen 1997; Wysocki and Whittle 2000, 592–3). The people deposited in the various long cairns seem to have made different use of carbohydrates and meat (cf. Richards 2000; Richards and Hedges 1999), and to have been subject to varying nutritional deficiencies and physiological stresses.

Monuments

Although there is a rich array in Wales of what are conventionally called chambered tombs, many of the other monumental forms found in the rest of Britain and Ireland are lacking. In many cases this has simply led to Wales being ignored in general considerations of the period, instead of enabling a debate on why Neolithic people in

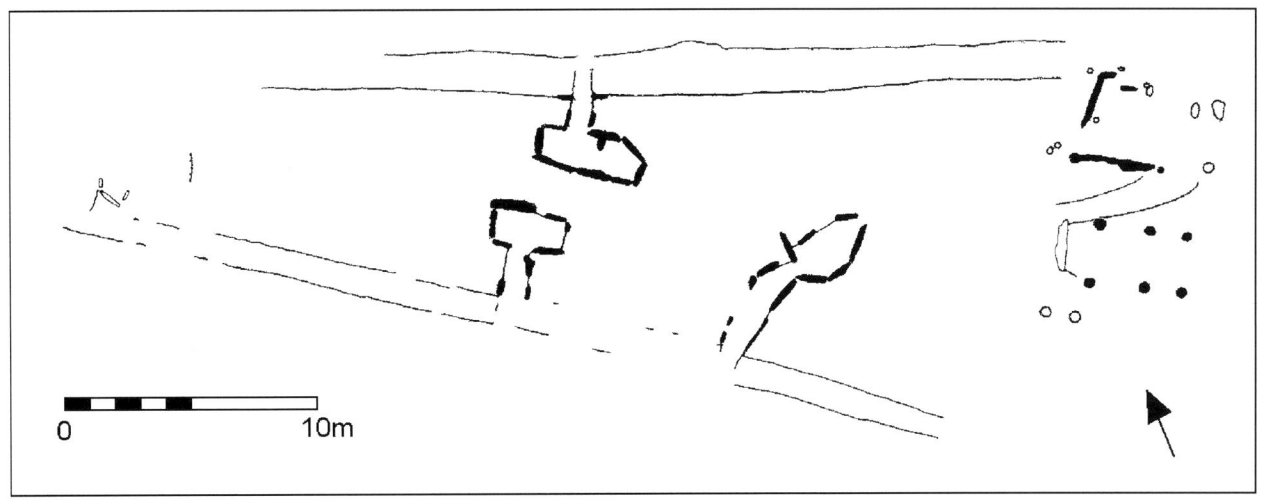

Figure 1.3 The wooden structure underneath the cairn at Gwernvale (after Britnell and Savory 1984).

this area chose to build only some of the suite of monuments potentially available to them. The general absence of classic causewayed enclosures, henges, cursus monuments and pre-megalithic wooden mortuary structures seems to have marginalised the Welsh record from many discussions in the wider literature on the Neolithic.

It is worth briefly detailing some of the absences, from later to earlier phases. There are two henges at Llandegai in north Wales (Houlder 1968), and the chambered tomb of Bryn Celli Ddu on Anglesey may have been built over a henge-like monument, although this remains contested (Eogan 1983). Another potential henge site is that of Castell Bryn-Gwyn, also on Anglesey (Lynch 1991, 100). Harding and Lee (1987) list only another five sites in the whole of Wales which may be henges. Wales contains only five percent of the stone circles of the British Isles (Burl 1979, 254) and as such they rarely figure in considerations of the wider phenomenon (e.g. Bradley 1998c; Watson 2000), the focus being instead on the large circles found in the Peak District, Cumbria, Wessex and Orkney. Indeed, some of the Welsh circles are almost certainly Bronze Age in date, including the Penmaenmawr circles (Griffiths 1960; Lynch 1995). Similarly, only three definite cursus monuments have been found in Wales, each less than 1 km long, at Walton (Gibson 1999a), Sarn-y-bryn-caled (Gibson 1994a) and Llandegai (Houlder 1968). Gibson (1999a, 130) lists another five possible sites.

The case for difference is not confined to the middle and later parts of the Neolithic. No certain causewayed enclosures are known in Wales, although Norton, noted above, is a candidate (Burrow *et al.* 2001), and Bryn Celli Wen may be part of a wider diversity of enclosures in western Britain as a whole (Darvill and Thomas 2001; Thomas 2001). A number of monuments in southern Britain have evidence of wooden structures which pre-date subsequent earth or stone phases (Kinnes 1992). Similar monuments have been found further afield such as Lochhill and Slewcairn in south-west Scotland (Masters 1973; 1981). As yet, this type of evidence has not been found in Wales, with the exception of Gwernvale (Figure 1.3). Strikingly, none of the excavated monuments in western Wales have produced evidence of wooden structures, although pre-cairn activity was found at Trefignath on Holyhead. The absence of pre-cairn wooden structures might in part be the result of small-scale excavations or of excavation technique. But it may also be indicative of a different set of traditions at the beginning of the Neolithic, particularly in the west of the country. This is a theme we shall return to in the final chapter.

In contrast, Wales has a notable record of stone-built chambered monuments, many very well-preserved. We have included 104 definite or probable Neolithic monuments in this study, and more have been lost (see Barker 1992 and also Fleming 1999). The vast majority of sites are found in clusters in the south-west, north-west and south-east of Wales, and represent some of the densest concentrations of megaliths in Britain and Ireland as a whole. As already noted and long discussed, a wide variety of different monument styles is represented which includes portal dolmens, passage graves, Cotswold-Severn long cairns and a number which defy traditional classification systems. We discuss these in more detail in chapters 4–6. What emerge as particularly distinctive are the traditions in the western part of Wales, in both the south-west and north-west. It is worth stressing too that significant parts of mid- and eastern Wales appear to have no early Neolithic monuments at all. It does not seem to be the case that these were 'empty quarters', and a further distinctive worldview is implied. A parallel situation could be that of south-west Ireland in the early Neolithic (Cooney 2000). But the focus of this volume is on the three areas of Wales with megalithic concentrations.

It is worth drawing attention here to another part of the Welsh Neolithic record, which is often treated separately from megaliths: the production of stone axes (Figure 1.4–1.6). This documents not only activity in the landscape, as

6   *Vicki Cummings and Alasdair Whittle*

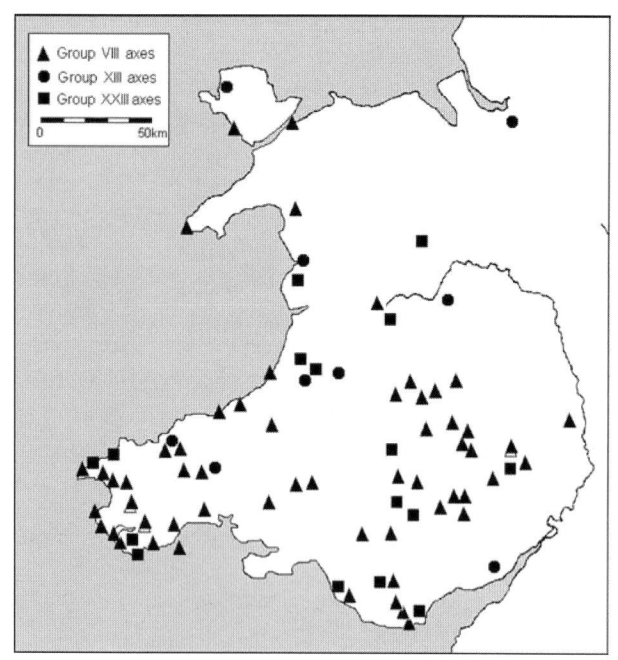

Figure 1.4 Distribution of southern Welsh axes (Groups VIII, XIII and XXIII) in Wales (after Clough and Cummins 1988).

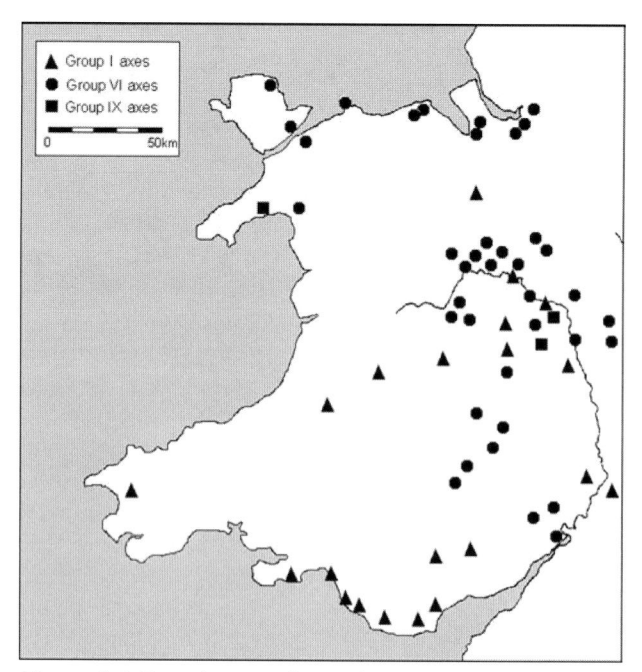

Figure 1.6 Distribution of axes from elsewhere (Groups I, VI and IX) in Wales (after Clough and Cummins 1988).

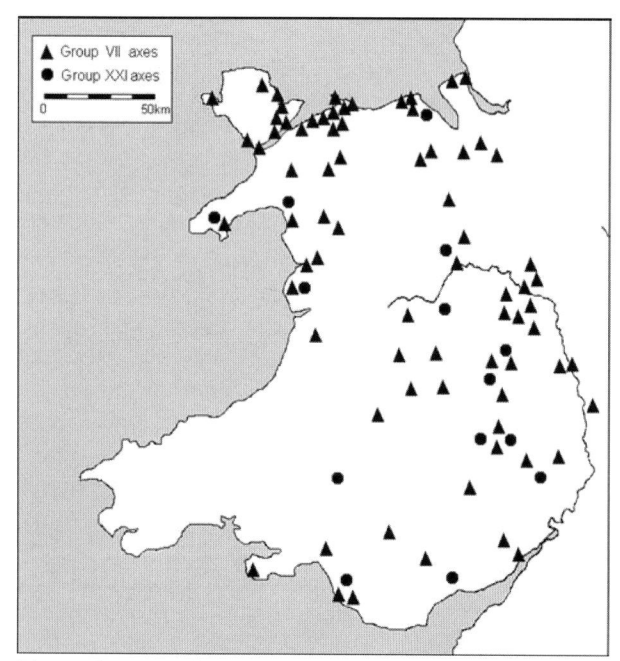

Figure 1.5 Distribution of northern Welsh axes (Groups VII and XXI) in Wales (after Clough and Cummins 1988).

noted above, but also another facet of a fascination with stone, as well as showing, importantly, some form of contact with more eastern parts of Britain.

Over 650 axes are recorded from Wales, of which almost 50% are grouped (Clough and Cummins 1988). The vast majority of axes in Wales are from Welsh sources, although axes from Cornish, Cumbrian and Northern Irish sources are also represented (Clough and Cummins 1988,

4–5). It is perhaps surprising how few Langdale (Group VI) axes have been found in Wales, particularly in comparison to the rest of Britain (see Map 6 Clough and Cummins 1988, 270) with a notable absence from southern Wales.

There are six known axe sources in Wales (see Figures 1.4 – 1.6). Three axe groups originate in south-west Wales (Group VIII, Group XIII and Group XXIII). Of these, Group VIII axes are definitely early Neolithic in date as examples of this axe group have been found at Hambledon Hill, Dorset, Carn Brea, Cornwall, and Windmill Hill, Wiltshire (Davis *et al.* 1988, 16). Little work has been done on the axe extraction site itself, which is thought to include the Preselis (around Carn Alw and Carn Meini) and outcrops on St David's Head and Ramsey Island (Barker 1992, 71), although two axehead manufacturing sites have been found at the base of the Mynydd Preseli. These sites produced axe roughouts, hammerstones and debitage (David and Williams 1995). The Preselis have long been recognised as having significance in the Neolithic as they are also the source of the Stonehenge bluestones (most recently commented on by Bradley 2000, 94, and discussed again in more detail in chapter 7). Group XIII and Group XXIII axes are generally considered to be later Neolithic or even early Bronze Age in date (Smith 1979, 19; Thorpe *et al.* 1991, 111–2) and there are fewer examples of these axes known from the British Isles. Again there seem to be multiple sources for these axes, from the Preselis to Strumble and St David's Head.

North Wales has two axe sources, Group VII at Graig Lwyd, Penmaenmawr and Group XXI at Mynydd Rhiw. Both of these sources have been excavated, the former to a lesser extent as it has been severely quarried in recent years. Graig Lwyd seems to have been quarried since the early Neolithic and Group VII axes have been found as far away as Windmill Hill, Wiltshire, the Isle of Man and Cairnpapple in West Lothian (Clough and Cummins 1988). At Mynydd Rhiw, shale was mined from a series of narrow pits which seem to have been in use since the Mesolithic (Lynch 1995, 26). However, few Group XXI axes have been found, and all are from Wales, suggesting this axe source was not as significant as Graig Lwyd. Group XII on the Shropshire/Montgomeryshire border has produced a number of battle-axes and axe-hammers, which are likely to be late Neolithic or early Bronze Age in date.

Just as people were moving parts of outcrops around in the form of stone axes, people were also utilising different stone types in the chambered monuments. At Carreg Samson in south-west Wales for example, two different stones were used in the construction of the monument. The first stone type is a local stone and can be found outcropping close to the monument. The other stone is not local and comes from further afield. This kind of selection occurs at a number of sites in Wales, although geological sourcing is required to explore this idea further. However, it does suggest that people were choosing particular stone sources and utilising them in particular ways, frequently moving them around the landscape as axes or in order to construct monuments. An additional connection between monuments and axes has been made elsewhere (Cummings 2002d) where it is suggested that both these forms of material culture employed distinctive textures to impart meanings to people who encountered or used them.

The final importance of the axe evidence lies in the sphere of interaction. Whatever the forms of exchange or other manner of distribution that were in play, the movement of axes shows contact, whether direct or indirect, between scattered and perhaps sometimes isolated communities. That web of contact extends beyond Wales. For example, around 30 Group VIII axes from south-west Wales are found in England with the distribution stretching to the southern coast, Norfolk and northern England. Likewise, Group VII axes from Penmaenmawr in north Wales are widespread throughout England (Clough and Cummins 1988). There must therefore have been knowledge of some kind of what went on in different areas from the early Neolithic onwards. This is significant when we consider again in chapter 7 the wider setting of the Welsh evidence.

Conclusion

Wales is frequently considered in relation to the southern British Neolithic or the Irish record, and in this light Wales is seen to lack many of the classic features of the Neolithic, such as causewayed enclosures and permanent settlements. These absences might be argued to relate to a relative lack of research in the region. We suggest, however, that they may relate to real differences in the way that people in the Neolithic on the eastern side of the Irish Sea thought about their world. This may go back in part to an earlier world of indigenous foragers, and it may be in part an expression of regional identity and difference from those communities around them, in the changing conditions of the start of the fourth millennium BC. It is to better understanding of that context, and of subsequent traditions stemming from it, that this volume is directed.

2 Places, monuments and landscapes: ways of seeing

Vicki Cummings and Alasdair Whittle

Landscapes of all the senses, and the role of seeing

In our own culture, we experience landscape primarily through sight, and the language that we use to describe the landscape is biased towards vision. However, it is clear that not all people experience the landscape primarily through vision and that the other senses, particularly sound and smell, can play a vital role in the understanding and experience of the world (Rodaway 1994). How then can we justify a study largely based on seeing and looking in the landscape?

Sound, for example, is essential to our lived-in world, for communication and for allowing us to identify place (Mills 2002). Sounds fill places and give them character. Sound also allows us to participate in the world, through listening and articulating (Rodaway 1994). Even the deaf use sound, in the form of vibrations, to assist them in everyday life. Unlike vision, sounds cannot be mapped, and sounds thus always seem to have a temporal aspect. Until writing was invented, we essentially lived in acoustic places (Schafer 1989). Sound is also different in character to vision. No light is needed to experience sound and we are also able to hear things behind our backs. So sounds are multi-directional and the body is always at the centre of sound. Sound is generally not considered an important part of the experience of a landscape in the western world. Yet ethnography suggests how important sound is in the active engagement of people with the lived-in world. The northern tribes of native Americans use sound extensively. In the winter darkness, sounds are much more revealing than sight and sounds can be used to hunt prey in the dark (Rodaway 1994). The Inuit, for example, describe place in acoustic terms and sound is used to mark land and resources, like a fence or a wall in our culture. For the Umeda of Papua New Guinea, who live in dense bush and forest, sound is much more important than vision (Gell 1995). The Umeda find it hard to conceptualise objects using vision alone; if something is hidden, it is silent. They also hunt by sound and an audible but invisible object is entirely present in a way that we find hard to understand (Gell 1995). As far as the wider surroundings are concerned, they have an acoustic landscape where features are grasped as movement and sound rather than as form. Even Umeda language is orientated towards sound and is highly iconic. Hence in Umeda a mountain is 'sis': the sound a mountain makes (Gell 1995).

Smell can also be an important aspect of experiencing the world. Smell is something that has in many ways been marginalised in western culture where many odours are negatively received and much effort is given to minimise them. Western languages do not have a very large vocabulary for describing smell (Classen *et al.* 1991). But even we associate certain smells with certain objects, and smell can be useful when an object is out of sight and sound. We also associate certain smells with people and places, so smells can be evocative and activate the memory. Smells can refer specifically to our own biography and life experiences, and can help form very strong bonds between individuals and place. Elsewhere, smell has a more significant role. The Aborigines, for example, use smell when hunting (Rodaway 1994). Bodily difference, including smell, is one source of sexual attraction between Lese farmer men and Efe forager women in central Africa (Grinker 1994, 80–1).

Touch – the haptic sense – is also vital to our understanding of the world but is one of the least studied senses (Cohen *et al.* 1994, 305). Touch has also been marginalised in some ways in some parts of western society where it has become desirable to maintain clear distances from other people (Rodaway 1994, 59). Although touch is primarily experienced through the fingers and hands, the entire body is a haptic sense organ with the skin being the single largest organ of the body (Rodaway 1994, 43). Furthermore, although touch can be both passive and active, it is absolutely essential in creating a bond between ourselves and the wider world (Ackerman 1991). Touch allows us to ascertain the size, weight, shape, density and temperature as well as the texture of an object. It also enables us to confirm that objects are three-dimensional, a characteristic which cannot necessarily be established through vision alone. As such, it plays an important role in the experience of landscape, particularly the immediate landscape (Cummings 2002d). We clearly live in, and engage with, a multi-sensual world.

The dominance of vision in the western world goes back to the sixteenth century and the growth of empiricism (Duncan 1993; Ingold 2000). Vision was considered the most reliable form of representation and led to the growth of the printed word, painted pictures (such as landscapes) and maps. Since then, vision has become increasingly important in the way we understand the world. European culture as a whole gives primacy to sight, although also at times being suspicious of it (Daniels and Cosgrove 1993).

There can be little dispute that our culture is dominated by vision, which dictates the way in which we use our eyes and how we interpret our visual experience. Landscape studies have been particularly affected by the dominance of vision (Bender 1998, 5), from the way we talk about landscape, to the way we represent it (see also chapter 3) and engage with it. The term landscape began its life as a word to describe a type of painting, as we set out in more detail in an endnote to this chapter,[1] and thus it automatically referred to something visual. Our discourse is also dominated by visual language; alternative words to landscape are *view*, *scene*, *vista*, *panorama* or *scenery*, all of which refer to a visual way of experiencing the world. In this sort of research context, seeing has come to have something of a bad press. Western landscapes have now become objects for visual consumption. Vision can be seen as seeking a 'total view' of social reality which of course is in fact unobtainable (Thomas 1993b). Sight only gives us access to surfaces; it is through the other senses that we learn to understand the further nature of objects (Rodaway 1994). The dominance of sight may also give the impression that we are detached observers. Smith (1993, 79) claims that we are all 'Olympian' spectators which rewards us with the pleasures of detachment and distance. Sight, finally, may be seen to marginalise the sensuality of the body and to distance us from the world in which we are engaged.

Several reflections on these debates are vital to the position we adopt in this study. Landscapes are not just visual fields, and lived-in landscapes can only be understood fully by paying attention to all the senses. We will note the significance of sound, for example that of the sea in certain settings, and we will detail what seem to us significant and deliberate choices of different textures in the constructional elements of some monuments, which evokes the sense of touch (and see Cummings 2002d). The dominant part of our treatment, however, concerns seeing. There are different ranges and kinds of seeing. The literature critical of 'totalising' vision, for example, is concerned with the encompassing gaze or panorama, and Gell (1995, 240) has suggested a 'landscape of articulation' for the Umeda in which 'the acoustic modality' binds together and makes accessible a sense of things wider than what is in view at intimate close range. We seek to deal with both looking out from and looking into places, with views which go both into the far distance and can be restricted – in our opinion recurrently and deliberately – in one or more directions. We are concerned with the immediate settings of places as well as with the middle and far distance. Although we look at instances of orientation on particular elements and features of the landscape, given principally by the axes of monuments, much of what we describe and discuss seems to involve a kind of sideways looking, a drawing in of things and features within the field of vision but not necessarily central to it. There is no need to reduce experience of the world to a single dimension or a single style of apprehending it. It is our claim that vision began to be more important from the beginning of the Neolithic onwards, but this was not a kind of seeing that can neatly be equated with that of the early modern world noted above. It belonged in part to an older, pre-Neolithic world, but was given more importance as places and monuments came to prominence. It may have varied from region to region, the major distinction being between the west and east of the area we consider in this study. Seeing in the Neolithic was often partial, referential, ambiguous, and probably also in some ways seasonal. These factors alone are enough to begin to mark out its distinctive character.

Places, and monuments

We experience the landscape from certain *places* within it. Johnson *et al.* (1994) characterise place as a portion of geographical space occupied by a person or thing. Curry (1998) defines place as simply a location which has a set of individuals attached to it. But how do we actually define what a place is? How do places come into being and why are they meaningful?

The term 'place' does actually translate into (and out of) western languages and typically means, in most non-European languages, a locality which has significance for a person or thing (Tuan 1978, 7). It might be seen as having near-universal significance, and certainly offers a vast field of comparison. We could say that places are simply unique, familiar and socially constructed (Massey 1995), defined by those actively involved in those places. Certainly many places do not have boundaries and some places appear to have a centre yet no perimeter. Other places have floating boundaries, changing over time and space and according to who is experiencing that place. Many places overlap. Place may simply be a pause in movement (Chapman 1997; Tilley 1993; 1994; Tuan 1977), and thus places are always changing, never fixed or bounded. This is particularly relevant if we consider that places are only really experienced from the inside (Thomas 1993b). In this way, it is possible to see places as having centres yet no boundaries (Ingold 1993; Gramsch 1996). Furthermore, although places are constructed in the memory, they are not frozen in time. Places are always in a state of flux and change, dependent not only on aspects like the built form of a place, but also on how people are viewing and using that place. Most places, then, are constantly being altered, either by humans, the environment or simply the passage of time.

Places come into being by encounter and this involves the human body being in a place, experiencing it first hand (Tuan 1977). This often involves moving around a place as it is through movement that we get to experience a place. After encounter comes association; once we have experienced a place we begin to associate it with something or someone. We quickly assign values to the places we encounter (Tilley 1996). Once a place has been experienced for the first time, a place usually becomes embedded in memory (Ashmore and Knapp 1999, 10). Places are thus constructed in the memory where they may gain added significance or additional associations. A place encountered in the past may become associated with the people or events that happened in that place (Massey 1995). As such, a place can be more about what happened there than its actual physical form. Places are often created through repeated encounter, repetitive experience and complex associations (Relph 1989, 26). Tuan (1977) claims that places only exist for us as places when they are familiar. A sense of belonging is important to a sense of place along with a sense of permanence and security. Places, then, are created through encounter, association, memory and experience.

Places that are important to us are often named, and a name may help to create a place. Names create a sense of permanence and also give a place a personality (Curry 1998, 49). 'Home' is one of the most emotive names for a place, as it implies familiarity, comfort, ease and security. While some names may be 'merely' descriptive, most are embedded in the history of an area, and the experiences of those who spend time there. The naming of places confirms the significance of particular locations which can be preserved over long periods of time (Bradley 2000, 158). For example, when many Iberian rock carvings were Christianised during the medieval period, those which were left unaltered often retained enough significance to be named (Bradley 2000, 74).

Places exist for different people at different levels and at different spatial scales. Places may have separable meanings and values for individuals and groups of people. While one type of place can be personal, most places are obviously to do with groups of people or collectivities in general. This is not to claim that people experience places in exactly the same way, as experience of place is rarely identically shared, but that most places gain their prominence and character from being communal. It becomes clear, then, that we are immersed in a world of places, which are socially constructed and in a state of flux. A landscape is full of places and the importance of the landscape may well relate to the significance of the places from which the landscape is being experienced. Places can be distinguished within the landscape on a conceptual level, but they are an integral part of the landscape itself. Places are locations *within* the landscape, where the actual body in space is situated.

For the purposes of this study, we take monuments to be places. Monuments themselves need not be reduced to single propositions (cf. Bloch 1977, 284; Strathern 1987, 29). They can be variously seen as statements of fact, ideas, suppositions, fixed for all time and immutable, transitory and ongoing projects, drawing in the world, creating distance from mundane existence, guiding and controlling experience, or opening up possibilities for creative play (e.g. Barrett 1994; Bender 1993a; Bradley 1993; 1998c; Richards 2003; Thomas 1993b; Tilley 1994).

We will argue later that the character of monuments in west Wales was largely different to that of those in the south-east. But all monuments can be regarded as places. They are built in selected settings, often, but not always, already marked out by previous use. Even short-lived constructions were probably there for a generation at least, and it is the character of many monuments that they endured in the landscape. Monuments were clearly not the only places of significance in the landscape, and we will make some reference to settlements, paths, places of deposition and natural places (cf. Bradley 2000), but monuments do serve as places from which to begin.

Landscape

It is clear from the history and origins of the term 'landscape' that we are dealing with a slippery and somewhat elusive concept. The word 'landscape' did not even exist in English until the seventeenth century and it is only comparatively recently that it has come to hold its present definition. We detail this now well known development at the end of this chapter.[1] Furthermore, many cultures in the world do not have a word analogous to landscape; it is an inherently Western concept and is enshrined in the discourse of western modernity (Ingold 2000; Thomas 1993b). This has led some to question whether we can usefully use the word landscape when talking about the past. Certainly, other words could be used in place of landscape such as environment, scene, panorama, view, vista or setting, but none of these terms seems to carry the same weight or meaning as landscape. Although landscape carries with it a range of overlapping and to some extent competing meanings, it is this very spectrum that adds to the potency and emotive nature of the word. In line with what we have already argued, we wish to retain this sense of variability and layered ambiguity. A brief note on historical development helps first to put this in context.

Landscape and archaeology

The term landscape has been used in archaeology for many years, although it is only in recent years that people have begun to look at landscape as an important part of the context of individual sites. In the 1920s, aerial photography promoted a general interest in landscape (Crawford and Keiller 1928; Crawford 1929). One of the earliest texts which actually looked at the effect of the landscape on people was Fox's *Personality of Britain* (1932), which expounded the ways in which the physical environment of Britain influenced early populations (Darvill 1997a); in Wales, Grimes (1936b) noted the overall landscape setting of the megalithic monuments. In the 1940s, World War Two led to a vast number of aerial photographs being produced, which increased interest in the landscape (Barker and Darvill 1997). The 1940s and 1950s saw authors such as Clark playing with ideas such as culture, biome and habitat (1952, 7), and Jacquetta Hawkes (1946, 17) discussing the impact of man on the natural landscape. However, there remained little specific work purely on landscapes. With the advent of New Archaeology in the 1960s, the word landscape was utilised much more extensively by archaeologists, adopted from (new) geography which had undergone a similar theoretical revolution in the 1950s. However, the landscape around an archaeological site (perceived as a bounded entity in processualism) was rarely considered as an important part of the site itself. It was mostly a backdrop; passive, static and unchanging. The term landscape became virtually synonymous with the term environment (see Evans *et al*. 1975; Limbrey and Evans 1978). Environmental reconstructions were used to suggest the type of land that surrounded a site and much effort was expended examining how people could utilise the landscape efficiently (using ideas such as site catchment analysis (Higgs and Vita-Finzi 1972) and optimal foraging strategies (see Ashmore and Knapp 1999, 7 for a review)).

By the early 1980s the definition and identity of the term landscape had been called into question in cognate disciplines (Ashmore and Knapp 1999; Darvill 1997b; Meinig 1979b). After a familiar timelag, by the early 1990s a number of texts were published which re-examined the importance of landscape in archaeological contexts. Particularly influential were Bender's *Landscape: politics and perspectives* (1993b) and Tilley's *A phenomenology of landscape* (1994). Both provided archaeological case studies, in the latter instance including both south-west and south-east Wales, as well as addressing the theoretical implications of a landscape archaeology and calling into question the term landscape itself. It was argued that this still related to a form of painting and a way of altering the earth (landscaping) which implied a distance between the individual and the world. This perceived distance enabled the viewer to have a privileged viewpoint, with the power to compose the view, while the object became increasingly distanced and manipulated (Rodaway 1994). Furthermore, since the term landscape had been adopted from a geography which used maps and other pictorial forms to *represent* the landscape (see Meinig 1979b), it also implied that the landscape could somehow be objectively studied and quantified.

Such unease with objectivity has in fact been problematic. Phenomenology is not concerned with whether phenomena are real or not, but how people experience and *understand* the world and things in the world. It draws heavily on Heidegger's concepts of dwelling and the relationship between *sein* (being) and *dasein* (being-in-the-world) (see Collins and Selina 1998; Karlsson 1997; Thomas 1996). Being-in-the-world resides in the process of objectification in which people set themselves apart from the world (Tilley 1994, 12). However, there is no straightforward external world that is separate from one's knowledge of it. Thus people attempt to bridge the gap to the external world through perception, bodily actions and movement. In essence, phenomenology is the study of the active engagement with the world by individuals exercising their capacity to make choices and impose meanings (Hammond *et al*. 1991; Ingold 1993). Consequently, we are not spectators of the world, but are directly involved with the world. Phenomenology is therefore trying to chart a middle ground between empiricist objectivism and cognitive idealism, simplistically between pure objectivity and pure subjectivity. And it is through the body that we mediate between thought and the world; the body is basically the vehicle for being-in-the-world (Tilley 1994, 14).

This may seem rather abstract in relation to the landscape, but Tilley (1994) has argued that a phenomenological approach assists us in understanding the multiplicity of perception and the experience of the landscape; we are always engaged with the world and cannot hope to stand outside of either space, time or our own conceptions and perceptions of the world. A phenomenological approach gives primacy to our own *perception* which is essential to our understanding of landscape (Ashmore and Knapp 1999, 1). Furthermore, a phenomenological approach explores the ways in which people experience and understand their world and allows the material record to be both ambiguous and polysemic and thus open to a multitude of interpretations (Brophy 1998). On the one hand, for study to go on, a consistent procedure of observation and inference must be adopted, as *A phenomenology of landscape* itself demonstrates, and even if multiple possibilities of interpretation are aired (e.g. Bender *et al*. 1997 on Leskernick), there comes a point when selection of a particular viewpoint has to be justified. This difficulty is amplified in the next chapter, on the methodology of the present study.

Whatever the outcome of this debate, following on from the initial studies of Bender and Tilley, a much wider range of interpretive possibilities has been asserted and become known to archaeologists, and we believe that it is useful to summarise some of these here. But it will quickly be seen that these overlap and in some cases compete with one another. We will discuss further below ways in which alternating ideas might be held within an overall worldview.

Defining landscape

Landscape is clearly an ambiguous and polysemic term and as such considerable effort has been invested in trying to define and sharpen the meaning of the word. We now consider these meanings in more detail, linking the theoretical points to the specific case study, showing that landscape is about memory, identity and biography, but is also mythological and temporal, issues we return to in chapter 7.

Landscape can be seen not as a container for action, a passive backdrop for activity, but as a medium for praxis (Thomas 1993b; Tilley 1994). For many years, landscape was seen as a kind of backcloth to the whole stage of human activity (e.g. Appleton 1975, 2). People undertook projects in the landscape, but the landscape itself had little impact on these activities. This view tends to deny any role for the active human agent and the intimate relationship that person has with the world (Barrett 1997). Landscape is thus given meaning by being altered by people (Gramsch 1996, 25). Furthermore, landscape is literally the medium through which social life is conducted (Darvill 1997a, 78) and is also the context for social action; it is thus socially constructed (Barker and Darvill 1997, 5). All human activity takes place in the landscape; landscape is not simply a backdrop to this, but is directly involved in how people undertake their everyday activities. In the Neolithic in Wales, we would argue, the landscape would have been an integral part of the experience of everyday places and things, directly affecting how and where activities were undertaken. Ethnographically, the hunter-gatherer group of Mbuti Pygmies see the forest in which they live as both mother and father, providing them with food, warmth, shelter and clothing (Ingold 1996; 2000). Every single activity or action undertaken by these people is influenced by the way in which they view the landscape. All social activity is undertaken in the landscape and is directly influenced by their underlying belief system. Thus, the forest is the medium in which all social relations are played out. The landscape does not contain, it enables. We could envisage a similar situation in Wales, with everyday settlements as well as monuments being positioned in relation to particular landscape features, and references made to particularly significant landforms in a variety of different practices.

It has been asserted that people create meaningful landscapes which in turn helps people to create a sense of identity (Ashmore and Knapp 1999, 14–6; Basso 1984; Bender 1993a). The landscape can be sedimented with human experiences which are highly subjective and personal to each individual. How people understand and engage with the world is dependent on the specific time and place of encounter and the individual's own age, gender, and social, economic and political position (Bender 1992; 1993a). Everyone is different and thus no two experiences of the landscape will ever be quite the same (Darvill 1997a, 75). Thus, landscape can help to form personal biographies and assist in the constitution of self-identity (Gramsch 1996, 29; Tilley 1996). The formation of self-identity among the Fijians is so inextricably linked to the landscape that individuals are virtually a manifestation of the place where they were born (Toren 1995). People are constantly re-negotiating their own sense of being and people can rework their sense of identity through a constant engagement and re-engagement with the landscape (Bender 1998, 25). For the Wintu of northern California, personal identity is embedded in the landscape; the landscape provides a series of images whose meaning has influence on each individual's daily activities, spiritual life and ethical considerations (Theodoratus and LaPena 1994). The unique and characteristic aspects of the Welsh landscape may equally have forged identities amongst Neolithic communities. In later chapters we argue that mountains seem to have been particularly significant in the Neolithic, and the presence of these on the horizon may have been in some sense a significant part of a person's identity. Connections with particular landscape features may also have decided the appropriate location for the burial of particular individuals at the end of their lives.

The play between individual and collective is problematic. Individuals obtain their frame of reference for understanding landscape from their own cultural circumstances, and the meaning of landscape can be broadly similar for people with a shared cultural background; landscape can act as shared cultural artefact which can be drawn upon by different people within the same cultural group (for example see Basso 1996, 60). Group identities can also be formed in and by the landscape. In Australia, groups perceive a very strong bond between themselves and the area of the landscape in which they live (Morphy 1995, 196; Tilley 1994). Likewise, the Apache have a close relationship with the landscape which not only supplies them with food but also provides moral guidance (Basso 1984, 44). Bender (1998) has shown how different groups of people in Britain have appropriated the landscape of Stonehenge into their own group identities. This also means that many landscapes become contested, as different groups seek to create links with particular places (see papers in Bender and Winer 2001, and below).

Places can also develop biographies (Kirk 1997). A landscape may be viewed as having a beginning; in the case of the Aborigines, the landscape was formed in the Dreamtime, when the ancestors who first walked the earth left evidence of their actions in the form of topographic features (Morphy 1995, 188). The topography can thus be 'read' like a biography. Landscape can be seen as embodying history, as the landscape has a transformative nature which is never frozen in time. The Maori of New Zealand believe that the *waahi tapu*, those parts of the landscape that are of special significance, provide them with a direct historical link to the ancestors (Matunga 1994, 221). Landscapes are involved in an endless historical process (Bender 1993c) and as such have a history: a past, a present and a future. In the same way that landscapes are historical, the human use and experience of the landscape are also radically historical (Thomas 1993a, 17; Lowenthal 1979, 104). In this sense, landscapes can be seen as a palimpsest of previous activity. We argue for elements of considerable continuity in the meanings of particular landscape features in later chapters, and suggest that places such as mountains and rivers were connected with an essentially Mesolithic understanding of the world. Just like people, places in a Neolithic world may well have had their own histories and biographies, which people knew, perhaps through oral tradition. It may have been these histories and stories, at least in part, that people were referencing from the monuments.

To understand and engage with the landscape requires

a sense of time. We have already seen how biographical encounters are created over time and how the landscape is an historical encounter. Landscape, in many ways, is time made visible (Chapman 1997); landscapes can reveal to us in material form the historicity of previous human encounters with the world. Places are created, named and used through time and landscapes achieve their identity over time (Curry 1998). Movement through the landscape is movement through both space and time. Landscapes are also never static (Bender 1993c), but changing from moment to moment, and thus time depth is a fundamental part of the experience of place and landscape. However, time does not form a container within which social life is played out but constitutes a medium through which social relations are produced and reproduced (Shanks and Tilley 1987). The experience of the landscape structures time and time structures the way we experience the landscape. Landscape and time are thus inseparable and in a constant dialectic and dynamic relationship with one another. Ingold (1993) discusses the importance of time and its relationship with landscape. He suggests that as people go about their everyday lives doing tasks they engage with other people and places, which, in combination with time and the landscape, forms a 'taskscape' (Ingold 1993). The landscape is thus both agency and time embodied (Ingold 1993; 2000). In this way, the landscape is always changing and altering, and because we cannot stand back and observe the passage of time, we are all always involved in a 'taskscape' (and see below). We very much favour the idea of the landscape as being of a crucial part of everyday life, with perhaps a sharper focus on specific landscape features at particular times or events and at specific places such as monuments. The temporality of the landscape is another issue to which we return in detail in chapter 7.

To follow on from this, we would see the engagement with landscape on an everyday basis as about dwelling. Landscape as dwelling involves the relationship between inhabited space and social being-in-the-world (Karlsson 1997; Kirk 1997; Thomas 1996). This theoretical approach based on the work of Heidegger suggests that spaces open up by virtue of the dwelling of people. In this way, dwelling links place, praxis, cosmology and nurture (Tilley 1994, 13). Essentially, dwelling removes the distance between people and things. It allows people to be actively engaged with places continuously. Ingold (1995), building on his 1993 paper, sees the world become a meaningful environment through being lived in. Dwelling allows an intimate relationship between individuals and the world in which they live. People understand their world through living in it. By being immersed in the landscape on a day to day basis the landscape gains its meaning.

As much as landscapes may have been engaged with and dwelt in on an everyday and continuous basis, landscapes also work on other, more abstracted levels. Landscapes can be particularly important in evoking memory. Küchler (1993) has suggested that landscape is the most generally accessible and widely shared *aide mémoire* and assists in the understanding of both the past and the future. Landscape can invoke memory in a number of ways (Ashmore and Knapp 1999, 13–14): through direct association with a particular place that may have been used or visited in the past, or by more indirect association such as a smell or emotive view. Memories are often contradictory and do not necessarily refer to the actual events as they occurred. Bachelard (1994) refers to the 'land of motionless childhood', where one cannot always remember precise details, for example how old one was when an event happened, but one has a sense of place that is still deeply rooted in the memory. Landscapes are filled with memory. We learn to negotiate our way around places and spaces by accessing memories; memory is like experience. Schama (1995) describes landscape as the work of the mind, where scenery is built up as much from strata of memory as from layers of rock. Thus, the landscape gains its meaning from memory. In addition, landscape essentially reminds us of our place in the world.

> Every part of this country is sacred to my people. Every hillside, every valley, every plain and grove has been hallowed by some fond memory or some sad experience of my tribe (Chief Seattle quoted in Hubert 1994, 16).

In the same way that the landscape can be rich in memories, it is also often filled with myths. Myths can both shape and be shaped by the land (Cosgrove 1993, 281). To the Aborigines of Arnhem Land, the landscape is inextricably linked to the mythological past (Taçon 1991; Tilley 1994). As mobile hunter-gatherers, they are continually moving around the landscape, but when people move into a new area, they do not impose their own myths on the land, rather they act as if the myths of the land take over them. It is not simply that the landscape is a sign system for mythological events, rather that the landscape is the referent for much of the symbolism (Morphy 1995, 186). In the same way, the Black Hills in the USA are considered sacred among many groups of native Americans (Sundstrom 1996). The hills are associated with constellations and also relate to the myth of the Falling Star. When new tribes moved into the area in the past they simply adopted the myths associated with particular locales in the Black Hills (Sundstrom 1996). Myths assist in giving meaning to landscape and in tying one's own personal history to that of the land. We suggest that the landscapes of Wales evoked both mythological understandings of the past and also memories of perhaps more recent events. The construction process of a monument and its subsequent use would also add to the range of memories associated with particular places and landscapes.

Landscape is a frame of discourse that encourages the development of metaphors (Morphy 1993, 205; Tilley 1999). The landscape is an ideal canvas for the application of metaphors, partly because its features so readily evoke other forms. Metaphors are almost always contextually and culturally specific and tie in with broader ideologies and cosmologies. The Aborigines view Uluru (Ayer's Rock) as the manifestation of the ancestors; in this way it can be viewed as both a myth and a metaphor (Morphy 1995). Tilley (1994, 30) describes paths through the landscape as metaphors for journeys, patterns of exchange or social relations. All sorts of other features in the landscape can be seen as metaphors: trees, water and so on (and this is discussed in more detail later).

It has been suggested that it was through narrative that places and landscape retained their significance. Narrative is essential in giving meaning to landscape and also in allowing us to make sense of the past (Children and Nash 1997a). Narrative may have been used in the past to articulate the importance of the landscape in the everyday lives of individuals (Schafer 1989). Aboriginal art, for example, is decorative but it also has hidden meanings and narratives, often providing information on local resources such as waterholes. Chapman (1997) claims that it is through their insertion into a narrative that places assume active meanings and that it is through the linking of places in a sequence (be it temporal or spatial) that a narrative is itself constituted. Places help to recall stories that are associated with them and places only exist by virtue of their employment in a narrative (Tilley 1994, 33). By using narrative, the features of the landscape act as mnemonic pegs on which moral teachings hang (Basso 1984, 44; 1996, 66; Tilley 1994, 33). We could envisage not only a series of narratives being connected to landscape features and monuments, but also the monuments themselves acting as a kind of grammar for understanding and utilising those narratives.

Landscape, culture and nature

It has been argued that landscape is a cultural process (Hirsch 1995; Lewis 1979; Schama 1995). This suggests that the landscape is a natural phenomenon which can be turned into a cultural landscape through human agency (Coones 1992). In this way, it is possible to see culture (people) as the agent, working with nature (the natural world) as the medium. This approach assumes that culture and nature are polar opposites, and results in one of the fundamental paradoxes in the term landscape; landscape is seen as both cultural and natural at the same time (Johnston 1998). Landscape is natural in the way that it incorporates aspects of the natural world, but it is also cultural, in the way that people have altered the landscape over the millennia. This makes the concept of landscape problematic as it seems therefore to be both cultural (altered by people, assigned meaning by people) and natural (as the natural world).

However, it is increasingly obvious that a rigid culture/nature dichotomy may not be appropriate in dealing with landscapes of the past. Culture and nature have not always been polar opposites. Nature originates from the Latin *nascere* which means to be born, to come into being: it is a *potential* rather than an actual event (Olwig 1993, 313). Culture stems from the Latin *colere* which meant to inhabit, to cultivate and to honour with worship; it also implied cyclical processes and the agricultural 'scaping' of the land by people (Olwig 1993, 313). Culture and nature as polar opposites originate in the Renaissance and have had much the same history as the word landscape. Adopted wholeheartedly in western philosophy during the Enlightenment, the Cartesian modernist dichotomies of culture/nature, mind/body, environment/society and objective/subjective time came to shape the way we look at the world. It was believed that it was possible to 'convert' nature into culture; the conversion of the land by agriculture was seen to be similar to the application of cooking to raw meat (Shanks 1992, 121). Empiricism, where increasing emphasis was put on experience, observation and description, seemed to promote this view of the world. It was considered clear that people *did* have an effect on nature; people *could* subjugate nature into culture. However, the dichotomy between science and the arts further promoted the idea of nature and culture as polar opposites. Science studied nature (geology, geography, biology) which was rooted in empiricism, while the arts studied culture (archaeology, anthropology) which is still considered much more subjective and open to interpretation. We are now at the stage that both culture and nature have a taken-for-granted status (Strathern 1995, 154) even though there seems to be no unified concept of either (Kuper 1999). Culture and nature are so enshrined in our language that it seems difficult to move beyond them.

However, a culture/nature dichotomy may simply be insufficient when discussing the past. Indeed, some cultures have no concept of a culture/nature dichotomy (MacCormack 1980). The people of Mount Hagen, for example, do not understand the concept of nature versus culture. They have both wild and domesticated animals, but the wild is not subjugated by things tame. They have a sense of culture, by differentiating themselves from outsiders, but what is missing is the underlying relationship with nature that our culture implies (Strathern 1980). The western view implies a state of changing or becoming, where nature can *become* culture, and the wild can *become* tame. Again this state of becoming is missing from the people of Mount Hagen's worldview (Strathern 1980). In presenting the not dissimilar example of the Chewong, foragers and to a limited extent cultivators in the Malay tropical rainforest, Howell (1996, 128) comments, 'we have been flooded in recent years with ethnographically founded denials of operative oppositions between nature and culture. There is no need to flog this particular dead horse'. On the other hand, while the Chewong do not generally make distinctions between themselves and other beings, or between a natural world and a cultural world, within their own environment of the forest, they do conceptualise some things as not personages, and do to some extent differentiate between 'us' and 'them', including the dangerous world outside the forest (Howell 1996, 141–2). Seeking to define operative categories and boundaries (cf. Sharples 2000, 114) may be a more fruitful way of proceeding in the archaeological study here, rather than imposing a universalist order.

Frames of reference

We have already given a preliminary discussion of the role of seeing in relation to the other senses, and argued the central position of the concept of place, embodied here in the form of monuments. The brief review of landscape concepts has opened a further very wide frame of reference. If landscapes can be so many different things – multi-sensory, embodied, biographical, crucial in the everyday lives of people, subjective, collective, timeless and mythical yet historically constituted, political, ideological and contested – how can we choose between the competing possibilities and their potential changes through time? Can we hope to grasp this range, when our first concern is with landscape as basic form, in the shape and relationships of hills, mountains, rivers, valleys and sea?

Our justification must rest in several levels. Landscape 'works' in many different ways. For the most part, landscape is experienced as part of everyday existence, perhaps familiar and knowable, regularly experienced or evoked in stories. On certain occasions, however, when moving around the landscape at times of heightened significance or when visiting special places, landscape becomes the focus of extra attention. It is this sharp focus on landscape which may have occurred at monuments in the Neolithic. We can attempt to understand an intimate or immediate landscape by closely examining the settings of groups of monuments. But that in turn grades into a middle and far distance, and these several scales also operate temporally as well as spatially. Looking out involved much broader networks, tied to local understandings of the world but also to history and different ways of doing things elsewhere. We will discuss local and regional aspects in relation to the wider context in chapter 7.

It is important to recognise that some of the possibilities raised by our review of landscape concepts may be incompatible. If landscape is to be seen as dominant ideology or political proposition, for example, it may at the same time less easily constitute an emblem of collective identity or personal biography. On the other hand, this may be to fall into the reductionist trap of seeking single propositions or a single point of view (Bloch 1977, 284; Strathern 1987, 29). People may think within a series of nodes or concepts, each of which may be part of a broader worldview though rarely explicitly connected (Bloch 1992). With reference to social relations and especially to the significance of myth in parts of Papua New Guinea, Wagner (1978) and Weiner (1988) have exploited the idea of 'obviation', or successive elaborations and replacements of ideas. As Weiner has put it (1988, 10), '…any symbolic operation that exposes the simultaneously differentiating and collectivizing modes of a tropic equation can be defined as *obviation*'. The effects will be different, depending on whether the dominant social convention is uniformity or differentiation. Here then, in brief, are two ways of thinking differently about competing points of view. Adapting Gell's language (1995), we could articulate differing modalities, which may allow us to move more freely between scales and concepts, from the local setting, particular stones, individual bodies, specific events, and named places, to the wider view, broader history, timeless myth, and general context.

We will return to these and other possibilities in chapter 7. But first, we set out how to go about things, and then try to tease out what is in the frame.

Note

1   The word landscape did not exist in the English language until recently and The Shorter Oxford Dictionary cites 1632 for its first actual usage in English. It is generally considered that the term originated from the German *Landschaft* and the Dutch *landschap* or *landskip*, which signified a unit of human occupation and referred to anything that might be considered a pleasing object of depiction (Hirsch 1995; Schama 1995). These terms also conveyed an element of place, province, territory, district or tract of land (Coones 1992, 23). It was introduced into the English language as *landscipe*, a technical term used by painters to describe a new and increasingly popular form of art work, the genre of landscape painting (Hirsch 1995). Before the Renaissance, landscape paintings were not very realistic and were usually simple, static and rather two-dimensional backdrops; the main focus were the subjects or objects depicted in the foreground (Clark 1949). The change towards the depiction of more realistic landscapes is often attributed to Leonardo da Vinci, but other painters such as Piero di Cosimo and Giovanni Bellini may equally have been responsible (Simmons 1993a, 84).

The Renaissance also began to promote a new way of looking at and understanding the world. Humans, and the environment in which they lived, began to be separated out as distinct entities (Cosgrove 1989, 121). The separation of humans from their environment and the image of nature as 'other' stemmed from the development of the empirical sciences from the sixteenth century onwards (Gramsch 1996, 24). In this period, science gave increasing primacy to experience, observation and painstaking description which further promoted the idea of landscape as external from people and landscape as a separate quantifiable entity. It is also claimed that in the Renaissance the land itself became viewed as something to be exploited, like a machine that would never break, however hard it was used (Schama 1995). This may in part be due to the invention of the fixed-harness plough (Schama 1995) and the intensification of agriculture across

Europe. Landscape art and painting became firmly established in the seventeenth century. Landscape, in this period still a synonym for nature, began to be viewed as the moral corrective for the corruption of culture, the court and city (Schama 1995). However, protagonists of the Enlightenment also believed that progress was achieved by man's control over nature. The view of man and nature as separate reached its height in late eighteenth-century Romanticism, where nature and landscape were seen as pure and good, a baseline against which to measure corruption (Meinig 1979a). This can clearly be seen in the work of a number of poets writing at this time:

> These beauteous forms,
> Through a long absence, have not been to me
> As is a landscape to a blind man's eye:
> But oft, in lonely rooms, and 'mid the din
> Of towns and cities, I have owed to them... Wordsworth (1798)

Landscaped gardens by people such as Capability Brown became increasingly popular in this era. As Europeans discovered more and more of the world, especially the New World and Africa, the peoples they encountered were viewed as free from culture, closer to nature and in a primitive state of happiness (Samuels 1979). Although viewed as lower in the scale of evolution, these people were seen as noble savages and became a therapeutic image for the European (Duncan 1993, 45).

By the nineteenth century, the meaning of the word had ceased to be applied directly to the signifier, the painting genre, and became transferred to the external referent of those paintings, the environment (Olwig 1993, 319). By this point, culture and nature were firmly entrenched as polar opposites in Western discourse. This made landscape a contradiction (Johnston 1998), as landscapes were both natural (situated in the natural world) and cultural (altered by people). It was not till the late nineteenth century that the word actually came to mean a portion of land or territory which the eye can comprehend in a single view (Johnson et al. 1994). This meaning has remained more or less intact till the present day, with The Concise English Dictionary describing it as "a natural or imaginary scene, as seen in the broad view".

3 Methodology

Vicki Cummings

Introduction

Having discussed theoretical aspects of seeing, place and landscape in the previous chapter, we now focus on the methodology involved in doing a particular landscape archaeology. In contrast to the quantity of books and papers on landscape theory, very little has been written on the practice of examining the landscape settings of sites. Here we discuss the selection of the sites in our study, and the recording and analysis methods employed.

Fieldwork

The selection of sites

Only definite or probable Neolithic chambered monuments were included in this study. The inventory lists the 104 sites considered. We deliberately did not include a few of the more recent discoveries, including the new long barrows found in the Black Mountains (Olding 2000) and the Lower Luggy long barrow (Gibson 2000), or other non-megalithic barrows identified by the Welsh Trusts, because as yet these sites have not produced megalithic remains. Only one non-megalithic long barrow has been included in the study, that of Cross Lodge in the Black Mountains, which almost certainly contains megalithic remains. The inventories of known chambered tombs were provided by Barker (1992) for south-west Wales, Lynch (1969b) for north-west Wales, and Corcoran (1969a) and RCAHMW (1997) for south-east Wales. Sites were plotted on 1:50,000 maps and every one was visited in the field. Other possible sites must be the focus of future research.

Landscape recording in the field

Most sites were visited on more than one occasion and at all sites the landscape setting was recorded in a number of different ways. First, a simple 360° representation of the landscape was drawn on to a blank circle (Figure 3.1).

This method was developed previously in a doctoral thesis on the landscape settings of sites in south-west Wales and south-west Scotland, in order to show the regularities, continuities and main emphases in the placing of sites in the landscape (Cummings 2001). They have the advantage of being quick to produce, allowing the whole landscape setting to be depicted in a single diagram. In addition, the

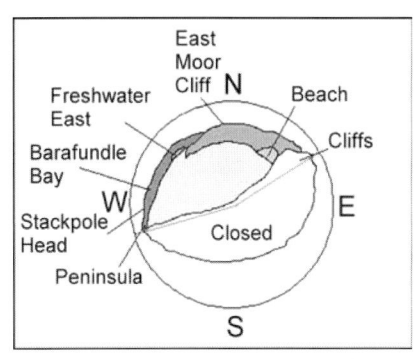

Figure 3.1 A schematic representation of the landscape setting around the King's Quoit, south-west Wales which represents how the landscape looks to all points of the compass when standing at the monument. This can be viewed next to a plan of the monument which can show the orientation of the landscape in relation to the monument.

orientation of the various landscape features was recorded so that it is possible to see in which direction mountains or hills lie. Disadvantages of this method are discussed below. Secondly, the entire landscape setting was also recorded descriptively (e.g. 'The beach at Freshwater East can be seen to the NW'). Finally, a 360° photographic panorama was taken at each site. Elsewhere, these photographic panoramas have been digitally stitched together to produce electronic landscape strips that can be viewed on a computer (Cummings 2000a; 2000b; 2001), but this was not done for all the sites here. The general location of each site or monument was also recorded as well as other potentially interesting features such as distinctive natural outcrops. Finally, the surrounding landscape was examined for any notable features, as well as any changes in the landscape setting. It was noted at many sites that the landscape setting was quite different just a few metres away from the site itself. Sea vistas, for example, disappeared from view, or mountains became no longer visible, and at a number of sites this was systematically recorded (see control samples section below).

GIS

In addition to the sites being visited and recorded in the field, a GIS viewshed from each site was also generated (Figure 3.2). GIS has been used increasingly in landscape-based projects as it offers a range of useful tools which

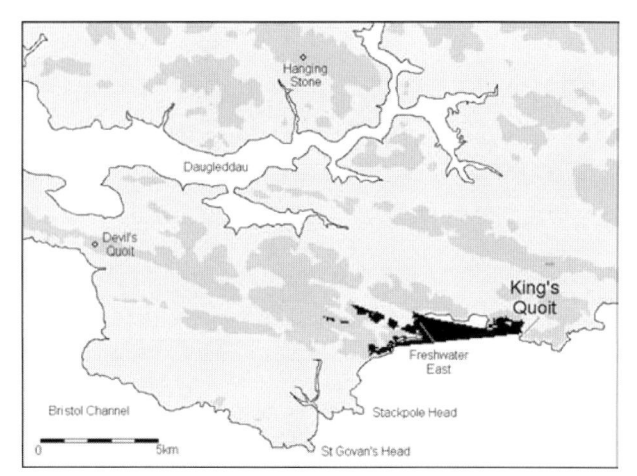

Figure 3.2 A GIS viewshed of the King's Quoit, south-west Wales. The black area is the part of the landscape visible from the monument. Reproduced by kind permission of Ordnance Survey. © Crown copyright NC/03/20516.

can assist in the analysis and interpretation of the landscape (Gillings *et al.* 1999; Johnson and North 1997; Wheatley *et al.* 2002). By inputting maps and contour data, as well as site locations, GIS can generate simple distribution maps as well as more complex diagrams, such as viewsheds, the areas of the landscape which are visible from certain locations (Gillings 1998, 118). For example, Mithen and Lake (1998) used GIS to show that Mesolithic sites on the island of Islay in Scotland were not specifically placed to have wide-ranging views over the landscape. In order to demonstrate this the known Mesolithic sites were plotted on a digital elevation map (DEM) and the views from each site were calculated (Lake *et al.* 1998). 1000 locales on the island were then randomly generated to see if they also had similar wide-ranging viewsheds. As the randomly generated sites also had expansive views, it was argued that Mesolithic sites cannot be seen to have been uniquely or distinctively positioned to overlook broad tracts of land (Lake *et al.* 1998; Mithen and Lake 1998).

In this study, contour data were downloaded from Edina (www.edina.ac.uk) for the whole of Wales at 1:50,000. The 'tiles' of data were then put into GIS software, in this case ArcView 3.2, and were stitched together to form a large Digital Elevation Model. All the monuments were added to the DEM from which the viewsheds were generated (Figure 3.3). GIS was used in two different ways, specifically as a tool to assist in addressing particular research questions, not as a technique for its own sake. First, a viewshed was produced for each of the megaliths in the study. In this way, GIS was able to back up and reinforce the observations made in the field, and this was particularly useful as results could be compared with the landscape schematics that were drawn in the field, as well as the photographic panoramas, reinforcing and supporting the readings and landscape observations. Furthermore, a few sites visited were positioned close to modern features which block out the view of the landscape, such as houses or thick forestry plantations, so that it was possible to demonstrate which parts of the landscape may have been visible at sites where this is no longer possible at the site itself. Secondly, GIS was also used to produce a series of control samples.

Control samples

In order to assess the validity of the claims formed on the basis of observations made at the monuments (i.e. that megaliths were carefully positioned in relation to specific landscape features), a series of comparative control samples was constructed. Three different types of control sample were used in this project, with varying degrees of success. Each will be discussed in turn.

Other monuments

A series of Bronze Age cairns was visited in south-west Wales in order to act as a control sample against which to compare the chambered monuments. Structures dating to different periods have been used elsewhere as control samples (e.g. Phillips 2002; Williams 1999). There are a number of Bronze Age cairns in south-west Wales and many of these occur in the same general area as the chambered monuments. The Bronze Age cairns in the vicinity of the Neolithic megaliths were visited and their landscape settings recorded. Virtually all these cairns are set on top of hills or mountains, and consequently have quite different settings to the megaliths (Figure 3.4). The settings of the Bronze Age cairns are contrasted to the megaliths in the next chapter and discussed in detail there. However, it should be noted here that although the Bronze Age cairns are located in quite strikingly different landscape settings to the megaliths, this relationship may be in part an issue of preservation. The cairns visited are unlikely to be a representative sample of all the Bronze Age locations used for the construction of a cairn. Those found on the top of hills and mountains may survive because these are the most inaccessible parts of the landscape, and although they provide a useful control sample, their preservation is likely to have biased the record. So a series of stone circles were also visited throughout Wales, again to act as a control sample against which to compare the megaliths. Although the stone circles of Wales seem to be both Neolithic and Bronze Age in date (Burl 1995), it is likely that at least some of these were in use at the same time as the megaliths, or soon after. It was only the stone circles that are found in the same general area as the megaliths which were visited, so the stone circles of Mid Wales were not visited, as they could not be directly compared to any nearby megaliths. These monuments are found in quite different parts of the landscape to the Bronze Age cairns, with a higher survival rate in lower areas. The results of these comparisons are also presented in the following chapters.

3 Methodology   19

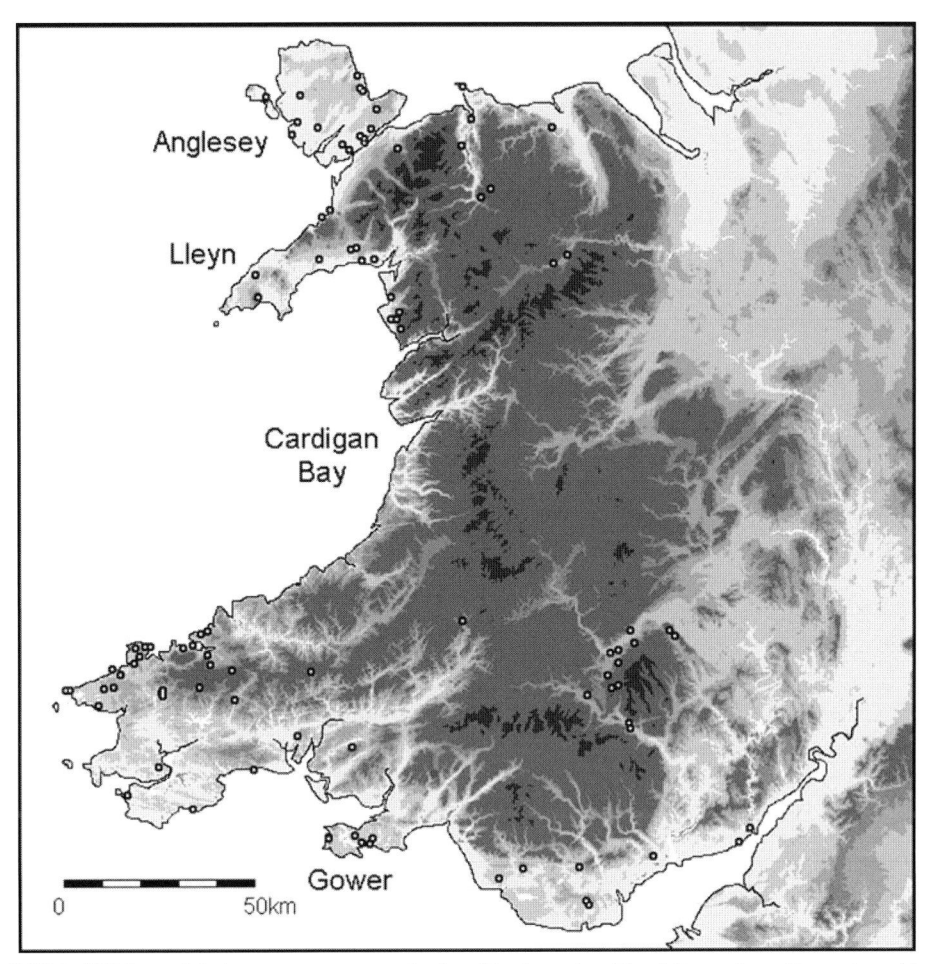

Figure 3.3 The DEM of Wales, with the monuments marked as black spots with white centres. Reproduced by kind permission of Ordnance Survey. © Crown copyright NC/03/20516.

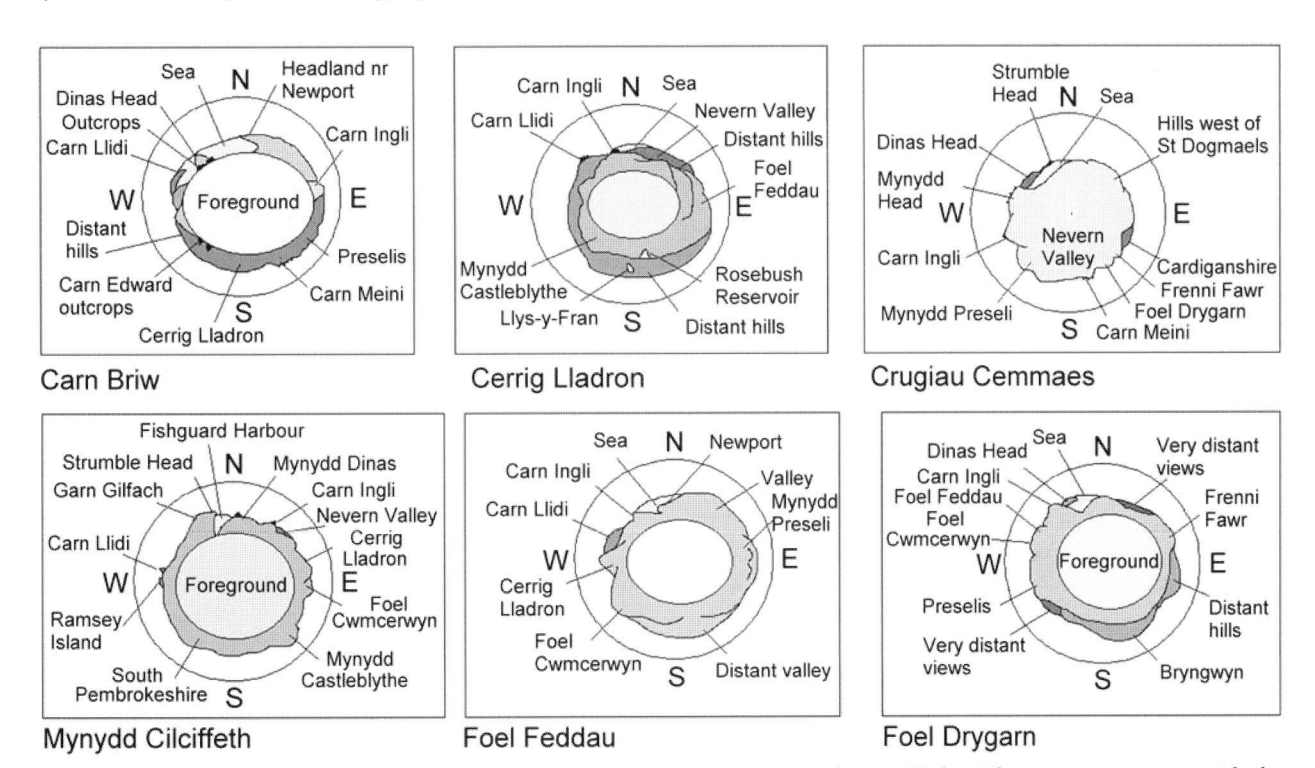

Figure 3.4 The landscape settings of a number of Bronze Age cairns in south-west Wales. These views contrast with the settings of the monuments.

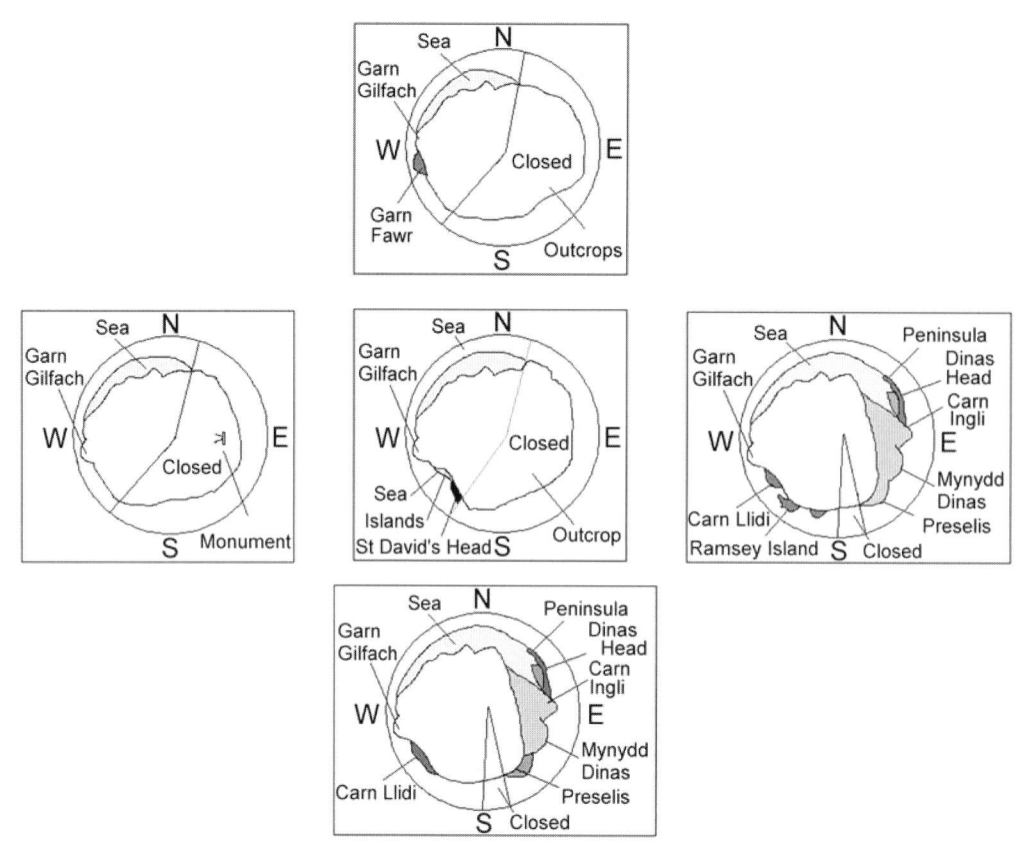

Figure 3.5 Control samples taken around Carn Wnda. At the centre is the view from Carn Wnda itself, and to the north, south, east and west the views taken in those directions at 60 paces from the site (approx 50m).

Control samples around the monuments

At a number of the megaliths control samples were actually taken around the sites. This was not possible at some sites, primarily due to difficulties of gaining access to the surrounding landscape. At sites such as Carn Wnda, for example, the landscape setting of various points a short distance from the monument itself was recorded. At this site, points at 60 paces (approximately 50 metres) to the north, south, east and west were visited and recorded (Figure 3.5). Just 50 metres from the monument in these four directions, the landscape views are quite different. For example, Carn Wnda seems to have been located so that there are views of the sea to the north and south-west and a view of the islands to the south-west and St David's Head. However, had the monument been built just 50m to the west of its present location the sea, islands and St David's Head would no longer have been visible. Likewise, had the site been built 50m to the east or south, a whole range of different landscape features would have been visible such as the Preselis, Carn Ingli and Dinas Head, but only a very small portion of the view would have been restricted; as will be seen, such restriction or closing of the view is recurrent and significant. In chapter 7 we will argue that the combination of landscape features visible from each site was carefully orchestrated, and that sites were carefully positioned to have a range of different features visible. Taking control samples from the immediate vicinity of the monuments demonstrates how moving a site only a few metres from its present location radically alters the views. A series of these control samples is presented in the following chapters.

GIS control samples

A series of control samples using GIS was also generated for a number of the megaliths. Viewsheds were created at three points to the north, south, east and west from the megalith, at 200m, 500m and 1km distances (Figure 3.6). This method produced mixed results. First, there are a number of problems with the detail of the viewsheds (see below). In these cases, the actual viewshed produced at each control point was too crude to be meaningfully compared with the view from the monument itself. For example, one of the relationships noted at Pentre Ifan was that there were clear views up to the outcrops of Carnedd Meibion Owen which appear skylined on the horizon (Tilley 1994, 105). Using GIS we hoped we could demonstrate that this relationship was not purely chance, and that by placing the monument in a slightly different part of the landscape, these outcrops would no longer have been visible. A series of viewsheds were generated around this site and compared with the viewshed from the site itself.

3 Methodology

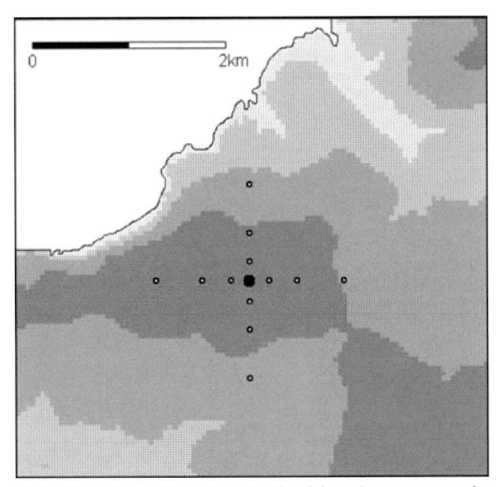

Figure 3.6 The site of Llech y Dribedd with a series of control points around the monument. Reproduced by kind permission of Ordnance Survey. © Crown copyright NC/03/20516.

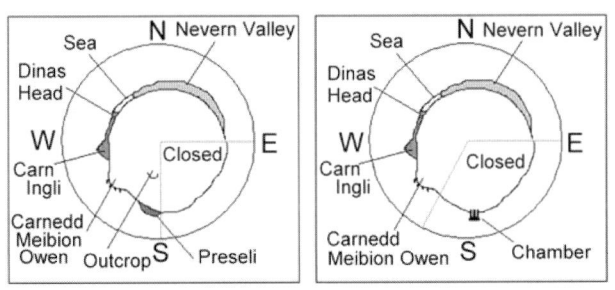

Figure 3.7 The landscape setting around Pentre Ifan (left) and the landscape from the tail of the long cairn at Pentre Ifan (right). From the tail of the long cairn the Preselis are no longer visible.

The results were rather unclear, for a number of reasons. First, the outcrops are not marked on the DEM as it is too coarse so that we had to 'best-guess' the location of the outcrops. Second, the control viewsheds are too crude to be meaningfully compared with the view from the monument itself. Finally, because it is not possible to work out how the outcrops would actually have *looked* from these control points, one cannot tell whether they would have been skylined from the control points. The GIS control samples suggested that the outcrops remained visible for 500m in all directions but it is unclear how they would have appeared to a viewer (for example, moving 500m to the north may have meant that the outcrops were still visible, but they may have no longer been visible on the skyline and may have blended in with the rest of the topography, effectively meaning that these features were no longer dominant features on the horizon). At Pentre Ifan it was not possible to actually visit the control points on the ground (because of access to private land) but simply looking at the landscape from the tail of the long cairn showed that from here the Preselis are no longer visible (as is the case from the chamber) and that by moving only a few tens of metres north again the outcrops of Carnedd Meibion Owen would almost certainly no longer be visible (Figure 3.7).

A critique of GIS

Many now well rehearsed criticisms have been leveled at GIS in recent years (for a review see Wheatley and Gillings 2000). In summary, GIS is essentially characterised by Cartesian notions of space, which is abstracted, timeless and passive (Thomas 1993b). By using maps as the basis for GIS, the observer is removed from a lived-in world and ends up seeing literally everything from nowhere, what Haraway (1991, 189) describes as the 'God-trick'. As a consequence, the space of GIS becomes a neutral backdrop with no cultural value (Gillings and Goodrick 1996). This is in complete contrast to the notions of space and place being propounded by many archaeologists (for example see Bender 1998). The experience of the world is reduced to information (Curry 1998, 56). In addition, GIS relates entirely to views and not to perception and as a consequence does not account for the difference between the two (Pollard and Gillings 1998). Thomas argues that we 'cannot reconstruct a past world of meaning from a Cartesian template of geometrical form' (Thomas 1996, 88). The analysis of abstracted spatial data does little to inform how people in the past may have experienced and interpreted landscape features. Other criticisms leveled at GIS include the charge that it encourages environmentally, functionally and technologically deterministic analytical viewpoints (Woodman 2000, 91). It also privileges vision, an issue already raised in the previous chapter and discussed again in chapter 7.

In the application of viewshed analysis, the most common use of GIS at present, a number of problems have become apparent. The contour data used in GIS are still quite crude, typically set at 10m intervals. This is not a sufficient resolution to pick up smaller landscape features which seem to be referenced at so many of the sites examined (such as rocky outcrops: see above and the next chapter). Furthermore, small-scale variability *within* sites cannot be calculated, for example the different views from the tail-end of a long cairn in contrast to the façade. The user also has to state the radius of the view (e.g. 2km, 5km, 10km and so on) and since no account is taken of the curvature of the earth, results can be misleading. When examining viewsheds, the landscape is split into cells of 50 square metres, each of which is given a set height. This is too coarse to pick up the subtleties of the location of a site and its wider landscape views. This problem was particularly apparent at a number of sites where the viewshed suggested that parts of the landscape were visible when in fact they are not. For example at the site of Cist Cerrig in north-west Wales the viewshed suggests that it is possible to see the mountains of Ardudwy, yet these are the features which are restricted from view by a nearby outcrop (Figure 3.8).

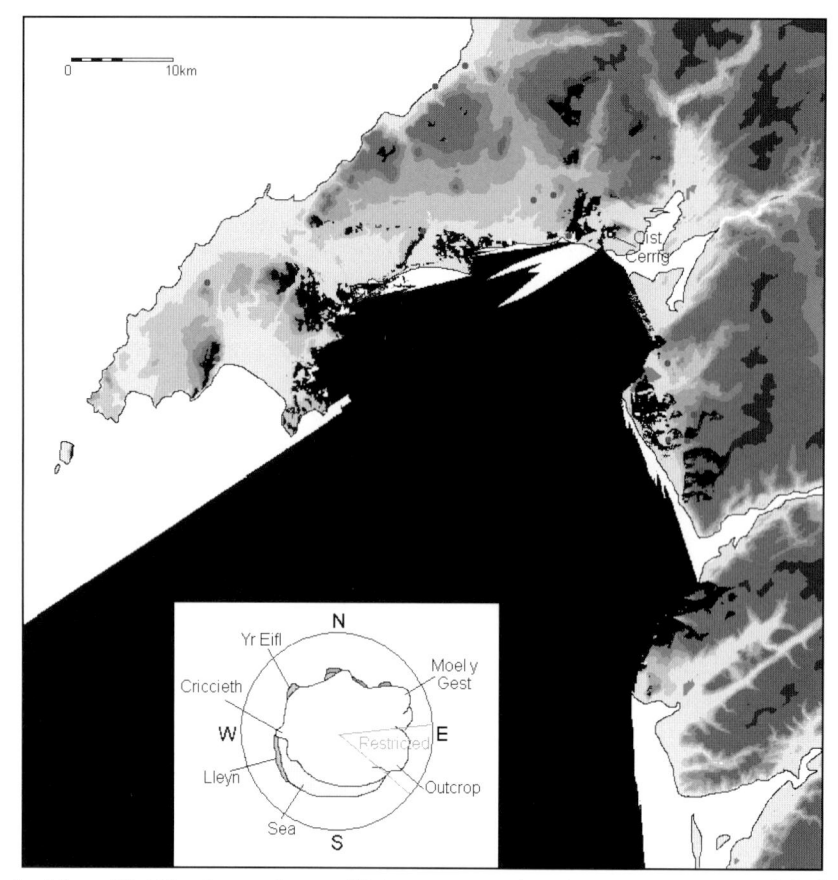

Figure 3.8 The viewshed from Cist Cerrig, north-west Wales, suggests that the mountains around Ardudwy are visible from the site. However, a visit to the monument shows that this is not the case (see embedded landscape schematic). Reproduced by kind permission of Ordnance Survey. © Crown copyright NC/03/20516.

Furthermore, the structural remains of the site cannot easily be included in the program, so GIS would not be able to present how the landscape looked in combination with the structural remains. In short, GIS simply cannot, at present, replicate the experience of being in the landscape. In addition to this there is the assumption that one can see a particular site from the points which are visible *from* the site (the issue of 'views to and views from'; see Wheatley and Gillings 2000, 7–8). This point is illustrated by Woodman's GIS exploration of Orcadian chambered tombs. Here she notes that the sites have exceptionally wide-ranging views of the landscape. As a consequence, the monuments should be visible from many places in the landscape. However, it is not until she visited some of the monuments in the field that she realised that this is not the case; many sites are not actually visible in the landscape, instead blending into their surroundings (Woodman 2000, 95).

Even with these limitations, however, there are advantages to GIS analyses which are presently being explored. As already stated, GIS does allow some field observations to be verified, and it has the potential to allow researchers to show that sites were placed in the landscape differently to randomly generated sites (Lake *et al.* 1998). In the future, more refined or detailed GIS studies than have been possible here may be able to show that sites were specifically positioned to have views of particular features of the landscape. More sophisticated GIS viewsheds are also now being generated which take into account experience and the different visual ranges of the human eye (see for example Wheatley and Gillings's (2000) 'Higuchi viewsheds'). GIS also provides an administrative framework where information can be efficiently organised (Pollard and Gillings 1998, 146) and there is also now the potential for it to be used to integrate different data sets (Mills 2000) as well as more complex landscape reconstructions (Higginbottom *et al.* 2001; see also Goodrick and Gillings 2000). However, the production of these 'integrated media' remains at a time-consuming, experimental stage, and was beyond the scope of this particular study.

The presentation of the landscape

Another key problem with landscape archaeology is the way in which the landscape is presented. Traditionally, the landscape has been depicted using photos, plans and descriptions, and more recently, GIS viewsheds. In this section we assess ways of representing the landscape and outline some of the methods employed in this volume.

A phenomenology of landscape (Tilley 1994) contained a series of black and white photographs which aimed to illustrate the main points of the book, but their poor quality of reproduction limits their ability to convey a sense of place (Cummings 2000a; 2000b). Other, more innovative uses of photography have been published, inspired by the work of David Hockney (1984) amongst others. Shanks in particular has used photographic collages to illustrate a sense of place and also embed temporality into an image (see for example Shanks 1992, 123). Intimate details of particular places are also included, and this photographic style has recently been used successfully by Mark Edmonds who co-authored a volume on the Peak District with a photographer. Here Edmonds and Seaborne (2001) include many images of distinctive natural places and modern features to give the reader a real sense of the landscapes described. Bradley (1998c; 2000) has made effective use of Mark Johnston's distinctive circular photographs as the front covers of books. Within this volume we use traditional photographs as well as photographic strips (see below). In addition, there is an associated website which contains a number of images not printed in the book (www.cardiff.ac.uk/hisar/archaeology/reports/megaliths/).

Diagrams have also been used to depict landscape settings, frequently simplified maps or sketches (for example, see Wainwright 1982 for sketches of north Wales, and Bradley 1998, 125) or even modified distribution maps. In addition to this there are landscape strips, which may have their origins with Alfred Wainwright's landscape drawings of the Lake District (e.g. Wainwright 1960). Landscape panoramas similar to Wainwright's landscape strips appear in a number of publications (e.g. the landscape around Stonehenge: Cleal *et al*. 1995, 38–9). However, these strips are often unwieldy. It is also often difficult to make out the finer details of the landscapes they depict. A variation of these landscape strips has been published which compresses and stretches the landscape strip into a single image (Cummings 2000a, fig 3). This method is also problematic, since it compresses the entire 360° panorama into a single diagram and it is hard not to think of this as a single view.

A whole series of alternative drawings have been produced in an attempt to illustrate the landscape settings of sites. Schematic diagrams have already been described above and are used throughout this volume. However, they are not without their problems. Abstracted and schematic, they offer only a two-dimensional representation of landscape. More recently, these landscape diagrams have been slightly modified, specifically to show the overall asymmetrical location of monuments (see figures in Cummings *et al*. 2002), something not relevant to many of the monuments in Wales and thus not employed here. In another consideration of landscape setting, Williams (1999) demonstrates that the Anglo-Saxon barrow of Lowbury Hill was placed to have wide-ranging views of the surrounding landscape. He illustrates the extent of the view using a schematic diagram showing the distances of the horizon to 16 cardinal points. Interestingly, this contrasts with the GIS viewshed from the site which does not demonstrate the perception of the landscape as commanding in all directions (Williams 1999, 63). Williams also illustrates the views from a series of control samples which do not have such wide-ranging views. Similar control samples were also used by Watson (2000) in his consideration of the landscape settings of stone circles in Britain. Here, Watson demonstrates that many stone circles are located in visually 'circular' landscapes and contrasts the view from the monument with a series of control points to show the overall impression of the horizon. These diagrams are not used here as the megaliths of Wales do not actually seem to be located in order to have wholly unrestricted views, reducing the usefulness of this method. This suggests that the way we present the landscape must be in part specific to the research project and the results of that project.

An increasing range of computer-generated landscape figures is also available. GIS viewsheds have already been discussed above. Using a computer it is also possible to blend together long photographic strips that would otherwise be impossible to stick together or reproduce in a book. A method for doing this has been published elsewhere (Cummings 2000a; 2000b) and a series of panoramas for the monuments of south-west Wales has been produced (Cummings 2001). However, we decided not to include these photographic strips as part of this volume due to the costs of adding a CD to the volume. Computers are also offering a whole range of new ways of representing the landscape and we have already briefly discussed the future of GIS, and there is also the potential of Virtual Reality. Exon *et al*.'s (2001) computer study of the landscapes around Stonehenge which incorporates GIS viewsheds and moving landscape representations is one way in which landscapes may be represented in the future.

4 The monuments of south-west Wales and their landscape settings

Vicki Cummings

The monuments of south-west Wales

With 33 monuments, south-west Wales (Figure 4.1) has one of the densest concentrations of megalithic structures in England and Wales, comparable only to Anglesey and the Cotswolds. The majority of sites in the study area can be found in the north of Pembrokeshire. There are three sites in southern Pembrokeshire and only six sites throughout Carmarthenshire. Other monuments are also found in the study area including two definite stone circles (Barnatt 1989; Burl 1995; Grimes 1938), a cupmarked slab (Trefael: Barker 1992, 52) and a large number of standing stones which it has been suggested are Bronze Age in date (Lewis 1966). A number of monuments may have been destroyed in this area (Fleming 1999, 120), and a full inventory of possible and lost sites is given by Barker (1992). More monuments may of course still be discovered. The relative absence of monuments in the southern half of the area

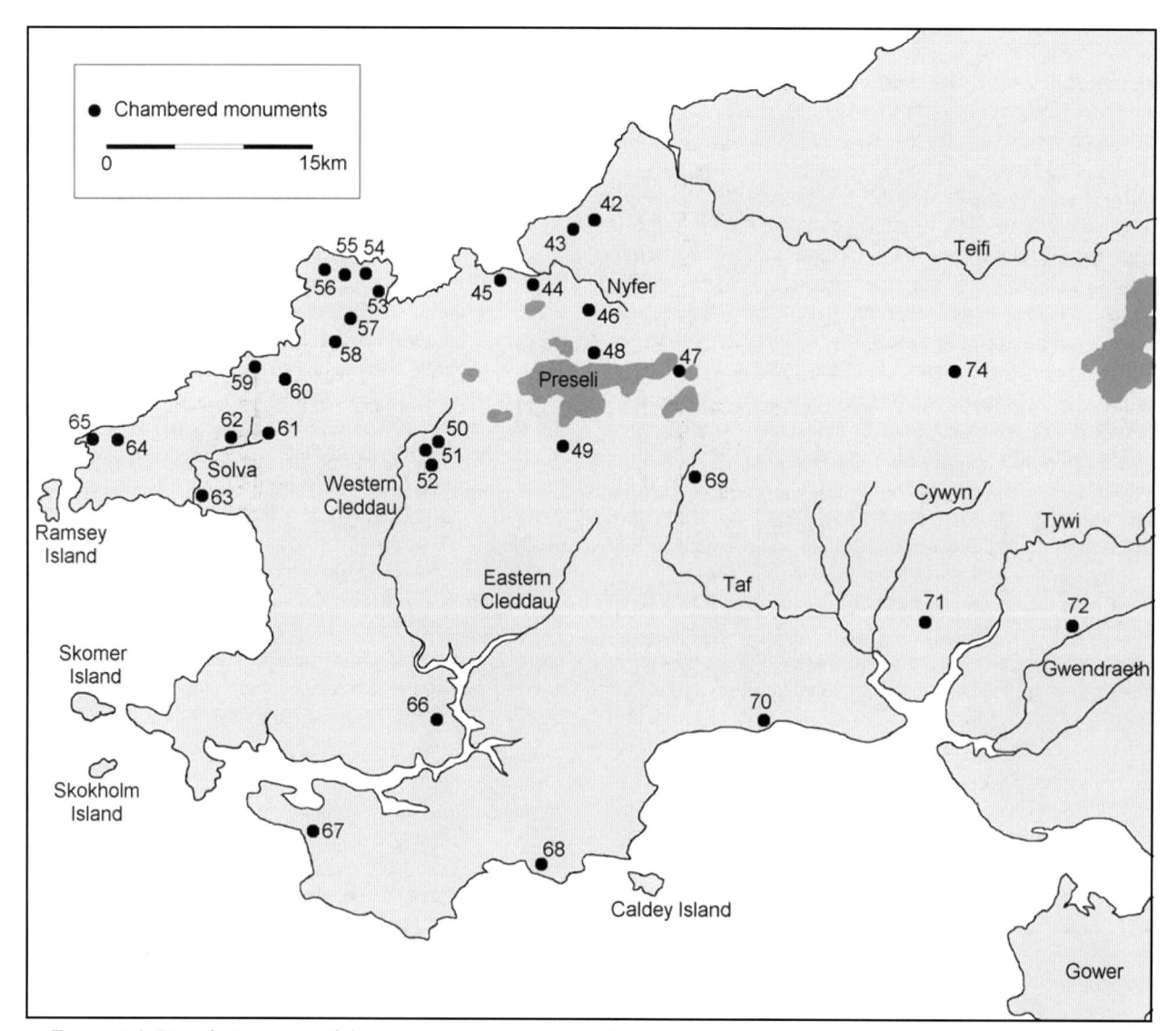

Figure 4.1 Distribution map of the monuments in south-west Wales. Dark shading indicates land over 1000ft (304m).

could be the result of more dense modern settlement there, but it is tempting to see the concentration of sites in the north of Pembrokeshire as genuine, particularly as possible and lost monuments are also concentrated in that part of the region.

Excavations

Only six Neolithic monuments in south-west Wales have been excavated to a reasonable standard, one of these being the stone circle at Meini Gwyr. This site once consisted of 17 stones enclosed within a bank (Grimes 1938). The circle was entered through a grand entrance lined with orthostats. A Bronze Age hearth and pottery sherds were found under one of the stone holes suggesting that the site had been destroyed or at least abandoned in the Bronze Age.

Only five megalithic monuments have been properly excavated. Pentre Ifan was investigated in 1936 and 1937 and again in 1958 and 1959 (Grimes 1948; 1960). The excavations revealed that the site had incorporated a long cairn or low platform (see later discussion) with horns surrounding a forecourt area, and that the crescentic façade and at least some of the cairn/platform were built at the same time. The large chamber was set over a deep pit. Furthermore, the western side of the chamber had once been bounded by two orthostats, while the east was lined by dry stone walling. The chamber had been disturbed prior to excavation but a few flint flakes and four sherds from the neck of a carinated bowl were found. The pottery was similar to that found at Dyffryn Ardudwy in north Wales (Lynch 1969b, 167). In the forecourt, a flint arrowhead and a few fragments of pottery were also found. To the east of the chamber, charcoal and flint flakes were found near to a slab which may once have stood upright. No human bone was found.

Carreg Samson was excavated in 1968 (Lynch 1975a) revealing that the chamber had also been set over a large pit or hollow. Additional stone holes showed that the gap to the north-east was filled with a stone and a passage had once existed to the north-west, which was at least 2m in length. The chamber had been disturbed, but finds included a microlith, a red deer tooth and sherds of pottery. The sherds all came from the same pot which would have been complete when deposited. It was unlike the pottery found at Clegyr Boia or Dyffryn Ardudwy (Lynch 1969a, 149–53) but may be early Neolithic in date. A few small pieces of a cremation burial were also found.

Twlc y Filiast in Carmarthenshire was excavated in 1953, exposing a chamber and antechamber with an elongated cairn or platform (Savory 1956b). A hollow in the floor of the chamber was found which contained dark earth and charcoal flecks. Another hollow was found in the antechamber which contained charcoal and burnt bone. A few finds were found beneath the cairn including a flint scraper, a stone pendant and some fragments of pottery (Savory 1956b, 304).

Carreg Coetan was excavated in 1979 and 1980 (Rees 1992) and although not yet published, the site did produce a series of radiocarbon dates, clustering around 3500 BC (CAR 391–4). Its stone construction was enclosed or incorporated within a round cairn or platform. The chamber itself had been disturbed but did produce sherds of Beaker and Grooved Ware as well as cremated human bone. The area outside the chamber had been paved and on the unsealed old ground surface two patches of cremated human bone and pottery similar to that at Clegyr Boia were found (Barker 1992, 20–21). Finally, the site of Bedd yr Afanc, consisting of two parallel rows of stone enclosed at either end, produced no finds (Grimes 1939a).

In addition to these more recent excavations, a number of sites were investigated by antiquaries, of which six are documented. The chambers at Cerrig y Gof were emptied revealing charcoal, pieces of 'rude' pottery, some particles of bone and black sea pebbles (Fenton 1810, 554–5). At Carn Wnda, Fenton (1848, 284) found red and black ashes mixed with burnt bone and fragments of pottery. There were similar finds at Garn Gilfach. Both chambers at St Elvies were excavated by Oswald without significant result (Barker 1992, 35), as was the monument of Coetan Arthur (Baring Gould et al. 1898, 130). Three of the four chambers at Morfa Bychan were investigated in 1910 (Ward 1918) producing a few flint finds. One further site, that of Ffynnondruidion, was destroyed in 1830 by the tenant farmer, but produced an axe and an adze (Barker 1992, 50).

Morphology and typology

The classification of the monuments of Pembrokeshire has been a matter of debate for many decades. Many scholars have attempted to classify the monuments but agreement has been limited. Over 60 years ago Grimes (1936a, 114) wrote 'I have neither the courage nor the insight to place them in any particular group'. This sentiment has continued through to the present day with Tilley (1994, 90) claiming that they 'do not fit into any neatly recognisable groups', while Fleming (1999, 120) describes the monuments as 'typologically eccentric'. Grimes was one of the first writers to advance any theories on the typology of the south-west Welsh tombs. Although he felt that they essentially could not be classified, he believed that monuments like Pentre Ifan were part of the Irish Sea series, diffused from centres in north-east Ireland and south-west Scotland (Grimes 1948); they fitted more generally into the western long cairn tradition. Likewise, the five chambers at Cerrig y Gof had similarities with sites in south-west Scotland, while passage graves such as Hanging Stone came from Brittany or Ireland (Grimes 1960, 10). Bedd yr Afanc was believed to be a wedge-shaped passage grave (Grimes 1960, 128), although Grimes changed his mind after excavating the site (Grimes 1939a).

Daniel (1950) was one of the few scholars to have actually attempted to classify the monuments, which he

Figure 4.2 The 'classic' portal at Pentre Ifan.

laid out in his seminal work *Prehistoric chamber tombs of England and Wales*. The first class of monument is his 'sub-megalithic' tomb, where the capstone is literally dug out of the earth and propped up. Garn Gilfach, Carn Llidi and The King's Quoit are examples of this type of site in south-west Wales and they can be found more widely in Wales with comparable sites in the Gower and north Wales. A variation of this is the 'earth-fast' chamber, where only one end has been propped up, such as Carn Wnda and Coetan Arthur. This type of monument is also referred to as 'rock-cut' (Daniel 1950, 48). The second class mentioned are passage graves (in their 1950s sense) with polygonal chambers. In south-west Wales, only two monuments of this type could be clearly assigned to this group, Carreg Samson and Hanging Stone. Bedd yr Afanc is described as a gallery grave (again in its 1950s sense), an interpretation which continues to the present day (Children and Nash 1997, 39; Rees 1992). Finally, the remaining sites are simply referred to as the 'Dyfed group', which are claimed to have an Irish origin (Daniel 1950, 154).

The monuments of south-west Wales did not feature extensively in Piggott's (1954) discussion on Neolithic Britain and the focus in the 1960s was primarily on the development of Cotswold-Severn monuments as well as the broader Clyde-Carlingford type (see review in Cummings 2002b). The south-west Welsh monuments were considered in passing by de Valera (1960, 79) who saw connections between these sites and Irish monuments. However, the south-western monuments were not considered at all in *Megalithic enquiries in the west of Britain* (Powell *et al.* 1969), though those of the north were (Lynch 1969b).

In 1972, Francis Lynch re-examined the monuments of the Nevern Valley and suggested that they were part of the broader Irish Sea portal dolmen building tradition (1972, 69). She had already outlined a model for the north Welsh monuments (Lynch 1969b) and suggested that a similar incursion of people may have occurred in south-west Wales, as argued for northern Wales. All monuments in the Nevern Valley are seen as portal dolmen types, although they break into three different groups. First, there are the 'classic' portal dolmen sites (Carreg Coetan, Llech y Dribedd and Trellyffaint), which she claimed were established at an early date in Pembrokeshire (Lynch 1976, 65). Secondly, there are internally developed types of portal dolmen such as Cerrig y Gof, which was the local answer to the need for more burial space (Lynch 1972, 81). The third group was that which illustrated evidence of contact with new, incoming ideas, and this was seen to be found at the site of Pentre Ifan. Lynch believed that this monument began its life as a large portal dolmen (Figure 4.2) set in a square cairn. At a later date (probably in the middle Neolithic) the façade was added and the cairn was lengthened as new ideas arrived from Ireland (Lynch 1972, 71). Sites such as Carreg Samson, Hanging Stone and Gwal y Filiast are described as small chamber

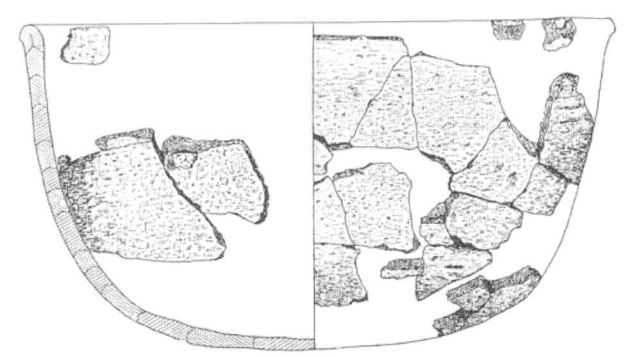

Figure 4.3 The early Neolithic pot from Carreg Samson (after Lynch 1975a).

and passage tombs, following on from Daniel's classification (Lynch 1976, 75). However, Lynch suggested that the rest of the monuments of Dyfed could not be usefully classified.

Bar her construction sequence at Pentre Ifan, Lynch's classifications remained mostly undisputed until 1992 (see Houlder 1974; Savory 1980; Rees 1992), when Barker critiqued in some detail all previous attempts at classification. Barker supported Lynch's suggestion that Pentre Ifan represents a 'genuine' portal dolmen monument, but believed it is the only example in the study area (1992, 76). All the other portal dolmens claimed by Lynch are 'developed, devolved or derivative forms'. Barker does believe, however, that monuments with rectangular chambers and portal entrances do represent a distinct form of monument. Following on from Lynch (1975a, 31), Barker also recognises a second type of monument. These are polygonal chambers with short entrance passages, such as Carreg Samson, and while they are not uniform in shape, he suggests they do represent a different group from the portal-type monuments. Long cairns, monuments next to outcrops and multiple chambered sites are seen as significant but do not constitute typological classes (1992, 77–8). Barker's discussion is the last attempt to classify the monuments of south-west Wales. Tilley (1994) and Fleming (1999) do not attempt any new classification, while Children and Nash (1997a) rather loosely follow Daniel's and Barker's typologies. Even though Barker suggests several groupings, his conclusion remains much the same as Grimes' (1936) sixty years earlier: 'the chambered tombs of SW Wales do not fit neatly into recognised typological groups' (Barker 1992, 78).

Chronology

The chronology of the monuments in south-west Wales remains equally poorly understood. This is partially due to problems with the morphology and the lack of an inferred typological sequence, as well as a meagre quantity of artefactual evidence from the monuments and associated radiocarbon dates. In fact, only one monument in south-west Wales has any radiocarbon dates: those from Carreg Coetan clustering around 3500 BC (CAR 391–4). In addition, the pit in Coygan Camp (Wainwright 1967) has a date of 4000–3650 cal BC (NPL–132). Otherwise, dating sequences have been inferred from the pottery. The settlement site of Clegyr Boia produced pottery similar to that at Dyffryn Ardudwy which implies an early Neolithic date (Lynch 1969a, 169–70; Lynch 1976, 65; Vyner 2001). However, pottery found at Carreg Samson (Figure 4.3) was not comparable to that found at Clegyr Boia, although Lynch still believed that it is early Neolithic in date (Lynch 1976, 65). Pentre Ifan produced a fragment of a bowl with the rest of the pottery undiagnostic. Carreg Coetan has produced pottery, but it still remains unpublished. Here pottery similar to that at Clegyr Boia was found as well as pottery reminiscent of Abingdon Ware (Lynch 1984, 108), corded Beaker and Grooved Ware (Barker 1992, 20).

There is a general consensus that portal dolmen monuments as well as the simple passage graves belong early in the Neolithic (e.g. ApSimon 1986; Barker 1992, 79; Cooney 2000; Lynch 1975a; Lynch 1976, 65; Masters 1981; Sheridan 1986). Lynch in particular has seen portal dolmens as early in the sequence, with the addition of the façade at Pentre Ifan a middle Neolithic phenomenon. There is virtually no discussion on the dates of monuments other than portal dolmens and passage graves, although most commentators seem to agree that Bedd yr Afanc and Cerrig y Gof are late Neolithic monuments.

Monuments in the landscape

Setting the scene

South-west Wales has a variety of contrasting landscapes, with much of Carmarthenshire and southern Pembrokeshire consisting of gently rolling hills now dominated by farmland. By contrast, northern Pembrokeshire is much more hilly with the Preseli mountains a major landscape feature (colour plate 1). Another prominent aspect of northern Pembrokeshire are the rocky outcrops. Many of these outcrops are quite small, and erupt out of hillsides and agricultural land. The four rocky knolls on top of Carnedd Meibion-Owen close to Pentre Ifan, for example, are some of the most distinctive outcrops in the area. There are also larger outcrops across northern Pembrokeshire, frequently set on top of hills, such as the outcrops along Strumble Head and on St David's Head. By comparison, southern Pembrokeshire and Carmarthenshire have few outcrops. Pembrokeshire in particular is well-known for its spectacular coastline, with rugged headlands, small bays and harbours, and offshore islands.

Previous work on landscape

A number of scholars have commented upon the role of the landscape when examining the monuments in south-west Wales. Grimes noted that stone circles are located in very different places to monuments (1936a, 106–10), and observed that monuments are frequently located near to rocky outcrops (1936a, 132). Furthermore, monuments are often placed along the flanks of valleys, avoiding the upland interiors (1936a, 114). Lynch (1972) noted that portal dolmens favour facing up-slope, which may have been more important than compass direction. Lynch also produced one the first 'phenomenological' papers when she addressed the impact of the landscape on prehistoric people, predating Tilley's discussion by 20 years (Lynch 1975b). Although not concentrating specifically on south-west Wales, Lynch did refer to the majesty of Carn Meini and discuss the location of monuments in other parts of Wales.

The landscape setting of monuments in Wales was examined more generally by Roese (1982), who noted that sites occur in low altitude positions close to water. Although their preferred locations are coastal, monuments are always set back from the shoreline. In conclusion, the topography of the region may have determined the siting and orientation of the tombs (Roese 1982, 774). Barker added little to this list, although he believes that the soil type and underlying geology may have been significant (1992, 73). It is perhaps Tilley (1994) who has given the most attention to the importance of landscape, as he included a case study on south-west Wales in his influential study of experiencing landscapes. Here, Tilley describes the location of monuments as highly structured and repetitive, focussing on bays, outlets and peninsulas. Tombs are not sited for maximum visibility or to be intervisible, but are related instead to rocky outcrops and to the coast. Furthermore, monuments may have been located along paths or trackways which allowed people to move through the symbolic geography all around them (Tilley 1994, 105). In another book on landscape, Children and Nash (1997a) follow Tilley's argument closely, arguing that monuments are orientated on rivers, headlands, mountain peaks and the sea. They differ from Tilley by suggesting that the landscape was actually reflected in the plans of the monuments, so that topographic features were symbolically incorporated into each site (1997a, 28). They also stress local variation, so that each regional group of monuments focuses on topographic features in the vicinity.

Critically reviewing Tilley's examination of the landscapes of south-west Wales, Fleming (1999, 120) suggests that the diversity of monuments and the apparent destruction of so many sites create a poor data set with which to work. The relationship between tombs and rocky outcrops is purely due to the fact that sites in such locations would be more likely to remain untouched than in agricultural areas. And finally, the claimed symbolic importance of Carn Ingli is criticised, as Fleming argues (1999, 121) that it would be impossible to site a monument in the Nevern Valley without referencing this mountain. These are the only problems noted with this data set; however, he has many more criticisms of Tilley's Black Mountains case study in south-east Wales (1999, 121–3), which is reviewed in chapter 6.

General location

The monuments of south-west Wales are found in discrete areas of the region. The distribution map (Figure 4.1) shows that the densest concentration of sites is in northern Pembrokeshire, with considerable 'blank' areas south of the Preselis and west of Haverfordwest. There are a number of isolated monuments spread through southern Pembrokeshire and throughout Carmarthenshire. The majority of monuments are located on what is now agricultural land (61%), with the remainder found on marginal land (39%). This relationship is only meaningful if we assume, for argument's sake, that the modern land usage reflects potential prehistoric conditions in some sort of way. The monuments which are located on rougher land are frequently those which are positioned right up against outcrops (see below), such as those set along Strumble Head and the monuments on St David's Head. Sites are located on average at 124m OD, although there are some striking anomalies. Carreg Coetan is the lowest-lying monument at just 10m OD, while the site of Mountain is positioned at just over 250m OD. The vast majority of sites (81%) are also located out of river valleys. Although no systematic fieldwork has been conducted in the interior of south-west Wales, it seems likely that the river valleys may have been one of the areas used for settlement. The river valleys would have provided a wide range of resources for both short-stay or longer-term settlement, and similar river valleys elsewhere seem to have been the focus for settlement in other areas of the Britain such as the Black Isle in north-east Scotland (Phillips and Watson 2000). Instead, most monuments are set up and out of the river valleys, although a few sites overlook rivers (see below). It seems, then, that most monuments were set away from areas which may have been the primary focus for settlement activity, while still being set on what is now good agricultural land. A smaller number of sites are located right up against large outcrops on the top of hills, away from the low-lying areas.

Geology

South-west Wales has an extremely complex geology, consisting of a diverse range of rock types. North Pembrokeshire has the most complex geology of the area, consisting of sandstone, Ordovician rocks and grits and shales, broken up by contemporaneous and intrusive rocks. In contrast, southern Pembrokeshire and Carmarthenshire have a gentler landscape consisting of Old Red Sandstone and carboniferous limestone, with igneous rocks only to the north (George 1970). Over half of the monuments in south-west Wales are located on intrusive igneous rocks. This may not seem remarkable, yet intrusive igneous rocks are by no means the most common rock type. They mostly occur in northern Pembrokeshire, where the densest concentration of monuments is found. While it could be argued that people had an intimate knowledge of their

Figure 4.4 The rock outcrops visible on the horizon from Pentre Ifan.

topography and were deliberately choosing to build monuments in these geological areas, it is likely that this preference for certain geological zones may be due to the characteristics of these rocks. For example, the reason that many sites are positioned in relation to intrusive igneous rocks may be that this is the rock type that creates the distinctive outcropping in northern Pembrokeshire.

Rocky outcrops

Tilley (1994, 94–105) described the relationship between monuments and outcrops in some detail in his study of the area. He discusses the location of the 'cemeteries' of Carn Wen and Morfa Bychan (sites with multiple chambers), which are arranged alongside 'linear' outcrops. He also suggests that other monuments may have been positioned in relation to the smaller 'circular' outcrops that are found in the area. He suggests that these outcrops may have been focal points in the landscape, keying the monuments into the wider landscape (Tilley 1994, 99). Carreg Samson, located between two outcrops, may have been situated on a pathway between these outcrops. Tilley also notes that Pentre Ifan is situated near the four prominent outcrops of Carnedd Meibion-Owen (Figure 4.4). Although Tilley thus discusses the relationship between outcrops and monuments in some detail, still more can be said.

A considerable number (some 36%) of monuments in south-west Wales have rocky outcrops visible on the skyline. As Tilley observed, this relationship is most pronounced at Pentre Ifan, but it occurs at other sites as well. For example, the striking outcrops of Great Treffgarne are visible on the skyline when standing in the façade at Garn Turne (Figure 4.5). Sites further afield such as Hanging Stone in southern Pembrokeshire are positioned so that an outcrop is just visible on the horizon, and a similar situation occurs at the White House monument. Had these monuments been located further down the slope on which they stand, the outcrops would not have been visible on the skyline (see chapter 3). Furthermore, the architecture appears to be designed so that these outcrops are visible at key moments in the use of a site. At Carreg Samson, the architecture of the monument seems to refer to the outcrops in the landscape. One of the outcrops here is on the alignment of the passage, while the other would have been visible when leaving the chamber. At Pentre Ifan the skylined outcrops are visible as one leaves the orthostatic façade. At these sites, then, monuments seem to have been built so that outcrops were not in the immediate vicinity but visible on the horizon (Cummings 2002a, 110–11), designed to be seen as one entered or left the chamber area.

The rocky outcrops that are visible from sites such as Carreg Samson and Hanging Stone are the smaller outcrops which erupt from flat land. In contrast, other sites in southwest Wales are positioned right up against outcrops (24%). These include the two 'cemeteries' discussed by Tilley, but also the sites found along Strumble Head, on St David's Head, and Mynydd Llangynderyn in Carmarthenshire (colour plate 3). These outcrops are quite different in nature from the outcrops that were skylined at other sites. These outcrops are part of larger hills; indeed, Tilley notes that the monuments set against these outcrops are not easily visible in the landscape, but the outcrops on which they stand are (Tilley 1994, 99). Not all these large

Figure 4.5 The Great Treffgarne rocks are visible on the skyline from Garn Turne.

Figure 4.6 Carn Wnda stands up against rocky outcrops.

outcrops have monuments against them. Strumble Head has a row of seven hills with outcrops on their summits running across the headland, but only three of these outcrops have monuments built against them. These are sites such as Carn Wnda which is positioned right up against the outcrops of Garnwnda (Figure 4.6). The monuments positioned right up against outcrops are morphologically quite different from the other monuments in south-west Wales, and we will discuss the classification of these sites in more detail below. The remainder of the monuments in south-west Wales (39%), many of these in or around the Nevern Valley, are not positioned in relation to outcrops.

Mountains

Before we discuss the significance of the mountains of south-west Wales, we would like to briefly define what a mountain is. Traditionally, a mountain was over 1000ft (304m) and it is this definition which has undoubtedly led to the description of the Preselis (with the highest point being only 536m OD) and the Black Mountains (highest

Figure 4.7 Carn Ingli visible behind Llech y Dribedd.

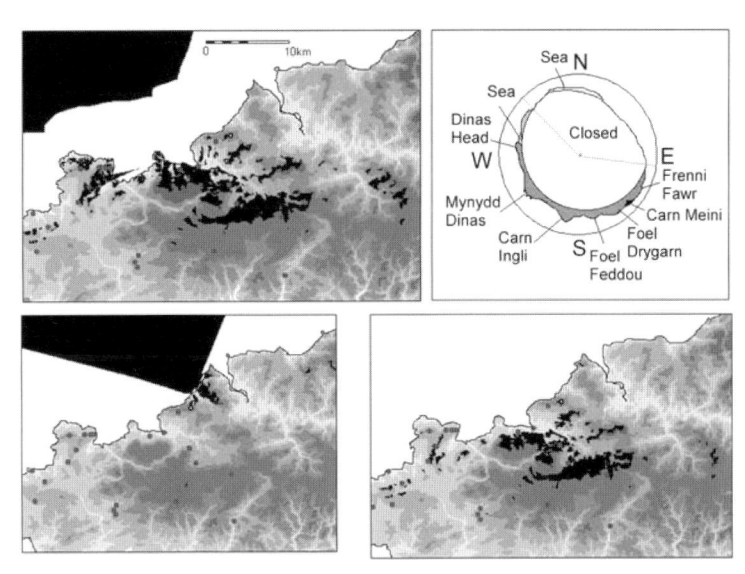

Figure 4.8 GIS control samples from Llech y Dribedd. The top left image is the viewshed from the monument, with the schematic representation of this view top right. Bottom left is a viewshed taken 200m to the north of the monument. From here it is no longer possible to see the Preselis. Bottom right is the viewshed 200m to the west of the monument, and from here it is no longer possible to see the sea. Reproduced by kind permission of Ordnance Survey. © Crown copyright NC/03/20516.

point 811m OD) as 'mountains'. We will therefore stick to this definition of a mountain throughout the text, while acknowledging that nowadays mountains are usually considered higher.

A number of the mountains in Pembrokeshire are visible from many of the monuments. Tilley (1994, 105) discusses the significance of Carn Ingli in relation to sites in the Nevern Valley, suggesting that Pentre Ifan (colour plate 5), Llech y Dribedd (Figure 4.7) and Trellyffaint may have been positioned so that they overlooked this particular mountain. Carn Ingli is visible from a total of seven sites in south-west Wales, mainly those in the Nevern Valley as well as Carn Wen and Parc y Cromlech above Fishguard Harbour. From these sites, Carn Ingli is an impressive mountain, dominant in the Nevern Valley. From sites like Llech y Dribedd (7km away) and Trellyffaint (6km away) the summit of Carn Ingli is a distinctive tipped peak on the horizon. At other sites such as Pentre Ifan, situated 3.5km away to the east, the whole length of the mountain is visible on the horizon. However, Fleming (1999, 121) questions the significance of this relationship, claiming that it would be difficult to avoid a view of Carn Ingli in this area of Pembrokeshire. However, one monument in the area manages just that. The monument of Bedd yr Afanc (admittedly by general consensus later in date) is 5km from Carn Ingli, yet the mountain cannot be seen. Likewise, had Llech y Dribedd been positioned a few hundred metres to the north or east, Carn Ingli would no longer have been visible (see Figure 4.8). It seems then, that monument builders had a choice regarding the precise location of each monument in the landscape, and that a view of Carn Ingli was not guaranteed when building a monument in the Nevern Valley. Furthermore, the topography of the Nevern Valley is gently undulating, meaning that Carn Ingli is frequently out of sight when moving through this area. The significance and possible meaning of Carn Ingli and other peaks will be discussed in depth in chapter 7.

Other mountains are visible from Neolithic sites. The Preselis are visible from ten sites in south-west Wales. This includes sites such as Llech y Dribedd, Trellyffaint and Pentre Ifan (see Figure 4.9) which are set only 10km from the Preselis as well as sites set further away. From Carreg Samson there are clear views of the Preselis which are visible on the skyline aligned on the passage and a nearby outcrop. The Preselis are also visible from the Devil's Quoit almost 40km away and in chapter 7 we will discuss the fact that a number of monuments in north Wales also have views of the Preselis. The Preselis are the largest mountains in south-west Wales although they are quite compact compared to the Brecon Beacons or Snowdonia, stretching lengthways for only 15km from Cerrig Lladron to Frenni Fawr. The highest summit in the Preselis is Foel Cwmcerwyn at 536m OD, although it is the rocky outcrops to the east which are more visually arresting than the highest point. Indeed, it is the summit of Carn Meini, the source of the Stonehenge bluestones and a Neolithic stone axe quarry, which seems to have been a primary focus for the monument builders (Bradley 1998c; 2000). Carn Meini is visually spectacular (Figure 4.10), consisting of a number of dramatic outcrops erupting from the hilltop. Among them are a series of natural forms which resemble built structures, including standing stones and chambered tombs (Cummings 2002a). Contrasting with the dark volcanic outcrops is a distinctive row of bright white quartz boulders which run across the summit. The nearby outcrops of Carn Bica, Carn Sian, Carn Breseb and Carn Alw are also visually spectacular. The importance of the Preselis seems to have continued into the late Neolithic in south-west Wales as the two stone circles of Gors Fawr and Meini Gwyr were built with clear views of the range, in particular the summit of Carn Meini (Figure 4.11). Both stone circles may have been placed along the route the bluestones could have taken on their journey to Wiltshire. Again, the significance of the Preselis and Carn Meini will be discussed in detail in chapter 7.

It is therefore interesting that one site in south-west Wales seems to specifically block or exclude views of the

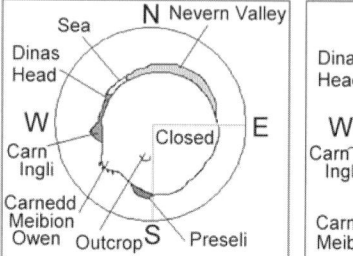

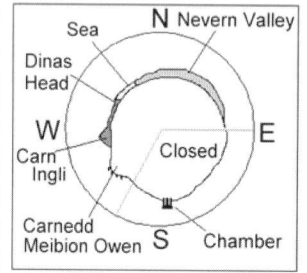

Figure 4.9 Schematic views of Pentre Ifan. Left is the view from the chamber, right is the view from the tail-end of the long cairn. The tail of the cairn is set downslope from the chamber and from this point the Preselis can no longer be seen on the horizon. Just beyond the tail the ground drops away quite steeply meaning that the monument as well as the outcrops of Carnedd Meibion Owen would no longer be visible when approaching from this direction.

Figure 4.10 The outcrops on the summit of Carn Meini.

Figure 4.11 The stone circle of Gors Fawr with Carn Meini in the background to the right.

Mynydd Preseli. The site of Garn Turne has a restricted view towards the east which blocks out the view towards the Preselis. When standing in the façade, the Preselis are blocked from view by the immediate hillslope, yet standing on the capstone, or a few metres uphill of the façade, the Preselis appear on the horizon (Figure 4.12). At this site, a restricted view in this direction means that the mountains cannot be seen at all from the site.

The other summit which is visible from a number of sites is Carn Llidi (colour plate 6). This hill can be seen from six sites in south-west Wales, including Garn Turne over 24km away (although the Preselis only 10km away cannot be seen). Two small monuments were actually built on the side of Carn Llidi. Carn Llidi is the largest hill to the west of the Preselis, and at 181m OD is higher than the hills with monuments which run across Strumble Head. Standing on St David's Head, Carn Llidi is a distinctive peaked hill with outcrops on the summit which overlooks an otherwise quite flat landscape.

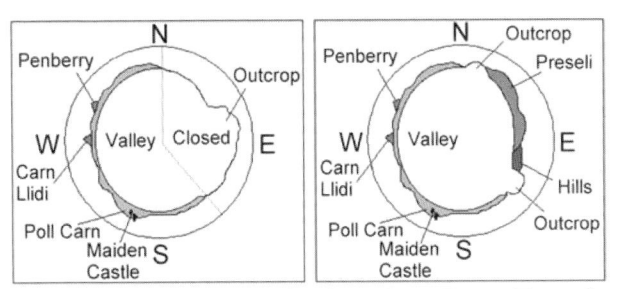

Figure 4.12 Control samples from Garn Turne. From the site itself the Preseli mountains are not visible, but a few metres uphill of the façade and they are visible.

Views of the sea

Tilley (1994, 93) noted that many of the monuments of south-west Wales have a complex relationship with the coastline, with 54% of sites placed within 1km of the sea. However, although monuments are located close to the sea, many do not seem to make this the focus of the view. Tilley emphasises this point with the example of St Elvies, which is located only a short distance from the sea (500m), but from the site there is only a view inland (1994, 93). Indeed, although many of the sites have a general coastal distribution, only 72% of sites have a view of the sea. From many of these sites, only a very small portion of the coastline is visible. This is particularly noticeable at sites such as White House and Treffynnon where there is a narrow view of the sea. These two sites are located 4km inland but seem to have been specifically located so that there was a view of the sea (Figure 4.13). However, it seems that although it may have been desirable to build a monument from which the sea was visible, this view should not be too expansive. Sites such as Carreg Coetan and Carreg Samson (colour plate 4) are located only a few hundred metres from the sea, yet they are not positioned to have wide views of the coast. In contrast, the smaller monuments set up against outcrops have wide-ranging views of the sea. From sites such as Coetan Arthur and Carn Wnda there are sweeping coastal vistas.

Rivers

It has already been noted that monuments are generally set away from the river valleys. 39% of sites are not positioned in relation to a river at all (the nearest river

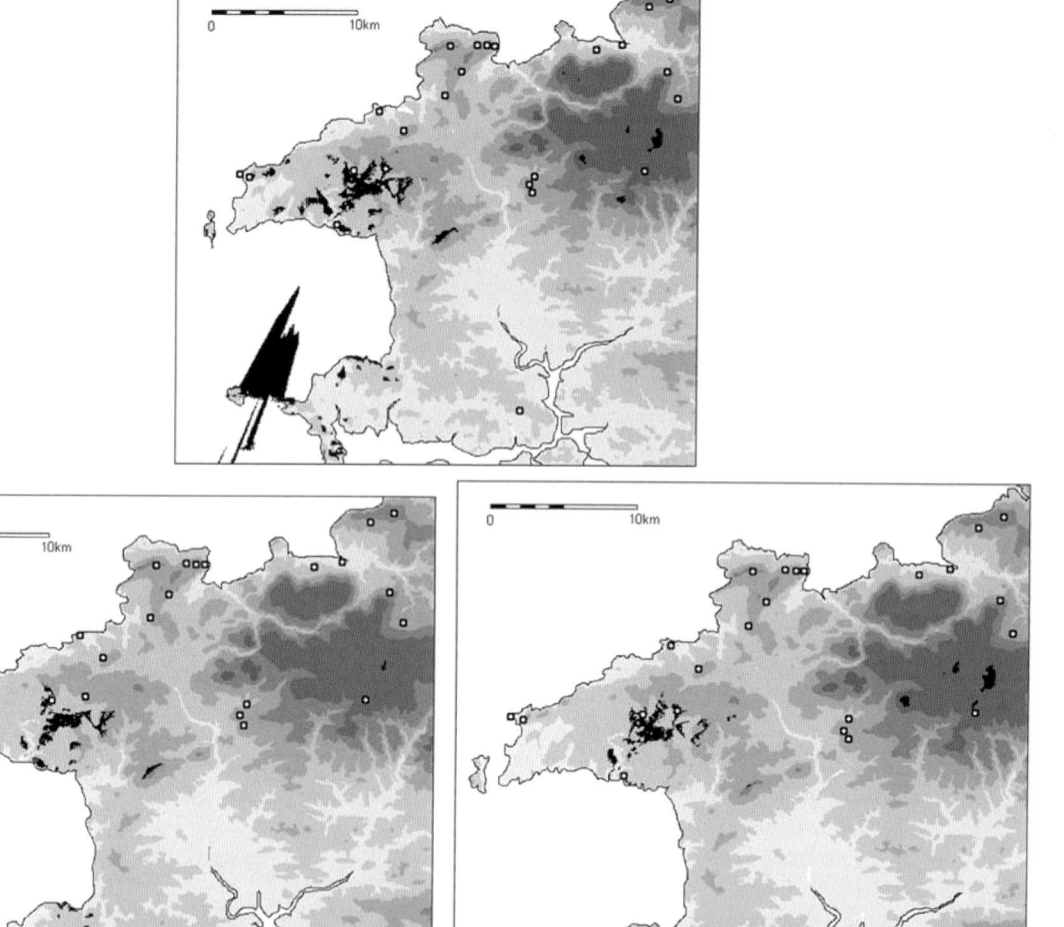

Figure 4.13 GIS control samples from White House. The top image is the viewshed from White House. From this site one can clearly see the sea and the Preselis. However, 500m to the west (bottom left) or 500m to the south (bottom right) this view of the sea is lost, as is the view of the Preselis to the west. Reproduced by kind permission of Ordnance Survey. © Crown copyright NC/03/20516.

being over 5km away). The vast majority of these sites are those positioned right up against the outcrops on Strumble Head, St David's Head and in southern Pembrokeshire. The rest of the monuments are on average 1.3km from the nearest river. Of these, six sites could be said to have been placed directly in relation to a river. Carreg Coetan is positioned to overlook the point where the Afon Nyfer joins the sea (colour plate 2). Mountain in the Preselis is set at the source of the Eastern Cleddau, while Colston is located just above the point where the Afon Anghof meets with the Western Cleddau. Hanging Stone in southern Pembrokeshire is positioned 4km from the point where the Eastern and Western Cleddau rivers meet (the Daugleddau), but has clear views of this estuary. Gwal y Filiast in Carmarthenshire is located right next to the Afon Taf; indeed, Tilley suggests this particular monument is positioned such that the rapids below can be heard from the monument (Tilley 1994, 109). The site of Gelli, one of the outliers in Carmarthenshire, is positioned close to the Afon Towy. It seems then, that most monuments are located rather generally in relation to rivers, but are mostly set at a distance from these so that they *overlook* river valleys. In six cases, however, sites seems to have been located in direct relation to certain rivers.

Harbours, inlets, bays, springs and streams

Tilley (1994, 93) briefly commented on the relationship between monuments and bays and inlets, suggesting they must have been an important factor in site location. This relationship is pronounced at 33% of sites, and obviously has no bearing on the location of the inland monuments. Carreg Coetan is close to Newport Bay, while Parc y Cromlech and Carn Wen are both located with clear views

Figure. 4.14 The King's Quoit overlooks the sea at Manorbier.

of Fishguard Harbour. Further along this coastline, Carreg Samson is close to the harbour at Abercastle, which provides a natural sheltered bay. Likewise, St Elvies is less than a kilometre from Solva Harbour. The King's Quoit in southern Pembrokeshire overlooks Manorbier Bay (Figure 4.14). Finally, three sites have views of wide expanses of beach, with Coetan Arthur and Carn Llidi being close to Whitesands Bay, and the Morfa Bychan chambers overlooking Pendine Sands. A quarter of the monuments are positioned within 250m of a spring, and a third of sites have a stream nearby. Sites such as Treffynnon, White House and Mountain all have springs close by. However, although this relationship may be simply fortuitous, springs could conceivably have been used for deposition or have been significant in their own right.

Islands

There are four sizeable and distinctive islands along the south-west Wales coastline: Ramsey Island off St David's Head, Skomer and Skokholm Islands to the south, and Caldey Island near Tenby. However, these islands do not appear to be key reference points in the landscape as only a few monuments have views of them. From the site of White House, the islands of Skomer and Skokholm are visible over 20km away. A short distance from White House, the site of Treffynnon also has views of Skomer and Skokholm Islands as well as Ramsey Island. Ramsey Island is clearly visible from the sites of Coetan Arthur (Figure 4.15) and Carn Llidi, both of which are located only a few kilometres from this island. When standing on the capstone at St Elvies, Ramsey Island is visible. However, at ground level the island cannot be seen. The lack of monuments in the southern half of the area means that only the site of Morfa Bychan has views towards Caldey Island. People undoubtedly visited Caldey Island in the Neolithic, however, as human bone has been found here (Schulting 1998; Schulting and Richards 2002)

Other land forms

There are other prominent land forms in the landscape which seem to have been a focus for the monuments. Seven monuments have views of Dinas Head (Figure 4.16), although no monuments are built on or near the headland itself. Pentre Ifan, Llech y Dribedd, Trellyffaint and Carreg Coetan all have clear views towards this distinctive headland. St David's Head may also have been important as three sites have clear views of the headland while another is actually built on it. The headland was the focus for later activity, with extensive prehistoric field systems and settlements (Murphy 2001).

A number of the monuments are located near to other natural features which may have been important in the

Figure 4.15 Coetan Arthur with Ramsey Island in the distance.

Figure 4.16 Dinas Head.

Neolithic. This relationship is primarily found at those monuments which are positioned right up against outcrops (see above). Around the sites on Strumble Head for example, there a number of natural features which resemble the nearby monuments. This issue has been discussed in more detail elsewhere (Cummings 2002a), where it is suggested that the status of these outcrops may have been rather ambiguous in the Neolithic. The likeness of natural features to monuments confused many of the antiquaries examining these sites, who mistook natural features for monuments (see Barker 1992). This relationship is particularly complex at Carn Wnda and Garn Gilfach, where there are many rocky forms which resemble built structures. The King's Quoit is also placed against a series of natural slabs which appear to be part of the monument itself. Antiquaries were unsure whether 'this particular object were a cromlech at all, and not simply an accidental formation' (Barker 1992, 38). This site is also near a number of other distinctive natural features including blowholes and deep chasms.

Restricted views

One of the most characteristic features of monuments throughout this region and beyond is that they all have a restricted view in one direction. The positioning of the monument on the side of a hill or slope means that one vista faces an immediate landscape, thus creating a restricted view. No distant landscape features can be seen beyond this immediate setting, which is normally visible for only a few tens of metres. All bar two (94%) of the monuments have a restricted view in one direction, and the exceptions, Bedd yr Afanc and Cerrig y Gof, may be later in date. It may seem difficult to demonstrate that a restricted view is meaningful, as this could simply be a by-product of these sites being placed on the side of a hill. However, not all sites that have a restricted view are located on the side of a hill. Sites such as Ffyst Samson and St Elvies seem to be carefully placed in the landscape so that there is dead ground visible in one direction. Furthermore, other types of Neolithic site are positioned with wide-ranging views in all directions which suggests that the presence of a restricted view may indeed be meaningful. Stone circles in Pembrokeshire (e.g. Gors Fawr and see Figure 4.17) and beyond have been shown to have long-distance views in all directions (Bradley 1998c, 116–31; Richards 1996b; Watson 2000). This is often not achieved by placing the site on the top of a hill. Instead, at sites like Gors Fawr, the monument is positioned on an open expanse where the surrounding topography appears to be distant in all directions. It is thus of interest that the sites of Bedd yr Afanc and Cerrig y Gof do not have restricted views. We will discuss the classification of these sites in more detail below. Restricted views are a recurrent feature in all our study areas in Wales, and also beyond, and we return to their possible significance in chapter 7.

These restricted views from monuments are to all points

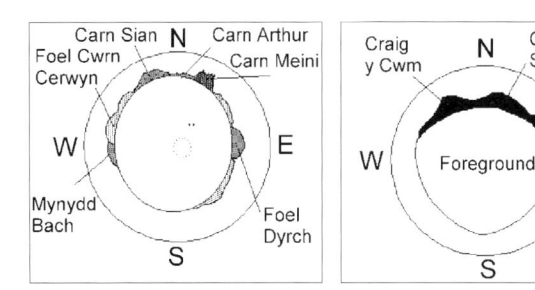

Figure 4.17 The landscape settings of the stone circles of Gors Fawr (left) and Meini Gwyr (right).

of the compass, although the north and the east are generally favoured. The percentage of the outlook which is restricted from wider view varies considerably, but the parameters may have been significant. Only two sites (Mountain and White House) have a restricted view which is less that 90°. Most monuments have a restricted view anywhere between 90° and 180° of the outlook, although there are a few exceptions. Sites which have over half of the view restricted are those which are positioned right up against outcrops, such as Carn Wnda and Garn Gilfach. This may be a result of the sites being set right up against the outcrops, but it also meant that over half of the view was closed from view for people encountering these sites.

Intervisibility

Tilley notes that very few of the monuments are located so as to be intervisible with one another (1994, 93). Pentre Ifan is visible across the valley from Llech y Dribedd and Trellyffaint, although the latter two monuments, only 2km apart, are not intervisible. A similar relationship can be found further west; Carreg Samson is visible across the valley from Ffyst Samson and Trewalter Llwyd, although the latter two monuments again are not intervisible. The similarity in form of these sites, in combination with their intervisiblity, could suggest that they were contemporary and specifically located in order to have views of other sites. The smaller chambers at Carn Llidi and Coetan Arthur on St David's Head, only 1km apart, are also intervisible. Although the chambers of the sites which are positioned right up against outcrops are not intervisible at most sites, the outcrops upon which the chambers are placed are; it has already been noted that Carn Llidi is visible from several sites in Pembrokeshire. Garn Gilfach also has a monument on it and the outcrop on which it stands is highly visible throughout the surrounding landscape even though the monument itself is not. Tilley (1994, 99) also comments on this relationship, suggesting that the outcrops draw attention to the location of the monuments, even if the sites themselves cannot be seen.

Location in relation to Mesolithic sites

It has been suggested that the location of the Neolithic

38   *Vicki Cummings*

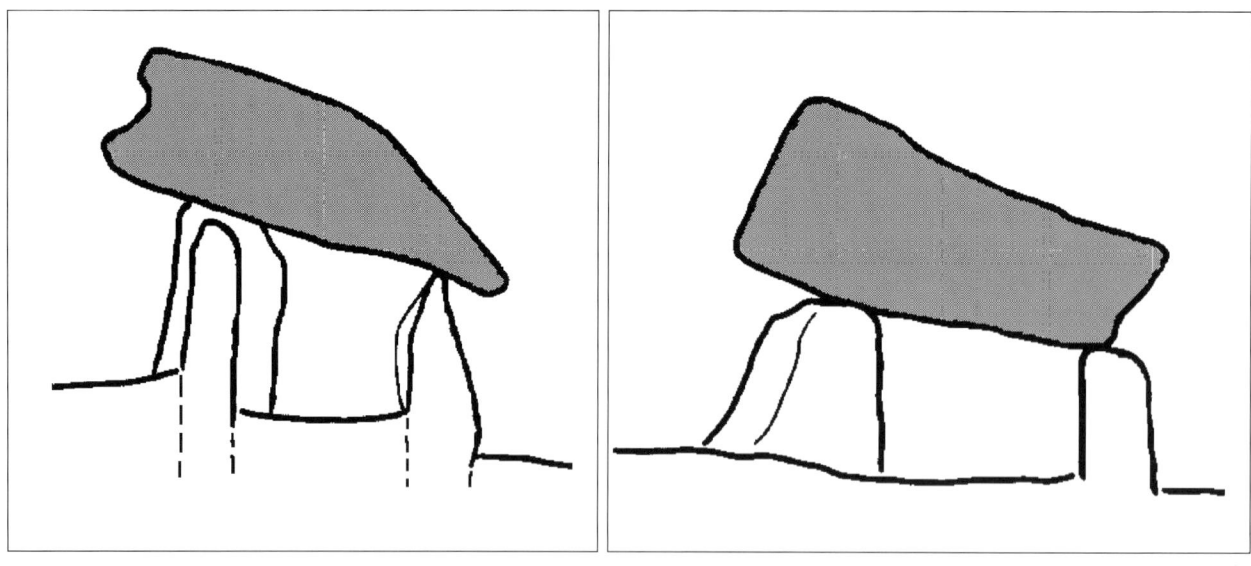

Figure 4.18 The distinctive capstones at Carreg Coetan and Llech y Dribedd (after Barker 1992).

monuments may be related to Mesolithic occupation sites (Tilley 1994, 87). A few sites are actually located next to Mesolithic locales, such as Carreg Samson, Carreg Coetan, the Devil's Quoit and the King's Quoit. Furthermore, several sites have clear views towards areas that were used extensively in the Mesolithic. Carn Llidi, for example, has clear views out over many of the Mesolithic locales found around St Brides Bay. We also know that Pembrokeshire as a whole was utilised throughout the Mesolithic and it is highly likely that the monuments were located in relation to a landscape already filled within meaningful, possibly mythical, places (Cummings 2000; and see chapter 7). It is striking, however, that there are no known monuments for over 15km from Nab Head, perhaps one of the most important Mesolithic sites in the area (David 1990).

Back to classification

Now that we have outlined the major landscape features which are visible from the monuments in south-west Wales, we can reconsider the classification of these sites. We suggest that the structural remains *in combination* with the landscape settings of the monuments can actually inform the classification of these structures.

On this basis, the monuments of south-west Wales can be divided rather roughly into two different classes. First, there are the larger monuments, which seem to be primarily influenced by the portal dolmen tradition found throughout the Irish Sea zone. There are three main concentrations of these: in the Nevern Valley (including sites such as Llech y Dribedd, Pentre Ifan and Carreg Coetan); the inland group (including Garn Turne, Mountain and Gwal y Filiast); and the Mathry group (including White House, Carreg Samson and Trewalter Llwyd).

The excavations at Carreg Coetan (Rees 1992), Carreg Samson (Lynch 1975a) and Pentre Ifan (Grimes 1948) all suggest that these sites are early Neolithic in date. Previously it has been argued that monuments such as Carreg Coetan, Carreg Samson and Pentre Ifan are typologically rather different. Carreg Coetan has been classed as a dolmen (Lynch 1972), but it has now been shown not to have the classic portalled entrance (Barker 1992, 20). The presence of a small passage at Carreg Samson has led to this site being affiliated to the passage grave tradition (Lynch 1975a), whereas Pentre Ifan has been considered a portal dolmen with an Irish façade set within a long cairn (Lynch 1976). However, these rather rigid classifications seem to ignore the fact that these sites also share many similarities. There are several factors to support the argument that these sites are essentially similar in nature. Each site consists of a large bulky capstone set on top of a number of smaller uprights thus creating a small box-like chamber area. At all these sites, the capstones appear to be almost floating above the ground (Figure 4.18; Cummings 2001; Whittle 2003b; and see chapter 7). The question of the form of cairns or platforms is also discussed further in chapter 7; we do not believe these were prominent. Indeed, the primary aim of these monuments in south-west Wales may have been to display particularly distinctive capstones (Whittle 2003a; 2003b; and see chapter 7). Some of these sites may have had small passages leading to the chamber area such as at Hanging Stone and Carreg Samson, while others such as Llech y Dribedd and Carreg Coetan seem to have had only a simple chamber. The small size of chambers does not suggest that these sites were primarily designed for the deposition of large amounts of human remains as in the Cotswold-Severn monuments further east. However, the presence of cremated remains at Carreg Coetan may suggest that some at least of these places were still connected with the deposition of the dead or became so at some point in their history. The sparse quantities of material culture recovered from these sites may suggest that it was the construction of these sites, and the creation of a permanent location in the landscape, that were critical.

These sites also share many similarities in landscape location which further supports this generalising classification. One of the key features of these monuments is that they have views of rock outcrops, either closer at hand such as those immediately above Pentre Ifan or further away, such as those on Carn Ingli and the Preselis. These sites are also almost exclusively located on what is now reasonable or good agricultural land, but set up and away from the river valleys. In this sense, they are positioned on the margins of the low-lying landscape, which may have been one of the focal areas for settlement, and thus may have been designed to be seen and approached from these areas. Many of these sites have a view of the sea, but this view is almost always only a small part of the vista. These sites also have views of other similar sites and potentially highly symbolic landscape features, such as the beginnings of rivers or springs. Furthermore, all have a restricted view in one direction, but this never exceeded half of the view.

Thus there seems to be a distinctive set of monuments in south-west Wales which take elements of the portal dolmen tradition to create individual sites that are fitted into local settings. At present it is a plausible hypothesis that these sites are early Neolithic in date and combine elements of a broader Irish Sea tradition in a localised fashion. It is possible to suggest that the overall experience of encountering these sites in the landscape is remarkably similar across south-west Wales.

The second distinctive class or group in south-west Wales are the 'earth-fast' monuments, in the terminology of Daniel (1950). This description remains appropriate, as all these sites have one end of their capstone touching the ground. All have thin capstones, which contrast with

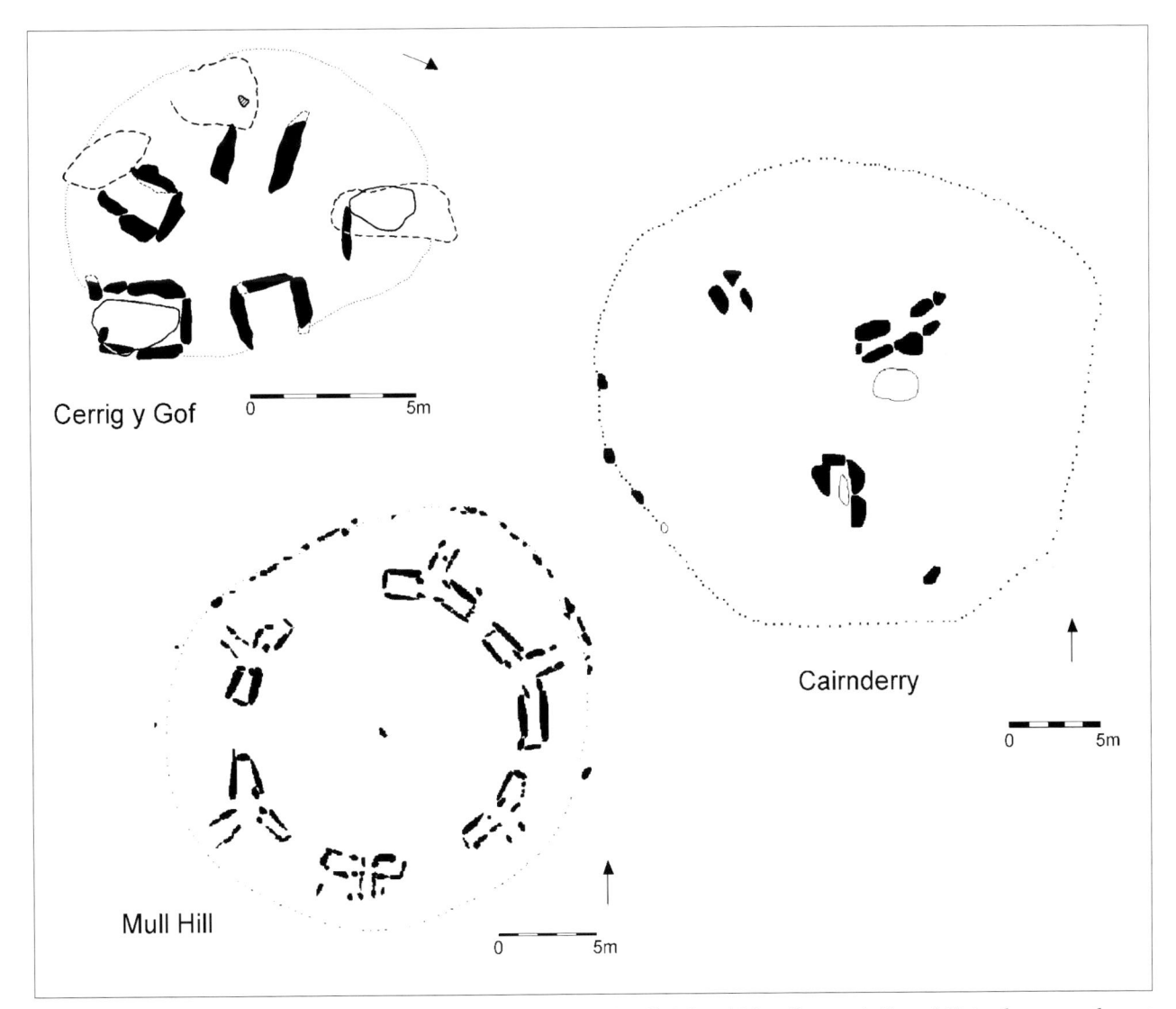

Figure 4.19 Plans of Cerrig y Gof, Pembrokeshire (top), Mull Hill, Isle of Man (bottom left) and Cairnderry, south-west Scotland (bottom right) (after Barker 1992; Burrow 1997 and Henshall 1972).

the bulky capstones on the portal dolmen sites. Their form creates much smaller chamber areas than the portal dolmens. Perhaps their most distinctive feature is their location right next to rocky outcrops, which distinguishes this group from the other monuments in south-west Wales. These megaliths were not, like the others, fitted into the landscape in relation to a whole variety of important symbolic features, but were literally placed on top of some of the most dramatic features in the landscape. This seems to be the dominant principle in the location of these sites. The lack of modern excavation at them means that there is no indication of the date of these monuments. Elsewhere it has been suggested that they could be later Neolithic in date (Cummings 2001), but equally they may be contemporary with the portal dolmen monuments. Excavation is required to address this issue.

There remain a few sites which do not fit into either of these two classifications, and it is worth briefly discussing these (and see discussion in chapter 7). The five-chambered site of Cerrig y Gof is typologically unparalleled in Wales (Figure 4.19), and it has been suggested that this site could be linked to Mull Hill on the Isle of Man (Darvill 2000, 376; Lynch 1972, 80–2) or the Bargrennan monuments of south-west Scotland (Darvill 2000, 376). This site could represent a later import of a more exotic kind of construction, perhaps an attempt to create links with other, more distant places. The site of Bedd yr Afanc has been described as a gallery grave (Grimes 1939a) and its position in an upland area of Pembrokeshire might support the idea that it is Bronze Age in date. Parallels with stone rows elsewhere should not be dismissed (Cummings 2001). The monuments at Morfa Bychan are also problematic as they are structurally quite different from any other monuments found in the study area. They are also in a rather unusual landscape position with clear views out over the Gower. We tentatively suggest that these sites are large Bronze Age cists. They too are placed very close to an outcrop, suggesting an element of continuity from the Neolithic into later periods.

Conclusions

The monuments of south-west Wales seem to have been carefully positioned in the landscape in relation to a range of particular landscape features. People visiting and encountering these monuments would have been able to see a whole range of important landscape settings which may have imbued them with individual meanings as well as tying them into the wider area. The combination of specific place and landscape setting is likely to have been an integral part of the way in which these sites were understood and used, and we have suggested here that this can also inform our classification of these sites. The broader significance and meaning of places, the landscape settings of these monuments, and the nature of the constructions themselves, will be further discussed in chapter 7.

5 The monuments of north-west Wales and their landscape settings

Vicki Cummings

The monuments of north-west Wales

For our study, north-west Wales incorporates the large area of the former counties of Caernarvonshire, Denbighshire, Merionethshire and Anglesey. There are 43 monuments here, distributed in clusters (Figure 5.1). In particular, there are a large number of sites on Anglesey: 16 definite or probable monuments, with many more possible ones (see Lynch 1969b). This is one of the densest distributions in Britain. Monuments are also found on the Lleyn peninsula (9 sites) and clustered around Ardudwy (6 sites) with the remainder inland. There are other monuments in the area including stone circles such as those on Penmaenmawr (Griffiths 1960), the henge monument at Llandegai (Houlder 1968) and enclosures such as Bryn Celli Wen on Anglesey (Thomas 2001). Even when taking into account the potential for lost or destroyed sites, the density of sites on Anglesey is impressive. The principal areas which lack monuments today may also have been devoid of them in the Neolithic; these are the mountainous and inaccessible parts of north-west Wales where one could, other things being equal, expect a high survival rate.

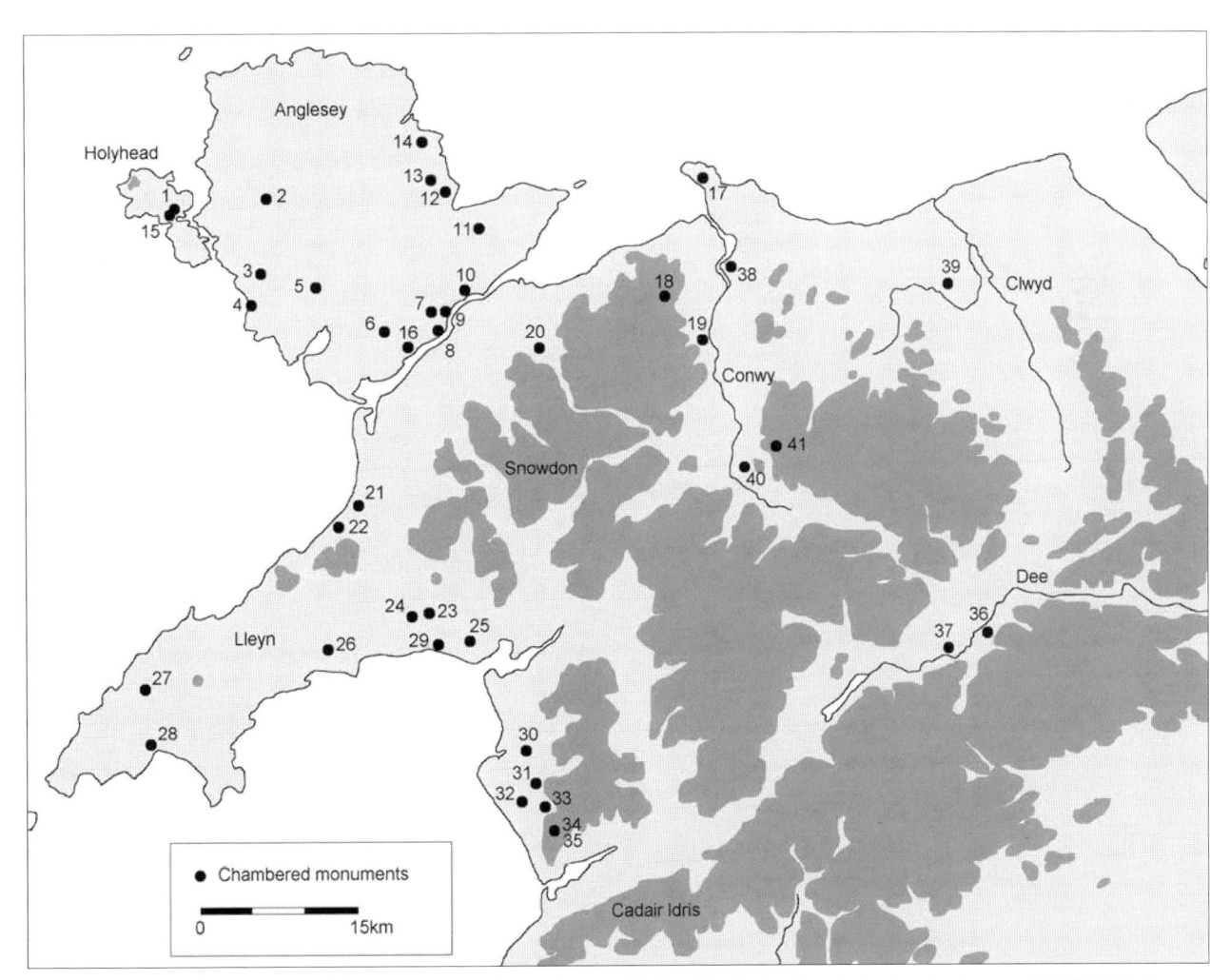

Figure 5.1 Distribution map of the monuments in north-west Wales. Dark shading indicates land over 1000ft (304m).

Excavations

A total of 12 sites in north-west Wales have been excavated of which eight are on Anglesey and Holyhead. The most recent excavations are those of Trefignath and Din Dryfol (Smith and Lynch 1987). Trefignath on Holyhead Island was excavated between 1977–9 and revealed a remarkably well-preserved multi-phase monument. Activity began at the site with a hearth, post-holes (which may have been part of a structure) and a small assemblage of finds, all of which predate the construction of the monument. The pottery from this pre-cairn activity is undecorated Irish Sea ware (globular and carinated bowls), comparable to other early assemblages in Wales (Smith and Lynch 1987, 77). A radiocarbon date on charcoal from the old ground surface with a range of 3980–3690 BC (HAR–3932) suggests that the first (western) chamber was built at this time (Smith and Lynch 1987, 45). At a later date, another chamber was added to the east of the first, and both chambers were set within a long wedge-shaped cairn or platform (Smith and Lynch 1987, 19; and see chapter 7). Both these chambers had been robbed out in antiquity, although some Grooved Ware was found, probably from a later context. Finally another chamber was built to the east, in the forecourt of the central chamber, and the cairn was extended to incorporate this chamber. Pottery and a flint sickle were found, and there was an arc of stakeholes and a pit in the forecourt of the eastern chamber (Smith and Lynch 1987, 26).

Din Dryfol on Anglesey was excavated in 1969 and 1970, and again in 1980. It comprises a number of chambers set within a long cairn which have been interpreted as the remains of a multi-phase monument (Smith and Lynch 1987). The western chamber may have been constructed first, and it contained the cremated remains of two individuals and flint. Another chamber may then have been constructed to the east. This chamber combined wood and stone elements, and human bone, pottery and flint were found in this chamber and in the surrounding cairn (Smith and Lynch 1987, 110). It has been suggested that an additional two chambers were built to the east, and the shattered butt of a polished stone axe was found in this area. The entire monument was enclosed in a long cairn with the addition of what has been described as a monumental façade.

The two large passage graves of Barclodiad y Gawres and Bryn Celli Ddu on Anglesey have also been excavated. Barclodiad y Gawres consists of a stone-built cruciform chamber and passage set within a round cairn (Powell and Daniel 1956). Five of the stones are decorated (Lynch 1967). Considerable parts of the chamber had been robbed prior to excavation, but fragments of cremated bone, representing two young adult males, and animal bone, charcoal and antler pins were found. At the centre of the chamber was a hearth which contained the remains of a 'stew' consisting of wrasse, eel, whiting, frog, toad, natterjack, grass snake, mouse, shrew and rabbit (Powell and Daniel 1956, 17).

Bryn Celli Ddu was excavated in the 1920s (Hemp 1930) and revealed a complex monument which appeared to have been constructed in a series of phases. Underneath the stone-built chamber were the remains of a henge or a henge-related monument, and the general consensus is that this represents the first phase at the site (Lynch 1991; O'Kelly 1969: but see Eogan 1983). This monument seems to have consisted of a bank and ditch and a circle of stones (O'Kelly 1969). There was a series of cremation pits associated with this phase and a large pit was found at the centre of the enclosure. Subsequently, a megalithic monument was built within the enclosure. This monument consisted of a chamber with a north-easterly passage set within a round cairn bounded by a kerb of stones. The chamber contained a single upright 'pillar' stone and a decorated slab was found to the rear of the chamber. The contents of the chamber had been disturbed by earlier activity; antiquarian reports suggest that the chamber had once been filled with human bone, and in 1865 Lukis found burnt human bone around the pillar stone (Hemp 1930, 180). Hemp (1930) found the remains of human bone, both burnt and unburnt in the chamber and passage, as well as shells, white quartz pebbles and a chert scraper. In the forecourt area two hearths were found, as well as a row of five post-holes and a shallow pit containing an ox burial (Hemp 1930, 195). The passage and forecourt had been blocked and also contained cremated bones and quartz.

Pant y Saer on the east side of Anglesey was originally investigated in 1875 and further excavated in 1932 (Scott 1933). The excavations revealed a rectangular pit cut into the limestone over which a chamber was constructed. A passage was also cut into the limestone and ran from the chamber to a forecourt area. The forecourt was cut through solid rock and much of the floor had disintegrated through burning; this feature was surrounded by a broad, low wall (Scott 1933, 197). A peristalith surrounded a small mound. The earlier excavations had uncovered a cist set into the main chamber. Human and animal bone, pottery and sea shells had also been recovered from the chamber. Scott (1933) found considerable quantities of material culture, much of it having been disturbed in the previous excavations. The remains of an estimated 54 people were found as well as animal bones, arrowheads, a sandstone disk, iron pyrites, shale, a bone point, quartz pebbles, charcoal and shells. The early Neolithic pottery was compared to that found at Windmill Hill (Scott 1933, 208) and Beaker. Pottery, a scratched pebble, a portion of a human skull and animal bones were deposited at the entrance which was eventually blocked. The complete closing of the forecourt by a dry wall remains unique in Britain (Scott 1933, 220).

Around the same time the chamber deposits at Ty Newydd were investigated, a little inland on the west side of Anglesey (Phillips 1936). The chamber contained beach pebbles, broken white quartz, flint flakes, a barbed and tanged arrowhead, a chip of a polished axe and Beaker

Figure 5.2 The first phase chamber at Dyffryn Ardudwy.

pottery. The excavator also found surviving traces of a passage. Earlier accounts of the site suggest that a passage, or even another chamber, as well as a cairn once existed at the site (Daniel 1950, 185). Bryn yr Hen Bobl on the southern coast of Anglesey was investigated between 1929 and 1934 (Hemp 1935b). The excavations revealed a single chamber set within a kidney-shaped cairn with a forecourt area. There was also a large 'terrace' to the south of the cairn and an elaborate series of walls was found underneath the cairn and terrace. The chamber contained fragments of human bone, representing at least 20 people, and animal bone and a bone pin. Considerable quantities of pottery were found underneath the terrace and cairn as well as scraps of human and animal bone and flint flakes, cores and arrowheads. Flakes of Graig Lwyd stone were also found as well as four polished stone axes (Lynch 1969a, 166). Other finds included a bone and a stone ball, shells and a stone with a pecked triangle (Hemp 1935b). There are also extensive earthworks outside the cairn (Leivers 1999).

Finally, the site of Lligwy on the east coast of Anglesey was investigated in 1908 (Baynes 1909), although the area around it may have been investigated previously in the nineteenth century. A 'sub-megalithic' chamber was found which contained what appeared to be *in situ* deposits. Considerable quantities of finds including inhumations were found. The chamber contained a layer of mussel shells over a layer of black earth mixed with bones, worked flint and pottery. Above this was a layer of paving followed by more black soil with human bones, flint and pottery (Baynes 1909, 224). This was covered with a layer of limpet shells. North of the chamber more deposits were found including human and animal bone, flint and a bone pin. Between 15 and 30 people are represented and the presence of Beaker and Grooved Ware has led Lynch to suggest a late Neolithic date for the site (Lynch 1995, 19).

Four sites have been excavated on the mainland of north Wales. Excavation of Dyffryn Ardudwy in 1960 revealed a well-preserved multi-phase monument (Powell 1973). First, a small stone chamber (Figure 5.2) was built which was set in an oval cairn or platform (see chapter 7) with a defined forecourt area. A pit was found in front of the portal stones which contained portions of several Neolithic vessels (Irish Sea fine plain ware). At a later date another chamber was built to the east and both chambers were incorporated into a long cairn. The eastern chamber had a 'portico' (or porch) which contained sherds of pottery, and pottery also came from the eastern chamber itself, representing several Neolithic and Bronze Age vessels. The small amount of surviving deposit in the eastern chamber consisted of fine dark earth with a small concentration of cremated bone, representing a single individual. There were also two broken shale pendants from the group XXI axe source of Mynydd Rhiw on the tip of the Lleyn peninsula (Powell 1973, 18), probably the remains of a Bronze Age wristguard (Burrow 2001). Seven flints were found among the cairn stones and a broken flint arrowhead at the eastern end of the cairn.

Capel Garmon in the Conwy Valley is generally considered to be an outlier of the Cotswold-Severn tradition and consists of a lateral chamber set within a trapezoidal long cairn. It has been investigated a number of times, principally in 1925 (Hemp 1927). The chamber area had been cleared out prior to excavation, so the only finds were a flint flake and some Beaker pottery (Hemp 1927, 24). The more recent work at Capel Garmon revealed pre-cairn activity consisting of a post-hole and cuts (Yates and Jones 1991). A skull fragment was also found.

The small site of Bachwen on the Lleyn peninsula was restored in the 1920s and during this process a paving of cobbles was found in the chamber with what appeared to be the remains of a fire (Hemp 1926). The site of Four Crosses also on Lleyn was reconstructed in 1936 (Daniel 1937b). There were no finds. It is reported that Tyddyn Bleiddyn to the east of the distribution of sites in north Wales produced human bones when investigated in the nineteenth century (Davies 1929). The main chamber area was cleared out and produced skulls as well as other human bones, representing at least 12 people. In the second cist were the remains of more people as well as the broken jaw of a roebuck and the remains of a goat (Davies 1929, 66).

Morphology and typology

The classification of the monuments of north-west Wales, like their south-western counterparts, has been debated and contested for many years. In 1936, Grimes felt able to assign some monuments to broader classifications. Bryn Celli Ddu was grouped with passage graves in Scotland, Ireland and Brittany, while Capel Garmon was considered part of the Cotswold tradition (Grimes 1936b, 115). Trefignath and two other sites on Anglesey were classed as 'segmented cists' while other sites in north-west Wales were considered portal sites or dolmens (Grimes 1936b, 120). Grimes divided the monuments more generally into long cairns and round cairns, identifying two groups within the former, those around Merioneth and the small series in the Conwy Valley.

In 1950, Daniel classified the monuments of north-west Wales into several different groups. The first of these was the Anglesey Group which consisted of passage graves and 'B-dolmens' (simple polygonal chambers) which included sites such as Bryn Celli Ddu and Plas Newydd (Daniel 1950, 54). These were seen as a colonising extension of the Boyne culture (Daniel 1950, 147). The rest were classified as the Gwynedd Group, part of the Irish Sea group, which contained a number of sub-groups. Trefignath was now described as a gallery grave (Daniel 1950, 86). Other sites such as Dyffryn Ardudwy were classed as terminally-chambered long barrows and were compared to the Cotswold-Severn group. Capel Garmon was considered a laterally-chambered tomb (although not directly associated with the Cotswold monuments), with those at Carneddau Hengwm intermediate between the lateral and terminal chambers. The remainder are considered 'free-standing rectangular chambers' (A-dolmens). Some of these, such as Gwern Einon were classed as portalled A-dolmens (Daniel 1950, 150). Elsewhere, other sites such as Lligwy were described as part of the 'sub-megalithic' group.

This rather confusing array of classifications continued in use when Piggott reviewed the British Neolithic in 1954. Here the monuments of north-west Wales were either considered as outliers of the Clyde-Carlingford culture, such as Trefignath, Lligwy, Pant y Saer and Bryn yr Hen Bobl (Piggott 1954, 179), or as outliers of the Cotswold-Severn group such as Capel Garmon, and the rest were classified as miscellaneous (Piggott 1954, 270). Lynch's (1969b) substantial reconsideration of the north Welsh monuments reclassified the monuments of Anglesey either as passage graves, such as Bryn Celli Ddu and Bodowyr, or as long graves, which included Trefignath and Hen Drefor. However, five sites were unclassified and two sites were described as 'variants'. On mainland north-west Wales, sites were classified either as portal dolmens (or related to the portal dolmen group), or Cotswold-Severn monuments, such as Capel Garmon and the Carneddau Hengwm, or remained unclassified. The precise origins of these various monuments, however, remained problematic. Lynch has not altered these basic classifications in later considerations of the area (Lynch 1991; 1995; 2000a), although the publication of the excavations at Trefignath and Din Dryfol (Smith and Lynch 1987) made the long grave classification slightly more complex than had been previously thought, due to the multi-phase construction sequences at these sites. In the most recent reconsideration of the monuments of north-west Wales, Leivers (1999) follows previous classifications of these sites and suggests that there are five main types of monument: simple unicellular box-like structures; simple passage graves; portal dolmens; multi-phase and multi-chambered monuments; and passage graves. However, these classifications are only useful as an aid to interpretation and sites should be understood as a local variation on a common theme (Leivers 1999).

Although the monuments of north-west Wales have been difficult to classify, geographically there are a number of distinct groupings. There is a concentration of sites on Anglesey and Holyhead, particularly to the south of Anglesey (hereafter the Anglesey group). A number of sites are found along the coasts of the Lleyn peninsula (hereafter the Lleyn group), and there are six sites on the Ardudwy peninsula to the south (hereafter the Ardudwy group). There are also a number of sites found along the river valleys to the east of Snowdon (hereafter the inland group, although these are much dispersed).

Chronology

The chronology of the north-west Welsh monuments is still poorly understood. As with sites in south-west Wales this is partly because of the diversity of the monuments and the lack of an agreed typological sequence. The single radiocarbon date from Trefignath on Holyhead, noted above, may suggest a relatively early date for the first-phase monument there. There are radiocarbon dates from other Neolithic sites in north-west Wales. Charcoal from a posthole and a hearth in the henge at Llandegai provided dates of 4350–3700 BC (NPL-223) and 3950–3000 BC (NPL-220) (Houlder 1968). The complex of hut circles at Moel y Gerddi produced three Neolithic dates of between 3650–2900 BC from the palisade and hearth (CAR-525, CAR-397 and CAR-527) while pits at the hilltop site of Capel Eithin, Anglesey produced dates of 3700–3350 BC (CAR-481) and 2859–2207 (CAR-446). A hearth from the same site had a date of 3340–2781 BC (CAR-488: Lynch 1991, 394). Two Bronze Age sites have also produced Neolithic dates. The barrow of Bedd Branwen produced a date in the early Neolithic from the charcoal from a pre-barrow hollow, of 3946–3530 BC (BM-452: Lynch 1991), while Brenig 53 (Lynch 1993) produced an early Neolithic date of 4250–3650 BC from a pre-barrow deposit (HAR-1436). This range of other dated activity may suggest, apart from variation in the monuments themselves, the likelihood of a sequence of constructions in the area.

The substantial quantities of pottery recovered from the excavated monuments also enable a more general chronology of the sites to be postulated. Early Neolithic pottery was found at the first phase at Dyffryn Ardudwy and later Neolithic and Bronze Age pottery from the second chamber (Powell 1973). Beaker pottery at Dyffryn Ardudwy, Ty Newydd, Pant y Saer and Capel Garmon shows later use of some kind. Early Neolithic bowls of the Irish Sea ware tradition were recovered from the second chamber at Trefignath (Smith 1987, 74) and Peterborough Ware from the final chamber. Lligwy (Lynch 1969a, 157–9) produced early Neolithic bowls of the Irish Sea ware Group and pottery similar to Grooved Ware. Considerable quantities of pottery were also found at Bryn yr Hen Bobl including early Neolithic bowls and later Peterborough Wares (Leivers 1999, chapter 6), although their precise nature and relationship with the monument is somewhat unclear (Peterson 1999).

Monuments in the landscape

Setting the scene

The landscapes of north-west Wales are quite varied. One of the visually most impressive landscape features of the area are of course the mountains (colour plate 7). The mountain range of Snowdonia stretches from Betws y Coed in the east to the Lleyn peninsula to the west, with Snowdon itself the highest peak at 1085m OD. These mountains dominate a large part of the landscapes of north-west Wales and no monuments have been found amongst them. The other visually striking mountain range is Cadair Idris, to the south of the study area, although no monuments are found near this peak. There are also a number of impressive and craggy mountains on the spine of the Lleyn peninsula, which is otherwise a fertile landscape with sandy beaches and coves. The small Bardsey Island lies off the southern tip of Lleyn. In contrast to the mainland, the large island of Anglesey is generally rich and fertile with gently undulating hills. It is separated from the mainland by the Menai Straits which are no wider than a river in places (in Welsh the Afon Menai: the river Menai). The smaller island of Holyhead, to the west of Anglesey, is rockier and more marshy and also has the highest point of the two islands: Holyhead Mountain at 220m OD. There are a number of smaller islands off the coast of Anglesey and Holyhead, most notably Puffin Island to the east. The northern river valleys contrast with the nearby mountains. The presence of modern towns such as Llandudno, Rhyl, Prestatyn and Bangor along the northern coast of north-west Wales may have affected the survival of monuments.

Previous work on landscape

There has been very little work on the landscape settings of the monuments of north-west Wales. A number of authors have commented in passing on the setting of the monuments. Grimes (1936b, 114) talked in general about the location of sites, suggesting a general preference 'for comparatively low-lying sites on valley flanks and spurs'. The general setting of the Merioneth sites was discussed in their inventory by Bowen and Gresham (1967), while Savory (1980, 221) suggested that the setting of the portal dolmens on 'less desirable land' can indicate that they are not early in date. In an influential paper, Lynch (1975b) discussed the location of prehistoric sites in relation in the landscape. In particular she emphasised the location of Bronze Age monuments on passes in north Wales. Lynch (1969b; 1991) also discussed the landscape setting of monuments as part of the overall understanding of sites, and detailed a number of cases. She described the setting of Presaddfed on Anglesey, for example, which is located on low land on the floor of a valley, which is the siting more typical for a portal dolmen (Lynch 1991, 87). She also noted that simple passage graves such as Bodowyr were built in commanding locations on the summit of a low hill (Lynch 1991, 65). Leivers (1999) notes the coastal distribution of monuments and their location on major route-ways across headlands and mountains, following on from the discussion of route-ways by Gresham and Irvine (1963). He also notes the locations of both Trefignath, on the highest point of an outcrop, and Din Dryfol, within a local setting. However, unlike in south-west Wales and south-east Wales (Tilley 1994; Fleming 1999), the landscape settings of these sites have not been further considered in any detail.

General location

The monuments of north-west Wales are found in quite specific parts of the landscape. Over three-quarters of the sites are located on what is now agricultural land, with 22% on marginal land. However, this relationship is only meaningful if modern land use reflects prehistoric conditions, and there are likely to have been substantial alterations of some of these areas in more recent years. In north-west Wales sites are set on average at 104m OD, but this does not reflect the differences between the separate concentrations. Sites on Anglesey and Holyhead are located in much lower parts of the landscape, on average at 45m OD. Barclodiad y Gawres is the lowest-lying monument in north-west Wales at only 10m OD. The monuments on the Lleyn peninsula are also set in low-lying parts of the landscape, on average at 65m OD. In contrast, those on the Ardudwy peninsula are set much higher up in the landscape, at an average of 174m OD. Likewise, those found along the rivers and in inland north-west Wales are typically on high ground (161m OD on average). Maen y Bardd and Maen Pebyll are the two highest monuments in the area, at 330m OD and 350m OD respectively.

Geology

The geology of north-west Wales is quite varied. There are large areas of Silurian and Ordovician rocks as well as large areas of Cambrian rocks around Ardudwy, and schists and gneisses of the Mona complex on the tip of Lleyn and across Anglesey. There are also smaller patches of contemporaneous and intrusive igneous rocks across north-west Wales with coal measures and trias rocks to the east. The monuments are found in most geological zones, although the two commonest rock types, Silurian and Ordovician, are under-represented with just 5% of sites on each. 27% of sites are found on the igneous rocks, with 22% of sites on carboniferous limestone and 22% of sites on schists and gneiss, all the latter on Anglesey. 19% of sites are found on Cambrian rocks, including all those around Ardudwy. As with the monuments in south-east Wales, the monuments are not built in the areas with coal measures and are constructed instead in the less common igneous and limestone areas.

Mountains

The vast majority of sites in the area have views of mountains. Only seven sites in north-west Wales do not have views of mountains and these are primarily those sites found tucked away in river valleys (see below). This

Figure 5.3 From the site of Hen Drefor there is a clear view of Snowdonia.

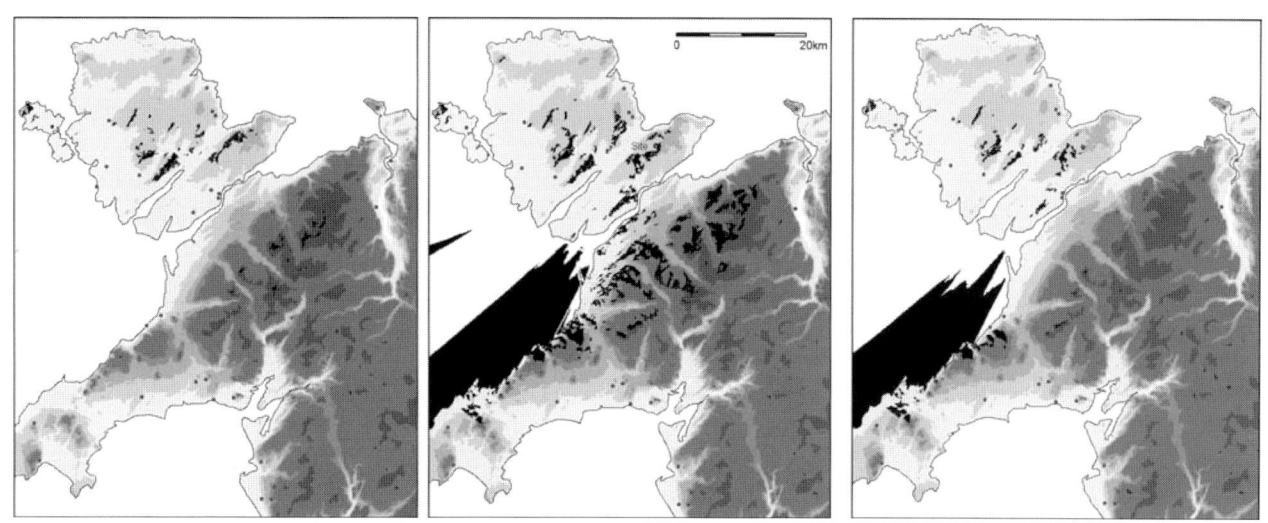

Figure 5.4 Viewsheds from around Hen Drefor. The image to the left is 500m to the north from the monument. Most of the views of the mountains are lost as well as the view of the sea. The centre image is the view from the monument itself. The image to the right is 500m to the south. Here the view of the sea is maintained, but all views of mountains are lost. Reproduced by kind permission of Ordnance Survey. © Crown copyright NC/03/20516.

Figure 5.5 Holyhead Mountain, visible behind the final phase chamber at Trefignath.

includes sites such as the two monuments along the River Dee as well as Din Dryfol on Anglesey. Two-thirds of sites in north-west Wales have views of Snowdonia (Figure 5.3), and over 60% have views of the distinctive ridge of mountains found along the Lleyn peninsula. Once again, there are differences between the monuments of the different areas. Virtually all the sites on Anglesey have views of Snowdonia; only two sites, Din Dryfol and Presaddfed, do not. From the other sites the views of Snowdonia, clearly visible on the horizon, are very striking (colour plate 8). The pass between Carnedd Dafydd and Elidir Fawr is particularly distinctive, although it is of interest that this is not visible from Bryn Celli Ddu. From all the sites along the southern coast of Anglesey, the Snowdonia mountain range completely dominates the view. It is possible to demonstrate that had some of these sites been located slightly differently in the landscape, Snowdonia would not have been visible (Figure 5.4). A number of the sites on Anglesey also have views of the mountains on Lleyn (69%) and a further 38% have views of Holyhead Mountain. Holyhead Mountain may have been a feature of more local significance. At Trefignath it is quite distinctive on the horizon and the final structure seems to have been positioned in relation to it; Holyhead Mountain appears directly behind the final-phase portal stones (Figure 5.5).

All but one of the sites on the Lleyn Peninsula have views of other mountains on Lleyn. None of the monuments

Figure 5.6 The mountains visible from Bachwen.

are actually set on the mountains themselves, although the two most south-westerly of the sites are set on the side of these hills. Mynydd Cefn Amwlch is set on the side of the hill of the same name, and Tan y Muriau is located on the eastern side of Mynydd Rhiw, although this distinctive summit is not visible from the site itself. The site of Bachwen is positioned with stunning views of some of the more northerly mountains, Bwlch Mawr and Gyrn Ddu (Figure 5.6). The sites on the south-easterly side of Lleyn, perhaps unsurprisingly, have views towards the mountains on Ardudwy. Two sites on the southern side of Lleyn also have views of Moel y Gest. This is quite a distinctive hill and it has the site of Cist Cerrig set on its lower slopes.

The group of six monuments on the Ardudwy peninsula has views of a number of different mountains. All these sites have views of the mountains on the Lleyn peninsula and all but one site, Dyffryn Ardudwy, have views of Snowdonia. Most of these sites also have views of Moelfre, one of the most distinctive mountains in the area. This mountain has a distinctive domed profile. At some sites, the architecture of the monuments seems to have been constructed in relation to Moelfre. For example, at Carnedd Hengwm North the two lateral chambers are directly aligned on Moelfre (Figure 5.7). As one approaches the southern chamber Moelfre is skylined above the mass of the cairn. Moelfre would have been visible upon exit from the northern chamber. From these sites it is also possible to see the Preseli mountains in south-west Wales. The significance of the Preselis, and of this long-range view, will be discussed in chapter 7.

As already mentioned, the inland river valley group does not, for the most part, have views of mountains at all, monuments being located in river valleys and surrounded by hills on either side which effectively block out views of the mountains beyond. Four sites in this group do, however, have views of Snowdonia. These are Maen y Bardd and Hendre Waelod close to the point where the Afon Conwy meets the sea, and Capel Garmon and Maen Pebyll further inland. The partial view of Snowdonia to the north-west is particularly striking from Capel Garmon as the site is enclosed on most sides by quite restricted views (see below).

Views of the sea

Over three-quarters (76%) of sites in north-west Wales are located with views of the sea. Once again, this varies from area to area. 94% of monuments on Anglesey have views of the sea, though in many cases this is actually of the water of the Menai Straits. Sites such as Trefignath and Lligwy have sweeping views of the open sea to the north and east respectively. Barclodiad y Gawres has the most extensive views out to sea as the site is set right on the edge of a cliff overlooking the open sea. Only one site on Anglesey, Bodowyr, does not have a view of the sea. Bryn Celli Ddu has a very subtle view of the sea. This is not immediately obvious when visiting the site as the thin sliver of the sea which is visible above a hillside frequently blends into the sky. However, as one approached the passage and chamber, the sea would have been visible

5 *The monuments of north-west Wales and their landscape settings* 49

Figure 5.7 The peak of Moelfre, aligned on the lateral chambers at Carnedd Hengwm North.

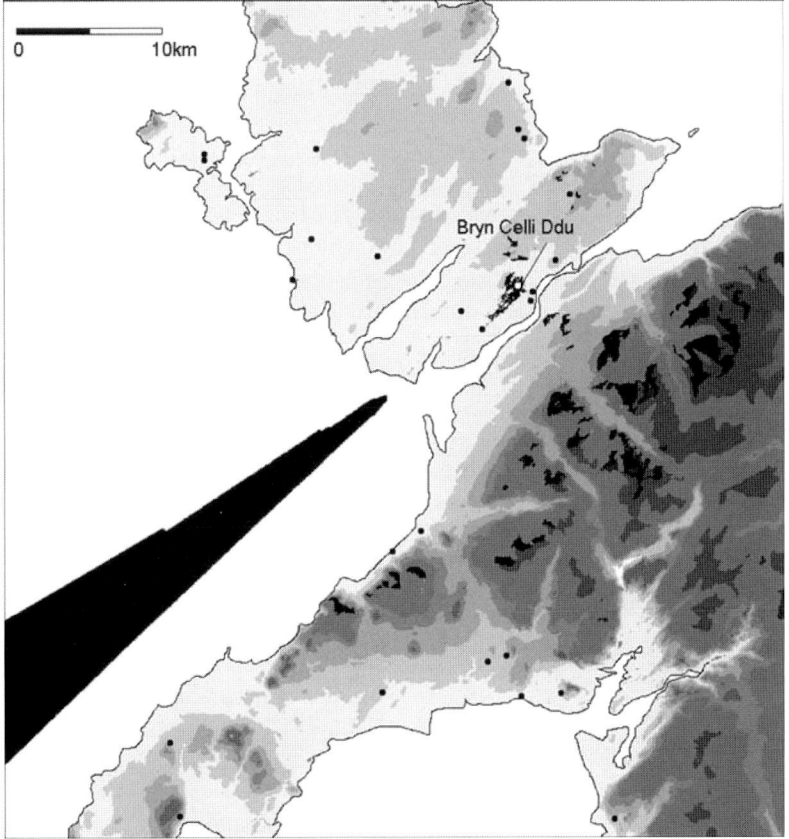

Figure 5.8 The viewshed from Bryn Celli Ddu, showing the visibility of the sea. Reproduced by kind permission of Ordnance Survey. © Crown copyright NC/03/20516.

Figure 5.9 Maen y Bardd, with clear views over the Afon Conwy.

behind the monument (see also Fowler and Cummings 2003). All the sites on the Lleyn peninsula have views of the sea. Again, the site of Ystuim Cegid Isaf has only a very small sliver of the sea visible, in a very similar way to the situation at Bryn Celli Ddu (Figure 5.8), and it has been suggested that this may have been a passage grave similar to Bryn Celli Ddu (Daniel 1950, 55). All other sites on Lleyn have more extensive views of the sea, and many sites have very impressive and sweeping views out over the water. The site of Bachwen on the northern side of the Lleyn peninsula, for example, is set only a short distance from the sea and has wide and expansive views of water. All the sites set on the Ardudwy peninsula also have views of the sea, and at these sites the sea appears behind the monument as one approaches the forecourt or front of the monument. This striking effect results in the stone monument being framed by water (Fowler and Cummings 2003; and see Scarre 2002a; 2002b). Unsurprisingly, only one site of the inland group has views out to sea, the site of Maen y Bardd on the north-eastern edge of Snowdonia.

Rivers, river valleys and streams

Throughout our study areas, the association between monuments and rivers is varied. In north-west Wales, some sites on the Lleyn peninsula and Anglesey (less than a quarter of the total) are more than 5km from any river. There are no rivers on Holyhead Island, or on the southern tip of Lleyn. The remainder of the monuments of north-west Wales are on average 0.8km from a river. This does not suggest a close association with a watercourse. However, some sites do seem to be in closer association with rivers. Six of the inland group are located along the Afon Conwy. This is the largest river in north-west Wales and runs from the heart of upland north Wales to Conwy Bay to the east of Snowdonia. The landscape around the Afon Conwy is quite different to that of Snowdonia as there are few long-distance views of mountains and the valley is surrounded by gentle rolling hills. Gresham and Irvine (1963, 56) have suggested that the Conwy may have been an important route through north Wales in prehistory, linking the north-west with more southern parts of Britain, perhaps including for the movement of Graig Lwyd axes. The site of Hendre Waelod is positioned only a short distance from, and in clear sight of, the Afon Conwy. Here, the river appears behind the portal stones as one approaches the site from uphill. Although the monument itself would not have been highly visible when actually standing at the riverside, Hendre Waelod is located on a distinctive-shaped hill which would have been a recognisable landmark from a distance. The monument of Maen y Bardd is set higher up the Afon Conwy but has impressive views of the river snaking its way through the valley floor (Figure 5.9).

Two monuments, Branas Uchaf and Tan y Coed, are found along the Afon Dyfrdwy (River Dee) to the east of Bala. Tan y Coed is positioned about 500m from the Dee

Figure 5.10 The outcrops beneath and around Din Dryfol.

and has views over the river valley with the hills of the Mynydd Mynyllod behind. This part of the north Welsh landscape is also completely different to the mountains of Snowdonia and the Lleyn to the west. Other isolated sites are located along river valleys. The site of Tyddyn Bleiddyn is positioned close to the Afon Elwy, while Sling is close to the Afon Ogwen. It is the Ogwen which flows to the east of the Llandegai henges. The monuments of Ardudwy are found on average 1.4km from the Afon Ysgethin, which therefore does not seem to have been of significance. However, the site of Cors y Gedol is only 300m from this river, although the river itself cannot be seen. Gwern Einon, also on the Ardudwy peninsula, is 1km from the Afon Artro and it has been suggested that the mouth of the Artro was an excellent harbour for craft coming from Ireland (Gresham and Irvine 1963).

The relationship between rivers and the monuments on Anglesey is even more tantalising. Seven sites are on average 1.1km from the Afon Braint which runs along the southern edge of Anglesey. This is not a substantial river, and Bryn Celli Ddu is closest to it at a distance of 200m. Several monuments also have clear views of the Afon Menai. Although part of the sea, the straits are not much wider than a river and might have been understood as such. The sites of Plas Newydd and Bryn yr Hen Bobl both have clear views of the Afon Menai and are only a few hundred metres from its shores.

Almost two-thirds of the sites in north-west Wales are also located close to a stream (63% within 500m). In most cases, the monuments are not placed directly alongside the stream but within their general vicinity. Since probably few points in this landscape are very far from a stream, this is not initially very encouraging. But a few sites might have a slightly closer relationship. It has already been mentioned that Bryn Celli Ddu is only 200m from the small Afon Braint. There is also a smaller tributary of the Braint 100m to the west of Bryn Celli Ddu. This effectively means that the monument is surrounded by water on three sides, to the east, south and west. The Carneddau Hengwm on the Ardudwy peninsula are also located close to a stream which runs to the north of the monuments. This stream runs from Bwlch y Rhiwgyr to the sea at Hengwm. This route through Bwlch y Rhiwgyr was a main thoroughfare in previous centuries (Lynch 1995, 29). Cefn Isaf is located right next to a stream and the site of Maen Pebyll is also close to a stream which runs past the monument to join the Afon Conwy.

Other natural features including rocky outcrops

A number of sites are located in relation to other natural features that may have been significant. The site of Barclodiad y Gawres is found close to the harbour at Porth Trecastle. It has been suggested that this may have provided a safe harbour for boats travelling to and from Ireland (Powell and Daniel 1956). Pant y Saer is just over 1km from another safe landing place for boats on the eastern side of Anglesey (Scott 1933).

Figure 5.11 The restricted view at Penarth.

Sites in north-west Wales are also found in the vicinity of outcrops although this relationship is not as pronounced as it is in south-west Wales. Trefignath and Din Dryfol (Figure 5.10) were both built on large and prominent outcrops. At Trefignath, pre-cairn activity was found scattered over the outcrop, suggesting that this may already have been a significant place. Other sites were built over outcrops but these can no longer be seen. This is the case, for example, at Ty Newydd (Phillips 1936). Other sites were built in the vicinity of outcrops. There is a large distinctive domed outcrop visible from Bryn Celli Ddu (colour plate 9), and Cist Cerrig is only few metres from some outcrops. The outcrops near Cist Cerrig have a line of cupmarks running down one of the surfaces (Hemp 1938). Capel Garmon in the Conwy Valley is also located next to distinctive outcrops, composed of 'cleaved volcanic dust of Rhyolitic character (containing)....flakes of green biotite' (Hemp 1927, 43). This rock type is only found in the crag to the south-west of the cairn.

The islands off the coasts of south-west Wales do not seem to have been key reference points in the landscape for the monuments in that area (but see Cooney 2003), and the same could be said of the islands of north-west Wales. The island of Anglesey may not have been conceptualised in the same way as other islands due to its size and because the Menai Straits are so narrow. Holyhead Island is only separated from Anglesey by a very narrow stretch of water. Bardsey Island off the Lleyn peninsula is visible from the Ardudwy monuments, but not from the two monuments on the southern tip of Lleyn, suggesting it may not have been a significant reference point. Puffin Island off the eastern tip of Anglesey is visible from Lligwy.

Restricted views

It has already been noted that one of the characteristics of virtually all megalithic constructions is that they have a restricted view in one direction (Figure 5.11). This is also the case with the north-west Welsh sites, of which 90% have a restricted view in one direction. This restricted view is almost always created by locating the monument on the side of a hill or a gentle rise, although at sites like Din Dryfol the view from the north-east round to the south-west is restricted by virtue of the monument being right up against a large outcrop. The view is also restricted by outcrops at Cist Cerrig. The site of Capel Garmon has a restricted view for three-quarters of the circumference, and this is unique in Wales (although see the setting of Parc le Breos Cwm on the Gower). The site is tucked away amongst outcrops and almost all of the view is of the immediate topography. This means that the monument is hidden from view. This is particularly interesting given the fact that it is generally considered to be an outlier of the Cotswold-Severn monument tradition. This site and Parc le Breos Cwm on the Gower, which is also set in a hidden location, will be discussed in more detail in the chapter 7. The view which is open and wide-ranging at Capel Garmon

Figure 5.12 Capel Garmon, in the Conwy valley.

is that of Snowdonia, linking this monument with the wider north-west Welsh landscape (Figure 5.12). At many of the sites with a restricted view, the builders of the monuments seem to have deliberately avoided building the site on the summit of the hill, thus ensuring a restricted view in one direction. There does not seem to be any patterning in the direction of the restricted view at the monuments. The restricted view is found to all points of the compass. A few sites have half of the view restricted by the hillsides on which they stand, and in all these cases, the restricted view is either north to south, or south to north.

There are four notable exceptions which do not have a restricted view in any direction. These are the passage graves on Anglesey of Bryn Celli Ddu and Barclodiad y Gawres and the possible passage grave of Ystium Cegid Isaf (see above). At these three sites there is no restricted view in any direction. This is particularly pronounced at Bryn Celli Ddu, which seems to be set at the centre of a circular landscape (cf. Bradley 1998c; Richards 1996b; Watson 2000). At the site of Barclodiad y Gawres the monument is also carefully placed so that there are wide-ranging views in all directions. Had the monument been placed just 50m in any direction this would not have been achieved (Figure 5.13). The settings of these sites can be compared in general to those of passage graves in Ireland, many of which are set on top of hills and consequently have wide-ranging views in many directions. The other site which does not have a restricted view in any direction is Bachwen on the northern side of the Lleyn peninsula. The implications of this will be discussed below. It is relevant, however, that the passage graves would presumably have been covered by considerable mounds in prehistory, in contrast to the other monuments discussed which may never have been covered by substantial cairns

or mounds (see chapter 7). At both Barclodiad and Bryn Celli, the mound itself blocks out many of the views of the surrounding landscape, so that as one approaches the site, the view ahead become closed.

Intervisibility

Very few monuments in north-west Wales are intervisible. A few have views over areas which contain other monuments, but these are not counted as intervisible here as it would not have been possible to actually see the other sites. In fact, given the density of monuments in southern Anglesey it is perhaps surprising that none of these sites are intervisible. Only four sites elsewhere are intervisible. Trefignath and Trearddur on Holyhead have views of one another, and Maen y Bardd overlooks the Afon Conwy which has Hendre Waelod along its banks. This situation contrasts with both south-west and south-east Wales where a number of monuments are intervisible. In those two areas, however, the monuments which have views of others are all clustered around wide valleys, a location not available in north-west Wales.

Back to classification

A great many of the sites in north-west Wales can be considered part of the broader portal dolmen tradition. Some of these sites may be understood as 'classic' portal dolmens, such as the first phase at Dyffryn Ardudwy, Gwern Einon, Cist Cerrig and Carnedd Hengwm South. However, many sites do not have the characteristic portalled entrance, and in this sense they are remarkably similar to sites in south-west Wales. These sites also create a

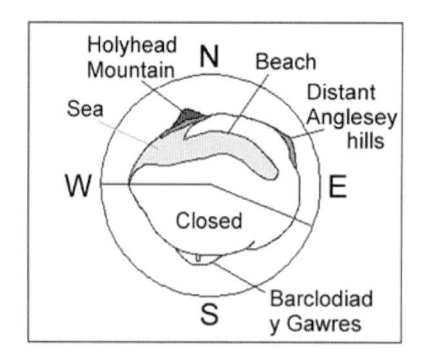

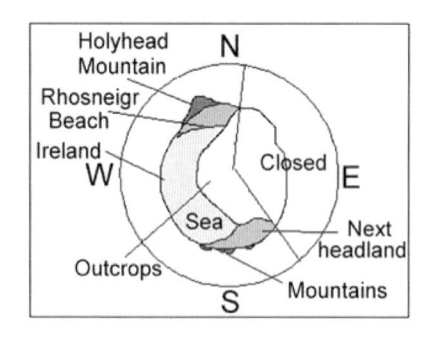

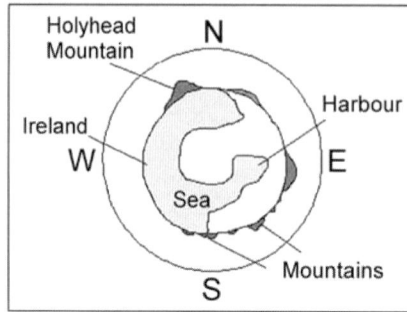

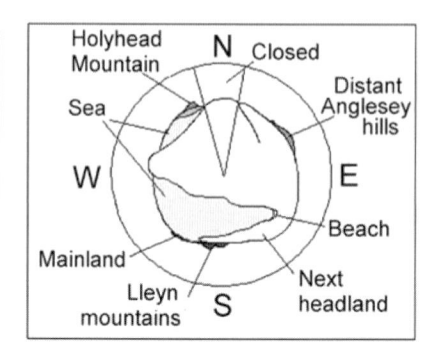

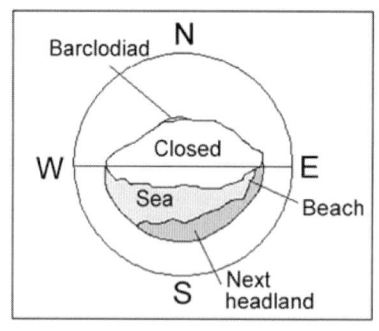

Figure 5.13 Control samples taken around Barclodiad y Gawres. Just 50m to the north (top), south (bottom), west (far left) or east (far right) radically changes the view of the surrounding landscape when compared with the view from the monument itself (centre).

small enclosed box-like chamber using sizeable stones. Like their counterparts in south-west Wales, many of these sites have distinctive and broad capstones. This includes sites such as Maen y Bardd, Cefn Isaf and Mynydd Cefn Amwlch. In this group we could also include monuments which may have had a small passage like Bodowyr and Ty Newydd on Anglesey, as the actual structure of these sites is remarkably similar to the portal dolmens. We might also include in this group the first phase of sites like Trefignath and Din Dryfol, which also created small box-like chambers set within round cairns. These sites in turn bear a striking similarity to the first phase at sites like Mid Gleniron in south-west Scotland (Corcoran 1969b), and may have been part of a broader desire to create a small chamber within the landscape. Pant y Saer might also be understood as a variation on this theme. It is perhaps no surprise that the chambers which bear a resemblance to those in south-west Scotland are in northern Anglesey, while the portal dolmens are found in southern Anglesey and mainland north-west Wales, particularly on Lleyn,

the Ardudwy peninsula and along the upper reaches of the Conwy Valley.

At some point, the simple boxes and some of the portal dolmens were elaborated and additional chambers were built. These sites were subsequently incorporated into long cairns or platforms, and this seems to have happened right across the area, from Carnedd Hengwm South in the south to Trefignath in the north. It seems possible that all the Ardudwy sites may have been incorporated into long cairns or platforms. Many of the sites on Anglesey may also have been elaborated, with the addition of a second chamber, as may have been the case at Plas Newydd, Presaddfed and Hen Drefor.

The passage graves of Bryn Celli Ddu and Barclodiad y Gawres may not have been the only substantial passage graves in north Wales. It is possible that Ystium Cegid Isaf was also a large passage grave that has since been severely robbed (although see Lynch 2001a). Also on Lleyn, Bachwen is a rather unusual site, both architecturally and in its landscape setting. It has a remarkably thin and small capstone for a portal dolmen (as classified by Lynch 1969b), even for a site in north Wales. There is no evidence of the classic portalled entrance that is found at sites like Dyffryn Ardudwy and Gwern Einon. There are also cupmarks on the upper surface of the capstone, and this is again unique in north Wales, although rock art is found at Barclodiad and Bryn Celli Ddu. The landscape setting of Bachwen is perhaps most unusual of all, as there are wide-ranging views in all directions. Its position on the side of the Lleyn peninsula would also mean that from it, like Barclodiad, there would be views of Ireland on a clear day. Is it possible, therefore, that this site is another, very badly damaged passage grave?

There are still a number of sites which do not fit into either of these two groups, and which remain hard to classify. As noted, Capel Garmon shares striking similarities with Cotswold-Severn monuments, although it is tempting to suggest that it may have begun life with the western chamber standing alone, which subsequently had the other chamber and passage added and set within a long cairn. We could suggest that this occurred around the same time at which other sites elsewhere were being elaborated and long cairns or platforms added. If this were the case, Capel Garmon would have borne a striking similarity to Tan y Coed and Branas Uchaf in its first phase, sites that are also set along rivers, with what appear to be simple polygonal chambers. Lligwy remains unparalleled. It might be seen as one of a number of local monuments which draw on notions of monumentality from elsewhere. Cerrig y Gof in south-west Wales and Mull Hill on the Isle of Man could be cited as other possible examples. Some of the remaining sites are too badly damaged for simple classification, such as Trearddur and Perthiduon, but their landscape settings suggest that they may belong to the dolmen tradition of this area.

Conclusions

As in south-west Wales, monuments appear to have been carefully positioned in the landscape, and the importance of place is again suggested. Broadly speaking, the monuments of north-west Wales seem to be located in two contrasting landscape settings. Monuments are usually positioned in relation to the mountains and the sea with clear views of both. This relates primarily to those sites on Anglesey, the Lleyn peninsula and around Ardudwy. The second group are located in relation to rivers and are positioned in quite different landscapes. From these sites the sea and the mountains are not visible; instead they are set within much more gentle and rolling countryside. Architecturally, there seems to be two main forms of monument in north-west Wales. Monuments in the portal dolmen tradition (which may include the simple boxes and other simple chamber forms) are found both along the river valleys and in places with views of the mountains and the sea. It is those found along the coast that seem to have been elaborated at a later date. The few passage graves are found only on Lleyn and Anglesey, in the latter case set within landscapes that encircle the monument.

6 The monuments of south-east Wales and their landscape settings

Vicki Cummings

The monuments of south-east Wales

For our purposes, south-east Wales covers a broad stretch of country, incorporating the former counties of Glamorgan, Monmouthshire and Brecknockshire. The 29 Neolithic monuments are found in three clusters within this region, with six sites on the Gower peninsula, 14 sites concentrated around the Black Mountains in Brecknockshire (with two further sites in neighbouring Herefordshire), and the rest dispersed in the lowland belt between Swansea and Chepstow (Figure 6.1). Other monuments are also found in this area, including two possible Neolithic ditched enclosures at the west end of the Vale of Glamorgan (Burrow *et al.* 2001), the possible stone enclosure on Gray Hill (Burl 1995, 174–80), and a few stone circles such as Cerrig Duon. As with other areas of the country,

it is likely that a number of monuments will have been destroyed by farming and later settlement, among other processes, including around what are now Cardiff and Newport. The distribution of monuments around the Black Mountains remains striking.

Excavations

Twelve monuments have been excavated in south-east Wales, and another four sites subject to antiquarian exploration: over half of the sites. In the Black Mountains, eight sites out of 14 have been excavated and have revealed quite remarkable evidence. Ffostyll North and South long cairns were partially excavated by Vulliamy in the 1920s (Vulliamy 1921; 1923). At Ffostyll North, Vulliamy found

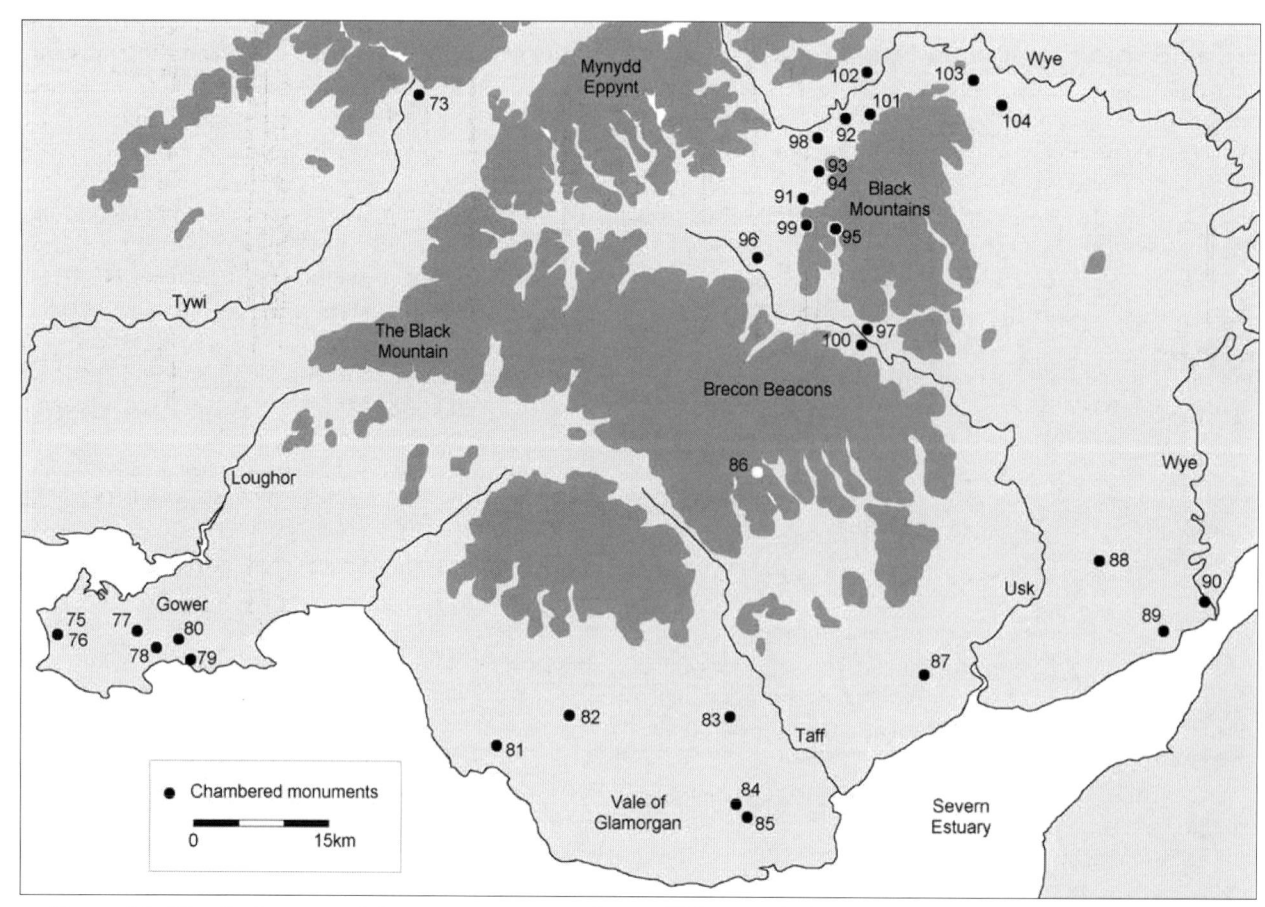

Figure 6.1 Distribution map of the monuments in south-east Wales. Dark shading indicates land over 1000ft (304m).

that the eastern chamber had been emptied prior to excavation, but the central chamber contained the bones of six or seven humans as well as horse, dog, ox and pig remains with pottery and flint (Vulliamy 1923). An additional chamber to the west was found which contained more human bone from at least four individuals, as well as animal bones and a flint flake. At Ffostyll South, the single chamber produced human and animal bone, and the cremation of a child along with animal bone, pottery and flint were found in the body of the mound (Vulliamy 1921). At least nine individuals were uncovered from this site, although it is claimed that human bone had been recovered from the site prior to excavation (RCAHMW 1997, 41). Vulliamy (1929) also excavated at Little Lodge where he uncovered a large central chamber containing the remains of eight individuals as well as charcoal and animal bone. A pair of smaller chambers was also found to the south of main central chamber, although these produced only one flint flake (RCAHMW 1997). Penywyrlod Llanigon was excavated around the same time (Morgan and Marshall 1921) and produced the remains of at least 20 individuals, pottery, animal bone and flint. However, it seems that there were three phases at this site, and it is not clear to which phase or phases these finds belong (RCAHMW 1997, 61).

Ty Isaf was excavated in 1938 by Grimes (1939b), who uncovered a wedge-shaped cairn with a horned façade and false portal entrance. Within the cairn were two lateral chambers set opposite one another and a larger chamber set at the southern end within a rotunda. A fourth and badly-damaged chamber was found at the southern end of the cairn (Grimes 1939b, 122). The forecourt contained burnt material, fragments of bone and a few flints, and had been filled. Beyond the limit of the forecourt filling, the butt of a polished stone axe was found buried (Grimes 1939b, 126). The chambers contained substantial deposits. Of the two lateral chambers, the western chamber contained the remains of at least 17 people and leaf-shaped arrowheads, a stone axe, a bone pin and pottery. The bones were found mostly in groups 'consisting frequently of the cranium, lower jaw and one or two long bones carefully placed against the side-stone and sometimes pushed into angles and crevices' (Grimes 1939b, 126). The eastern chamber contained the bones of only one individual, but the remains of two individuals were found in the passage. This chamber also contained pottery and a small sandstone pendant. The large central chamber contained the remains of nine people and pottery. The southern chamber contained cremated bone and a Bronze Age urn (Grimes 1939b, 130). A more recent examination of the human bone from Ty Isaf has shown that a broad range of ages is represented here, and suggested that carbohydrates (cereals) may have played little part in these people's diets (Wysocki and Whittle 2000).

The excavation of Pipton in 1950 revealed another wedge-shaped cairn with a horned façade and dummy portal (Savory 1956a). The forecourt had been deliberately filled in and the horn-core of an ox was found wedged into the socket of the eastern portal stone. Two chambers were uncovered, the first of which was divided into three compartments with a long angled passage. The chamber contained a pit and human bone from at least two individuals, animal bone, flint, hazelnuts and decayed organic matter (Savory 1956a, 23). The second chamber uncovered was a smaller enclosed cist with no passage, which contained seven discrete heaps of human bone representing at least nine people, with each group containing the mixed remains of different people (Wysocki and Whittle 2000).

More recently the sites of Gwernvale and Penywyrlod Talgarth have been investigated and published (Britnell and Savory 1984). Gwernvale has been excavated a number of times over the years with the south-east chamber being emptied out in 1804 (RCAHMW 1997, 56–60). The excavations in 1978 revealed three additional chambers which were set within a trapezoidal long cairn with a false portal. The human bone represented at least three people and flint and pottery were also found. Pre-cairn activity was also found under the cairn at Gwernvale, including Mesolithic and Neolithic flint assemblages and from the latter period, traces of buildings, pottery and organic remains (for full details see Britnell and Savory 1984). Penywyrlod Talgarth was only discovered in 1972 despite being the largest long cairn in the area at over 60 m (Savory 1973). It was found as the site was being quarried away, revealing one chamber to the south-west and three chambers to the north-east, all set within a large cairn with a false portal. Only chamber NE II was fully excavated, but discrete deposits of human bone were found representing six individuals. Again, each pile of bones consists of the remains from two or three people (Wysocki and Whittle 2000). An examination of the teeth from Penywyrlod Talgarth suggests that this population may have consumed cereals more frequently (Wysocki and Whittle 2000). One of the ribs from chamber NE III has a flint tip from an arrowhead embedded in it, and the lack of bone regrowth indicates that the person died shortly after being shot (Wysocki and Whittle 2000). Other finds include animal bone, a flint knife, pottery and a possible bone flute (Britnell and Savory 1984).

On the Gower, two sites have been excavated. Parc le Breos Cwm was excavated in 1869 (Lubbock 1871) and again in 1960–1 (Atkinson 1961; Whittle and Wysocki 1998). The excavations uncovered the remains of at least 40 inhumation deposits as well as cremations. Domesticated and wild animal bones were found as well as 32 knapped pieces of flint and pot sherds (Whittle and Wysocki 1998). An examination of the human bone suggests that the bone from the chambers had been exposed before being deposited. Stable isotope analysis suggests that people buried in the monument had not been eating marine resources (Richards in Whittle and Wysocki 1998), while an examination of the bones themselves hinted that the males had been more mobile than their female counterparts. Nicholaston was excavated in 1939 and revealed a long cairn covering a single chamber (Williams 1940). The only find was charcoal.

Tinkinswood near Cardiff was excavated in 1914 (Ward 1915; 1916), showing a series of rows of upright stones within the long cairn as well as a walled pit containing animal bones. The large main chamber, which had been disturbed prior to the investigations, was excavated, producing the remains of at least 50 people (RCAHMW 1976, 37). There were other finds of flint implements, bone pins and pottery. The forecourt area had been paved and was covered with broken pottery before being infilled. Lastly, Thornwell Farm in Chepstow was discovered recently and excavated in 1990–1. A chamber contained the remains of four adults and two children as well as early Neolithic pottery and flint tools (Children and Nash 1996, 38).

Antiquarian excavations were conducted at Heston Brake overlooking the Severn Estuary. At Garn Goch in the Black Mountains it is claimed that a cist or cromlech was uncovered in 1847 which contained human remains (RCAHMW 1997, 54). The chamber at St Lythans was emptied out in 1875 and human remains and pottery were found (RCAHMW 1976, 39). Finally, minor investigations at Penmaen Burrows on the Gower uncovered bone (RCAHMW 1976, 32).

Morphology and typology

In contrast to their difficulties with the monuments of south-west Wales, scholars have shown little hesitation in classifying those in south-east Wales. Many of the monuments in the area, particularly those in the Black Mountains, have long been assigned to the broader Cotswold-Severn classification. This monumental form was originally described as a 'Cotswold long cairn' (Crawford 1925; Grimes 1936a), but in discussing the morphology of Parc le Breos Cwm, Daniel (1937a) described this broader category of monuments as 'Cotswold-Severn', incorporating sites from south-east Wales, Gloucestershire, Oxfordshire, Wiltshire, Somerset and Berkshire. Cotswold-Severn monuments are typically characterised by the presence of a long cairn, typically trapezoidal or horned, with a clearly defined forecourt area. The forecourt frequently leads to a terminal single or transepted chamber. For example, at Tinkinswood the forecourt leads directly to a simple, box-like chamber whereas at Parc le Breos Cwm two pairs of smaller compartments face one another across a passage. A number of Cotswold-Severn monuments have lateral chambers, where the chambers are positioned along the sides of the long cairn. At these sites, such as Gwernvale and Ty Isaf, the lateral chambers are small and reached along a short passage. Sites with lateral chambers usually have a 'false portal' entrance in the façade as at Penwyrlod Talgarth. Since Daniel coined the term 'Cotswold-Severn', there has been considerable debate about the Cotswold-Severn monuments in general (e.g. Corcoran 1969a; Daniel 1950; Darvill 1982; Piggott 1954; Saville 1990), and in particular the question of how these sites relate to chambered tombs elsewhere (Daniel 1941). Cotswold-Severn monuments have long been seen as part of a broader tradition of monument construction, originally with origins in France (Daniel 1941; 1950, 156; Piggott 1954, 150). However, the actual classification of the Black Mountains group has not been seriously challenged as the structural similarities between these and monuments found further east seem unequivocal.

Other sites in south-east Wales have been classified as Cotswold-Severn monuments. The sites of Gwern y Cleppa and Heston Brake in Monmouthshire, and Parc le Breos Cwm and Penmaen Burrows on the Gower have been assigned to the Cotswold-Severn tradition (Corcoran 1969a; Whittle and Wysocki 1998), as have Pentyrch and Tythegeston in Glamorgan (Corcoran 1969a, 20; RCAHMW 1976, 25). Both Tinkinswood and St Lythans have also been classified as Cotswold-Severn cairns with a simple terminal chamber (Corcoran 1969a), although the chambers at these sites both bear a striking resemblance to portal dolmens found further west (discussed in more detail below).

A few sites in south-east Wales have been classified as portal dolmens, in particular several monuments on the Gower. Sweyne's Howe North and South were both considered to be portal dolmens (Corcoran 1969a, 67) and Whittle and Wysocki suggested that with its low cairn, Parc le Breos Cwm may have 'something of its design in common with Irish Sea portal dolmens' (1998, 170). The site of Gaer Llwyd 6km south-east of Usk and Coity near Bridgend have also been tentatively assigned to the portal dolmen tradition (Corcoran 1969a, 276). A few sites have also defied easy classification. Corcoran (1969a, 66–7) had a group of 'hybrid and miscellaneous' cairns which included Arthur's Stone and Ty Illtyd in the Black Mountains, and Arthur's Stone and Nicholaston on the Gower, although Daniel classed Arthur's Stone on the Gower in his 'sub-megalithic' class (1950, 47).

Chronology

Our understanding of the chronology of sites in south-east Wales has improved a little in recent years, as a number of sites have been radiocarbon dated. Dates are already available from Gwernvale, where the pre-cairn activity dates to around 3900 cal BC (CAR-113–6), and from Penywyrlod Talgarth, where human bone has produced a date of 3980–3630 cal BC (HAR-674) (Britnell and Savory 1984); further dates have been produced from the latter in a programme initiated by Alasdair Whittle and Michael Wysocki (cf. Wysocki and Whittle 2000), which range from 3940 BC to 3030 BC (OxA-11287–90; 11305; 11419). There is also a set of twelve radiocarbon dates from Parc le Breos Cwm, which suggest a date for construction and use of around 3800–3500 BC (OxA-6487–6492) (Whittle and Wysocki 1998); two dates fell a little later (OxA-6495 and OxA-6497), and two dates from animal bone were Mesolithic in age (OxA-6499–6500). These results, taken in combination with the results from other Cotswold-Severn monuments further east (Whittle and Wysocki 1998) could suggest that the lateral Cotswold-Severn monuments of south-east Wales may be relatively early in the regional sequence; other dates are awaited from Ty Isaf and Pipton, part of the programme noted above. Four new dates from human bone at Tinkinswood place deposition around 3700 BC (OxA-11406–9), but are too few for the place of terminal-chambered monuments, anyway rare in south-east Wales, reliably to be established in the regional sequence. There are, as yet, no dates for the portal dolmens in the region (see discussion below).

Over the past few decades there has also been discussion regarding the possibility of multi-phase construction sequences at the monuments in south-east Wales and further afield (e.g. Corcoran 1972). A few monuments in south-east Wales may be the result of different phases of construction. The original excavator, Grimes, thought that Ty Isaf was a unitary design, and explicitly stated that he could see no join in the stone work between the rotunda and the long cairn (Grimes 1939b, 138). However, Corcoran (1969a, 84) raised the possibility that the site could have been built in several phases. He suggested that the rotunda and its chambers may have been constructed prior to the addition of the long cairn and its lateral chambers; alternatively, the rotunda and its chambers may have been inserted into a laterally-chambered cairn. Corcoran supported the latter of the two propositions, and suggested that Pipton may also have seen a similar sequence (Corcoran 1969a, 87). He also suggested that Pen-y-wyrlod Llanigon and Heston Brake may have been constructed in more than one phase (Corcoran 1969a, 80; 1972, 43). However, other authors have called the idea of multi-phase construction sequences into question; Britnell and Savory (1984) consider the issue as contentious. They found no evidence for multiple phases at Gwernvale or Penywyrlod Talgarth and caution against understanding sites with multiple chambers as representing multiple phases (Britnell and Savory 1984, 7). Another possibility is of extended building processes, in which some 'chambers' stood alone for periods of time before eventual incorporation in cairns and mounds (Lesley MacFadyen, *pers. comm.*). This would serve to blur the distinction between single- and multi-phase construction, as well as reinforcing the importance of local place. We return to these points in chapter 7.

Monuments in the landscape

Setting the scene

South-east Wales incorporates a range of different landscapes. To the west, the Gower Peninsula has long sandy beaches, spectacular coastlines and caves all along the southern shore. The Gower also contains smaller upland areas such as Cefn-y-Bryn which has Arthur's Stone set close to its summit and Rhossili Down at the western tip of the Gower which is covered with Bronze Age cairns and has wide views of the sea, Carmarthenshire and Worms Head. In contrast, the Vale of Glamorgan, stretching from Swansea to Cardiff, is quite different in nature. The Rhondda and Neath valleys are hilly with narrow valleys following the main watercourses, but these areas seem devoid of Neolithic monuments. Instead it is the rich coastal plain with its gently undulating land around Bridgend and Cardiff which has a limited number of monuments. A couple of monuments are also set at the mouth of the River Severn, an estuarine landscape with views towards the hills of Somerset. The Brecon Beacons are part of the broader range of mountains and hills which stretch from Merthyr Tydfil to Ammanford, incorporating Forest Fawr and the Black Mountain. These hills effectively mark the northern edge of south Wales. There are no monuments around these hills, and instead the distribution is centred exclusively on the Black Mountains. Both the Brecon Beacons and the Black Mountains have a series of river valleys running through them. The Brecon Beacons have the larger peaks, while the Black Mountains are more rounded and lower (colour plate 10). It is perhaps the overall Black Mountains escarpment which is most distinctive rather than the individual mountains, with some notable exceptions such as Mynydd Troed and Hay Bluff.

Previous work on landscape

The monuments of south-east Wales have been the focus of discussion since Crawford (1925, 11) and their landscape setting has been commented on many times. Crawford himself noted that many of the sites in the Black Mountains are positioned on the edge of valleys. Grimes (1936b, 113) commented on the location of the Black Mountains group as 'between valley and hill' and suggested that the monument builders preferred low-lying and less conspicuous positions (Grimes 1939b, 121). Daniel (1950, 30) noted that sites such as Gwern y Cleppa and Heston Brake were positioned in commanding positions with wide views, but that other sites such as Parc le Breos Cwm and Sweynes Howes were inconspicuously positioned even when there were commanding positions nearby (colour plate 11). The landscape setting of Parc le Breos Cwm has been commented on by many authors (references in Whittle and Wysocki 1998). Daniel also noted a general preference for sites being close to sources of stone and water (the sea and rivers), which he took as evidence of seaborne colonisation (1950, 33). Piggott noted that the Black Mountains group was set in valleys among thick oakwood (1954, 149) and Corcoran (1969a) again noted the location of sites on the slopes of valleys (1969, 23).

The landscape settings of the monuments in the Black Mountains were also discussed in Tilley's *A phenomenology of landscape* (1994), where a chapter detailed their position in relation to the hills and rivers of the area. Tilley argued that the overall axis of each long cairn had been specifically built in order to point towards particular landscape features. The significance of river valleys and prominent spurs was emphasised, and Tilley suggested that the monuments specifically highlighted views towards these highly symbolic and important features. Nash's (1997) paper on the Black Mountains replicated Tilley's arguments, and added the view that the architecture of the monuments was designed to mimic or otherwise reproduce important features of the landscape.

Fleming (1999) has explored potential problems with Tilley's argument, suggesting that many of the Black Mountains cairns were not oriented on hills or spurs. Likewise, the orientation of cairns in relation to rivers was also criticised. Instead Fleming suggested that natural features such as trees or local events prior to construction may have been significant in the location of individual sites. Most recently, Cummings *et al.* (2002) have considered the landscape setting of the Black Mountains monuments as part of a broader study of the notion of 'sidedness' in the creation and experience of megalithic monuments. It is suggested that the monuments were positioned in the landscape in order to divide the view along the axis of the cairn so that the two different sides of each monument had opposing landscape views (Cummings *et al.* 2002). Instead of simply highlighting single topographic features of note, the axis of each site seems to emphasise points of transition between contrasting parts of the landscape. This is also reflected in the architecture and the deposits made in the chambers.

General location

The great majority (79%) of monuments in south-east Wales are found on what is now agricultural land, mainly in pasture. This includes all the sites along the coast from Heston Brake to Tythegeston (hereafter the coastal group) and all but one of the sites around the Black Mountains. However, in contrast to this all but one of the Gower monuments are located in more upland locations. Even the exception, Parc le Breos Cwm, situated in a narrow valley, is not in an area suitable for extensive agriculture. On average, sites in south-east Wales are positioned at 141m OD, but this average differs in each area. In the Black Mountains monuments are on average at 200m OD, with Gwernvale the lowest-lying site at 69m OD and the two Ffostyll cairns the highest at 312m OD. In the Gower, the average height for a site is 101m OD, with Arthur's Stone at 145m OD and Parc le Breos Cwm at 20m OD. On average the sites of the coastal group are much more low-lying (76m OD) with the portal dolmen site of Gaer Llwyd the exception at 215m OD. It has been noted that the monuments are found between the good free-draining soils and wetter soils (Corcoran 1969a, 17; Olding 2000, 10).

Geology

The geology of south-east Wales divides up reasonably neatly into bands of different rock types (George 1970). There is a large band of coal measures which stretches from Kidwelly in the west to Pontypool in the east, but this is the area devoid of monuments. The Gower consists of Carboniferous Limestone with patches of Old Red Sandstone, and there are large swathes of the latter north of Cardiff and Newport, with the Black Mountains and the Brecon Beacons consisting entirely of Old Red Sandstone. The most complex geological zone is between Cardiff and Bridgend which consists of a combination of Trias, Limestone, Sandstone and Lias. Over half of the monuments in south-east Wales (66%) are located on Old Red Sandstone, with another 17% positioned on Carboniferous Limestone.

Mountains and hills

A number of the monuments in south-east Wales seem to be located in relation to mountains and hills, in particular the Black Mountains. The relationship between these monuments and the Black Mountains has already been discussed by Tilley (1994), who suggested that the long cairns were oriented towards the spurs of the Black Mountains. He considered views of the Black Mountains, and of rivers, to be of the greatest significance, and highlighted the importance of Mynydd Troed, visible from 50% of the sites. Fleming (1999) has criticised Tilley's claim that certain long cairns 'point' at particular mountains. Cummings *et al.* (2002) suggest that Tilley's overall hypothesis was correct in the sense that monuments are positioned in relation to the Black Mountains. They suggest instead that the long axes of the cairns actually point towards the edge of spurs and escarpments. The relationship between the monuments and the Black Mountains is clearly an important one, and more can be said.

First, all the monuments have views of the Black Mountains escarpment. As Tilley notes, these views focus on the hills of Twmpa (Lord Hereford's Knob), Y Das, Mynydd Troed, Hay Bluff and the southern peaks of Table Mountain and Sugar Loaf. These are not the highest hills in the range; Waun Fach at 811m OD is the highest peak, and is surrounded by other high mountains such as Pen y Gadair Fawr and Pen Trumau. Those highest hills lie in the heart of the Black Mountains and do not seem to be the primary focus of the monuments. Instead it is the smaller but prominent peaks of Hay Bluff and Mynydd Troed which stand out in the landscape as seen from below, and which may have been the significant landmarks for local monuments builders. For example, from Clyro the peaks of Hay Bluff, Twmpa and Y Das are prominent (Figure 6.2), as well as Mynydd Troed in the distance. From Ffostyll North and South, Twmpa, Y Das and Mynydd Troed are also prominent on the skyline.

The main thrust of Tilley's argument was the way in

Figure 6.2 The Black Mountains escarpment, as visible from Clyro.

which the monumental architecture seems to interact with the Black Mountains. While it is actually the case that the long axes of the long cairns do not literally 'point' at these mountains (see Fleming 1999), the axis of any particular site does seem to be positioned in relation to these hills. At the Ffostyll cairns, for example, both sites have one axis pointing to one side or edge of the Black Mountains. At Ffostyll North the eastern long axis is not oriented precisely on Twmpa, but the edge or side of this mountain. Likewise at Ffostyll South the long axis of the cairn does not point directly at Mynydd Troed, but to one side of the mountain. A similar situation can be found at Penywyrlod Talgarth, Pipton and Little Lodge. It is these escarpment edges which are so visually distinctive in the landscape (Figure 6.3). Tilley has also suggested that terminal chambers were aligned in the same directions as the long cairns themselves (1994, 138–9). However, this too must be contradicted, since in each case, as with the long cairns themselves, the chambers are not exactly aligned on spurs. Instead, when entering or exiting these chambers, the direct line of sight is towards escarpment edges. Elsewhere it has been suggested that these terminal chambers may have been positioned to create asymmetrical views of the landscape as one entered or exited the chambers, in order to refer to a broader notion of 'sidedness' (Cummings *et al.* 2002). Tilley further discussed the relationship between hills and chambers at the laterally-chambered sites (1994, 140). He suggested that it is the middle of the escarpments which are visible when entering these lateral chambers, and discussed in detail how the passage of Arthur's Stone is aligned on Hay Bluff. This latter claim has also been doubted by Fleming (1999, 121). With regards to the idea that the lateral chambers point at the middle of escarpments, this is certainly true in some cases. For example, the two lateral chambers at Ty Isaf are both directed towards the centre of Mynydd Troed and Pen Trumau respectively. However, at other sites this is not the case. For example, the large asymmetrical chamber at Pipton changes its axis a number of times, yet each time the axis changes it is pointing towards the edge of the escarpment. We should also take into account the issue of multiple phases at these sites. At Ty Isaf, for example, it is possible to suggest that the passage and chambers set within the rotunda pre-dated the long cairn with its two opposing lateral chambers. If this was the case, the entrance to the passage leading to the chambers within the rotunda could be seen as aligned in a general fashion on the gap between Mynydd Troed and Castell Dinas. This has implications for other possible multi-phase sites such as Penywyrlod Talgarth, Pipton, Gwernvale and Ffostyll North, where the significant landscape features may have changed over time and be marked in the changing alignments of the chambers.

It is not only the Black Mountains which are visible from these monuments but also, at a greater distance, the

Figure 6.3 The long mound at Penywyrlod Talgarth is aligned on the edge of Mynydd Troed.

Brecon Beacons. 50% of sites in the area, such as Penywyrlod Talgarth, the Ffostyll pair and Clyro, have views of the Brecon Beacons. It has already been noted that Ty Illtyd is more closely related to the Brecon Beacons than to the Black Mountains (Tilley 1994, 124). This site is 6.5km to the west of Mynydd Troed and has clear and impressive views of the Brecon Beacons including the two highest peaks of Pen y Fan and Fan y Big (Figure 6.4). At Penywyrlod Talgarth the Brecon Beacons are visible from the western side of the cairn. Here, the very substantial cairn seems to have been carefully positioned so that there is a view of the Brecon Beacons; had the site been a few tens of metres to the east of where it now sits, the Brecon Beacons would not have been visible on the horizon. Its position and alignment also offer a line of sight to the edge of Mynydd Troed, as noted, a view to the escarpment to the east, a wide vista over the Wye valley, and a portion of restricted view to the immediate southwest. The careful orchestration of views of the mountains is clearly shown at the two Ffostyll cairns. From the northern site a wide expanse of the Brecon Beacons can be seen, yet from the southern cairn just 50m away only a much smaller portion of the Brecon Beacons is visible (Cummings *et al*. 2002, figure 3).

It is striking that there is no concentration of monuments around the Brecon Beacons, nor around the south and eastern edges of the Black Mountains. Nor is the eye-catching outlier of the east side of the Black Mountains, the Skirrid, referenced by any of the surrounding monuments. We have already suggested variation in focus or concern through time, and there may have been a further variability in what was deemed significant or appropriate in the first place. Could it be that in some way the landscape around the Brecon Beacons was not thought of as so suitable as the Black Mountains for the placing of monuments? The Black Mountains are surrounded on all sides by river valleys and usable lowland, whereas the Brecon Beacons have a much more upland feel to them. To the south are a series of boggy and craggy hills, while the mountains of Forest Fawr are found directly to the west. Mynydd Llangynidr and the western edge of the Black Mountains are to the east, leaving the Usk Valley to the north. Gwernvale and Garn Goch were constructed close to the Usk but further east. This can only be a partial explanation of difference, since there is no obviously different character to either the north side of the Brecon Beacons or the south-east side of the Black Mountains, where monuments are also apparently missing. It is hard to penetrate other possible factors such as distribution of population, local mythologies, or taboos.

The monuments in the other areas of south-east Wales do not seem to have such a close affinity with hills and mountains as those in the Black Mountains. The monuments on the Gower have views of some impressive local

Figure 6.4 From Ty Illtyd there are clear views of the Brecon Beacons.

Figure 6.5 The wide ranging views from Arthur's Stone on the Gower.

hills, such as Llanmadoc Hill and Rhossili Down. Arthur's Stone is actually set on the large central hill that runs through the heart of the Gower (Cefn y Bryn). It is also possible to see all the way to the Preselis from Arthur's Stone, as well as to the Black Mountain to the north-east (Figure 6.5). The significance of this will be further discussed in chapter 7. Of the coastal group it is only Tythegeston that has views of distant hills, in this case those of the Rhondda, while the three monuments found along the Severn have views of the hills of Somerset.

Figure 6.6 The view of the Severn from Heston Brake.

Rivers and streams

Tilley (1994) discussed the relationship between the monuments of the Black Mountains and rivers in some detail. He noted that the major rivers of the area, the Wye and the Usk, or their tributaries, are visible from all the sites. A number of sites are actually positioned so that their long axes run parallel to waterways (Clyro, Cross Lodge, Gwernvale, Pipton and Ty Illtyd: Tilley 1994, 124), and sites are also located in 'associated pairs' on opposite sides of rivers. Tilley suggested that, with mountains or hills, views of rivers were of essential importance and significance (1994, 136). Fleming has criticised these observations, suggesting that only three sites (Clyro, Cross Lodge and Gwernvale) are oriented on rivers and that at sites like Gwernvale, which Tilley claimed was deliberately aligned on the Usk, the orientation of the long cairn may have been influenced by other factors such as pre-cairn activity (Fleming 1999, 123).

A brief glance at the distribution map of sites in the Black Mountains (Figure 6.1) shows that monuments are roughly located in relation to river valleys and rivers (i.e. none are placed on top of mountains or away from the river valleys). However, the relationship between rivers and monuments is rather more complex than Tilley has implied. Sites are on average 1.1km from the nearest river or tributary, but some sites are much closer than this. Gwernvale is only half a kilometre from the Usk, while Mynydd Troed is 3km away from the Llynfi. However, the Llynfi is only a stream near Mynydd Troed and can hardly be classed as a river or even a major tributary. This leaves Mynydd Troed many kilometres from the nearest river. The two Ffostyll cairns are also 2km from the Llynfi. The two sites to the north of the distribution, Arthur's Stone and Cross Lodge, are only 2km from the Wye. However, it is not possible to actually see the Wye or the Wye Valley from either of these sites, as the view in that direction is restricted by the immediate topography. Instead there are views down towards the Dore, but again this is only a stream in this part of the landscape. Other sites are much more closely associated with rivers. Ty Illtyd has clear views of the Usk, and Clyro overlooks the Wye. Penywyrlod Llanigon, which is 3km from the Wye, has clear views of the river.

It seems, then, that monuments in the Black Mountains, as in south-west Wales, are rather variably positioned in relation to rivers and river valleys. Only Gwernvale and Garn Goch are positioned in the river valley itself; most of the other sites are positioned overlooking river valleys but are set up and away from the river valley. *Contra* Tilley, it is not possible to actually see the nearby river from all sites, especially if we envisage some tree cover (further discussed in chapter 7). In addition, a number of the rivers in the Black Mountains are ignored. There are no monuments near the lower stretches of the Dore, or along Escley Brook, the Afon Honddu or the River Monnow. However, none of these river valleys provides the combination of land and views of the Black Mountains in the way that the Wye and the Usk do.

A connection between monument architecture and rivers is much harder to sustain. If the long cairns do seem rather variably oriented along river valleys, this may be as much to do with the way that they appeared on the horizon as one approached from the river valleys as a sense of monument echoing river course. Fleming has argued this in relation to Penywyrlod Talgarth (1999, 121). The other group of monuments which seems closely associated with rivers in south-east Wales are the three sites found along the River Severn. These are Gwern y Cleppa, Thornwell Farm and Heston Brake and all have wide-ranging views of the Severn (Figure 6.6). Gwern y Cleppa is 4km inland from the Severn but has wide views; Heston Brake is 1km from the Severn and has very impressive views of the estuary for almost half of the view; and from Thornwell Farm it is possible to see where the River Wye meets the Severn.

The remainder of the coastal group in south-east Wales do not seem to be closely related to rivers. Sites are on average 3.3km from the nearest river which suggests that sites were placed away from the river valleys but still in the fertile band of land to the south of the region. The site of Coity, however, is placed in the triangle of land between the Afon Ogwr to the west, the Afon Ewenni to the east and south, and streams to the north. The monuments on the Gower are not close to any rivers as there are none in the area. Instead, the Gower is surrounded by the sea to the north, west and south.

A number of the monuments in south-east Wales are positioned close to a stream. 72% of sites are located within 500m of a stream. The comments in chapters 4 and 5 can be noted again. This possible association is more pronounced on the Gower, which lacks any rivers, where all but one site is located close to a stream (on average sites are less than 200m from a stream). The site of Parc le Breos Cwm is actually positioned in a valley which may have had a stream running right next to the cairn in the Neolithic (Whittle and Wysocki 1998). All bar two of the coastal group are close to streams, with many of the sites being positioned close to the start of a stream. Some of the Black Mountains sites seem to be positioned in relation to streams (some of Tilley's tributaries) such as Little Lodge which is only 50m from a stream and Ty Isaf which overlooks the stream which forms the Afon Rhiangoll. Other sites are not located near to streams at all such as Pipton and Ty Illtyd.

Views of the sea

All the monuments in the Black Mountains are inland and it is not possible to see the sea from them, though the upper Severn estuary can be seen from the higher parts of the Skirrid. The sea can be seen from only one of the coastal group monuments; from Tythegeston a very small patch of sea is visible to the south-west. However, some of the other monuments in south-east Wales are more closely associated with the sea. All the monuments on the Gower except Parc le Breos Cwm have views of the sea. Arthur's Stone has views of the sea to the north, out towards Carmarthen Bay, while the rest of the monuments have views of the southern coast. Both Nicholaston and Penmaen Burrows look out over the sea near Oxwich Bay, although this view can no longer be seen at the latter due to more recent dune formation. From the two Sweyne's Howe monuments it is possible to see the sea, again around Oxwich Bay. From Sweyne's Howe North it is also possible to see the sea to the north, approximately the point where the Afon Llwchwr meets the sea. However, from Sweyne's Howe South the mass of Sweyne's Howe North blocks out this view of the sea. Furthermore, had these two sites been positioned on top of the ridge of Rhossili Down just 200m to the west, there would have been wide views out over Carmarthen Bay and to the west.

Other natural features

Other natural features may be a significant feature of the surroundings of a number of the monuments in south-east Wales. Heston Brake, Tythegeston and St Lythans (colour plate 12) are all positioned on the top of quite prominent knolls. Heston Brake, for example, is located on the summit of a protruding knoll that can be seen from many directions (Figure 6.7). This means that the site is skylined when approached from most directions. In addition to this the long thin chamber lies across the knoll, following the contour of the hill, with the two portal stones directing the participant out to a spectacular view of the Severn estuary. Arthur's Stone on the Gower may also have been built so that it was visible from a number of locations along the northern coast of the Gower and from the opposite shore. Tinkinswood is positioned next to some quite distinctive outcrops that were probably the source of the stone for the monument itself. Many of these outcrops resemble built structures. The site of Parc le Breos Cwm is located only a short distance from Cathole Cave. It has also been suggested that the cairn of Mynydd Troed may have been deliberately sited next to the pass immediately below it (Fleming 1999).

Restricted views

In the two previous chapters it was noted that the great majority of sites in south-west and north-west Wales have a restricted view in one direction. This is where the viewer can only see the immediate landscape and no distant features are visible on the horizon. In south-east Wales 86% of sites have a restricted view in one direction. All the monuments on the Gower are positioned so that there is dead ground close to them. Parc le Breos Cwm is a different case in that it has restricted views in all directions (Figure 6.8). In the Black Mountains all the sites except Garn Goch, which is not certainly a Neolithic monument, have a restricted view. 69% of these sites have a closed view to the north which restricts the views beyond the Wye Valley. Over half of the sites in the Black Mountains also have a restricted view which is less than 90°. This may be partly because many of these sites are not located on the side of hills which would otherwise create dead ground for approximately half of the view. Instead it is the gentle undulations in the topography which create a restricted view at these sites. Two of the sites in the coastal group do not have a restricted view. Both of these,

Figure 6.7 The skylined profile of Heston Brake, seen from the north.

Figure 6.8 The enclosed setting at Parc le Breos Cwm.

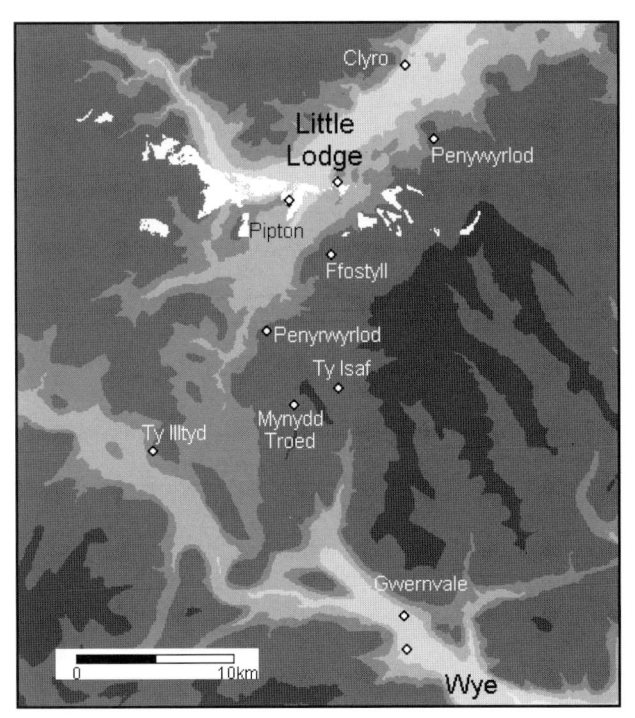

Figure 6.9 The viewshed from Little Lodge, showing intervisibility with Pipton. Parts of the landscape visible from the site are shown in white. Reproduced by kind permission of Ordnance Survey. © Crown copyright NC/03/20516.

Tythegeston and Heston Brake, are set on top of hills or knolls, giving wide-ranging views in all directions. The presence of a restricted view may even have influenced the architectural form of some monuments. At Arthur's Stone, on the north-east side of the Black Mountains, the chamber and the innermost part of the passage are aligned roughly NNW, which more or less coincides with the direction of the restricted view (to the north). Had people exited the monument at this point they would have been presented with a restricted view. Instead the passage turns almost 90° to the west. Exiting the monument along this axis means that a participant would instead have seen the edge of the Black Mountains escarpment straight ahead.

Intervisibility

It has already been noted that the Cotswold-Severn monuments of this area are sited in pairs (Piggott 1954, 130). Tilley (1994) has also discussed in some detail the issue of intervisibility in relation to the Black Mountains monuments. He suggested that the five monuments at the centre of the Black Mountains distribution are intervisible (Ffostyll North, Ffostyll South, Little Lodge (Figure 6.9), Penywyrlod Talgarth and Pipton). Otherwise, intervisibility is restricted to 'between pairs of monuments' (Tilley 1994, 127). Other sites seem to be deliberately sited so as not to be intervisible. Tilley suggests that Penywyrlod Llanigon was located so that Clyro could not be seen across the valley (1994, 134). Likewise the Ffostyll cairns were located so that Pipton and Little Lodge were not visible. Fleming (1999, 122) has dismissed these claims, suggesting that it is only a coincidence that some sites are intervisible and that it is unlikely that Penywyrlod Llanigon was sited so that Clyro was not visible. There are certainly problems with the issue of intervisibility which must relate in part to the sequence of construction of these sites. Nevertheless, Tilley's claim that the five central sites would have been intervisible, especially if we perhaps envisage fire and smoke at these sites, remains valid, although it is difficult to show that they were positioned specifically in order to be intervisible. On the Gower, Penmaen Burrows and Nicholaston are intervisible and further east Tinkinswood and St Lythans are also intervisible.

Location in relation to Mesolithic sites

Since the monument of Gwernvale overlies a Mesolithic occupation, it may be legitimate to suppose that this influenced the location of subsequent Neolithic activity (Britnell and Savory 1984), even though the interval between Mesolithic and Neolithic uses of this place is not known. The absence of evidence from other sites makes it hard to sustain the suggestion that all monuments may have been positioned in relation to earlier activity. Certainly areas that were exploited in the Mesolithic such as the Glamorgan uplands and Waun Fignen Felen (Tilley 1994, 112; Barton *et al.* 1995) did not see later Neolithic monument construction. Nevertheless, Tilley's original suggestion (1994) that Mesolithic locales which were part of a broader symbolic understanding of the landscape were later marked out by Neolithic monuments remains a relevant one.

Back to classification

In chapters 4 and 5, we suggested that the landscape settings of sites in south-west and north-west Wales were able to inform the classification of the monuments in those areas. In contrast to the situation in south-west and north-west Wales, the classification of the great majority of the monuments in south-east Wales has not been considered a problem. The Black Mountains group are considered part of the broader Cotswold-Severn classification and their location in the landscape supports the idea that they form a coherent group, which is a regional variation on a common theme. Virtually all the monuments in this area are placed in similar locations in the landscape: variously set along the river valleys with clear views of the Black Mountains escarpment. The architecture of each individual monument seems to be carefully constructed so that landscape and monument interact and form a vital part of the experience of each site. There are only two sites which seem to be positioned in slightly different parts of the landscape: Garn Goch and Mynydd Troed. Both may be

Figure 6.10 The chamber at St Lythans. The landscape around this site consists of gently rolling hills.

round cairns and are not certainly Neolithic monuments. A number of the monuments beyond the Black Mountains are located in similar locations in the landscape; Tythegeston, Penmaen Burrows, Gwern y Cleppa, Heston Brake and Thornwell Farm can also be considered a local variation on the Cotswold-Severn theme, and are set in broadly comparable settings to the Black Mountains monuments.

The portal dolmens in south-east Wales seem to be positioned in quite different parts of the landscape. Arthur's Stone (Gower), Gaer Llwyd, Sweyne's Howe North and Sweyne's Howe South are all located in more upland locations. The last three sites seem to be tucked away in the landscape, in what may have been quite hidden locations. In contrast, Arthur's Stone is set on one of the highest points on the Gower, with views out to south-west Wales, where there is a concentration of portal dolmens, many of which have views of the Preselis (see chapter 4). Perhaps the siting of Arthur's Stone was a deliberate attempt to make a connection with this area and the form of monumentality found there.

Four monuments in the coastal group of south-east Wales are set in rather unspectacular settings. The sites of Coity, Pentyrch, Tinkinswood and St Lythans are all found in unremarkable locations (Figure 6.10). However, they are all set within the coastal strip found in this part of Wales, and contrast with sites such as Heston Brake and Tythegeston which are located in conspicuous positions in the landscape. These sites bear a striking resemblance to both portal dolmens and Cotswold-Severn monuments. Tinkinswood has a large single chamber with an enormous capstone supported by several large uprights. However, this chamber is set within a long cairn and has the distinctive forecourt area found in Cotswold-Severn monuments. Architecturally, this monument might be seen as a combination of both portal dolmen and Cotswold-Severn styles, and this duality might be reinforced by its landscape setting. Is it possible that all four sites present a combination of the form and setting of Cotswold-Severn and portal dolmen monuments? If this was the case, it has implications for the origins of monumentality in this area, since the date of Tinkinswood would imply the prior existence of both other Cotswold-Severn monuments and portal dolmens.

Conclusions

The monuments found in south-east Wales are quite diverse in both their overall landscape setting and form. The emphasis here is more on diversity. The monuments along the coasts of south-east Wales are usually located with views of the sea and also of local hills, while the position of the Black Mountains group seems to link the architecture of the long cairns with the topography of the surrounding mountains and hills. With the Black Mountains group there is also more emphasis on pairing and intervisibility. What is perhaps most striking about these monuments is the contrast they provide, in both architecture and location, to the western tradition of monument construction. This is one of the key themes returned to in chapter 7.

7 Stones that float to the sky: seeing place, myth and history

Vicki Cummings and Alasdair Whittle

Places and beyond

In chapter 2 we discussed the importance of place, and argued that monumental constructions can be seen as places. The evidence presented in chapters 4–6 and in the inventory can stand as a catalogue of particularity to reinforce this claim. Such places may not always have been the same. Some are distinguished by setting, as we have extensively discussed, and others by the history of their use. Signs of earlier use of places can be found sporadically across our study areas (in part the product of excavation techniques), and with examples from all areas and from all the main kinds of constructions (thus, from Trefignath, Gwernvale and Bryn Celli Ddu), do not appear to be confined to any one kind of monument. In his critique of Tilley's *A phenomenology of landscape*, Fleming (1999, 124) also argued powerfully for the importance of place and immediate locality. While also considering other possibilities such as sitings deliberately away from daily life, to overlook routeways, or to make an association with natural features other than rivers, hilltops or rock outcrops, Fleming strongly suggests the significance of place as linked to events, and of the immediate locality or folk territory. There is no need to disagree with these arguments in themselves, but the evidence and discussions presented in our study surely make it hard to confine the significance of monuments to place and immediate locality alone; and Fleming's argument in fact also admits the same point. If, from a theoretical point of view as discussed in chapter 2, places do not necessarily have fixed boundaries, or can be seen as pauses in movements, being the product of encounter with the human body, then there is every justification for seeking to combine a sense of place with wider perspectives.

An older conception of monuments that does in fact go beyond place and immediate locality is that of the territorial marker (Renfrew 1976; 1979). In this the monument stands for and in a sense draws in a range of land, and the resources contained within it, from the area round about. This has been perhaps unfairly discounted in recent discussions of monuments, in which the emphasis has tended to be either on the individual monument, and especially the kind of experience generated within it, or on the totality of the surrounding landscape, almost universalised and abstracted. The idea of the territorial marker at least invites consideration of the land round about particular sites, and of the relations between constructions in any one area. Alternatives which consider gradations in relationship to domestic and wild expressed in lower and higher settings in the landscape, as suggested for Rousay (Jones 1998), do not consider the wider distributions and spacings (nor indeed the variations in view or perspective that lower and higher settings might have afforded). The emphasis of the territorial marker model was on fixed settlement and the establishment of ownership or rights to resources within defined tracts of land. In some landscapes, for example the tracts of stone-walled enclosures or fields at Behy-Glenulra, Co. Mayo (Caulfield 1983; Caulfield *et al.* 1998) and other locations in western Ireland dated to the early Neolithic (Cooney 2000), where there are dispersed court graves or cairns, this might be an appropriate role for monuments. Elsewhere it seems much more problematic. Perhaps there is simply too little secure evidence in Wales as a whole to make judgements (see chapter 1). Where there appears to be a little more evidence and the beginning of possible pattern, there may be separation between the main distributions of occupation material and the major concentrations of monuments. The north-east side of the Black Mountains is an interesting case in point (Olding 2000), suggestive perhaps of the scenario mooted by Fleming but explicable also in many other ways. And in many other situations, a lack of long-term fixity in residence and land-use makes the idea of territorial markers problematic. As often observed, the model works best for the situation in which all the monuments of a given distribution have been built, and is much weaker for the early stages of a sequence. Nonetheless, something of this older approach can be kept in mind when thinking about the relationship of specific places and localities to what lay beyond.

Visions in the woods

Another dimension of this relationship is the extent of visibility in woodland settings. While woodland cover has often been seen as a problem for any kind of seeing out, or looking in, we suggest that there is much variability, including seasonal difference, and that woodland was an integral part of the experience of monuments, place and locality. The argument is set out with generalised reference to all parts of our study area and to all kinds of monument. In the next section, we focus on particular monuments, beginning with portal dolmens and related constructions.

The significance of the relationship between monuments

in general and landscape features such as mountains, hills, outcrops and horizons in general has long been called into question because we are unsure of the extent to which vegetation and trees would have affected visibility. This question is particularly pertinent in relation to early Neolithic sites as it is clear that much of Britain, including Wales, would have been covered with woodland. Our own inventory of sites indeed notes many instances where the view is blocked or partially obscured by present-day vegetation.

In the early Neolithic much of Wales, and Britain as a whole, is thought to have been covered with woodland which would have variously comprised oak, ash, alder, lime, elm, hazel, birch, poplar and yew (Caseldine 1990; Linnard 2000). There are a number of non-megalithic locations which have produced environmental evidence which enable us to construct an overall picture of the environment in Wales, as already briefly noted in chapter 1. Environmental analysis at a number of the megalithic monuments in Wales enables us to reconstruct the environmental setting of these constructions with a little more precision. A number of sites seem to have been set in quite wooded environments. Soil pollen from the first phase at Dyffryn Ardudwy in north-west Wales suggests that there was woodland around the monument, although this was either disturbed or secondary (Dimbleby 1973). This woodland was rich in hazel and oak, and the poor representation of grasses and herbs led to the suggestion of the presence of a dense canopy of trees (Dimbleby 1973, 4). Land molluscs from Penywyrlod Talgarth and Ty Isaf in the Black Mountains and Bryn yr Hen Bobl in north Wales suggest that there may also have been shady conditions around these sites (Caseldine 1990, 52; Kennard 1935, 280). However, other monuments seem to have been set within much more open environments. Trefignath on Holyhead in north Wales is set on top of a rock outcrop and seems to have been surrounded by grassland (Greig 1987). Barclodiad y Gawres sits on a headland on the west coast of Anglesey and it has been suggested that when the site was built it was surrounded by light woodland as well as more open grassy habitats (Powell and Daniel 1956, 24). In the Black Mountains in south-east Wales, the Mynydd Troed long barrow was built in an area of heathland and open woodland (Crampton and Webley 1966). Carbonised plant remains and the presence of disturbed soil beneath the cairn at Gwernvale in the Black Mountains also suggest that this monument could have stood within a reasonably clear environment (Britnell and Savory 1984).

If some sites were located in woodland, while others were positioned in much more open conditions, it also seems likely that there was considerable variation over time. Some sites may have been built in wooded settings which were gradually cleared. At others, woodland may have grown in cleared areas. For example, at Dyffryn Ardudwy an area of ground was cleared for the construction of the earliest phase of the monument. However, by the time the second phase was built, secondary woodland had grown around the monument (Dimbleby 1973, 6). This is a pattern repeated at sites in southern Britain (Austin 2000, 74).

So it is legitimate to suggest that at sites which were set within open conditions, the surrounding landscape would have been visible, and the environmental evidence suggests that at least some monuments were positioned in predominantly open conditions. At these sites people would have been able to see landscape features such as mountains and outcrops. However, it also clear that a number of monuments – perhaps the majority – may have been built in quite wooded conditions, and that woodland regeneration took place around certain sites.

We tend to assume that this would mean that a site was surrounded by dense woodland. However, there are a number of assumptions about the nature of woodland which need to be addressed. First, there was likely to have been considerable variability in Neolithic woodlands. Some woodland may have been quite dense while other areas may have had much thinner tree cover. We know that woodland was altered by people from the Mesolithic onwards (Finlayson and Edwards 1997; Simmons 1993b) and it is possible that earlier people had thinned out considerable tracts of woodland (as at Waun Fignen Felen: Smith and Cloutman 1988). There is also evidence which now supports the idea that some woodland at least was not primary and unaltered in the early Neolithic. Extensive research in the Somerset Levels, not far from south-east Wales, has revealed that there may have been quite complex uses for woodland already in place by the early Neolithic (Coles and Coles 1986). The Sweet Track contains trees of different ages; some timbers were from large oaks, while others were from much younger trees, which suggests that some of the woodland had been cleared about 100 years before (Coles and Orme 1984, 12). There is also evidence that people were coppicing woodland in the Neolithic. For example, a seven-year coppice cycle has been suggested from the hazel evidence on the Somerset Levels (Coles and Coles 1986, 56). Coppiced trees would show up in pollen diagrams but would not have created a dense canopy of leaves. There is also the question of the size of the trees that make up woodland (cf. Rackham 1980). For example, quite small oak trees produce pollen which may give a misleading impression of the vegetation since we tend to envisage mature woodland when interpreting pollen diagrams. This might be particularly relevant at sites like Dyffryn Ardudwy where it seems that secondary woodland surrounded the site. All of this suggests that the landscape would not necessarily have been entirely blocked from view even if the pollen evidence suggests that there was woodland around a site.

We have also made observations in the course of this study which show that it is possible to see landscape features *through* trees. Close to Pentre Ifan is the ancient oak woodland of Ty Canol, and in the summer it is still possible to see landscape features such as Carn Ingli through quite dense oak canopies. However, distant landscape features are clearly visible through this woodland in the winter months when there are no leaves on the trees (see colour plates 13 and 14). All the landscapes around Ty Canol woods were visible at this time of the year. These findings have interesting implications for the significance of the landscape at monuments surrounded by woodland. In the summer months features such as Carn Ingli may have been just discernible through the trees while other parts of the landscape may not have been visible at all. However, in the winter months it may have been possible to make out all the landscape features around a site. It seems, then, that even if trees did surround a monument, this did not mean that the surrounding landscape was always blocked from view.

Trees may even have added to the symbolism and meaning of monumental places. Woodland and trees are likely to have been potent symbols in the Neolithic. Not only were wooded environments used as part of a seasonal round, plausibly involving the movement of livestock (Edmonds 1999), but they would have provided a medium through which people could think about the world (Evans *et al.* 1999; Ingold 2000; Rival 1998). People were living in woodland, modifying woodland (coppicing, cutting down trees, burning woodland) and moving through woodland. There may have been focal points in forests created by natural tree-throws or clearings, as well as by human clearances, and further enhanced by the coming together of people, for more mundane 'settlement' or less routine aggregations for feasting and exchange. Wood was also routinely used for hafting axes, for making bows and for firing pottery.

Timber was used in the construction of many early Neolithic monuments. Timber mortuary structures are of course found at a number of sites in southern England such as Wayland's Smithy (Whittle 1991), Fussell's Lodge (Ashbee 1966), Haddenham (Hodder and Shand 1988), and further afield at Streethouse, Cleveland (Vyner 1984) and Lochhill, Dumfries and Galloway (Masters 1973). These sites were clearly associated with the deposition and transformation of the dead (Kinnes 1992). At Wayland's Smithy, for example, successive deposits of the dead were placed on a pavement between two great split oaks (Whittle 1991, 70). This suggests that wood was a highly potent substance, and that monuments constructed from wood drew their meaning, in part, from the social and symbolic significance of trees (Austin 2000). But wood does not seem to have been much used in the construction of monuments in Wales (although see Smith and Lynch 1987, 110 on possible use of wood at Din Dryfol). Given its prevalence elsewhere, this is an interesting and, we assume, significant opposition. With reference to the later Neolithic of southern England, the argument has been made that wooden monuments could have marked out arenas for the living, while stone-built monuments created places for interactions with the dead (Parker Pearson and Ramilisonina 1998). The reality may have been more complicated than this, but this model at least supports the plausibility of some kind of play, opposition or complementarity between stone and trees or timber in the early Neolithic monuments of Wales.

There is ethnographic evidence which reinforces the suggestion that woodland and trees may have been significant in the past. For example, in the Arctic sacred places are frequently marked by trees; groves are also important, and the birch is a particularly potent tree (Ovsyannikov and Terebikhin 1994). Specific trees may have been named and incorporated into an inscribed and symbolic landscape (Basso 1996). Particularly distinctive trees may even have been tied to local myths and legends. In many cultures, woodland and trees are thought to be the dwellings of spirits or ancestors (Rival 1998). Trees can also have a more ambiguous status, providing both resources and danger (Bird-David 1992; Whittle *et al.* 1999, 384). Trees are also potent metaphors for broader conceptions of the cosmos. For example, to the Mdembu of Zaire the tree is a rich symbol and stands as a sign of strength and permanence (Davies 1988, 34). Other peoples believe that a tree stands at the very centre of the world where the roots represent the underworld, the branches represent heaven, and the trunk stands for this realm (Davies 1988; Ovsyannikov and Terebikhin 1994). This 'world tree' is thus a conceptual ordering of the universe. We could imagine monuments being located in order to draw upon this metaphor, with monuments themselves being an entranceway to the underworld. For the Zafimaniry of Madagascar, wood is a crucial metaphor for the body and life cycles (Bloch 1995). Similarly, the Yolngu of Arnhem Land, Australia, connect tree-trunks with bone and leaves with flesh (Keen 1990).

Finally, the seasonality of the vegetational cycle may also relate to how these sites were actually used and perceived. At the least, alterations in mood can be seen as linked to seasonal changes in the character of the landscape (e.g. Harris 2000; Harrison 2001). Monuments surrounded by trees in the summer could have been used for the burial of fleshed bodies and the presence of leaves on the trees may relate in part to the flesh on the body. In this way the highly potent and polluting act of burying a fleshed body would have been hidden from the wider community, as many of the views into and from the wider landscape would have been blocked or obscured. It has been suggested that monument builders deliberately created areas of darkness and light within the chamber (Bradley 1989; Jones 1999). The presence of differing densities of trees around a monument could also create effects of dark and light outside a monument as well as inside, and this would have been particularly a summer effect (Figure 7.1). In contrast, the winter might have been a time for the deposition, movement or other treatment of defleshed bones. Now the leaves were gone from the trees, leaving the bare trunk, a possible analogy for the removal of flesh from the bones. The wider landscape would also have been visible, and the monument visible from the landscape,

Figure. 7.1 The woodland setting of Gwal y Filiast, south-west Wales.

enabling the movement of bones or essences throughout the landscape. This seasonal use of monuments and movement of bodies may have tied into other movements: of people, of stock and of objects, and it could also tie into the seasonal use and management of woodland. It is this interest in the seasons which seems to have been formalised at later Neolithic monuments, such as Stonehenge, where mid-summer and mid-winter were actually marked out in stone.

Achievements of special virtue: stones that float to the sky

In the task of relating place to locality and beyond, we have to give more thought not only to the nature and effect of the woodland setting but also to the character of the monumental constructions in question. Most past models have tended to take the character of monuments for granted in discussions of this kind. In what we could call neutrally an older or pre-processual literature, the concerns were understandably for typology and sequence. Grimes's account of Pentre Ifan (1948) makes intriguingly suggestive remarks about the possible significance of the pit underlying the main stone construction and of the originally free-standing monolith stone IX, but otherwise restricts itself to detailed description, and discussion of

sequence. The same concerns can be found in Powell's discussion of Dyffryn Ardudwy (e.g. Powell 1973, 31–3), and continue as a dominant theme in Frances Lynch's valuable papers (Lynch 1972; 1975a). The general assumptions of the time are reflected in the reference to a 'widespread Neolithic desire to provide a lasting and monumental home for their dead' (Lynch 1975a). Commenting on the enormous capstone at Llech y Dribedd, Lynch strikingly reflected (1972, 77) that 'The lifting of such unnecessarily huge stones must have been an achievement of special virtue to the builders of Portal Dolmens...', but otherwise the discussions are almost wholly in terms of sequence, incoming populations and their landings and penetration inland, and subsequent relative dispersal and isolation. Nor is there much more consideration in the more recent, post-processual, literature of the character of monuments themselves. As Fleming has noted (1999, 119–20), Tilley's account tended to downplay the structural diversity of monuments in south-west Wales, and while Tilley (1994) sought to examine the links between constructions and landscape forms, there is curiously little discussion of the monuments themselves.

We would like to concentrate in the first place on portal dolmens and related monuments (see also Whittle 2003b), since despite the honourable tradition of discussion in the specialised Welsh literature they have been largely neglected in wider discussions of monumentality until very recently (see Bradley 1998b; 1998c; 2000; Tilley 1996; Tilley and Bennett 2001), and since there are by contrast many more recent discussions of Cotswold-Severn monuments and passage graves. Ultimately, however, we seek an interpretive and historical perspective within which all the monuments of Wales can be accommodated.

It is not hard to find the reasons for the comparative neglect in discussions of portal dolmens. They appear to be deceptively simple constructions. Their open character has made their original contents, if any, extremely vulnerable to disturbance and dispersal. They are hard to date, and were placed at first in the older literature at the end of the supposed developmental sequence. Crucially, and we would suggest correctly, Frances Lynch has advocated an early date, arguing from the associated pottery at monuments like Dyffryn Ardudwy (Lynch 1976, fig. 1) and from the sequences of construction to be found at Dyffryn Ardudwy, Pentre Ifan, Carnedd Hengwm South, and elsewhere (Lynch 1976). Evidence from Ireland can also be seen in the same light (summarised in Cooney 2000), though the sequences on either side of the Irish Sea need not necessarily have run in parallel, and it is not entirely clear whether the early radiocarbon dates on human bone from Poulnabrone, County Clare, directly date the construction of the portal monument (Cooney 2000, 96). Finally, portal dolmens and related monuments have of course proved hard to classify. A notion of 'typical' and 'classic' has been dominant but probably unhelpful. Neat, rectangular chamber, twin portal stones with closing slab, and substantial if not massive capstone have all been seen as defining characteristics. These serve to separate other monuments with more polygonal chambers, a lack of defined portals, and possible short passages or at least additional stones outside the main stone construction; Carreg Samson is obviously a good case in point (Lynch 1975a). But the notion of fixed types rapidly leads to difficulty. In discussing the monuments of the Nevern valley, Lynch claimed Carreg Coetan as the 'most classic' example of a portal dolmen (1972, 69), but from this perspective Llech y Dribedd 'clearly belongs to the Portal Dolmen tradition but it is not an entirely classic example' (Lynch 1972, 77). Likewise, Powell saw the first, western construction at Dyffryn Ardudwy firmly as a portal dolmen, but the second, eastern one as something else, though he ends by conceding that it could be considered as 'a form of enlarged Portal Dolmen...adopting some new concepts of what an impressive funerary monument should be' (Powell 1973, 35). All such differences may have been significant, from the point of view of both sequence and development, and experience and meaning. But at this stage it may be much more profitable to think in terms of a western tradition of construction which produced and allowed a spectrum of forms. In that spirit, we go on to discuss portal dolmens and related monuments as early, distinctive constructions.

Several features need re-emphasising. First, some monuments have large pits under them. Of that at Pentre Ifan, Grimes (1948, 13) conceded that 'it may be that the pit was not dug for entirely structural reasons', such as to get a level floor for the stone construction. The deliberately refilled stone in the pit, much of it of igneous type rather than the immediately local shale, could suggest, together with the act of digging in the first place, an interest in the properties of the earth itself. A similar pit was also found under the main stone construction at Carreg Samson (in conventional formal terms, a chamber and passage monument rather than a portal dolmen), but without the same kind of stony backfill; following the suggestion of Hogg, the possibility was mooted that the pit represents where the capstone was dug out of the earth (Lynch 1975a, 16). This is an attractive idea, and there are other stones still today partly buried, both close to Carreg Samson (Lynch 1975a, 16) and Pentre Ifan. If this kind of explanation is preferred, it is still striking that builders chose to commemorate the act of extraction from the earth by placing the resulting stone construction directly above, in what might not from a purely practical point of view have been the easiest location.

Secondly, uprights are obviously recurrent. Their arrangement in rectangles or other layouts may well have been significant, but this need not exhaust their significance. Uprights may have been important in their own right. The monolith stone IX at Pentre Ifan (Grimes 1948) might be seen as an earlier feature, following the model of Breton menhirs (Bradley 2002, and references). As noted in earlier chapters and in the inventory (see also Cummings 2001), there are significant variations in colour and texture among uprights, including in the example of Carreg Samson, suggesting further that these stones were also themselves meaningful (and see Cummings 2002c). But there is a sense also in which their significance may have been misinterpreted, through the employment of a common language for all types of megalithic and monumental construction (Tilley 1998). In this regard the near-universal assumption in the relevant literature on portal dolmens and related monuments is that uprights serve to define and create 'chambers'; missing stones or inadequate provision of side stones are regarded as problematic, as in the main stone construction at Pentre Ifan (Grimes 1948; Lynch 1972). That a chamber-like space results in many instances is not in doubt, but the spectrum of construction also frequently allows much less formality, and it is legitimate therefore to consider whether the overriding role of the uprights was to act as supports for the larger stone raised above them. At the least, these were not the same kind of chambers as in Cotswold-Severn monuments or in passage graves.

As often commented, the raised stones were often substantial. Lynch suggests weights of up to 50 tons (1972, 77) and Barker suggests the capstone at Garn Turne may be 60 tons (1992, 29). Many are thick, pregnant with their mass, but again there is a spectrum of variation, grading into the smaller and thinner examples at Dyffryn Ardudwy and Cors y Gedol and elsewhere. Carreg Samson (Figure

Figure. 7.2 Carreg Samson, south-west Wales.

7.2), formally a passage and chamber monument rather than a portal dolmen, shares the feature of a massive raised stone. Many are marked by a distinctive tilt on their upper surface. Sometimes this may just be the result of the shape of the stone dug out of the earth, but in others, as seems also often to be the case in Ireland, this feature is enhanced by subtle differential propping. It is even possible that some raised stones have been shaped rather than merely extracted from the earth. That at Pentre Ifan is one obvious candidate, and a wider study of this, though beyond the scope of the present study, would be timely. One of us has already drawn attention elsewhere to the visual effect of some of the raised stones (Figure 7.3), such as at Pentre Ifan and Llech y Dribedd, which seem to float in the air (Cummings 2001). Others, such as at Carreg Coetan (Figure 7.4), are rather different, giving the impression of either pressing down on the earth or a massive effort required to suspend them just above its surface.

Closely and directly linked to the use of the term 'chamber', the language employed on these stones has been universally that of 'capstones'. The easy assumption is made, often implicitly, that their principal structural purpose was to finish or close a chamber, rather in the manner of the beautifully engineered roofstones at Knowth, which was in turn to be covered by a cairn or mound. It is hard to separate this question from that of cairns and mounds. Once again, the easy assumption is usually made that a cairn was something which enclosed the whole, as is undoubtedly the case in Irish as well as north Welsh passage graves, and probably in the great majority or more of Cotswold-Severn monuments; Hazleton North retained traces of a pitched axial ridge right along the top of its cairn (Saville 1990). Discussing Pentre Ifan, Grimes (1948, 10) noted the idea of the covering cairn as coming to prominence in the nineteenth century. The radical alternative for many portal dolmens and related constructions is that cairns were often never more than low platforms. It is unwise to be dogmatic when there is clearly such scope for later denudation, but it is striking how often very little survives of cairn material in contrast to the larger uprights and capstones. Had stone robbing been universally the main instrument of decay and destruction, we might well have expected many fewer major stone constructions (conventionally 'chambers') to have survived. The cairn at Pentre Ifan was already a minor feature at the start of the seventeenth century (Grimes 1948), and putative robbing cannot be ascribed to intensifying land-use in more recent times. Frances Lynch (1972, fig. 4) has suggested the presence of a small, squarish, first cairn at Pentre Ifan. At only about 11 by 15 m, with the main stone construction on the uphill side, and reaching a height at the top of the downhill end of the capstone or raised stone (i.e. its lowest part) of some 3 m, it is hard to see how such a cairn could have been a covering one at all. In other instances, there may have been little by way of surrounding material, as seems to have been the case at Carreg Samson (Lynch 1975a). While some cairns may have had formal limits, as in the suggested second, more elongated phase at Pentre Ifan, or the rounded form of Carreg Coetan, others may have been much less well defined. At Pentre Ifan, there were signs of careful placing, diagonal stones alternating with smaller infill. To one side of the cairn at Twlc y Filiast (Savory 1956b, 303), there were 'large glacial blocks apparently still in their natural positions but mixed with a certain amount of material derived from the cairn'; the distinction between placed and natural may have been blurred (cf. Cummings 2002a; Tilley *et al*. 2000; Tilley and Bennett 2001). At Dyffryn Ardudwy, the thickest part of the cairn seems to have been due to a low bank connected to secondary blocking of the eastern stone construction (Powell 1973, 35–7).

While much variation can readily be envisaged, the separate strands of this discussion can be brought together in the following way. Surrounding cairns may often have had more the character of a low platform than a mounded and enclosing pile of stones, sometimes formally demarcated but on other occasions not rigidly separated from the natural stony surrounds. This is not unprecedented. Something of the kind may be seen in some at least of the Irish court tombs, and in late arrangements in some of the Orkney monuments. The emphasis is again on stone,

7 *Stones that float to the sky: seeing place, myth and history* 75

Figure. 7.3 Four different views of the capstone at Llech y Dribedd, south-west Wales.

Figure. 7.4 Carreg Coetan in south-west Wales.

Figure. 7.5 The 'floating' capstone at Pentre Ifan, facing uphill.

generally much smaller than that used in the main vertical construction, with some evidence of gradations and deliberate placings. Out of this surface of stone rise uprights, to varying heights, and above these sit, hang or float a series of raised stones. It is as though there is a narrative connecting all these elements: pits dug into the earth and refilled with stone, a surface of stone from which uprights rise, and finally the great raised stones themselves. How different our normal view of these raised stones might be if we could escape the confines of conventional terminology. Following ethnographic examples of the naming of places and features in the landscape (e.g. Basso 1996; Waterson 2000), we could at least make these constructions sound less familiar, for example on the following lines, with Welsh versions added for the sake of further unfamiliarity:

stones-that-float-to-the-sky (*cerrig sy'n ymestyn i'r awyr*)
places-where-the-creators-emerged (*y mannau lle yr ymddangosodd y creawdwyr*)
mountain-raised-by-the-ancestors (*mynydd a godwyd gan yr hynafiaid*).

While there is clear evidence, already cited, of modifications over time to particular sites, it may well be that these monuments were not the result of prolonged construction. Whatever the social circumstances surrounding the selection of stones, the mobilisation of labour, or the choice of propitious times (see Richards 2003), the building process as such is likely to have been a fairly swift one. The Pentre Ifan monolith might serve to extend the sequence of use of this site, seen also in its possible secondary cairn and façade (Lynch 1972; 1976), but on the whole secondary modifications to these sites take the form of repetition, as at Dyffryn Ardudwy, rather than the wider process of transformation and eventual closure seen for example in southern English long barrows. The single act of creation may have added to the renown of builders, and may, as discussed further below, relate to other acts of creation and bringing the world into existence.

Relatively little of the contents of these constructions has survived. This paucity might also be a significant aspect of the character of these constructions, serving to emphasise what could be seen from the outside and roundabout, rather than what was deposited within, but this is hard to put into perspective. We know of depositions of both unaltered and cremated human bone. We know very little of the relative histories of construction and deposition. There may be a connection with human ancestry and descent, but it remains unclear whether this was a principal focus. Irish portal dolmens and court tombs may also largely share the same ambiguity.

Even with portal stones and tilted raised stones, there is a sense in which these box-like, four-square constructions lack a single axis. In some cases, as set out in chapters 4–6 and the inventory, a prominent axis may be proposed; Pentre Ifan faces uphill (Figure 7.5). But it also faces in other directions, and the 'gunsight' model of monument orientation does not seem to apply, in the way discussed for Cotswold-Severn monuments (Fleming 1999; Tilley 1994). In this way, portal dolmens appear from their careful placings in chosen settings, as set out especially in chapters 4–5, to draw in a range of features of the surrounding landscape. Pentre Ifan affords views of outcrops, Carn Ingli, a partial view of the sea, and tracts of the Nevern valley. The prominent axis looks at the rising slope, with minor outcrops to one side, but other features are not excluded. Other discussions (Bradley 1998b; Tilley 1996; Tilley and Bennett 2001) have already usefully explored, in the context of south-west England, the resemblances between portal dolmens and natural landforms, especially

Figure. 7.6 The dolmen of Maen y Bardd, north-west Wales.

tors, and the portal dolmens of Wales can certainly also be thought of in the same sort of terms. But it seems hard to confine their significance to this one relationship. They are built from materials rooted in particular places and localities, and yet refer to a series of wider features.

Among these wider features, outcrops, hills and mountains on the one hand, and the sea on the other, appear to be of recurrent significance. Just as with the wooded setting, there is a significant range of ethnographic data suggestive of the possible meanings and associations of mountain and sea. Many groups of native North Americans, for example, view mountains as highly symbolic and sacred locales, which are part of creation myths and stories (Martin 2001; Sundstrom 1996) and which are key locales in the ceremonial use of the landscape (Price 1994; Reeves 1994). Mountains and hills are often connected with mythical beginnings (Martin 2001; Middleton 1960; Waterson 2000; Whitley 1998; and see more detailed discussion on the significance of mountains below). In Australia, many stone sources are considered to be the remains of ancestral beings formed during the Dreamtime (cf. Morphy 1995; Tilley 1994). To the Wamira of Papua New Guinea, many stones have a history, name and life of their own (Kahn 1990). Some stones represent where elders sat in the past while others are considered to be the ancestors themselves. The Wamira believe that stones and rocks actually move around by themselves. Stones representing named ancestors walk about, particularly at night, sometimes even disappearing for years at a time. In a similar way, the sea, the coast and foreshore are also significant and symbolic in many ethnographic cases (see below for more detailed discussion on the significance of the sea and water).

Portal dolmens may therefore be seen, for all their apparent simplicity, to have complex associations and meanings. They are rooted in particular places by the choice of setting and materials. They may draw in a range of other landscape features (Figure 7.6). As with other monuments, some of this may have been less visible in summer, and more obvious in winter. It is not clear in the case of portal dolmens whether their primary emphasis was on the remains of the human dead, and by association on notions of human descent and ancestry. Other sets of ideas are suggested. Construction itself emphasises stone from the earth, and presents great raised stones for display and contemplation. The achievement of construction must surely have been a source of worldly renown, but it may also have played on a powerful mythical dimension, of stories of creation of the earth and of original creator figures who arose from the earth and waters. These might also have been associated with the outcrops, hills, mountains and sea visible from portal dolmens. A kind of reflexive relationship is possible. The monuments stand in sight of landscape features redolent of beginnings, and the monuments themselves recreate central features of that narrative. The presence or absence of human remains may be of secondary importance in this perspective. For all we know, the tilt of raised stones might have been far more significant than human remains, reflecting the first rising of the earth, or portraying the inversion of normality in that first time, like the beings who walked upside down in Lugbara myth (Middleton 1960).

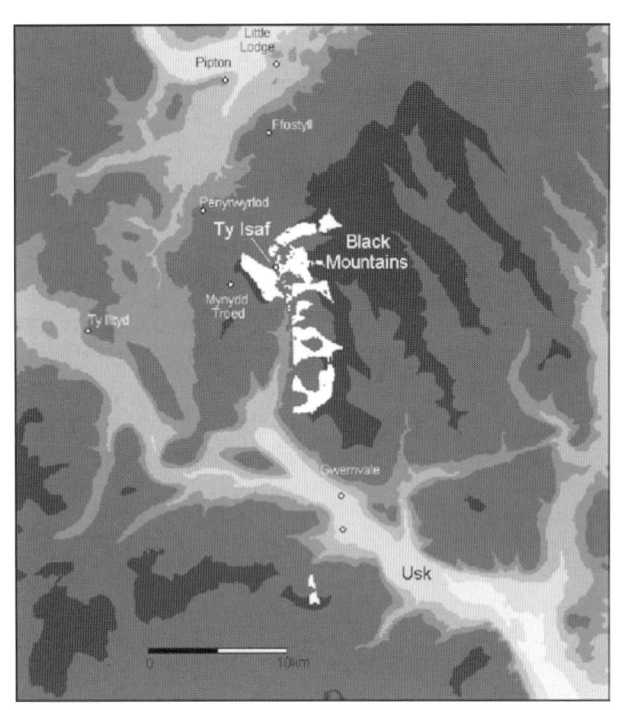

Figure. 7.7 The viewshed from Ty Isaf, with parts of the landscape visible marked in white. Reproduced by kind permission of Ordnance Survey. © Crown copyright NC/03/20516.

Other ways of seeing

This extended discussion of portal dolmens has served not only to suggest ways in which place and locality could be linked to the wider landscape, but to emphasise the particularity of different styles of monument. What may hold good for portal dolmens does not necessarily wholly apply to long cairns and passage graves. Portal dolmens could be seen as strongly local but linked to the wider landscape by mythology to do with the beginnings of the earth; outward appearance, rapidly constructed, may have counted for far more than contents, and despite minor typological differences, may have served much the same purpose across a number of areas (and indeed beyond west Wales itself). Long cairns can also be seen as strongly local. Gwernvale remains the best example of repeated (if episodic) use of a particular place. With this group, however, place and locality were perhaps more the expression of immediate difference than with portal dolmens. Within a short distance around the northern flank of the Black Mountains, there is much variation in setting and outlook, from the expansive vistas possible from Penywyrlod Talgarth to the more enclosed views from Ty Isaf (Figure 7.7). The Ffostyll cairns suggest variation in dominant axes through time. Human bones from these long cairns have also given a parallel series of indications of quite varied lifestyles (Wysocki and Whittle 2000). There was presumably a more or less conscious connection with Cotswold monuments to the east, given all the close architectural resemblances, but if so the link with wider fields was perhaps a more immediate one than in the case of portal dolmens, to do with recent, or comparatively recent, human histories of population dispersals and relationships. The building process can justifiably be seen as far slower and more extended than in the case of portal dolmens, and a far greater concern with contents can be seen not only in the architectural provision of small closed chambers but also of course in the human remains themselves, variously accumulated, sorted and treated, over what seems to have been long periods of time (as witnessed for example by new radiocarbon dates from Penywyrlod Talgarth).

The differing architecture of long cairns afforded differing perspectives of the landscape. As with portal dolmens, there is some sense in which wider features are made visible from some sites. The careful placings detailed in chapter 6 seem to bear this out. Penywyrlod Talgarth is again a useful example. Its wide-ranging views of the Wye valley (Figure 7.8), the Black Mountains scarp and the more distant Brecon Beacons would not have been possible in quite the same way if the monument had been placed slightly differently. Yet the more definite axes provided by long cairn architecture offered more focused sightings on features of the landscape beyond that which seems to have been the case with portal dolmens. In some cases big hills are avoided, though there appears to be a recurrent interest in features of the Black Mountain escarpment (Figure 7.9). Chapter 6 argued (cf. Cummings *et al.* 2002) for alignment in many cases on transitional points in the landscape of the scarp, a sense of sidedness which seems also to permeate the long cairn architecture and the treatment of human remains within.

In turn, passage graves present other differences. It is hard not to see the north Welsh examples as part of a wider and older story whose origins and central focus lay elsewhere, principally in Ireland. A different architectural style emphasises long passages, entrances and exits, and hidden contents. Both sites also have panels with rock art, not found at any of the other types of monument in Wales (although there are simple cupmarks on Trellyffaint in south-west Wales and Bachwen in north Wales, probably Bronze Age additions). Barclodiad y Gawres has five slabs with rock art comprising spirals, lozenges, chevrons and zig-zags which can be paralleled with rock art styles at passage graves in Ireland. There are rather different views of mountains and the sea at these sites as well. At Barclodiad the mound is set right on the western coast of Anglesey with views out over the sea and out to Ireland. At Bryn Celli Ddu the site has views of Snowdonia, but not the sweeping vistas found at other sites. Instead the view is more disembodied and the absence of a restricted view adds another contrast (Figure 7.10).

There are other types of monument in Wales which cannot be understood as part of the portal dolmen, long cairn or passage grave traditions, although ultimately they may be variations on one or more of these themes. The first of these are the earth-fast sites found exclusively in south-west Wales, defined by the propped capstone and

7 Stones that float to the sky: seeing place, myth and history

Figure. 7.8 The long cairn at Penywyrlod, Talgarth.

Figure. 7.9 The view of Table Mountain and the Black Mountains from Garn Goch.

Figure. 7.10 The passage grave of Bryn Celli Ddu.

landscape setting next to outcrops. These megaliths may be tied into a much more localised understanding of monumentality. Equally some of these sites may be later in date, a result of the fragmentation of more uniform ideas in the early Neolithic (Cummings 2001). These sites may equally be a result of the flexibility of the broader notion of monumentality, and may even represent essentially 'Mesolithic' attempts at constructing Neolithic monuments. The flexibility and variability of monumental style are well illustrated in south-east Wales as well. Here there are a number of sites which seem to share characteristics with both portal dolmens and long cairns. In chapter 5 we suggested that people were drawing from a broad range of different architectural styles in order to create a monument. We should perhaps not forget the complete exceptions to the rule, of which there are a few examples in Wales. These are sites which do not share similarities with other monuments either architecturally or in their landscape setting, including Bedd yr Afanc and Cerrig y Gof in south-west Wales and Lligwy in north Wales. These may be later monuments (late Neolithic or even early Bronze Age in date, most likely the case with Bedd yr Afanc) or perhaps a localised attempt at the broader idea of monumentality.

Places and landscape

In earlier chapters we outlined all the major landscape features that can be seen from the monuments in Wales. We will now discuss the possible significance of a number of these landscape settings, emphasising the role these features may have had in the local Neolithic cosmology. It seems that the builders of the Welsh megaliths preferred to place monuments in very specific parts of the landscape. The landscape settings of each site are not identical, however, and it seems that the monument builders had a range of different landscape elements from which to choose, some of which may have been more important to reference than others.

Outcrops

First, it seems that a number of sites in south-west Wales were located in relation to rocky outcrops. As already discussed, the relationship between monuments and outcrops is quite complex. The portal dolmens like Carreg Samson and Pentre Ifan are located so that there are outcrops visible on the horizon. At these sites the monuments were kept at a distance from the outcrops, so that they were visible on the skyline but not present in the immediate vicinity. These outcrops are not the coastal ones that seem to have been important in the Mesolithic

(Cummings 2001; Tilley 1994), but are smaller and inland, frequently protruding out of agricultural land. Many are quite striking in their appearance. Not only are they quite imposing within the local landscape, but many of them resemble built structures. People may not have been able to fully comprehend the difference between natural places that appear to be built and humanly constructed features (Bradley 1998c; 2000; Cummings 2002a). We suggest that these outcrops were highly symbolic, and may have been regarded as monuments in their own right. They may have been mistaken for humanly constructed megaliths, or perhaps they were thought to be the monuments of the ancestors (*mynydd a godwyd gan yr hynafiaid*). They may even have received ritual deposits as is known from outcrops in south-west England (Bradley 1991). Whether or not these outcrops were incorporated into the ritual use of the monuments, they seem to have been extremely important in the location of monuments. Therefore, sites such as Pentre Ifan, White Horse and Carreg Samson seem to have been specifically located so that outcrops were skylined.

In contrast, the earth-fast sites in south-west Wales such as Carn Wnda were built right up against outcrops. These outcrops are different again from the ones that are skylined. They are much more sizeable and visually dominating, set on top of hills and were visible from other Neolithic sites. These smaller chambered cairns did not simply reference these outcrops, but were built right up against them, suggesting that the symbolism of these outcrops was being appropriated by the monument builders. The outcrops were undoubtedly already highly symbolic places. First, they are all literally covered with 'natural' chambered cairns that resemble the earth-fast monuments (Cummings 2002a). Tilley (1994, 99) also notes that the smaller monuments are virtually invisible from a distance, and the outcrops against which they stand are highly visible across the wider landscape.

It is the monuments of south-west Wales which have the most striking relationship with outcrops. This seems to be a result of the unique topography of south-west Wales. The north and south-east do not have the number of upstanding and distinctive outcrops that are found in the south-west. Some sites elsewhere are positioned in relation to outcrops however, such as Din Dryfol on Anglesey and Trefignath on Holyhead. Tinkinswood in south-east Wales is also located near to outcrops. These may have been part of a local understanding of the landscape, perhaps with mythological associations going back to the Mesolithic (see below).

Rivers

Another recurrent locational factor for the position of many of the monuments in Wales seems to have been rivers. Several sites seem to have positioned specifically in relation to rivers. In south-west Wales, for example, the Eastern Cleddau has the site of Mountain at its source, while Colston is set at the point where the Afon Anghof and the Afon Glan-Rhyd meet to form the main Western Cleddau watercourse. We would like to suggest that the Cleddau rivers were the most important rivers in Pembrokeshire. The Eastern Cleddau links the Nevern Valley and the Mynydd Preseli with the south of Pembrokeshire and the Bristol Channel. Group VIII axes which originate from the Preselis may well have travelled along the Eastern Cleddau, as well as the Stonehenge bluestones. The site of Gwal y Filiast is located next to the Afon Taf at a point where there are rapids (Tilley 1994, 109). The Afon Taf may also have been an important river; its source lies only a couple of kilometres away from the source of the Cleddau, very close to the Mynydd Preseli. This may also have been used to access northern Pembrokeshire and the Preselis, but from the Carmarthenshire area. The site of Gelli is positioned close to the Afon Towy, a route from Carmarthen Bay into the uplands of mid Wales. Finally Carreg Coetan is positioned at the point where the Afon Nyfer meets the sea, and it is likely that the Nyfer was also significant. It runs through one of the richest valleys in northern Pembrokeshire with a dense concentration of Neolithic monuments.

In north Wales a number of sites are focussed around the Afon Clwyd. Close to the point where the river meets the sea three sites have clear views of the Clwyd: Hendre Waelod, Porth Llwyd and Maen y Bardd. Other sites further inland are more loosely associated with this river valley such as Capel Garmon. The Conwy creates a low-lying and passable valley which connects inland north Wales with Anglesey and the Irish Sea.

In south-east Wales it has already been noted that many of the Black Mountains group are positioned in relation to the Usk and Wye river valleys, and further south, three sites are located to have views of the River Severn. In the case of the Black Mountains sites it seems likely that the Usk and Wye were important rivers for movements around the landscape. Both rivers encircle the Black Mountains escarpment and run down to the sea, reaching it at Newport and Chepstow respectively. These fertile river valleys would not only have provided access into the interior of Wales from the south-east Welsh coast, but also provided agricultural land and a range of wild resources.

Water and rivers may have been important for a number of reasons. First, it is likely that water travel was the main way of covering long distances; inland areas may have been quite difficult to reach on foot. For this reason, the Irish Sea seems to have played a fundamental role in the early Neolithic for the spread of material culture and ideas (e.g. Bowen 1970; papers in Cummings and Fowler 2003; Herity 1970; Saville 1994; Sheridan 2000). South-west and north-west Wales may have been core areas in the Neolithic, even though they are now considered to be on the periphery (Cummings forthcoming). This is due to their central location in the Irish Sea area, and may well explain the dense concentration of monuments in both areas (other concentrations of monuments can be found in

Dumfries and Galloway, the Isle of Man and the eastern coast of Ireland). Therefore, both south-west and north-west Wales may have formed part of a broader network which distributed ideas and material culture along the Irish Sea area as well as being a focus of monument construction. In a similar way, the Wye and Usk may have facilitated contacts between south-east Wales and areas along the Severn Estuary.

Water is also a highly symbolic natural feature. Many Neolithic monuments such as henge monuments may have been seasonally surrounded by water (Richards 1996a) and other Neolithic monuments are associated with water, in particular cursus monuments (Brophy 1999). A whole series of burials have been found in rivers such as those along the River Trent (Pearce *et al.* 1997). Rivers also received deposits of material culture in late Neolithic contexts, including pottery and axes (Bradley 2000, 118; Thomas 1991; 1996, 117). Water, then was clearly a highly potent natural feature, surrounded with its own mythology (Fowler and Cummings 2003). Therefore, as well as being a highly symbolic metaphor in its own right (Richards 1996a), water may have provided links with the wider world.

Sea

Many of the Neolithic monuments also seem to have been situated to have a view of the sea. This is clearly not the case with the monuments which are inland (such as Garn Turne, Capel Garmon and the entire Black Mountains group). In south-west Wales all sites near the coast have views of the sea, usually of 90° or less. It is only the earth-fast sites which are positioned right up against outcrops, such as Carn Wnda and Carn Llidi, which have a view of the sea which exceeds 90°. In north-west Wales, all bar one of the monuments on Anglesey have a view of the sea, and most sites, like the dolmens in south-west Wales, have less than 90° of the view facing the sea. A notable exception is Barclodiad y Gawres which sits on a coastal headland with wide sea views. Elsewhere in north Wales monuments have more expansive views of the sea: the Ardudwy group for example.

The presence of a sea-view may have been another important factor in the location of a site. The potential significance of a sea-view is emphasised at sites like White House in south-west Wales, from which there is only a very small view of the sea. This site seems to have been positioned very carefully in the landscape; it has a restricted view in one direction, an outcrop skylined, as well as a small view of the sea. Otherwise this monument stands in a very nondescript landscape. Likewise at Ty Newydd in north-west Wales, the site looks out over the sea to the west, Holyhead Mountain and Snowdonia. Had the site been positioned a few metres to the north-east this combination of views would not have been possible, and the view of the sea lost. The site of Sweyne's Howe South on the Gower seems to be carefully positioned so that Sweyne's Howe North is visible on the skyline behind a small portion of the sea.

The relevance of a view of the sea may be partly connected to the importance of water in general. Water has cleansing properties (Douglas 1966) and may have been associated with renewal or rebirth. The sea has a rhythmical cycle which may have appeared to be timeless. The sea is also a liminal place, and the inter-tidal zone an interface between the land and the sea (Scarre 2002a). It provides life but also takes it away. Water, in particular the sea, may also have been a metaphor for journeying and travelling (Richards 1996a). The sea, then, could have been seen as a creator, a transformer and recycler of life (Kahn 1990, 59). Richard Bradley (2000, 12–3) details elements of the belief system of the Saami, who divide the world into three layers, the sky, the earth and the underworld which correspond to air, land and water. The underworld is associated with the dead and as such all things associated with water are potent. Equally, the presence of a sea-view may be referencing a (perceived or real) link between Pembrokeshire and the rest of the Irish Sea zone. A view of the sea may also be concerned with origins, particularly of monument construction. Equally, monuments may also be referencing the importance of the sea as a resource. In this respect, it is interesting that most sites seem to be concerned to have only a small portion of the sea visible. Could this refer in some way to the diminishing role of coastal resources in the diets of Neolithic people, as suggested by current stable isotope analysis (Schulting 1998)?

Mountains

Another factor that seems to have been considered important in the location of chambered cairns was their position in relation to specific hills and mountains. We will discuss the significance of mountains in relation to the three different areas of Wales. To begin there are two mountains which are repeatedly referenced by the monuments in south-west Wales: Carn Ingli and Carn Meini. The relationship between Carn Ingli and the monuments of the Nevern Valley has already been expounded by Tilley (1994, 105), who suggests that sites were located so that Carn Ingli dominated the view in a particular direction. This was criticised by Fleming (1999), who felt it was difficult to avoid a view of the mountain in that area. We would like to suggest that Carn Ingli *was* a highly significant and symbolic hill. There may have been a number of reasons why it was considered important. First, it may have been because the crag dominated the Nevern Valley that monuments were built around its base. Second, Carn Ingli is the only peak in south-west Wales which may have a Neolithic enclosure on its summit, and this may have added to its significance. It is possible to suggest that it may have played a crucial role in the rituals and funerary rites conducted in the region. It continued to be an important site in the Bronze Age as a number of huts can be found

Figure. 7.11 The view of Snowdonia from Bodowyr.

on its lower slopes. One of the most interesting features of Carn Ingli is that it appears to be a different mountain when viewed from different places. From each of the sites from which the mountain is visible, the summit looks different. From some sites only the uppermost crag is visible, while from others all the outcrops on the summit are discernible. Instead of being static and unchanging, could this feature have been fluid, changing its meaning and form as one moved around the landscape? Finally, from the summit of Carn Ingli there are clear views over the rest of Pembrokeshire. This might suggest that the mountain was considered to stand at the very centre of a Neolithic world in this area (Cummings forthcoming).

It is the Mynydd Preseli which seem to be the other important mountain range in the Neolithic, most specifically the summit of Carn Meini. Carn Meini was the source of Neolithic axes, (Groups VIII and XIII) and would ultimately become the source of the Stonehenge bluestones (Green 1997; Scourse 1997). We would like to suggest that the importance of this mountain range extends back to the beginning of the Neolithic, if not back into the Mesolithic. Such is the striking nature of this crag that it is likely that it would have been surrounded by myths. It may have been interpreted as the mountain of the ancestors, perhaps associated with origin myths and the place where the sky meets the earth.

The Preselis are also frequently shrouded in cloud or mist. An old Pembrokeshire saying goes:

'When Prescelly wears a hat
Pembrokeshire will weep for that'

Thus the mountains are visible as cloud throughout Pembrokeshire, even when they are invisible on the ground. It may also be of significance that Ireland is visible from the summit of Carn Meini (Miles 2001), which may have added to its symbolic nature, as well as linking it with far-away places (Cummings 2003; forthcoming). This would certainly be an appropriate reference point for a monument. Indeed, at Carreg Samson the passage is aligned first on a nearby outcrop as well as on a large outcrop a few kilometres from the chamber, with the Mynydd Preseli visible in the distance. A number of monuments in north Wales also have views of the Preselis, and part of the significance of these sites may have been the long distance view to south Pembrokeshire. The significance of the Preselis is one of the features which seems to endure into the late Neolithic. The stone circles of Gors Fawr and Meini Gwyr both have views of Carn Meini and it is in the late Neolithic that the builders of Stonehenge used the outcrop as the source of the bluestones. Only a place such as Carn Meini may have been appropriate for the most impressive construction in the country (Bradley 2000). There has been speculation over the years as to whether the bluestones were taken from a pre-existing monument. Such is the nature of Carn Meini that the builders of Stonehenge may have believed that they *were* taking stones

Figure. 7.12 The mountains on the Lleyn peninsula, from Mynydd Cefn Amwlch.

from a pre-existing monument. The symbolic importance of the Preseli landscape may have been such that the stones at Stonehenge may have been positioned to reflect their original provenance (Bradley 2000, 95).

Particular mountains in north Wales also seem to have been significant. Two-thirds of sites have views of Snowdonia (Figure 7.11), of which Snowdon is the largest mountain in Wales. The edge of Snowdonia was utilised in the Neolithic as the source of Group VII axes. Visually dominant from so many parts of the north Welsh coastline, Snowdonia also offers a range of spectacular mountains and passes into the heart of north Wales. Elsewhere it has been argued that part of the significance of Snowdon may also relate to its intervisibility with the rest of the Irish Sea zone; it is possible to see all the other key parts of the Irish Sea from the summit for Snowdon (south-west Wales, southern Ireland, northern Ireland, the Isle of Man, south-west Scotland and Cumbria: see Cummings 2003). The mountains on the Lleyn peninsula are also visible from many sites (Figure 7.12), and these mountains have a particularly distinctive shape. They are steep and abrupt mountains rising up out of the peninsula. One of these hills, Mynydd Rhiw, was also used a source of stone axes in the early Neolithic (Group XXI). Parts of this mountain also made it into the monuments: two plaques of Mynydd Rhiw stone were found at Dyffryn Ardudwy (Powell 1973), probably a Bronze Age wristguard (Burrow 2002). It is of interest that no monuments have views of perhaps the most distinctive mountain range in north Wales, Cadair Idris. Elsewhere it has been argued that this is because the area around these mountains does not offer the combination of landscape features preferred for a monument (Cummings 2003). Monuments in south-east Wales also cluster around mountains, particularly the Black Mountains group. Here, the Black Mountains escarpment is visually spectacular and visible from a number of the monuments as are the Brecon Beacons.

Mountains may have been significant for a number of reasons. Elsewhere it has been suggested that monuments may have views of mountains as this created connections across the landscape. In the eastern Irish Sea zone monuments have views of mountains which themselves have views out over the Irish Sea (Cummings 2003). So for example, monuments in north Wales have views out over Snowdonia, which in turn has views out over other parts of the Irish Sea. Thus the landscapes of the Irish Sea zone are connected through the intervisibility of its mountains.

Mountains also possess a unique range of properties beyond their physical appearance which make them distinctive places in the landscape. Mountains often have different weather systems to more low-lying areas. For much of the year mountains are shrouded in mist and cloud, or haze in the summer (Figure 7.13). The summits of mountains can be invisible or covered with cloud even

Figure. 7.13 Mountains emerge through the cloud.

when the surrounding valley areas are drenched in sunshine. Mountains seem to attract cloud. We know now that this is because air cools as it moves over mountains, causing clouds to form.

Being on a mountain also creates a series of unique experiences and these may have added to the significance of these places. We know that some people climbed mountains such as the Preselis and the lower slopes of Snowdonia as these were utilised for axe production. People were also capable of scaling higher mountains as shown by the utilisation of Langdale and Scafell Pike in Cumbria (Bradley and Edmonds 1993). The experience of being on a mountain is quite different to that of the low-lying areas. Often walking in cloud in the high mountains, there is also a noticeable temperature difference as one ascends. There can be snow on the mountains even when it has not snowed in the valleys. Conversely, it is also possible for higher elevations to be warmer than lower elevations when a strong area of cold high pressure is dominating the weather. Being in the mountains also gives a unique perspective on the lower areas (Figure 7.14). We tend to take for granted views from above, such as maps and aerial views, but in the Neolithic this would have been much more unusual. Being able to look down over large tracts of landscape would have been a rare and extraordinary experience. Mountains are also places where the land meets the sky, where one can stand in the clouds, or even overlook clouds when above the cloudline (Figure 7.15). Landscapes disappear and reappear when in the

Figure. 7.14 The wide-ranging views of the valley from the mountain.

Figure. 7.15 Mountains appearing and disappearing in cloud.

clouds. Mountains are also liminal and marginal places. These are also places of danger. Mountains, then, have a unique range of characteristics that sets them apart from other areas of the landscape. Mountains are also where water, earth, sky and stone meet, places perhaps where other worlds could be seen or entered. These otherwordly places would have been liminal and may consequently have been sacred places, perhaps connected with spirits and myths.

Ethnographically, mountains often have a central role in mythology and cosmology. Many groups of native North Americans view mountains as highly symbolic and sacred locales, which are part of creation myths and stories and which are key locales in the ceremonial use of the landscape (Price 1994; Reeves 1994). Mountains and hills are often connected with mythical beginnings. In Western Arnhem Land, Australia, many stone sources are considered to be the remains of ancestral beings formed during the Dreamtime (Taçon 1991). The unique properties of mountains and the significance assigned to them in many cultures may suggest, then, that mountains could have been considered highly sacred places in the Neolithic. Mountains may even have been understood as active entities or agents in their own right. As already described, mountains often disappear and reappear according to the weather. It seems likely that people in the Neolithic understood themselves as immersed in the world in contrast to somehow being separated or opposed to it. As such, mountains may have been an active part of that world, part of a spectrum of things and people that had consciousness, life and some kind of agency. We therefore suggest that mountains had a special place in a Neolithic cosmology.

Local features

Finally, the builders of the monuments of Wales clearly took local features into account when deciding where to build a site. Such features may have been significant in relation to individual sites and may have tied into local myths or legends. Features like springs, bays, harbours, caves, Mesolithic sites and headlands may only have been considered significant at a local level, but were important enough to reference in the landscape, if opportunity allowed. It may equally be the case that monuments were located in relation to features which are no longer visible in the archaeological record. Brightly coloured or specific flowers, trees, groves, animals and plants may all have played a part in the location of a site. Fleming outlines a number of these alternative perspectives which include factors such as overlooking routeways or being connected with the moon or sun (Fleming 1999, 124).

Looking in, looking out

Throughout this chapter we have discussed the views of the landscape from the chambered cairns. However, it is also important to consider the views of the monuments from the wider landscape. The monuments seem to have been predominantly placed on the side of hills, close to, but not on, the summit. If there was not substantial or only limited tree cover in the way (see above), this means that these sites would have been visible from the low-lying areas, which may have been the focus of settlement activity. The limited lithic evidence from Wales does not, at present, enable us to establish connections between the places used for everyday settlement and the monuments, but it is possible to suggest that the monuments may have been positioned, in part, so that they were visible on the horizon above the areas where people were living.

Monuments, then, seem to be positioned between the places utilised by the living and higher, more marginal and liminal places such as mountains. As such, monuments create places that are in between worlds. Monuments were consistently located at places of transition, where rivers began (Mountain), where rivers entered the sea (Carreg Coetan, Hendre Waelod) where tributaries joined (Colston) or between lower-lying areas and the uplands (Carneddau Hengwm; Pentre Ifan). Monuments may themselves have been regarded as liminal places, set away from the everyday locales of the living. This possibility is strengthened by the discovery of pits underneath some of the monuments which may have been spots where the underworld could be accessed (and see above). Other sites, particularly the earth-fast sites in south-west Wales, were positioned right up against outcrops; they were placed between rock and earth, as well as resembling caves (Tilley 1994, 96). To enter one of these chambers may have literally been to enter another world. Monuments, then, may have stood between the living and the dead at points of transition. Early Neolithic monuments also play out a whole series of oppositions within their landscape setting. In the landscape, oppositions were created between open and closed views, the coast and inland, and low-lying areas and the uplands (see Cummings *et al.* 2002). This effectively means that monuments created a place *in between* these oppositions. Monuments, then, were clearly places of interaction and of transition. They were places where people could negotiate and come to understand their own place in the world.

Composing places

People in the Neolithic had a choice concerning where they built their monuments. By the beginning of the Neolithic it seems likely that they inhabited a landscape which was already filled with symbolic and important places (Tilley 1994). Particular natural features such as outcrops, rivers and the sea would have been visited in the Mesolithic and assigned meaning, perhaps as part of a mythological understanding of the world. There were also a series of marked locales in the Mesolithic, potential forerunners to Neolithic monuments. The large shell middens on Oronsay, Scotland, may have been symbolic and special places in the landscape (as has also been argued for the Breton middens: Thomas and Tilley 1993, 228 and see J. Pollard 2000), the shells collected simply to create the shell middens or as part of ritual feasting. The remains created large, permanent places in the landscape and these were places which endured, 'persistent places' (Barton *et al.* 1995; J. Pollard 2000). Furthermore, like many Neolithic monuments, these shell middens were set in liminal places, in the case of Oronsay, between the land and sea. The similarities between these shell middens and Neolithic monuments are further strengthened by the presence of human bone in the midden at Cnoc Coig. Here the remains of at least seven individuals were found, with both children and adults being represented. However, whole skeletons were not found, as is the case in many midden burials in Brittany (Schulting 1996) and Scandinavia. Here the bones were primarily from the hands, feet and cranium (Mellars 1987, 290). This suggests that whole bodies were placed on the middens, perhaps as part of an excarnation ritual (T. Pollard 1996; J. Pollard 2000). This is clear evidence of the manipulation and use of human bones prior to the beginning of the Neolithic. Like Neolithic monuments, then, the Oronsay shell middens created permanent and enduring locales in the landscape which were repeatedly visited and used for, amongst other things, the transformation and deposition of human remains.

There is evidence of a commitment to place in the Welsh Mesolithic evidence. The Nab Head promontory in south-west Wales was visited a number of times throughout the Mesolithic period, and excavations have uncovered many thousands of worked flints, making this one of the largest Mesolithic sites in Britain. Several more exotic items have been found amongst the early Mesolithic assemblage, and these include 690 shale beads and two 'figurines'. The beads were clearly made at the site as drills, bead blanks and broken beads have been found (David 1990, 245). Later Mesolithic finds include three pecked and ground stone axes and a perforated stone disc. These finds are exceptional, and suggest a locale that was returned to time and again and marked with the deposition of special objects. The Caldey Island caves in south-west Wales also seem to represent a locale repeatedly visited and used, this time for the deposition of human and animal remains (Lacaille and Grimes 1955; Schulting and Richards 2002). Therefore, there seems to be a pre-existing connection to place and landscape prior to the construction of monuments in Wales.

The megalith builders seem to have positioned each site in relation to a whole plethora of significant features, some of which undoubtedly had connections back into the Mesolithic. There is direct evidence of this from Gwernvale, where the Neolithic monument was built over Mesolithic occupation debris (Britnell and Savory 1984). However, sites were not simply placed in locales which were already significant, or in relation to a single important landscape feature. A whole range of different landscape features were referenced from each monument. 90% of monuments have a restricted view in one direction, while 74% have a view of mountains and 59% have a view of the sea. Thus sites were frequently positioned in order to have a restricted view, a view of mountains *and* a view of the sea, a *combination* of features. Other features were important: 26% of monuments in Wales have a view of an outcrop, 22% of sites are intervisible and 19% of sites are located close to a river. These figures relate to more localised phenomena. 61% of sites in south-west Wales have a view of an outcrop, while 50% of sites in south-east Wales are intervisible. Each site, then, seems to have been 'fitted' into the local landscape so that a *range* of symbolic places could be referenced.

Histories of west and east

So far we have considered the landscape settings of the monuments in the south-west, south-east and north-west of Wales and discussed the overall location of monuments in general. However, there are similarities in the settings of sites both within these areas and across a broader area which need to be emphasised. As has already been suggested, the portal dolmens of south-west Wales, for example, share a number of characteristics in their overall landscape setting. These monuments are positioned in the vicinity of rocky outcrops, but these outcrops are always skylined on the horizon, in direct contrast to the nearby earth-fast sites (see below). Almost all sites have views of the sea and also of mountains (Fowler and Cummings 2003), such as the crag of Carn Llidi to the west or Carn Ingli and the Preseli Mountains to the east. All monuments are set on a gentle slope overlooking a valley area and they have a restricted view in one direction (Cummings 2001). The dolmens of south-west Wales, then, could be understood as a regionally distinctive group with the characteristic setting of outcrops, sea and mountains.

Other localised patterns can be seen. All the monuments on the Ardudwy peninsula in north-west Wales are located in remarkably similar locations. Located between Harlech and Barmouth, these sites are all positioned between the low-lying coastal strip and the higher ground to the east. All sites have a view of the sea which is visible in the background as one approaches the portal stones, and all have views of mountains. The summit of Moelfre seems to have been of particular significance in this area. From these monuments one can also look out over Cardigan Bay and there are views of the Preselis on a clear day. The similarities in form and setting of these sites suggest that they could be understood as a small regional grouping. However, they also share many characteristics with the dolmens of south-west Wales, suggesting a broader connection across this area. In fact, all of the dolmens in Wales are located in broadly similar landscape settings: with views of mountains and sea, a closed view in one direction and located on the side of a hill on a gentle slope overlooking a valley area.

This is in direct contrast to a number of the other types of monument in Wales. In south-west Wales, the earth-fast sites are located in completely different parts of the landscape to the nearby dolmens. As well as being morphologically different from the dolmens, they are also positioned right up against outcrops so that half of the view is completely dominated by a view of the nearby outcrop. We have already noted that in north-west Wales the two passage graves of Bryn Celli Ddu and Barclodiad y Gawres are located in very different parts of the Anglesey landscape to the other monuments on the island. But it is perhaps the Cotswold-Severn monuments of south-east Wales that contrast most significantly with the monuments of western Wales. As we have already suggested, these monuments are rather different to the portal dolmens. Built over a considerable period of time, these were places for careful working, reworking and texturing of different materials (Lesley McFadyen, *pers. comm.*). These were also places for the deposition of considerable quantities of human remains, which seem to have been carefully mixed, reordered and reworked over time. Architecturally, the substantial long cairns found at these sites create a rather different monument to the upstanding megaliths, capstone and small platform of the dolmens. The landscape setting of these sites is also different. Diversity here seems to be key, as already noted between the encircled setting of Ty Isaf in contrast with the wide vistas from Penywyrlod Talgarth. There is a concern with setting in relation to river valleys and mountains, but much less of a sense of an overall consistency in location as found with the dolmens. This leads us to suggest that there may have been two rather different histories of monument construction in Wales, with contrasts between east and west.

The broader setting

So far, discussion has largely been in terms of the territory of modern Wales. At this point, consideration of the wider context is desirable. It is scarcely possible here to present all the detail which could be mustered, but the wider context may be one of the keys to better understanding of the world to which the megaliths of Wales belonged, and an outline sketch will be attempted. While this perspective was appreciated in the older literature, it has largely been lost sight of in more recent discussions of Welsh monuments. The first emphasis here will be on west Wales and the Irish Sea, but a model linking west and east will also be offered.

As briefly described in chapter 1, for the purposes of this discussion we can date the beginnings of the Neolithic in western Britain and Ireland to around 4000 BC. It is still not clear how much variation there was in fifth millennium BC indigenous lifestyles up and down the coasts and interiors of western Britain and Ireland. Evidence from central and southern Ireland may indicate areas of relative or real absence, and something of similar patchy distributions can be seen in mid-Wales, parts of north Wales, and parts of south-west Scotland. By contrast, relative concentrations of population can be suggested in some areas, for example in south-west Wales and parts of north-east Ireland. The lifestyle may have involved degrees of seasonal, annual and lifetime mobility. The middens on Oronsay tended to be occupied at different seasons of the year, and one individual had a mixed diet which consisted of both marine and terrestrial proteins, showing considerable diversity of resource use (Richards and Mellars 1998). Diet as seen in isotopic analysis seems to have been dominated by marine foods (Richards 2000; Richards and Hedges 1999; Richards and Mellars 1998; Schulting 1998; Schulting and Richards 2002), but inland sites remind us that subsistence practices must have included terrestrial resources, and even at coastal sites like Ferriter's Cove there was a place for pig hunting alongside sea fishing (Woodman et al. 1999). In a world of scattered concentrations of population, relative isolation, and repeated movements, there was already a commitment to place (see above).

It may be a mistake to think of this as a uniform world. The distinctive natural history and situation of Ireland have been emphasised by Cooney (2000), and while this stands out perhaps as the largest single difference, there may have been other more subtle ones related to the form of coastlines, the relationship of coast to interior, and the distribution and movements of resources. It may also be a mistake to think of this as an unchanging world. The wider context to which the Oronsay occupations belonged appears to be one marked by change, with some kind of concentration of human presence on Oronsay in the latter part of the Meolithic sequence and relative absence or at least reduced archaeological visibility of human presence in other islands and areas roundabout (Mithen 2000a; 2000b). In this perspective, it is hardly surprising that there should now be evidence for contact between south-west Ireland and elsewhere, in the form of cattle bones from the middle to later fifth millennium BC at Ferriter's Cove (Woodman et al. 1999). Given that cattle were not part of the native Holocene fauna in Ireland, these few bones must have come from the outside, either in the form of a living animal or as a joint of meat. The excavators indicate that the most likely source would be domesticated cattle from north-west France (Woodman et al. 1999, 90), which the chronology would allow (see below), though the possibility that the animal in question was an auroch from elsewhere in western Britain cannot wholly be excluded.

It seems clear from the evidence of Ferriter's Cove itself and of other Irish sites that whatever immediate impact this contact had, it did not lead straightaway to other changes. But this find highlights the realities of contact and the potential for change. The case had perhaps been presaged in Brittany itself at an earlier date, when a pair of apparently domesticated cattle had been deposited in a pit later marked by the long cairn of Er Grah in the Morbihan, but radiocarbon dated to the late sixth or early fifth millennium BC (Tresset and Vigne forthcoming). At this date, the local context was probably Mesolithic rather than Neolithic, the transition perhaps coming around 4500 BC (Scarre 2002b). There is no other certain sign from the middens of Téviec and Hoëdic, dated to approximately the same time (Scarre 2002b, 29; Schulting and Richards 2001), for use of domesticates in the indigenous context. It may be significant, if the Er Grah deposit is an indigenous one, that these animals were not consumed. Rather, they may have been sacrificed as something both new and conceptually powerful. Other contexts or situations which might have afforded the potential for change through contact include seasonal long-range fishing trips (Clark 1977), and movements of individuals, for example possibly of women from the interior to the coast of Brittany (Schulting and Richards 2001).

The wider evidence from western France and northern Spain for indigenous communities can briefly be noted (Arias 1999; Scarre 2002b). It shares much of the character of that from western Britain and Ireland; patchy distributions, inland as well as coastal use, movement as well as commitment to place, and some variation in diet though with a tendency to strong marine signatures in isotopic analysis, can all again be found. Though this is not the place to discuss the issue in detail, we can note, with reference to commitment to place, special constructions and worldview, that it has been suggested that the middens of Téviec and Hoëdic could have been the result of special feasting attendant on mortuary rites (Scarre 2002b, 25) rather than simply occupations (Schulting 1996). It has been customary to characterise these 'well-established communities of fisher-hunter-gatherers' (Scarre 2002b, 25) as numerous and widespread, but their distribution may not have been either dense or ubiquitous. On the other hand, survey has shown the existence of inland Mesolithic groups, and the total presence of the indigenous population, even though not absolutely numerous, may have been sufficient to delay the encroachment, if that is the best interpretation, of agricultural populations from the Paris basin (Scarre 2002b). The Neolithic site of Le Haut-Mée in eastern Brittany (Cassen et al. 1998) can be dated to the early fifth millennium BC (Scarre 2002b, 32).

The indigenous world here was probably also not unchanging. The middens of Téviec and Hoëdic began to accumulate c. 5500 BC. Change in Brittany and elsewhere was undoubtedly accelerated by contact and influence from outside, both from the eastern world of the Paris basin, and the southern domain of the Mediterranean. A recent authoritative review of the western French evidence has suggested that in each of southern, northern and eastern Brittany the evidence for the beginning of the Neolithic is relatively abrupt, c.4500 BC, and that the case for indigenous continuity is relatively slight; in contrast, south of the Loire there may have been a longer history of contact with the south, and a greater indigenous role is possible (Scarre 2002b). The overall model, however, is of 'mosaic colonization, with scattered farming settlements linked together by exchange networks and co-existing for several centuries with indigenous hunter-gatherer communities' (Scarre 2002b, 41), with emphasis given to 'the power of Atlantic ideologies and cosmologies to absorb and transform' the ideas of 'suspected pioneer farming groups', which 'rapidly lost their separate identity, to become an indistinguishable part of the local and regional pattern' (Scarre 2002b, 55). Further afield, one view of the sequence in Cantabria in northern Spain is of indigenous acculturation leading to Neolithic beginnings c. 5000 BC, with the start of monumental constructions c. 4500 BC (Arias 1999).

There is much here that is relevant to the beginning of the Neolithic in western Britain and Ireland. One possibility is that the same processes repeated themselves, with some colonisation concentrated into particular areas of the Irish Sea zone, much contact with indigenous communities roundabout, and considerable absorption on both sides of the practices and worldviews of the others. Colonisation has been suggested for the distinctive setting of Ireland (Cooney 2000), but in contrast to western France and western Iberia (Scarre 2002b; Zilhão 2000), it is far harder to identify or suggest specific areas of colonisation on the eastern side of the Irish Sea, unless, in the style of the older literature, every potentially early monument is seen as the mark of incomers. It may also be that changes in Brittany were not quite so abrupt as Scarre has argued, and the potential indigenous contribution there was still considerable. It remains unclear from the state of the Breton evidence what sort of economy was introduced from the start of the Neolithic c.4500 BC. Representations of animals on the Table des Marchand-Gavrinis menhir (Whittle 2000) are only a tantalising hint, and limited isotopic analysis from late contexts at Téviec and Hoëdic could suggest mixed diets (Schulting and Richards 2001). The changes that are manifest lie in the realm of ideas, in the still uncertain sequence from menhirs to *tertres* to early passage graves. It is quite unclear whether any particular part of Brittany or of west and north-west France as a whole would have been the source for large budding-off populations by 4000 BC, and the destruction of some menhirs and the introduction of passage graves, themselves of uncertain date, cannot easily be seen as a single event producing a dispersal of Neolithic refugees (*contra* Sheridan 2000, 13). For one thing, menhirs might have been destroyed to protect rather than end their memory (Bradley 2002, 39).

That isotopic analysis has indicated a major shift from marine to terrestrial resources by an established phase of the early Neolithic in western Britain (Richards 2000; Richards and Hedges 1999; Schulting 1998; Schulting and Richards 2002) is undeniable, but it remains to be seen how swift changes in diet were in the first two to three centuries of the Neolithic and what variation can be found with wider sampling of the late Mesolithic. Even if there were immediate replacements, it is uncertain whether they must reflect incoming population. The substitution of domesticated animals and cereals for native resources might have been accomplished within the indigenous setting. Following domestic cattle rather than deer and aurochs, or harvesting cereals rather than seals or fish, might not have been a major conceptual step for knowledgeable, resource-oriented foragers: takers of opportunities, in Bird-David's phrase (1992, 40). As chapter 1 has already indicated, the evidence for Neolithic occupation remains slight, and at face value does not speak for extensive or rapidly growing populations in the early Neolithic. This is not wholly to exclude the possibility of either some filtered colonisation or of rapid diet change in the eastern Irish Sea zone at the start of the Neolithic, but to emphasise on the one hand the still persistent difficulties of the colonisation model and on the other the range of arguments in favour of a substantial indigenous contribution here to the formation of Neolithic communities.

It is then to this sort of context that the monuments of west Wales may belong in the early Neolithic. Many of these monuments, from portal dolmens and related constructions to earth-fast monuments, are distinctive. There are no compellingly similar antecedents in north-west France. There are good grounds, if so far largely unsupported by radiocarbon dating, for seeing at least some of the portal dolmens as early, and it was argued above that these constructions were on the whole swiftly carried out. If their meaning, as argued above, was to emphasise elements of a mythology involving the earth and creation or creators, it could be supposed that this refers best to indigenous belief systems, though of course the possibility of mutual influence and absorption (cf. Scarre 2002b, 55) cannot be discounted. The eastern part of the Irish Sea zone at the start of the Neolithic in the late fifth or early fourth millennium BC could have witnessed the reassertion and enhancement of indigenous beliefs in the face of and in reaction to the sets of changes in ideas and daily practices which had been affecting western Europe as a whole since the sixth millennium BC, and adjacent north-west France in particular since the mid-fifth millennium BC. This view might extend also to Ireland, *contra* prevailing Irish interpretations, and monuments and landscape could both have been part of a new sense of regional western community as argued above. On the other hand, the total distribution of Irish portal dolmens appears much wider than that of late Mesolithic populations on the island.

Long ago, Stuart Piggott (1955) posed the question of east or west, in relation to possible sources of the British Neolithic. The axes of identity and allegiance that he and Childe before him had indicated have remained the focus of research to this day. It is still legitimate to see major influences from the world of northern France, the Low

Countries and the Rhineland and beyond on the formation of the Neolithic of the whole of eastern Britain. It is definitely beyond the scope of this volume to detail this relationship, but the character of the early Neolithic in southern England and eastern Britain as a whole is relevant to the nature of the early Neolithic in the west. Piggott left the relationship *between* east and west alone. The presence in south-east Wales of long cairns of a very different tradition to the monuments of the west demands that this be examined. We have already sketched some major differences; we will now briefly reconsider relationships.

There are familiar difficulties in unravelling the competing claims for colonisation and acculturation in the eastern part of Britain. But there may be a case for seeing more colonisation here, by fissioning or filtering from the major established populations of the adjacent continent in the late fifth and earliest fourth millennium BC (cf. Schulting 2000). Diet change after the first two or three centuries may have been extensive, and there were few areas by this time without a Neolithic presence of some kind. East and west were certainly in contact, as seen in the movement of stone axes and in shared styles of pottery. The realm of ideas may have been rather different in the east. Memory of or reference to the old tradition of the LBK, in the form of the long mound and the ditched enclosure, was a dominant factor, absent in the west. On present chronology, however, this may not have come to the fore until at least two or three centuries after the start of the Neolithic, a still unexplained delay in cultural memory (cf. Bradley 2002). Early monuments in the east were on the whole modest affairs, small constructions of wood, stone, earth and chalk, that were not monumentalised until the setting up of large long mounds and cairns, and the digging of ditched arenas. They might often be seen as an enhancement of the importance of place, and the landscape setting in itself may have been of less importance. Much early activity of this kind may have been concerned with the deposition of human remains, and specific genealogies as well as generalised notions of ancestry may have been to the fore. The foci were on the one hand distant memories and on the other recent persons. A rather different sort of belief system may have been at work.

Bringing these two sets of possibilities together may further serve to underline the distinctive nature of what went on in the west in the early Neolithic. Communities in the Irish Sea area may have been reacting not only to ideas, events, contacts and new opportunities from over the sea, but also to changing populations and their ideologies in the lands to the east. It seems possible, then, that the Gower and the Black Mountains may mark the westernmost extension of the eastern system, though there is no need, given the apparent variability in the Black Mountains situation, to suppose that every inhabitant there was of direct continental descent. Instead, we could envisage considerable diversity, even in a small area such as the Gower or the Black Mountains, with influences from both east and west, manifest in the range of different monument forms.

A consideration of the Neolithic megaliths of Wales in their landscape settings can contribute significantly to understanding not only local and regional trajectories of change but also wider histories of west and east. It is these broader histories, and the manifestation of these differences *between* east and west, which seem to have defined the nature of the early Neolithic in Wales. This, in turn, would have impacted on the connections people made with the landscape, and their understanding of their place in the Neolithic world.

Bibliography

Ackerman, D. 1991. *A natural history of the senses.* London: Phoenix.

Appleton, J. 1975. *The experience of landscape.* Chichester: John Wiley.

ApSimon, A. 1976. A view of the early prehistory of Wales. In G. Boon and J. Lewis (eds), *Welsh antiquity,* 37–53. Cardiff: National Museum of Wales.

Arias, P. 1999. The origins of the Neolithic along the Atlantic coast of continental Europe: a survey. *Journal of World Prehistory* 13, 403–64.

Ashbee, P. 1966. Fussell's Lodge long barrow excavations, 1957. *Archaeologia* 100, 1–80.

Ashmore, W. and Knapp, B. 1999. Archaeological landscapes: constructed, conceptualized, ideational. In W. Ashmore and B. Knapp (eds), *Archaeologies of landscape: contemporary perspectives,* 1–30. Oxford: Blackwell.

Atkinson, R. 1961. Parc le Breos Cwm. *Archaeology in Wales* 1, 5.

Austin, P. 2000. The emperor's new garden: woodland, trees and people in the Neolithic of southern Britain. In A. Fairbairn (ed.), *Plants in Neolithic Britain and beyond,* 63–78. Oxford: Oxbow.

Bachelard, G. 1994. *The poetics of space.* Boston, Mass: Beacon.

Bagnall-Oakley, M. and Bagnall-Oakley, W. 1889. *An account of some of the rude stone monuments and ancient burial mounds in Monmouthshire.* Newport: Monmouthshire and Caerleon Antiquarian Association.

Barclay, G. 1996. Neolithic buildings in Scotland. In T. Darvill and J. Thomas (eds), *Neolithic houses in northwest Europe and beyond,* 61–75. Oxford: Oxbow.

Barclay, G. 2001. 'Metropolitan' and 'parochial/core' and 'periphery': a historiography of the Neolithic of Scotland. *Proceedings of the Prehistoric Society* 67, 1–18.

Barclay, G. and Maxwell, G. 1999. The Cleaven Dyke: a summary account of survey and excavation, 1993–96. In A. Barclay and J. Harding (eds), *Pathways and ceremonies: the cursus monuments of Britain and Ireland,* 98–106. Oxford: Oxbow.

Baring-Gould, S., Burnard, R. and Enys, J. 1898. Exploration of the stone camp on St David's Head. *Archaeologia Cambrensis* 16, 105–31.

Barker, C. 1992. *The chambered tombs of south-west Wales: a reassessment of the Neolithic burial monuments of Carmarthenshire and Pembrokeshire.* Oxford: Oxbow.

Barker, K. and Darvill, T. 1997. Introduction: landscape old and new. In K. Barker and T. Darvill (eds), *Making English landscapes,* 1–8. Oxford: Oxbow.

Barnatt, J. 1989. *Stone circles of Britain.* Oxford: British Archaeological Reports, British Series 215.

Barnatt, J. and Edmonds, M. 2002. Places apart? Caves and monuments in Neolithic and earlier Bronze Age Britain. *Cambridge Archaeological Journal* 12, 113–29.

Barrett, J. 1994. *Fragments from antiquity: an archaeology of social life in Britain 2900–1200 BC.* Oxford: Blackwell.

Barrett, J. 1997. Stone age ideologies. *Analecta Praehistorica Leidensia* 29, 121–29.

Barton, R., Berridge, P., Walker, M. and Bevins, R. 1995. Persistent places in the Mesolithic landscape: an example from the Black Mountain uplands of south Wales. *Proceedings of the Prehistoric Society* 61, 81–116.

Basso, K. 1984. "Stalking with stories": names, places, and moral narratives among the Western Apache. In E. M. Bruner (ed.), *Text, play and the story: the construction and reconstruction of self and society,* 19–55. Washington DC: American Ethnological Society.

Basso, K. 1996. Wisdom sits in places: notes on a Western Apache landscape. In S. Feld and K. Basso (eds), *Senses of places,* 53–90. Santa Fe: School of American Research Press.

Baynes, N. 1909. The excavation of Lligwy cromlech, in the county of Anglesey. *Archaeologia Cambrensis* 9, 217–31.

Baynes, N. 1932. Lligwy cromlech. *Transactions of the Anglesey Antiquarian Society and Field Club* 1932, 37–8.

Bell, M., Caseldine, A. and Neumann, H. 2000. *Prehistoric intertidal archaeology in the Welsh Severn Estuary.* York: Council for British Archaeology.

Bender, B. 1992. Theorising landscape and the prehistoric landscape of Stonehenge. *Man* 27, 735–55.

Bender, B. 1993a. Introduction: landscape – meaning and action. In B. Bender (ed.), *Landscape: politics and perspectives,* 1–17. Oxford: Berg.

Bender, B. (ed.) 1993b. *Landscape: politics and perspectives.* Oxford: Berg.

Bender, B. 1993c. Stonehenge – contested landscapes (medieval to present day). In B. Bender (ed.), *Landscape: politics and perspectives,* 245–79. Oxford: Berg.

Bender, B. 1998. *Stonehenge: making space.* Oxford: Berg.

Bender, B., Hamilton, S. and Tilley, C. 1997. Leskernick: stone worlds; alternative narratives; nested landscapes. *Proceedings of the Prehistoric Society* 63, 147–78.

Bender, B. and Winer, M. (eds) 2001. *Contested landscapes: movement, exile and place.* Oxford: Berg.

Bird-David, N. 1992. Beyond 'the hunting and gathering mode of subsistence': culture-sensitive observations on the Nayaka and other modern hunter-gatherers. *Man* 27, 19–44.

Bloch, M. 1977. The past and the present in the past. *Man* 12, 278–92.

Bloch, M. 1992. What goes without saying: the conceptualisation of Zafimaniry society. In A. Kuper (ed.), *Conceptualising society,* 127–46. London: Routledge.

Bloch, M. 1995. The resurrection of the house amongst the Zafirmaniry of Madagascar. In J. Carsten and S. Hugh-Jones (eds), *About the house; Lévi-Strauss and beyond,* 52–71. Cambridge: Cambridge University Press.

Bowen, E. 1970. Britain and the British Seas. In D. Moore

(ed.), *The Irish Sea province in archaeology and history*, 13–28. Cardiff: Cambrian Archaeological Association.

Bowen, E. and Gresham, C. 1967. *History of Merioneth, volume one*. Llandysul: Gomerian Press.

Boyd Dawkins, W. 1874. *Cave hunting. Researches on the evidence of caves respecting the early inhabitants of Europe*. London: Macmillan and Co.

Boyd Dawkins, W. 1901. On the cairn and sepulchral cave at Gop, near Prestatyn. *Archaeological Journal* 108, 322–41.

Bradley, R. 1989. Darkness and light in the design of megalithic tombs. *Oxford Journal of Archaeology* 8, 251–9.

Bradley, R. 1991. Monuments and places. In P. Garwood, D. Jennings, R. Skeates and J. Toms (eds), *Sacred and profane*, 135–40. Oxford: Oxford University Committee for Archaeology.

Bradley, R. 1993. *Altering the earth*. Edinburgh: Society of Antiquaries of Scotland.

Bradley, R. 1998a. Directions to the dead. *KVHAA Konferenser* 40, 123–35.

Bradley, R. 1998b. Ruined buildings, ruined stones: enclosures, tombs and natural places in the Neolithic of south-west England. *World Archaeology* 30, 13–22.

Bradley, R. 1998c. *The significance of monuments: on the shaping of human experience in Neolithic and Bronze Age Europe*. London: Routledge.

Bradley, R. 2000. *The archaeology of natural places*. London: Routledge.

Bradley, R. 2002. *The past in prehistoric societies*. London: Routledge.

Bradley, R. and Edmonds, M. 1993. *Interpreting the axe trade: production and exchange in Neolithic Britain*. Cambridge: Cambridge University Press.

Britnell, W. 1982. The excavation of two round barrows at Trelystan, Powys. *Proceedings of the Prehistoric Society* 48, 133–201.

Britnell, W. and Savory, H. 1984. *Gwernvale and Penywyrlod: two Neolithic long cairns in the Black Mountains of Brecknock*. Cardiff: Cambrian Archaeological Association.

Brophy, K. 1998. This is not phenomenology (or is it?): experiencing cursus monuments. *Third Stone* 30, 7–9.

Brophy, K. 1999. The cursus monuments of Scotland. In A. Barclay and J. Harding (eds), *Pathways and ceremonies: the cursus monuments of Britain and Ireland*, 119–29. Oxford: Oxbow.

Burl, A. 1979. *The stone circles of the British Isles*. New Haven: Yale University Press.

Burl, A. 1995. *A guide to the stone circles of Britain, Ireland and Brittany*. Yale: Yale University Press.

Burnham, H. 1995. *A guide to ancient and historic Wales: Clwyd and Powys*. Cardiff: CADW.

Burrow, S. 2002. Reuniting the Dyffryn Ardudwy pendants. *Archaeologia Cambrensis* 151, 203–206.

Burrow, S., Driver, T. and Thomas, D. 2001. Bridging the Severn Estuary: two possible earlier Neolithic enclosures in the Vale of Glamorgan. In T. Darvill and J. Thomas (eds), *Neolithic enclosures in Atlantic northwest Europe*, 91–100. Oxford: Oxbow.

Caseldine, A. 1990. *Environmental archaeology in Wales*. Lampeter: Cambrian Printers.

Cassen, S., Audren, C., Hinguant, S., Lannuzel, G. and Marchand, G. 1998. L'habitat Villeneuve-St-Germain du Haut-Mée (St-Etienne-en-Cogles, Ille-et-Vilaine). *Bulletin de la Société Préhistorique Française* 95, 41–75.

Caulfield, S. 1983. The Neolithic settlement of north Connaught. In T. Reeves-Smyth and F. Hamond (eds), *Landscape archaeology in Ireland*, 195–215. Oxford: British Archaeological Reports, British Series 116.

Caulfield, S., O'Donnell, R. and Mitchell, P. 1998. Radiocarbon dating of a Neolithic field system at Ceide Fields, County Mayo, Ireland. *Radiocarbon* 40, 629–40.

Chambers, F. 1983. The palaeoecological setting of Cefn Gwernffrwd – a prehistoric complex in mid-Wales. *Proceedings of the Prehistoric Society* 49, 303–16.

Chapman, J. 1997. Place as timemarks – the social construction of prehistoric landscapes in eastern Hungary. In G. Nash (ed.), *Semiotics of landscape: archaeology of mind*, 31–45. Oxford: British Archaeological Reports, International Series 661.

Childe, V. G. 1940. *Prehistoric communities of the British Isles*. Edinburgh: Edinburgh University Press.

Children, G. and Nash, G. 1996. *A guide to prehistoric sites in Monmouthshire*. Woonton Almeley: Logaston.

Children, G. and Nash, G. 1997a. *The anthropology of landscape: a guide to Neolithic sites in Cardiganshire, Carmarthenshire and Pembrokeshire*. Woonton Almeley: Logaston.

Children, G. and Nash, G. 1997b. Establishing a discourse: the language of landscape. In G. Nash (ed.), *Semiotics of landscape: archaeology of mind*, 1–4. Oxford: British Archaeological Reports, International Series 661.

Clark, J. G. D. 1952. *Prehistoric Europe: the economic basis*. London: Methuen.

Clark, J. G. D. 1966. The invasion hypothesis in British prehistory. *Antiquity* 40, 172–89.

Clark, J. G. D. 1977. The economic context of dolmens and passage graves in Sweden. In V. Markotic (ed.), *Ancient Europe and the Mediterranean: studies presented in honour of Hugh Hencken*, 35–50. Warminster: Aris and Phillips.

Clark, K. 1949. *Landscape into art*. Harmondsworth: Pelican.

Classen, C., Howes, D. and Synnott, A. 1991. *Aroma: the cultural history of smell*. London: Routledge.

Cleal, R., Walker, K. and Montague, R. 1995. *Stonehenge in its landscape: twentieth century excavations*. London: English Heritage.

Clough, T. and Cummins, W. (eds) 1988. *Stone axe studies: volume two*. London: Council for British Archaeology.

Cohen, S., Ward, I. and Enns, J. 1994. *Sensation and perception*. Fort Worth: Harcourt Brace College.

Coles, B. and Coles, J. 1986. *Sweet Track to Glastonbury: the Somerset Levels in prehistory*. London: Thames and Hudson.

Collins, J. and Selina, H. 1998. *Heidegger for beginners*. Cambridge: Icon.

Coones, P. 1992. The unity of landscape. In L. Macinnes and C. Wickham-Jones (eds), *All natural things: archaeology and the green debate*, 22–40. Oxford: Oxbow.

Cooney, G. 1997. Excavation of the portal dolmen site at Melkagh, Co. Longford. *Proceedings of the Royal Irish Academy* 97, 195–244.

Cooney, G. 2000. *Landscapes of Neolithic Ireland*. London: Routledge.

Cooney, G. 2003. Neolithic worlds; islands in the Irish Sea. In V. Cummings and C. Fowler (eds), *The Neolithic of the Irish Sea: materiality and traditions of practice*. Oxford: Oxbow.

Corcoran, J. X. W. P. 1969a. The Cotswold-Severn group. 1. Distribution, morphology and artifacts. In T. G. E. Powell, J. X. W. P. Corcoran, F. Lynch, and J. G. Scott, *Megalithic enquiries in the west of Britain*, 13–71. Liverpool: Liverpool University Press.

Corcoran, J. X. W. P 1969b. Excavation of two chambered cairns at Mid Gleniron Farm, Glenluce Wigtownshire. *Transactions of the Dumfries and Galloway Natural History and Antiquarian Society* 46, 31–90.

Corcoran, J. X. W. P. 1972. Multi-period construction and the origins of the chambered long cairn in western Britain and Ireland. In F. Lynch and C. Burgess (eds), *Prehistoric man in Wales and the west*, 31–63. Bath: Adams and Dart.

Cosgrove, D. 1989. Geography is everywhere: culture and symbolism in human landscapes. In D. Gregory and R. Walford (eds), *Horizons in human geography*, 118–35. London: MacMillan.

Cosgrove, D. 1993. Landscape and myths, gods and humans. In B. Bender (ed.), *Landscape: politics and perspectives*, 281–305. Oxford: Berg.

Crampton, C. and Webley, D. 1966. A section through the Mynydd Troed long barrow, Brecknock. *Bulletin of the Board of Celtic Studies* 22, 71–77.

Craster, O. 1953. *Ancient monuments of Anglesey*. London: Her Majesty's Stationery Office.

Crawford, O. G. S. 1920. Account of excavations at Hengwm, Merionethshire, August and September 1919. *Archaeologia Cambrensis* 20, 99–133.

Crawford, O. G. S. 1925. *The long barrows of the Cotswolds*. Gloucester: John Bellows.

Crawford, O. G. S. 1929. *Air photography for archaeologists*. Southampton: Ordnance Survey.

Crawford, O. G. S. and Keiller, A. 1928. *Wessex from the air*. Oxford: Clarendon Press.

Cummings, V. 2000a. Landscapes in motion: interactive computer imagery and Neolithic landscapes of the Outer Hebrides. In C. Buck, V. Cummings, C. Henley, S. Mills, and S. Trick (eds), *UK chapter of computer applications and quantitative methods in archaeology*, 11–20. Oxford: British Archaeological Reports, International Series 844.

Cummings, V. 2000b. The world in a spin: recreating the Neolithic landscapes of South Uist. *Internet Archaeology* 8 (http://intarch.ac.uk/journal/issue8/cummingsindex.htm).

Cummings, V. 2001. *Landscapes in transition? Exploring the origins of monumentality in south-west Wales and south-west Scotland*. Unpublished Ph.D. thesis: Cardiff University.

Cummings, V. 2002a. All cultural things: actual and conceptual monuments in the Neolithic of western Britain. In C. Scarre (ed.), *Monumentality and landscape in Atlantic Europe*, 107–21. London: Routledge.

Cummings, V. 2002b. Between mountains and sea: a reconsideration of the monuments of south-west Scotland. *Proceedings of the Prehistoric Society* 68, 125–46.

Cummings, V. 2002c. Building from memory: remembering the past at Neolithic monuments in western Britain. In H. Williams (ed.), *Archaeologies of remembrance: death and memory in past societies*, 25–44. London: Klewer Plenum.

Cummings, V. 2002d. Experiencing texture and transformation in the British Neolithic. *Oxford Journal of Archaeology* 21, 249–61.

Cummings, V. 2003. Connecting the mountains and the sea: the monuments of eastern Irish Sea zone. In V. Cummings and C. Fowler (eds), *The Neolithic of the Irish Sea: materiality and traditions of practice*. Oxford: Oxbow.

Cummings, V. forthcoming. Monuments at the centre of the world: exploring regional diversity in south-west Wales and south-west Scotland. In G. Barclay and K. Brophy (eds), *Regional diversity in the Neolithic of Britain and Ireland*. Oxford: Oxbow.

Cummings, V., Jones, A. and Watson, A. 2002. In between places: axial asymmetry and divided space in the monuments of the Black Mountains, south-east Wales. *Cambridge Archaeological Journal* 12, 57–70.

Curry, M. 1998. *Digital places: living with Geographic Information Technologies*. London: Routledge.

Daniel, G. E. 1937a. The chambered barrow in Parc le Breos Cwm, S. Wales. *Proceedings of the Prehistoric Society* 6, 71–86.

Daniel, G. E. 1937b. The Four Crosses burial chamber, Caernarfonshire. *Archaeologia Cambrensis* 92, 165–7.

Daniel, G. E. 1941. The dual nature of the megalithic colonisation of prehistoric Europe. *Proceedings of the Prehistoric Society* 7, 1–49.

Daniel, G. E. 1950. *The prehistoric chamber tombs of England and Wales*. Cambridge: Cambridge University Press.

Daniel, G. E. and Powell, T. G. E. 1949. The distribution and date of the passage-graves of the British Isles. *Proceedings of the Prehistoric Society* 14, 169–87.

Daniels, S. and Cosgrove, D. 1993. Spectacle and text: landscape metaphors in cultural geography. In J. Duncan and D. Ley (eds), *Place/culture/representation*, 57–77. London: Routledge.

Darvill, T. 1982. *The megalithic chambered tombs of the Cotswold-Severn region*. Highworth: Vorda.

Darvill, T. 1997a. Landscapes and the archaeologist. In K. Barker and T. Darvill (eds), *Making English landscapes*, 70–91. Oxford: Oxbow.

Darvill, T. 1997b. Neolithic landscapes: identity and definition. In P. Topping (ed.), *Neolithic landscapes*, 1–14. Oxford: Oxbow.

Darvill, T. 2000. Neolithic Mann in context. In A. Ritchie (ed.), *Neolithic Orkney in its European context*, 371–85. Oxford: Oxbow.

Darvill, T. and Thomas, J. (eds) 2001. *Neolithic enclosures in Atlantic northwest Europe*. Oxford: Oxbow.

Darvill, T. and Wainwright, G. 2002. SPACES – exploring Neolithic landscape in the Strumble-Preseli area of southwest Wales. *Antiquity* 76, 623–4.

David, A. 1990. Some aspects of the human presence in west Wales during the Mesolithic. In C. Bonsall (ed.), *The Mesolithic in Europe*, 241–53. Edinburgh: John Donald.

David, A. and Williams, G. 1995. Stone axe-head manufacture in the Preseli Hills, Wales. *Proceedings of the Prehistoric Society* 61, 433–60.

Davies, D. 1988. The evocative symbolism of trees. In D. Cosgrove and S. Daniels (eds), *The iconography of landscape*, 32–42. Cambridge: Cambridge University Press.

Davies, E. 1923. Some Lleyn antiquities. *Archaeologia Cambrensis* 78, 306–10.

Davies, E. 1929. *The prehistoric and Roman remains of Denbighshire*. Cardiff: William Lewis.

Davies, M. 1945. Types of megalithic monuments of the Irish Sea and north Channel coastlands: a study in distributions. *Antiquaries Journal* 25, 125–44.

Davis, R., Howard, H. and Smith, I. 1988. The petrological identification of stone implements from south-west England:

sixth report. In T. Clough and W. Cummins (eds), *Stone axe studies, volume two*, 14–20. London: Council for British Archaeology.

de Valera, R. 1960. The court cairns of Ireland. *Proceedings of the Royal Irish Academy* 60, 1–140.

Dimbleby, G. 1973. Report on two soil samples from Dyffryn Ardudwy. *Archaeologia* 104, 4–5.

Douglas, M. 1966. *Purity and danger*. London: Routledge.

Duncan, J. 1993. Sites of representation: place, time and the discourse of the other. In J. Duncan and D. Ley (eds), *Place/culture/representation*, 39–56. London: Routledge.

Edmonds, M. 1999. *Ancestral geographies of the Neolithic: landscape, monuments and memory*. London: Routledge.

Edmonds, M. and Seaborne, T. 2001. *Prehistory in the Peak*. Stroud: Tempus.

Eogan, G. 1983. Bryn Celli Ddu. *Antiquity* 57, 135–6.

Evans, C., Pollard, J. and Knight, M. 1999. Life in woods: tree-throws, 'settlement' and forest cognition. *Oxford Journal of Archaeology* 18, 241–54.

Evans, J. G., Limbrey, S. and Cleere, H. (eds) 1975. *The effect of man on the landscape: the highland zone*. London: Council for British Archaeology.

Exon, S., Gaffney, V., Woodward, A. and Yorston, R. 2001. *Stonehenge landscapes: journeys through real and imagined worlds*. Oxford: British Archaeological Reports.

Fenton, J. 1848. Cromlech at Llanwnda, Pembrokeshire. *Archaeologia Cambrensis* 3, 283–4.

Fenton, R. 1810. *A historic tour through Pembrokeshire*. London.

Finlayson, B. and Edwards, K. 1997. The Mesolithic. In K. Edwards and I. Ralston (eds), *Scotland: environment and archaeology 8000 BC–AD 1000*, 109–125. Chichester: Wiley.

Fleming, A. 1999. Phenomenology and the megaliths of Wales: a dreaming too far? *Oxford Journal of Archaeology* 18, 119–25.

Fowler, C. and Cummings, V. 2003. Places of transformation: building monuments from water and stone in the Neolithic of the Irish Sea. *Journal of the Royal Anthropological Institute* 9, 1–20.

Fox, C. 1932. *The personality of Britain*. Cardiff: National Museum of Wales.

Fox, C. 1937. The megalithic monuments of the Gower – their relation to topography. *Archaeologia Cambrensis* 92, 159–61.

Gell, A. 1995. The language of the forest: landscape and phonological iconism in Umeda. In E. Hirsch and M. O'Hanlon (eds), *The anthropology of landscape: perspectives on place and space*, 232–54. Oxford: Oxford University Press.

George, T. 1970. *British regional geology: south Wales*. London: Her Majesty's Stationery Office.

Gibson, A. 1994a. Excavations at the Sarn-y-bryn-caled complex, Welshpool, Powys and the timber circles of Great Britain and Ireland. *Proceedings of the Prehistoric Society* 60, 143–224.

Gibson, A. 1994b. Lower Luggy long mound. *Archaeology in Wales* 34, 51–2.

Gibson, A. 1995. First impressions: a review of Peterborough Ware in Wales. In I. Kinnes and G. Varndell (eds), *'Unbaked urns of rudely shape'*, 23–40. Oxford: Oxbow.

Gibson, A. 1999a. Cursus monuments and possible cursus monuments in Wales: avenues for research. In A. Barclay and J. Harding (eds), *Pathways and ceremonies: the cursus monuments of Britain and Ireland*, 130–40. Oxford: Oxbow.

Gibson, A. 1999b. *The Walton Basin project: excavation and survey in a prehistoric landscape 1993–7*. London: Council for British Archaeology.

Gibson, A. 2000. Survey and excavation at a newly discovered long barrow at Lower Luggy, Berriew, Powys. *Studia Celtica* 34, 1–16.

Gibson, A., Becker, H., Grogan, E., Jones, N. and Masterson, B. 2001. Survey at Hindwell enclosure, Walton, Powys, Wales. In T. Darvill and J. Thomas (eds), *Neolithic enclosures in Atlantic northwest Europe*, 101–10. Oxford: Oxbow.

Gillings, M. 1998. Embracing uncertainty and challenging dualism in the GIS-based study of a palaeo-flood plain. *European Journal of Archaeology* 1, 117–44.

Gillings, M. and Goodrick, G. 1996. Sensuous and reflexive GIS: exploring visualization and VRML. *Internet Archaeology* 1 (http://intarch.ac.uk/journal/issue1/gillingsindex.htm).

Gillings, M., Mattingly, D. and van Dalen, J. 1999. *Geographical Information Systems and landscape archaeology*. Oxford: Oxbow.

Goodrick, G. and Gillings, M. 2000. Constructs, simulations and hyperreal worlds: the role of Virtual Reality (VR) in archaeological research. In G. Lock and K. Brown (eds), *On the theory and practice of archaeological computing*, 41–58. Oxford: Oxbow.

Gramsch, A. 1996. Landscape archaeology: of making and seeing. *Journal of European Archaeology* 4, 19–38.

Graves-Brown, P. 1998. Ewenny, Beech Court Farm prehistoric enclosure. *Archaeology in Wales* 38, 111–2.

Green, C. 1997. The provenance of rocks used in the construction of Stonehenge. In B. Cunliffe and C. Renfrew (eds), *Science and Stonehenge*, 257–70. Oxford: Oxford University Press.

Greig, J. 1987. Pollen and plant macrofossils. In C. Smith and F. Lynch, *Trefignath and Din Dryfol*, 39–44. Bangor: Cambrian Archaeological Association.

Gresham, C. 1985. Notes on two Anglesey megalithic tombs. *Archaeologia Cambrensis* 134, 225–7.

Gresham, C. and Irvine, C. 1963. Prehistoric routes across north Wales. *Antiquity* 37, 54–8.

Griffiths, W. 1960. The excavation of stone circles near Penmaenmawr, north Wales. *Proceedings of the Prehistoric Society* 16, 303–39.

Grimes, W. 1936a. The long cairns of the Brecknockshire Black Mountains. *Archaeologia Cambrensis* 91, 259–82.

Grimes, W. 1936b. The megalithic monuments of Wales. *Proceedings of the Prehistoric Society* 2, 106–39.

Grimes, W. 1938. Excavations at Meini Gwyr, Carmarthen. *Proceedings of the Prehistoric Society* 4, 324–5.

Grimes, W. 1939a. Bedd y Afanc. *Proceedings of the Prehistoric Society* 5, 258.

Grimes, W. 1939b. The excavation of Ty-isaf long cairn Brecknockshire. *Proceedings of the Prehistoric Society* 6, 119–42.

Grimes, W. 1948. Pentre Ifan burial chamber, Pembrokeshire. *Archaeologia Cambrensis* 100, 3–23.

Grimes, W. 1960. *Pentre-Ifan burial chamber*. Cardiff: Ministry of Works.

Grimes, W. 1965. Neolithic Wales. In I. Foster and G. Daniel (eds), *Prehistoric and early Wales*, 35–69. London: Routledge and Kegan Paul.

Grinker, R. 1994. *Houses in the rainforest: ethnicity and inequality among farmers and foragers in central Africa.* Berkeley: University of California Press.

Hammond, M., Howarth, J. and Keat, R. 1991. *Understanding phenomenology.* Oxford: Basil Blackwell.

Haraway, D. 1991. *Simians, cyborgs and women: the reinvention of nature.* London: Free Association.

Harding, A. and Lee, G. 1987. *Henge monuments and related sites of Great Britain.* Oxford: British Archaeological Reports, British Series 175.

Harris, M. 2000. *Life on the Amazon: the anthropology of a Brazilian peasant village.* Oxford: Oxford University Press.

Harrison, S. 2001. Smoke rising from the villages of the dead: seasonal patterns of mood in a Papua New Guinea society. *Journal of the Royal Anthropological Institute* 7, 257–74.

Hawkes, C. 1940. *The prehistoric foundations of Europe to the Mycenean Age.* London: Methuen.

Hawkes, J. 1946. *Early Britain.* London: Collins.

Hemp, W. 1923. Maen Pebyll long cairn. *Archaeologia Cambrensis* 78, 143–7.

Hemp, W. 1926. The Bachwen "cromlech". *Archaeologia Cambrensis* 81, 429–31.

Hemp, W. 1927. The Capel Garmon chambered long cairn. *Archaeologia Cambrensis* 82, 1–43.

Hemp, W. 1930. The chambered cairn of Bryn Celli Ddu. *Archaeologia* 80, 179–214.

Hemp, W. 1935a. Arthur's Stone, Dorstone, Herefordshire. *Archaeologia Cambrensis* 40, 288–92.

Hemp, W. 1935b. The chambered cairn known as Bryn yr Hen Bobl near Plas Newydd, Anglesey. *Archaeologia* 85, 253–92.

Hemp, W. 1936. Carnedd Hengwm, Merionethshire. *Archaeologia Cambrensis* 91, 25–29.

Hemp, W. 1938. Cup markings on rock at Treflys, Caernarvonshire. *Archaeologia Cambrensis* 93, 140–1.

Hemp, W. 1952. Merionethshire cairns and barrows in Llandrillo and neighbouring parishes. *Bulletin of the Board of Celtic Studies* 14, 155–65.

Herity, M. 1970. The early prehistoric period around the Irish Sea. In D. Moore (ed.), *The Irish Sea province in archaeology and history*, 29–37. Cardiff: Cambrian Archaeological Association.

Herne, A. 1988. A time and a place for the Grimston bowl. In J. Barrett and I. Kinnes (eds), *The archaeology of context in the Neolithic and Bronze Age: recent trends*, 2–29. Sheffield: Department of Archaeology and Prehistory.

Higginbottom, G., Smith, A., Simpson, K. and Clay, R. 2001. Incorporating the natural environment: investigating landscape and monument as sacred space. In T. Darvill and M. Gojda (eds), *One land, many landscapes*, 97–104. Oxford: British Archaeological Reports, International Series 987.

Higgs, E. and Vita-Finzi, C. 1972. Prehistoric economies: a territorial approach. In E. Higgs (ed.), *Papers in economic prehistory*, 27–36. Cambridge: Cambridge University Press.

Hillson, S. 1996. *Dental anthropology.* Cambridge: Cambridge University Press.

Hirsch, E. 1995. Landscape: between place and space. In E. Hirsch and M. O'Hanlon (eds), *The anthropology of landscape: perspectives on place and space*, 1–29. Oxford: Oxford University Press.

Hockney, D. 1984. *Cameraworks.* London: Thames and Hudson.

Hodder, I. and Shand, P. 1988. The Haddenham long barrow: an interim statement. *Antiquity* 62, 394–453.

Houlder, C. 1968. The henge monuments at Llandegai. *Antiquity* 92, 216–21.

Houlder, C. 1974. *Wales: an archaeological guide.* London: Faber and Faber.

Howell, S. 1996. Nature in culture or culture in nature? Chewong ideas of 'humans' and other species. In P. Descola and G. Palsson (eds), *Nature and society: anthropological perspectives*, 127–44. London: Routledge.

Hubert, J. 1994. Sacred beliefs and beliefs of sacredness. In D. Carmichael, J. Hubert, B. Reeves, and A. Schande (eds), *Sacred sites, sacred places*, 9–19. London: Routledge.

Ingold, T. 1993. The temporality of the landscape. *World Archaeology* 25, 152–75.

Ingold, T. 1995. Building, dwelling, living: how animals and people make themselves at home in the world. In M. Strathern (ed.), *Shifting contexts*, 57–80. London: Routledge.

Ingold, T. 1996. Hunting and gathering as ways of perceiving the environment. In R. Ellen and K. Fukui (eds), *Redefining nature*, 117–55. Oxford: Berg.

Ingold, T. 2000. *The perception of the environment: essays on livelihood, dwelling and skill.* London: Routledge.

Johnson, I. and North, M. 1997. *Archaeological applications of GIS.* Sydney: University of Sydney.

Johnson, R., Gregory, D. and Smith, D. (eds) 1994. *The dictionary of human geography.* Oxford: Blackwell.

Johnston, R. 1998. The paradox of landscape. *European Journal of Archaeology* 3, 313–25.

Jones, A. 1998. Where eagles dare: landscape, animals and the Neolithic of Orkney. *Journal of Material Culture* 3, 301–24.

Jones, A. 1999. Local colour: megalithic architecture and colour symbolism in Neolithic Arran. *Oxford Journal of Archaeology* 18, 339–50.

Kahn, M. 1990. Stone-faced ancestors: the spatial anchoring of myth in Wamira, Papua New Guinea. *Ethnology* 29, 51–66.

Karlsson, H. 1997. *Being and post-processual archaeological thinking.* Goteborg: Gotarc Serie C, Arkeologiska Skrifter no. 15.

Keen, T. 1990. Ecological community and species attributes in Yolngu religious symbolism. In R. Willis (ed.), *Signifying animals: human meaning in the natural world*, 85–102. London: Unwin Hyman.

Kennard, A. 1935. Mollusca. In W. Hemp, The chambered cairn known as Bryn yn Hen Bobl near Plas Newydd, Anglesey. *Archaeologia* 85, 253–92.

Kinnes, I. 1992. *Non-megalithic long barrows and allied structures in the British Neolithic.* London: British Museum.

Kirk, T. 1997. Towards a phenomenology of building: the Neolithic long mound at La Commune-Séche, Colombiers-sur-Seulles, Normandy. In G. Nash (ed.), *Semiotics of landscape: archaeology of mind*, 59–70. Oxford: British Archaeological Reports, International Series 661.

Knowles, F. 1909. Report on the human remains from the Ifton Limestone Quarries, near Newport, Mon. *Archaeologia Cambrensis* 9, 5–16.

Küchler, S. 1993. Landscape as memory: the mapping process and its representation in a Melanesian society. In B. Bender (ed.), *Landscape: politics and perspectives*, 85–106. Oxford: Berg.

Kuper, A. 1999. *Culture: the anthropologists' account.* Cambridge MA: Harvard University Press.

Lacaille, A. and Grimes, W. 1955. The prehistory of Caldey. *Archaeologia Cambrensis* 104, 85–165.

Lake, M., Woodman, P. and Mithen, S. 1998. Tailoring GIS software for archaeological applications: an example concerning viewshed analysis. *Journal of Archaeological Science* 25, 27–38.

Larsen, C. 1997. *Bioarchaeology: interpreting human behaviour from the human skeleton.* Cambridge: Cambridge University Press.

Leivers, M. 1999. *The architecture and context of mortuary practice in the Neolithic period in north Wales.* Unpublished Ph.D. thesis: University of Southampton.

Lewis, J. 1966. The standing stones of Pembrokeshire. *Pembrokeshire Historian* 2, 7–18.

Lewis, P. 1979. Axioms for reading the landscape: some guides to the American scene. In D. Meinig (ed.), *The interpretation of ordinary landscapes: geographical essays*, 11–32. Oxford: Oxford University Press.

Limbrey, S. and Evans, J. G. (eds) 1978. *The effect of man on the landscape: the lowland zone.* London: Council for British Archaeology.

Linnard, W. 2000. *Welsh woods and forests: a history.* Llandysul: Gomer Press.

Lowenthal, D. 1979. Age and artifact: dilemmas of appreciation. In D. Meinig (ed.), *The interpretation of ordinary landscapes: geographical essays*, 103–28. Oxford: Oxford University Press.

Lubbock, J. 1871. Description of the Parc Cwm tumulus. *Journal of the Ethnological Society of London* 2, 416.

Lynch, F. 1967. Barclodiad y Gawres. *Archaeologia Cambrensis* 116, 1–22.

Lynch, F. 1969a. The contents of excavated tombs in North Wales. In T. G. E. Powell, J. X. W. P. Corcoran, F. Lynch, and J. G. Scott, *Megalithic enquiries in the west of Britain*, 149–74. Liverpool: Liverpool University Press.

Lynch, F. 1969b. The megalithic tombs of north Wales. In T. G. E. Powell, J. X. W. P. Corcoran, F. Lynch, and J. G. Scott, *Megalithic enquiries in the west of Britain*, 107–48. Liverpool: Liverpool University Press.

Lynch, F. 1972. Portal dolmens in the Nevern Valley, Pembrokeshire. In F. Lynch and C. Burgess (eds), *Prehistoric man in Wales and the west*, 67–84. Bath: Adams and Dart.

Lynch, F. 1975a. Excavations at Carreg Samson megalithic tomb, Mathry, Pembrokeshire. *Archaeologia Cambrensis* 124, 15–35.

Lynch, F. 1975b. The impact of the landscape on prehistoric man. In J. Evans, S. Limbrey, and H. Cleere (eds), *The effect of man on the landscape: the highland zone*, 124–27. York: The Council for British Archaeology.

Lynch, F. 1976. Towards a chronology of megalithic tombs in Wales. In G. Boon and J. Lewis (eds), *Welsh antiquity: essays mainly on prehistoric topics presented to H. Savory*, 63–79. Cardiff: National Museum of Wales.

Lynch, F. 1984. The Neolithic pottery: discussion. In W. Britnell and H. Savory (eds), *Gwernvale and Penywyrlod: two Neolithic long cairns in the Black Mountains of Brecknock*, 106–10. Bangor: Cambrian Archaeological Association.

Lynch, F. 1991. *Prehistoric Anglesey: the archaeology of the island to the Roman conquest.* Llangefni: Anglesey Antiquarian Society.

Lynch, F. 1993. *Excavations in the Brenig Valley.* Aberystwyth: Cambrian.

Lynch, F. 1995. *Gwynydd: a guide to ancient and historic Wales.* Cardiff: CADW.

Lynch, F. 2000a. The earlier Neolithic. In F. Lynch, S. Aldhouse-Green, and J. Davies (eds), *Prehistoric Wales*, 42–78. Stroud: Sutton.

Lynch, F. 2000b. The later Neolithic and earlier Bronze Age. In F. Lynch, S. Aldhouse-Green, and J. Davies (eds), *Prehistoric Wales*, 79–138. Stroud: Sutton.

Lynch, F. 2002. A fresh look at Ystum Cegid Isaf megalithic tomb. *Archaeologia Cambrensis* 151, 207–13.

MacCormack, C. 1980. Nature, culture and gender: a critique. In C. MacCormack and M. Strathern (eds), *Nature, culture and gender*, 1–21. Cambridge: Cambridge University Press.

Martin, J. 2001. *The land looks after us: a history of native American religion.* Oxford: Oxford University Press.

Massey, D. 1995. The conceptualisation of place. In D. Massey and P. Jess (eds), *A place in the world?*, 45–86. Oxford: Oxford University Press.

Masters, L. 1973. The Lochhill long cairn. *Antiquity* 47, 96–100.

Masters, L. 1981. Chambered tombs and non-megalithic barrows in Britain. In J. Evans, B. Cunliffe and C. Renfrew (eds), *Antiquity and man*, 161–76. London: Thames and Hudson.

Matunga, H. 1994. Waahi tapu: Maori sacred sites. In D. Carmichael, J. Hubert, B. Reeves and A. Schande (eds), *Sacred sites, sacred places*, 217–26. London: Routledge.

Meinig, D. 1979a. The beholding eye: ten versions of the same scene. In D. Meinig (ed.), *The interpretation of ordinary landscapes: geographical essays*, 33–48. Oxford: Oxford University Press.

Meinig, D. 1979b. Introduction. In D. Meinig (ed.), *The interpretation of ordinary landscapes: geographical essays*, 1–7. Oxford: Oxford University Press.

Mellars, P. 1987. *Excavations on Oronsay.* Edinburgh: Edinburgh University Press.

Mercer, R. 1981. Excavations at Carn Brea, Illogan, Cornwall, 1970–73: a Neolithic fortified complex of the third millennium bc. *Cornish Archaeology* 20, 1–204.

Middleton, J. 1960. *Lugbara religion: ritual and authority among an East African people.* Oxford: Oxford University Press.

Miles, D. 2001. The Presely Hills. *Rural Wales* 2001, 14–15.

Mills, S. 2000. An approach for integrating multisensory data: the examples of Sesklo and the Teleorman Valley. In C. Buck, V. Cummings, C. Henley, S. Mills, and S. Trick (eds), *UK chapter of computer applications and quantitative methods in archaeology*, 27–38. Oxford: British Archaeological Reports, International Series 844.

Mills, S. 2002. *The significance of sound in fifth millennium cal. BC southern Romania: auditory archaeology in the Teleorman River Valley.* Unpublished Ph.D. Thesis: Cardiff University.

Mithen, S. 2000a. *Hunter-gatherer landscape archaeology: the Southern Hebrides Mesolithic project.* Oxford: Oxbow.

Mithen, S. 2000b. Mesolithic sedentism on Oronsay: chronological evidence from adjacent islands in the southern Hebrides. *Antiquity* 74, 298–304.

Mithen, S. and Lake, M. 1998. The distribution of Mesolithic sites on Islay: field survey. numerical classification and viewshed analysis. Paper given at the 1998 Mesolithic conference in Leicester.

Morgan, W. and Marshall, G. 1921. Excavation of a long barrow at Llanigon, Co. Brecon. *Archaeologia Cambrensis* 79, 296–9.

Morphy, H. 1993. Colonialism, history and the construction of place: the politics of landscape in northern Australia. In B. Bender (ed.), *Landscape: politics and perspectives*, 205–43. Oxford: Berg.

Morphy, H. 1995. Landscape and the reproduction of the ancestral past. In E. Hirsch and M. O'Hanlon (eds), *The anthropology of landscape: perspectives on place and space*, 184–209. Oxford: Oxford University Press.

Murphy, J. 1999. Archaeology as folklore: the literary construction of the megalith Pentre Ifan in west Wales. In A. Gazin-Schwartz and C. Holtorf (eds), *Archaeology and folklore*, 240–54. London: Routledge.

Murphy, K. 2001. A prehistoric field system and related monuments on St David's Head and Carn Llidi, Pembrokeshire. *Proceedings of the Prehistoric Society* 67, 85–100.

Musson, C. with Britnell, W. and Smith A. 1991. *The Breiddin hillfort: a later prehistoric settlement in the Welsh Marches*. London: Council for British Archaeology.

Nash, G. 1997. Monumentality and the landscape: the possible symbolic and political distribution of long chambered tombs around the Black Mountains, central Wales. In G. Nash (ed.), *Semiotics of landscape: archaeology of mind*, 17–30. Oxford: British Archaeological Reports, International Series 661.

O'Kelly, C. 1969. Bryn Celli Ddu. *Archaeologia Cambrensis* 118, 17–48.

Olding, F. 2000. *The prehistoric landscape of the eastern Black Mountains*. Oxford: British Archaeological Reports, British Series 297.

Olwig, K. 1993. Sexual cosmology: nation and landscape at the conceptual interstices of nature and culture: or what does landscape really mean? In B. Bender (ed.), *Landscape: politics and perspectives*, 307–43. Oxford: Berg.

O'Neil, B. St. 1937. Excavations at Breiddin Camp, Montgomeryshire, 1933–35. *Archaeologia Cambrensis* 92, 86–128.

O'Neil, B. St. 1942. Excavations at Ffridd Faldwyn Camp, Montgomery, 1937–39. *Archaeologia Cambrensis* 97, 1–57.

Oswald, A., Dyer, C. and Barber, M. 2001. *The creation of monuments: Neolithic causewayed enclosures in the British Isles*. London: English Heritage.

Ovsyannikov, O. and Terebikhin, N. 1990. Sacred space in the culture of the Arctic regions. In D. Carmichael, J. Hubert, B. Reeves and A. Schande (eds), *Sacred sites, sacred places*, 44–81. London: Routledge.

Parker Pearson, M. and Ramilisonina. 1998. Stonehenge for the ancestors: the stones pass on the message. *Antiquity* 72, 308–26.

Pearce, M., Garton, D. and Howard, A. 1997. Dumping the dead in the late Neolithic. Paper given at TAG Bournemouth, December 1997.

Peterson, R. 1999. *The construction and use of categories of Neolithic pottery from Wales*. Unpublished Ph.D. thesis: University of Southampton.

Phillips, C. W. 1936. An examination of the Ty Newydd chambered tomb, Llanfaelog, Anglesey. *Archaeologia Cambrensis* 91, 93–99.

Phillips, T. 2002. *Landscapes of the living, landscapes of the dead: the location of chambered cairns of northern Scotland*. Oxford: British Archaeological Reports, British Series 328.

Phillips, T. and Watson A. 2000. Chambered cairns and settlement: the living and the dead in northern Scotland, 3600–2000 BC. *Antiquity* 74, 786–92.

Piggott, S. 1954. *The Neolithic cultures of the British Isles*. Cambridge: Cambridge University Press.

Piggott, S. 1955. Windmill Hill – east or west? *Proceedings of the Prehistoric Society* 20, 96–101.

Pollard, J. 2000. Ancestral places in the Mesolithic landscape. *Archaeological Review from Cambridge* 17, 123–38.

Pollard, J. and Gillings, M. 1998. Romancing the stones. Towards a virtual and elemental Avebury. *Archaeological Dialogues* 2, 143–64.

Pollard, T. 1996. Time and tide: coastal environments, cosmology and ritual practice in early prehistoric Scotland. In T. Pollard and A. Morrison (eds), *The early prehistory of Scotland*, 198–210. Edinburgh: Edinburgh University Press.

Powell, T. G. E. 1963. The chambered cairn at Dyffryn Ardudwy. *Antiquity* 37, 19–24.

Powell, T. G. E. 1973. Excavations at the megalithic chambered cairn at Dyffryn Ardudwy, Merioneth, Wales. *Archaeologia* 104, 1–50.

Powell, T. G. E. and Daniel, G. E. 1956. *Barclodiad y Gawres: the excavation of a megalithic chamber tomb in Anglesey 1952–1953*. Liverpool: Liverpool University Press.

Powell, T. G. E., Corcoran, J. X. W. P., Lynch, F. and Scott, J. G. 1969. *Megalithic enquiries in the west of Britain*. Liverpool: Liverpool University Press.

Price, N. 1994. Tourism and the Bighorn Medicine Wheel: how multiple use does not work for sacred land sites. In D. Carmichael, J. Hubert, B. Reeves and A. Schande (eds), *Sacred sites, sacred places*, 259–64. London: Routledge.

Rackham, O. 1980. *Ancient woodland: its history, vegetation and uses in England*. London: Edward Arnold.

RCAHMW 1960. *Inventory of the ancient monuments in Caernarvonshire: vol 2, central: the cantref of Arfon and the commote of Eifionydd*. London: Her Majesty's Stationery Office.

RCAHMW 1964. *Inventory of the ancient monuments in Caernarvonshire: vol 3, west: the cantref of Lleyn, together with the general survey of the county*. London: Her Majesty's Stationery Office.

RCAHMW 1976. *An inventory of the ancient monuments in Glamorgan: vol 1: pre-Norman. Part 1: the stone and bronze ages*. Cardiff: Her Majesty's Stationery Office.

RCAHMW 1997. *An inventory of the ancient monuments in Brecknock (Brycheiniog): the prehistoric and Roman monuments*. Stroud: Sutton.

Rees, S. 1992. *A guide to ancient and historic Wales: Dyfed*. London: Her Majesty's Stationery Office.

Reeves, B. 1994. Ninaustákis – the Nitsitapii's sacred mountain: traditional native religious activities and land use/tourism conflicts. In D. Carmichael, J. Hubert, B. Reeves and A. Schande (eds), *Sacred sites, sacred places*, 265–95. London: Routledge.

Relph, E. 1989. Geographical experiences and being-in-the-world: the phenomenological origins of geography. In D. Seamon and R. Mugerauer (eds), *Dwelling, place and environment*, 15–32. New York: Columbia University Press.

Renfrew, C. 1976. Megaliths, territories and populations. In S. de Laet (ed.), *Acculturation and continuity in Atlantic Europe*, 98–220. Bruges: de Tempel.

Renfrew, C. 1979. *Investigations in Orkney*. London: Society of Antiquaries.

Richards, C. 1996a. Henges and water: towards an elemental

understanding of monumentality and landscape in late Neolithic Britain. *Journal of Material Culture* 2, 313–36.

Richards, C. 1996b. Monuments as landscape: creating the centre of the world in late Neolithic Orkney. *World Archaeology* 28, 190–208.

Richards, C. 2003. Labouring with monuments: constructing the dolmen at Carreg Samson, south-west Wales. In V. Cummings and C. Fowler (eds), *The Neolithic of the Irish Sea: materiality and traditions of practice*. Oxford: Oxbow.

Richards, M. 2000a. Human consumption of plant foods in the British Neolithic: direct evidence from bone stable isotopes. In A. Fairbairn (ed.), *Plants in Neolithic Britain and beyond*, 123–35. Oxford: Oxbow.

Richards, M. and Hedges, R. 1999. A Neolithic revolution? New evidence of diet in the British Neolithic. *Antiquity* 73, 891–7.

Richards, M. and Mellars, P. 1998. Stable isotopes and the seasonality of the Oronsay middens. *Antiquity* 72, 178–84.

Rival, L. 1998. Trees, from symbols of life and regeneration to political artefacts. In L. Rival (ed.), *The social life of trees: anthropological perspectives on tree symbolism*, 1–36. Oxford: Berg.

Rodaway, P. 1994. *Sensuous geographies*. London: Routledge.

Roese, H. 1982. Some aspects of topographical locations of Neolithic and Bronze Age monuments in Wales. *Bulletin of the Board of Celtic Studies* 29, 763–75.

Samuels, M. 1979. The biography of landscape: cause and culpability. In D. Meinig (ed.), *The interpretation of ordinary landscapes: geographical essays*, 51–88. Oxford: Oxford University Press.

Saville, A. 1990. *Hazleton North: the excavation of a Neolithic long cairn of the Cotswold-Severn group*. London: Historic Buildings and Monuments Commission, Archaeological Report 13.

Saville, A. 1994. Exploitation of lithic resources for stone tools in earlier prehistoric Scotland. In N. Ashton and A. David (eds), *Stories in stone*, 57–70. London: Lithic Studies Society.

Savory, H. 1956a. The excavation of the Pipton long cairn Brecknockshire. *Archaeologia Cambrensis* 105, 7–48.

Savory, H. 1956b. The excavation of 'Twlc-y-Filiast' cromlech, Llangynog, (Carm.). *Bulletin of the Board of Celtic Studies* 16, 300–308.

Savory, H. 1973. Pen-y-wyrlod: a new Welsh cairn. *Antiquity* 47, 187–92.

Savory, H. 1980. The Neolithic in Wales. In J. Taylor (ed.), *Culture and environment in prehistoric Wales*, 207–31. Oxford: British Archaeological Reports, British Series 76.

Scarre, C. 2002a. A pattern of islands: the Neolithic monuments of north-west Brittany. *European Journal of Archaeology* 5, 24–41.

Scarre, C. 2002b. Contexts of monumentalism: regional diversity at the Neolithic transition in north-west France. *Oxford Journal of Archaeology* 21, 23–61.

Schafer, R. M. 1989. Acoustic space. In D. Seamon and R. Mugerauer (eds), *Dwelling, place and environment*, 87–98. New York: Columbia University Press.

Schama, S. 1995. *Landscape and memory*. London: Harper Collins.

Schulting, R. 1996. Antlers, bone pins and flint blades: the Mesolithic cemeteries of Téviec and Hoëdic, Brittany. *Antiquity* 70, 335–50.

Schulting, R. 1998. *Slighting the sea: the Mesolithic-Neolithic transition in northwest Europe*. Unpublished Ph.D. thesis: Reading University.

Schulting, R. 2000. New AMS dates from the Lambourn long barrow and the question of the earliest Neolithic in southern England: repacking the Neolithic package? *Oxford Journal of Archaeology* 19, 25–35.

Schulting, R. and Richards, M. 1999. Stable isotope evidence for similarities in the types of marine foods used by late Mesolithic humans at sites along the Atlantic coast of Europe. *Journal of Archaeological Science* 26, 717–22.

Schulting, R. and Richards, M. 2001. Dating women and becoming farmers: new AMS and stable isotope evidence from the Breton Mesolithic cemeteries of Téviec and Hoëdic. *Journal of Anthropological Archaeology* 20, 314–44.

Schulting, R. and Richards, M. 2002. Finding the coastal Mesolithic in southwest Britain: AMS dates and stable isotope results on human remains from Caldey Island, south Wales. *Antiquity* 76, 1011–25.

Scott, W. 1933. The chambered tomb of Pant y Saer, Anglesey. *Archaeologia Cambrensis* 38, 185–228.

Scourse, J. 1997. Transport of the Stonehenge bluestones: testing the glacial hypothesis. In B. Cunliffe and C. Renfrew (eds), *Science and Stonehenge*, 271–314. Oxford: Oxford University Press.

Shanks, M. 1992. *Experiencing the past: on the character of archaeology*. London: Routledge.

Sharples, N. 2000. Antlers and Orcadian rituals: an ambiguous role for red deer in the Neolithic. In A. Ritchie (ed.), *Neolithic Orkney in its European context*, 107–16. Oxford: Oxbow.

Sheridan, A. 1986. Porcellanite artefacts: a new survey. *Ulster Journal of Archaeology* 49, 19–32.

Sheridan, A. 2000. Achnacreebeag and its French connections: vive the 'Auld Alliance'. In J. Henderson (ed.), *The prehistory and early history of Atlantic Europe*, 1–15. Oxford: British Archaeological Reports, International Series 861.

Simmons, I. 1993a. *Interpreting nature: cultural constructions of the environment*. London: Routledge.

Simmons, I. 1993b. Vegetation change during the Mesolithic in the British Isles: some amplifications. In F. Chambers (ed.), *Climate change and human impact on the landscape*, 109–118. London: Chapman and Hall.

Smith, A. and Cloutman, E. 1988. Reconstruction of Holocene vegetation history in three dimensions at Waun-Fignen-Felen, an upland site in south Wales. *Philosophical Transactions of the Royal Society of London B* 322, 159–219.

Smith, A. and Morgan, L. 1989. A succession to ombrotrophic bog in the Gwent Levels, and its demise: a Welsh parallel to the Somerset Levels. *New Phytologist* 122, 145–69.

Smith, C. and Lynch, F. 1987. *Trefignath and Din Dryfol: the excavation of two megalithic tombs in Anglesey*. Bangor: Cambrian Archaeological Association.

Smith, I. 1979. The chronology of British stone implements. In T. Clough and W. Cummins (eds), *Stone axe studies*, 13–22. London: Council for British Archaeology.

Smith, J. 1993. The lie that binds: destabilizing the text of landscape. In J. Duncan and D. Ley (eds), *Place/culture/representation*, 78–92. London: Routledge.

Strathern, M. 1980. No nature, no culture: the Hagen case. In C. MacCormack and M. Strathern (eds), *Nature, culture and gender*, 174–219. Cambridge: Cambridge University Press.

Strathern, M. 1987. Introduction. In M. Strathern (ed.), *Dealing with inequality: analysing gender relations in Melanesia and beyond*, 1–32. Cambridge: Cambridge University Press.

Strathern, M. 1995. The nice thing about culture is that everyone has it. In M. Strathern (ed.), *Shifting contexts*, 153–76. London: Routledge.

Sundstrom, L. 1996. Mirror of heaven: cross-cultural transference of the sacred geography of the Black Hills. *World Archaeology* 28, 177–89.

Taçon, P. 1991. The power of stone: symbolic aspects of stone use and tool development in Western Arnhem Land, Australia. *Antiquity* 65, 192–207.

Theodoratus, D. and LaPena, F. 1994. Wintu sacred geography of northern California. In D. Carmichael, J. Hubert, B. Reeves and A. Schanche (eds), *Sacred sites, sacred places*, 20–31. London: Routledge.

Thomas, J. 1991. *Rethinking the Neolithic*. Cambridge: Cambridge University Press.

Thomas, J. 1993a. After essentialism: archaeology, geography and post-modernity. *Archaeological Review from Cambridge* 12, 3–27.

Thomas, J. 1993b. The politics of vision and the archaeologies of landscape. In B. Bender (ed.), *Landscape: politics and perspectives*, 19–48. Oxford: Berg.

Thomas, J. 1996. *Time, culture and identity: an interpretive archaeology*. London: Routledge.

Thomas, J. 1999. *Understanding the Neolithic*. London: Routledge.

Thomas, J. 2001. Neolithic enclosures: reflections on excavations on Wales and Scotland. In T. Darvill and J. Thomas (eds), *Neolithic enclosures in Atlantic northwest Europe*, 132–43. Oxford: Oxbow.

Thomas, J. and Tilley, C. 1993. The axe and the torso: symbolic structures in the Neolithic of Brittany. In C. Tilley (ed.), *Interpretative archaeology*, 225–72. Oxford: Berg.

Thorpe, R., Williams-Thorpe, O., Jenkins, D. and Watson, J. 1991. The geological sources and transportation of the bluestones from Stonehenge, Wiltshire, UK. *Proceedings of the Prehistoric Society* 57, 103–58.

Tilley, C. 1993. Art, architecture, landscape (Neolithic Sweden). In B. Bender (ed.), *Landscape: politics and perspectives*, 49–84. Oxford: Berg.

Tilley, C. 1994. *A phenomenology of landscape*. Oxford: Berg.

Tilley, C. 1996. The powers of rocks: topography and monument construction on Bodmin Moor. *World Archaeology* 28, 161–76.

Tilley, C. 1998. Megaliths in text. In M. Edmonds and C. Richards (eds), *Understanding the Neolithic of north-western Europe*, 141–60. Glasgow: Cruithne Press.

Tilley, C. and Bennett, W. 2001. An archaeology of supernatural places: the case of West Penwith. *Journal of the Royal Anthropological Institute* 7, 335–62.

Tilley, C., Hamilton, S., Harrison, S. and Anderson, E. 2000. Nature, culture, clitter. *Journal of Material Culture* 5, 197–224.

Toren, C. 1995. Seeing the ancestral sites: transformations in Fijian notions of the land. In E. Hirsch and M. O'Hanlon (eds), *The anthropology of landscape: perspectives on place and space*, 163–83. Oxford: Oxford University Press.

Tresset, A. and Vigne, J. D. forthcoming. Le dépôt d'animaux de la structure et d'Er Grah: une illustration de la symbolique des bovins à la charnière du Mésolithique et du Néolithique bretons? *Gallia Préhistoire*.

Tuan, Y. 1977. *Space and place: the perspective of experience*. London: Edward Arnold.

Tuan, Y. 1978. Space, time, place: a humanistic frame. In T. Carlstein, D. Parkes and N. Thrift (eds), *Timing space and spacing time: making sense of time*, 7–16. London: Edward Arnold.

Vulliamy, C. 1921. The excavation of a megalithic tomb in Breconshire. *Archaeologia Cambrensis* 76, 300–305.

Vulliamy, C. 1923. Further excavations in the long barrows at Ffostill. *Archaeologia Cambrensis* 78, 320–4.

Vulliamy, C. 1929. Excavation of an unrecorded long barrow in Wales. *Man* 29, 34–6.

Vyner, B. 1984. The excavation of a Neolithic cairn at Street House, Loftus, Cleveland. *Proceedings of the Prehistoric Society* 50, 151–96.

Vyner, B. 2001. Clegyr Boia: a potential Neolithic enclosure and associated monuments on the St David's peninsula, southwest Wales. In T. Darvill and J. Thomas (eds), *Neolithic enclosures in Atlantic northwest Europe*, 78–90. Oxford: Oxbow.

Wagner, R. 1978. *Lethal speech: Daribi myth as symbolic obviation*. New York: Cornell University Press.

Wainwright, A. 1960. *The southern fells: a pictorial guide to the Lakeland fells*. Kendal: Westmoreland Gazette.

Wainwright, A. 1982. *A north Wales sketchbook*. Kendal: Westmorland Gazette.

Wainwright, G. 1967. *Coygan camp: a prehistoric, Romano-British and Dark Age settlement in Carmarthenshire*. Cardiff: Cambrian Archaeological Association.

Ward, A. 1976. The cairns on Mynydd Llangynderyn: a focal point of the early Bronze Age in SE Dyfed. *The Carmarthenshire Antiquary* 12, 3–21.

Ward, J. 1915. The St Nicholas chambered tumulus, Glamorgan. *Archaeologia Cambrensis* 15, 253–320.

Ward, J. 1916. The St Nicholas chambered tumulus, Glamorgan, part two. *Archaeologia Cambrensis* 16, 239–67.

Ward, J. 1918. Some sepulchral remains near Pendine, Carmarthenshire. *Archaeologia Cambrensis* 18, 35–79.

Waterson, R. 2000. House, place and memory in Tana Toraja (Indonesia). In R. Joyce and S. Gillespie (eds), *Beyond kinship: social and material reproduction in house societies*, 117–88. Philadelphia: University of Pennsylvania Press.

Watson, A. 2000. *Encircled space: the experience of stone circles and henges in the British Neolithic*. Unpublished Ph.D. thesis: Reading University.

Weiner, J. 1988. *The heart of the pearl shell: the mythological dimension of Foi sociality*. Berkeley: University of California Press.

Wheatley, D., Earle, G. and Poppy, S. (eds) 2002. *Contemporary themes in archaeological computing*. Oxford: Oxbow.

Wheatley, D. and Gillings, M. 2000. Vision, perception and GIS: developing enriched approaches to the study of archaeological visibility. In G. Lock and K. Brown (eds), *On the theory and practice of archaeological computing*. Oxford: Oxbow.

Whitley, D. 1998. Finding rain in the desert: landscape, gender and far western North American rock-art. In C. Chippindale and P. Taçon (eds), *The archaeology of rock art*, 11–29. Cambridge: Cambridge University Press.

Whittle, A. 1991. Wayland's Smithy, Oxfordshire: excavations at the Neolithic tomb in 1962–3 by R. J. C. Atkinson and S. Piggott. *Proceedings of the Prehistoric Society* 57, 61–102.

Whittle, A. 1996. *Europe in the Neolithic: the creation of new worlds*. Cambridge: Cambridge University Press.

Whittle, A. 1997. Moving on and moving around: Neolithic settlement mobility. In P. Topping (ed.), *Neolithic landscapes*, 15–22. Oxford: Oxbow.

Whittle, A. 2000. 'Very like a whale': menhirs, motifs and myths in the Mesolithic-Neolithic transition of north-west Europe. *Cambridge Archaeological Journal* 10, 243–59.

Whittle, A. 2003a. *The archaeology of people: dimensions of Neolithic life*. London: Routledge.

Whittle, A. 2003b. Stones that float to the sky: portal dolmens and their landscapes of memory and myth. In V. Cummings and C. Fowler (eds), *The Neolithic of the Irish Sea: materiality and traditions of practice*. Oxford: Oxbow.

Whittle, A., Pollard, J. and Grigson, C. 1999. *The harmony of symbols: the Windmill Hill causewayed enclosure*. Oxford: Oxbow.

Whittle, A. and Wysocki, M. 1998. Parc le Breos Cwm transepted long cairn, Gower, west Glamorgan: date, contents and context. *Proceedings of the Prehistoric Society* 64, 139–82.

Whittle, E. 1992. *A guide to ancient and historic Wales: Glamorgan and Gwent*. Cardiff: CADW.

Williams, A. 1940. A megalithic tomb at Nicholaston, Gower, Glamorgan. *Proceedings of the Prehistoric Society* 6, 178–81.

Williams, A. 1953. Clegyr Boia, St. David's (Pemb.): excavation in 1943. *Archaeologia Cambrensis* 102, 20–47.

Williams, H. 1999. Placing the dead: investigating the location of wealthy barrow burials in seventh century England. In M. Rundkvist (ed.), *Grave matters*, 57–86. Oxford: British Archaeological Reports, International Series 781.

Woodman, P. 2000. Beyond significant patterns towards past intentions: the location of Orcadian chambered tombs. In C. Buck, V. Cummings, C. Henley, S. Mills and S. Trick (eds), *UK chapter of computer applications and quantitative methods in archaeology*, 91–105. Oxford: British Archaeological Reports, International Series 844.

Woodman, P., Anderson, E. and Finlay, N. 1999. *Excavation at Ferriter's Cove, 1983–95: last foragers, first farmers in the Dingle peninsula*. Bray: Wordwell.

Wordsworth, W. 1798. Lines composed a few miles above Tintern Abbey, on revisiting the banks of the Wye during a tour, July 13, 1798. In J. Stillinger (ed.), *Selected poems and prefaces by William Wordsworth*. Boston: Houghton Mifflin.

Wysocki, M. and Whittle, A. 2000. Diversity, lifestyles and rites: new biological and archaeological evidence from British earlier Neolithic mortuary assemblages. *Antiquity* 74, 591–601.

Yates, A. 2000. Ewenny, Beech Court Farm prehistoric enclosure. *Archaeology in Wales* 40, 89.

Yates, M. 1989. *Dyffryn chambered tomb*. CADW booklet.

Yates, M. and Jones, M. 1991. Excavation and conservation at Capel Garmon chambered tomb, Betws-y-Coed, Gwynedd, 1989. *Archaeology in Wales* 31, 1–5.

Yates, M. 1996. *Capel Garmon chambered tomb*. CADW booklet.

Yates, M. and Longley, D. 2001. *Anglesey: a guide to ancient monuments on the Isle of Anglesey*. Cardiff: CADW.

Zilhão, J. 2000. From the Mesolithic to the Neolithic in the Iberian peninsula. In T. Price (ed.), *Europe's first farmers*, 144–82. Cambridge: Cambridge University Press.

8 Inventory

Vicki Cummings

Introduction

This inventory provides a list of all the chambered tombs in Wales which were included in this study. This includes most of the definite monuments which have remains surviving on the ground. A few sites were omitted, primarily because their status as a Neolithic monument was in question, or they have not yet produced megalithic remains (such as the newly discovered long barrows at Lower Luggy: Gibson 1994b). An exception to this is Cross Lodge, included because it features in previous discussions of landscape setting (Cummings *et al.* 2002; Tilley 1994). A few sites that have been destroyed but are well documented are also included here, but we have not included most doubtful and probable sites: inventories of all sites including possible and doubtful sites can be found elsewhere:

> **North Wales**: Leivers 1999; Lynch 1969a; 1969b.
> **South-west Wales**: Barker 1992.
> **South-east Wales**: Corcoran 1969.

The inventory is listed by county, starting in north Wales. The county names, however, refer to the old Welsh counties (see Fig. 8.1) and not the more recent unitary authorities. We have chosen to list the monuments in this way as the codes for each monument (e.g. MON 1 = Monmouthshire 1) are based on these earlier counties.

The description of each site is not exhaustive but includes all key information. In particular if a site has been excavated, all the details are not included, but we list all the references for each site at the bottom of the entry. A plan is provided for most sites. Finally we describe the landscape setting of each monument and include, in most cases, a simple schematic diagram which depicts the landscape visible from the monument. At sites where it was not possible to produce a landscape schematic (for example if modern features such as houses obscured the view), a GIS viewshed is included instead. Viewsheds from all sites can be found online at:

http://www.cf.ac.uk/hisar/people/vc/megaliths/megaliths.html

For each site we give the name of the site as it is now commonly known and referred to in the literature, the sites classification code and the national grid reference. For information on access to those sites which are open to the public, the regional CADW guidebooks can be consulted: Burnham 1995; Lynch 1995; Rees 1992; E. Whittle 1992. Distribution maps are located in the main text (Figs 4.1, 5.1 and 6.1)

ANGLESEY

1   Trefignath
2   Presaddfed
3   Ty Newydd
4   Barclodiad y Gawres
5   Din Dryfol
6   Bodowyr
7   Bryn Celli Ddu
8   Bryn yr Hen Bobl
9   Plas Newydd
10 Ty Mawr
11 Hen Drefor
12 Glyn
13 Pant y Saer
14 Lligwy
15 Trearddur
16 Perthiduon

The following texts discuss the monuments of Anglesey. Some of these also have more detailed information on individual sites and these are listed at the end of each entry where relevant: Craster 1953; Daniel 1950; Grimes 1936; Leivers 1999; Lynch 1969a; 1969b; 1976; 1991; 1995; 2000a; 2000b; Yates and Longley 2001.

8 Inventory

Figure 8.1 Map of Wales showing pre-1974 counties in Wales (after Archaeology in Wales).

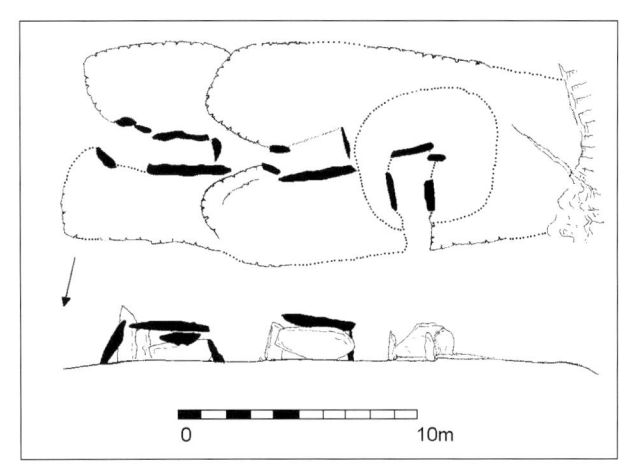

Figure 8.2 Plan and elevation and elevation of Trefignath (after Smith and Lynch 1987).

1. Trefignath (ANG 1) SH 259 806

Description: Set on top of a rocky outcrop at 20m OD in the midst of grazing land, the landscape that surrounds this monument is rather different to that of the rest of Anglesey. This is a landscape of rocky outcrops and knolls. One of the most distinctive features of this site is the outcrop over which the monument is built. The east and west chambers are well preserved, but the middle chamber is badly damaged. The site has been excavated (Smith and Lynch 1987) which revealed a multi-phase construction. The remains of hearths and a small assemblage of finds suggest that there was pre-cairn occupation of the site. The first chamber is the western chamber which was set within a small round cairn over a hollow in the outcrop (Smith and Lynch 1987, 11). A radiocarbon date from the old ground surface suggests that this chamber was built 3750–3500 BC (HAR-3932). The middle chamber was constructed next and the cairn was also enlarged to a wedge-shaped long cairn or platform incorporating both chambers. Finally the eastern chamber was constructed in the forecourt of the central chamber and the cairn or platform was extended. An arc of stakeholes and a pit were found in the forecourt of the eastern chamber. All the chambers had been robbed out in antiquity, although some secondary finds were recovered including Grooved Ware and flint (Smith and Lynch 1987, 26).

Landscape setting: This site has clear and impressive views out over Holyhead Mountain; this may have been an important local landmark. There are also wide views out over Holyhead Bay and Carmel Head. Trearddur is visible 500m to the south. However, much of the view is now obscured by the nearby aluminium factory and trees. However, it is still possible to see the mountains of Snowdonia on a clear day to the south and east of the site. The chambers also seem to be carefully positioned so that there are quite contrasting views along the axis. This is particularly pronounced with the largest and final chamber at the site. As you approach the portal stones of this chamber Holyhead Mountain is visible just above the capstone. To the left the view is restricted while to the right there are wide views out over the sea. This is particularly interesting given the fact that the portal stones are not aligned on the main axis of the chamber, instead being set at an angle.

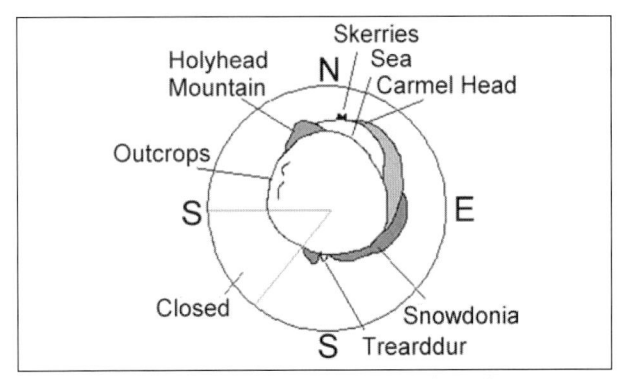

Figure 8.3 The setting of Trefignath.

References: Lynch 1969b, 113–5; Lynch 1991, 330–4; Lynch 1995, 10–11; Smith and Lynch 1987.

2. Presaddfed (ANG 2) SH 348 809

Description: Set in the middle of a pasture at 45m OD, this site is only a short distance from Llyn Llywenan lake. Apart from Din Dryfol it is the most inland of all the monuments on Anglesey. The larger of the two chambers is well-preserved although it has a wooden support to hold up the capstone. It consists of four uprights and a capstone. The second chamber has collapsed with the capstone leaning against two supporting stones. One of the most interesting features of this monument is that it is made from two different stone types. One is local as evidenced by a nearby outcrop and this is very similar to the stone used to construct Trefignath. Some of the uprights are conglomerates with large pebbles and quartz inclusions. Lynch (1969b) suggests that this site may have been a multi-phase monument like Trefignath.

Landscape setting: 'Its position in the bottom of a valley is unusual' (Lynch 1995, 11). The site is presently surrounded by trees and hedges in all directions. However, there would have been views out to the mountains of the Lleyn Peninsula, as well as a view of the sea to the northwest.

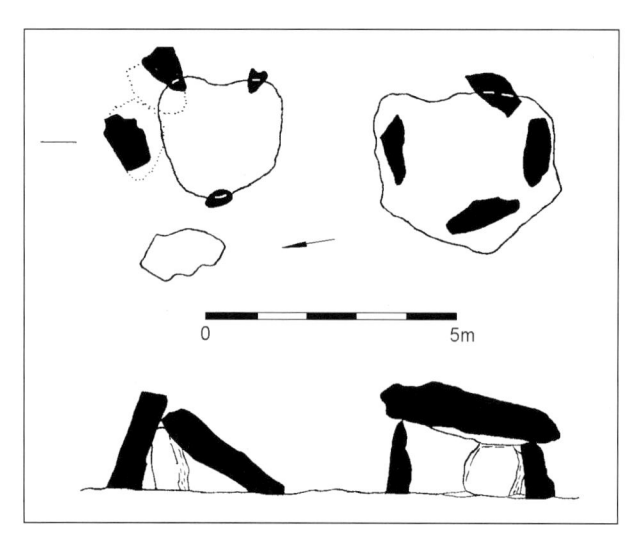

Figure 8.4 Plan and elevation of Presaddfed (after Lynch 1969b).

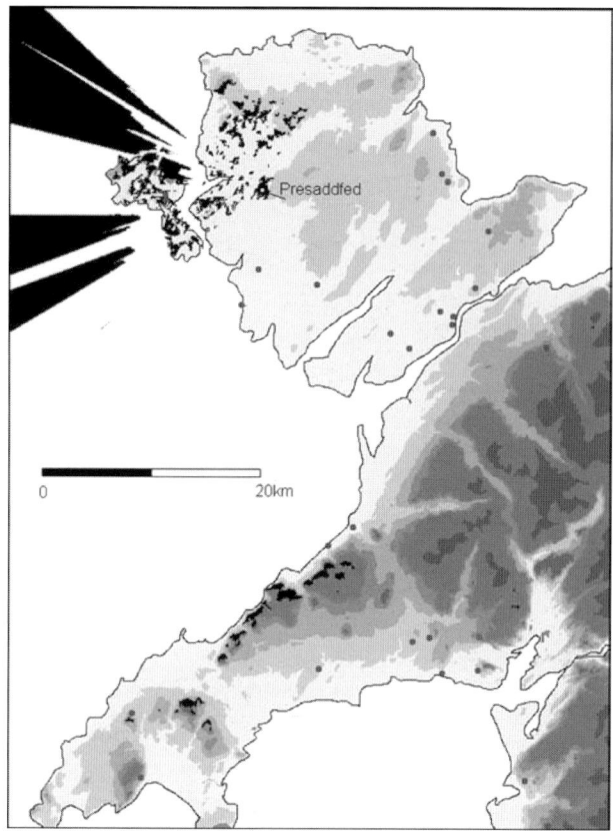

Figure 8.5 The viewshed from Presaddfed. Reproduced by kind permission of Ordnance Survey. © Crown copyright NC/03/20516.

References: Lynch 1969b, 123; Lynch 1991, 86–7; Lynch 1995, 11.

3. Ty Newydd (ANG 3) SH 344 738

Description: Set at 35m OD in the corner of an agricultural field a few kilometres inland from the coastline near Rhosneigr, this site has been badly damaged in the last few hundred years. It is set on top of an outcrop which is now completely grassed over. It has been claimed that the capstone broke in two when the tenant farmer lit a fire on top of the monument (Phillips 1936). The chamber survives as a combination of the original uprights and modern props, and the capstone is partly missing. Nevertheless, this would once have been an impressive site. Like Presaddfed, the chamber is made from two different stone types, a Ordovician pebbly sandstone and a single quartzite stone. The site was excavated in 1935 and beach pebbles, broken white quartz, flint flakes, a barbed and tang arrowhead, a chip of a polished axe and Beaker pottery were found. A spread of charcoal marked out the chamber area. Earlier accounts suggest that another chamber or possibly a passage survived here as well as a cairn (Daniel 1950, 185) and the excavator claimed a passage was found (Phillips 1936).

Landscape setting: The landscape setting of this site is quite spectacular. There are clear views out to sea to the west and views of Caergybi and Holyhead mountain to the WNW. There are wide views out over northern Anglesey to the north and also really clear views of mountains to the SE. There is a restricted view to the SW.

Figure 8.6 Plan and elevation of Ty Newydd (after Lynch 1991).

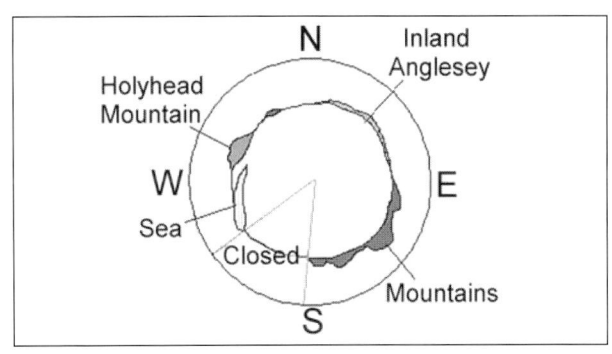

Figure 8.7 The setting of Ty Newydd.

References: Lynch 1969b, 116–7; Lynch 1991, 63–5; Lynch 1995, 13; Phillips 1936.

4. Barclodiad y Gawres (ANG 4) SH 329 707

Description: This monument is set on the end of a headland at 10m OD on the western side of Anglesey next to the harbour of Porth Trecastle. It has wide views out over the sea and the rocky coastline, and is located in a very different position to all other chambered tombs in the area. The site is very well preserved, with the chamber contained within a modern concrete dome. The entire chamber and passage survive. A number of the stones are decorated with a variety of rock art styles including spirals, chevrons and lozenges (Lynch 1967). Structurally the site is perhaps comparable only to Bryn Celli Ddu in Wales, although there are similarities with the Boyne Valley monuments in Ireland (Lynch 1969b, 110; Powell and Daniel 1956, 31). The monument has been described as a cruciform passage grave and has been fully excavated (Powell and Daniel 1956). At the centre of the chamber a hearth was found which had had a deposit containing wrasse, eel, whiting, frog, toad, natterjack, grass snake, mouse, shrew and rabbit bones poured over it. A deposit of limpet and oyster shells over which was a layer of small flat stones covered this. The southern end of the chamber had been robbed but did contain fragments of bone and charcoal. The western side chamber contained the cremated remains of two individuals with bone pins. The passage contained a small niche where a pillar of friable rock was found (Powell and Daniel 1956, 13). Pebbles of shale were found on the floor of the passage.

Landscape setting: The site is located on a headland, and there are wide views out to sea. The excavators noted that on a very clear day it is possible to see the Wicklow Hills 70 miles away (110 kilometres) to the west (Powell and Daniel 1956, 2). Because the site has been reconstructed, it is difficult to estimate how high the original mound would have been and therefore which mountains would have been visible on the horizon from the top of the cairn. The landscape panorama presented below is an estimation of the view, taken about half-way up the present artificial mound. However, standing lower down on what would have been the base of the mound, some of the mountains depicted disappear. Interestingly, the mountains in the Snowdon range are those that disappear from view, while those on the Lleyn peninsula remain visible around the site. There is also a clear view of Holyhead Mountain. Furthermore, standing at the back of the cairn it is possible to see the nearby harbour which the excavators claimed would have been one of the safest harbours on Anglesey (Powell and Daniel 1956). Standing at the entrance to the passage, however, this view is obscured by an outcrop. In addition, standing at the entrance gives a completely different perspective of the surrounding landscape as the views of most of the mountains are blocked from view. Approaching the monument by land the monument is continually skylined. Sometimes it disappears from view but always reappears on the horizon.

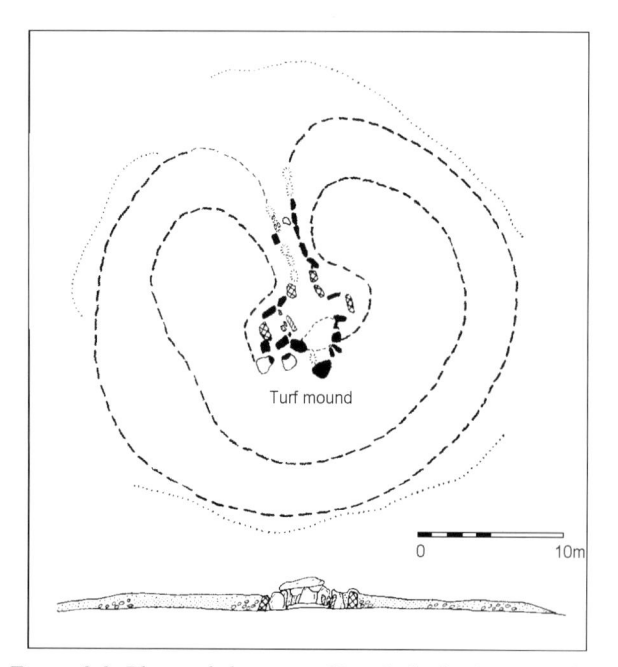

Figure 8.8 Plan and elevation of Barclodiad y Gawres (after Lynch 1969b).

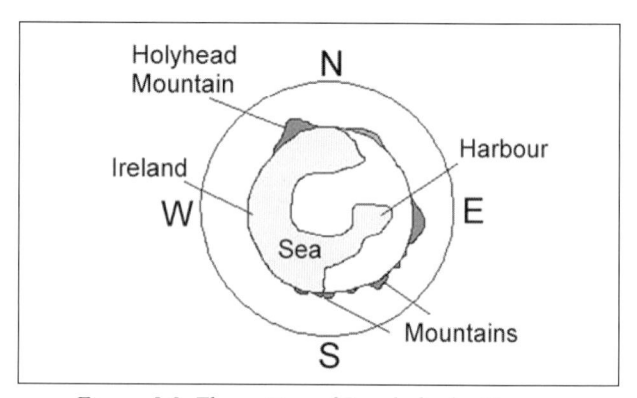

Figure 8.9 The setting of Barclodiad y Gawres.

References: Daniel and Powell 1949, 169–87; Lynch 1967, 1–22; Powell and Daniel 1956; Lynch 1969b, 110–11; Lynch 1991, 70–8; Lynch 1995, 11–12.

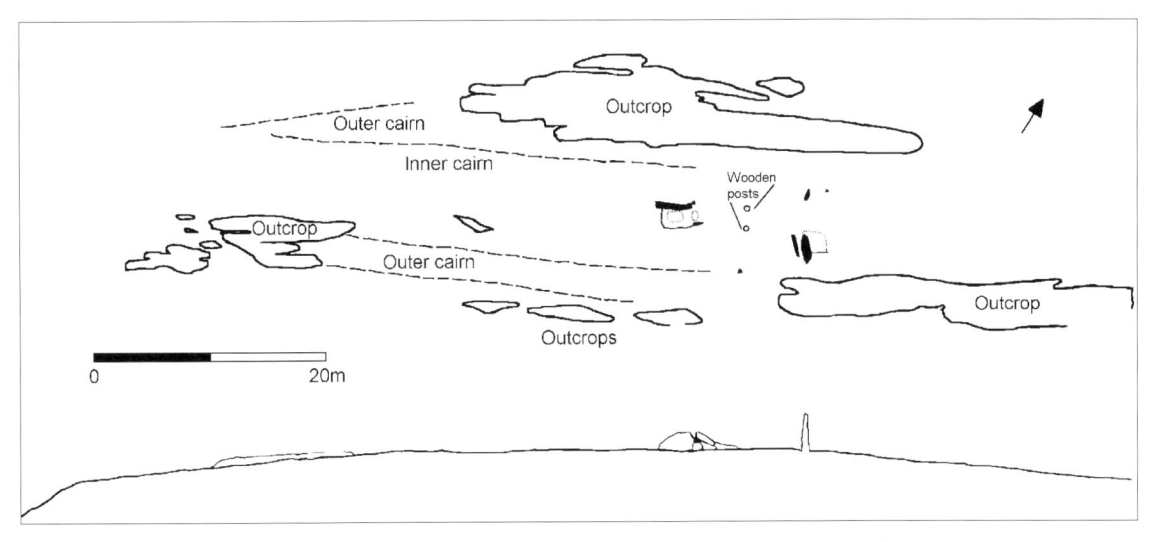

Figure 8.10 Plan and elevation of Din Dryfol (after Lynch 1991).

5. Din Dryfol   (ANG 5) SH 396 725

Description: This monument is located right up against a large rock outcrop in an area literally covered in rock outcrops at 45m OD. There are a series of prominent outcrops to the west and the site lies along the axis of a long thin outcrop just a few metres to the west of the chamber. A single chamber survives which has collapsed. In addition, what is described as part of a façade also survives, but these stones are really large, much larger than any of the stones used in the façades found along the eastern side of the Irish Sea. Structurally, the site is enigmatic, even after excavation (Smith and Lynch 1987). None of the stones were set in stone holes so the site remains difficult to reconstruct. It seems that the surviving western chamber (chamber 4) was constructed in the first phase, with the subsequent addition of a second chamber (chamber 3) with wooden entrance posts to the east. These two posts were removed before they rotted away, perhaps for the construction of another chamber (chamber 2). An additional chamber (1) may have been placed behind the portal stones, or perhaps a short passage stood there instead. The entire monument is set within a long thin cairn. The western chamber produced the cremated remains of two individuals plus flint. Pottery was also recovered from the site and is similar to that found at Dyffryn Ardudwy and Clegyr Boia. A burnt and broken polished stone axe was found in chamber 2 (Smith and Lynch 1987, 120).

Landscape setting: What is perhaps the most surprising aspect of the setting of this monument is that it has no long distance views in any direction. All views are of the local topography. Slightly over half of the view is completely restricted by the large outcrop that the site stands against. From the SSW to the NNE, the view looks out over other outcrops in the immediate vicinity. The viewshed analysis demonstrates that the sea is also visible to the SW. The outcrop on which the monument stands is the most visually distinctive of all of these outcrops, and it also means that if one approached from the east or south, the monument would be highly visible beneath the outcrop. This is in marked contrast to the rock-cut tombs of Pembrokeshire which blend into the outcrops under which they sit. The presence of the long rounded boulder next to the chambers must be significant.

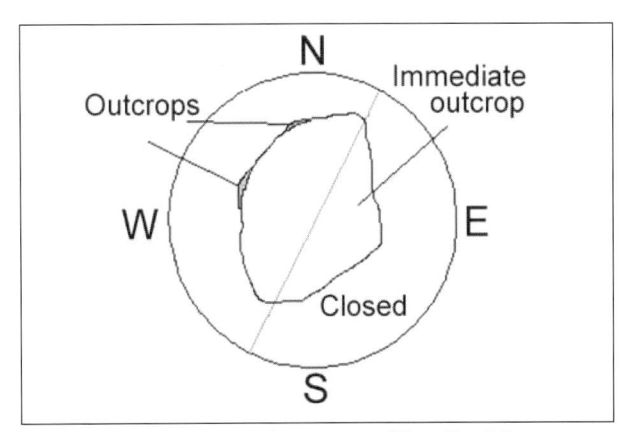

Figure 8.11 The setting of Din Dryfol.

References: Lynch 1991, 334–8; Lynch 1995, 13–14; Smith and Lynch 1987.

6. Bodowyr (ANG 6) SH 463 682

Description: Set at 35m OD almost on the summit of a gentle hill this site is set in rich agricultural land on the southern side of Anglesey. There are no distinctive features of note around the site although stone walls nearby suggest that there may have once been outcrops in the area. The site survives as a large triangular capstone on top of four uprights. There is a sill stone to the east which may originally have divided the chamber from a small passage (Lynch 1995, 14). The site has never been excavated.

Landscape setting: The landscape setting of the site is quite spectacular with wide and clear views of all the mountains in the Snowdon range from the east round to the south. There are also views of some of the northern Lleyn mountains to the south. There is a small restricted view to the SW. WSW to N the view is also restricted, at which point one can see out across northern Anglesey. If one were to approach and enter the monument along the axis of the passage, the view to the left would have been completely restricted while the view to the right looked out over the high mountains of Snowdon: a complete contrast.

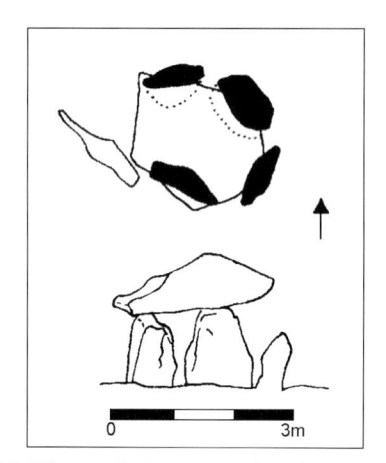

Figure 8.12 Plan and elevation of Bodowyr (after Lynch 1969b).

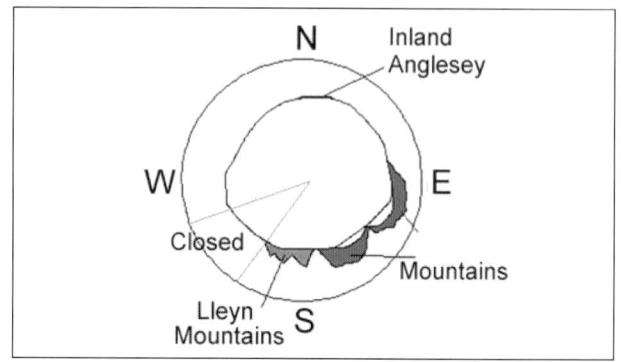

Figure 8.13 The setting of Bodowyr.

References: Lynch 1969b, 116–7; Lynch 1991, 63–4; Lynch 1995, 14.

7. Bryn Celli Ddu (ANG 7) SH 508 702

Description: This passage grave is located at 30m OD in gently rolling farmland. Plas Newydd is located just over 1km to the east. The landscape around the site is reasonably featureless except for a large domed outcrop to the west. The sea is only 1.5km away yet it cannot be seen and the site feels as if it is inland. The site has been partly restored and is well preserved although the main chamber has concrete beams. The decorated slab at the rear of the chamber is a replica, and the original can be seen in the National Museum in Cardiff. The site was excavated in the 1920s which revealed a series of different phases at this site. The first phase seems to have been the construction of a henge (or related) monument, consisting of a bank and ditch and a circle of stones (O'Kelly 1969). A number of the stones were associated with human remains and quartz. At a later date (enough time had passed for the ditch to silt up and be covered with turf) a passage grave was constructed. This was covered with a mound and bounded by a kerb of stones. Finally, the passage and entrance were blocked. When excavated the chamber had been severely disturbed by previous activity and although antiquaries report that the chamber was originally filled with bone, only a few pieces were found during the excavations. The chamber and passage also contained flint arrowheads, quartz pebbles and sea-shells. A large dressed pillar was also found in the chamber (Hemp 1930). Two hearths were found to flank the entrance as well as a cremation deposit. In the forecourt area postholes marked out a small enclosure which framed a pit containing an ox burial. At the rear of the chamber another ritual pit was found which had been burnt and contained a burnt human right ear-bone (Hemp 1930, 196). Next to this pit was a recumbent decorated slab.

Landscape setting: 'The siting of Bryn Celli Ddu close to the river on fairly level land is appropriate to a henge complex' (Lynch 1991, 101). This site is located with wide views in most directions. Most significantly there is no restricted view in any direction although the views from the east to the south are wider, looking out over mountains. Most of the monuments on Anglesey have quite specific views of Snowdonia, with the pass from Betws y Coed to Bangor clearly visible, but this pass is not visible from Bryn Celli Ddu. This site also has views of the sea but not of the Menai Straits.

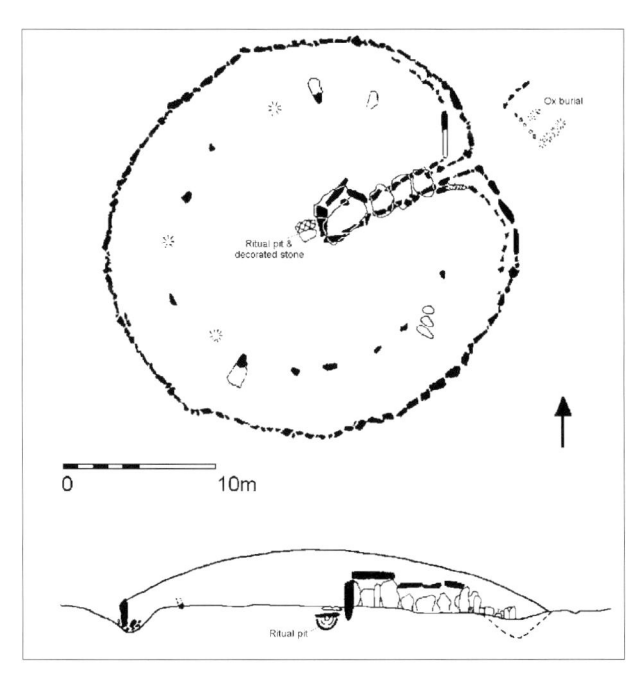

Figure 8.14 Plan and elevation of Bryn Celli Ddu (after Lynch 1969b).

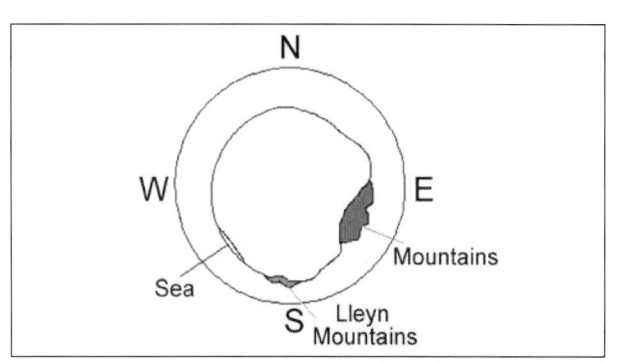

Figure 8.15 The setting of Bryn Celli Ddu.

References: Daniel and Powell 1949; Eogan 1983; Hemp 1930; Lynch 1969b, 110–12; Lynch 1991, 93–101; Lynch 1995, 14–16; O'Kelly 1969.

110　　　　　　　　　　　　　　　　　　　　　　　　　　　*Vicki Cummings*

8. Bryn yr Hen Bobl (ANG 8) SH 519 690

Description: Set at 35m OD in agricultural land above the Menai Straits, this monument survives as a large grassy mound with a poorly preserved chamber visible. The mound has several trees growing on it and the terrace is only just visible to the south. The site was excavated in the 1920s and 1930s (Hemp 1935) and revealed a complex structure. The single chamber had a forecourt to the west and although the stone which covers the entranceway to the chamber has two natural holes in it (now broken), it would not have been possible to enter the chamber this way. The chamber is set within a kidney-shaped cairn which also covers a number of dry-stone walls. Hearths were found in the forecourt with pottery; the chamber contained unburnt but broken human and animal bone, representing at least 20 people, and a bone pin (Hemp 1935, 259). The forecourt was also blocked with dry-stone walling. There is also a large terrace at the site which runs for 100m to the south of the site. This feature remains unparalleled in Britain. The old ground surface

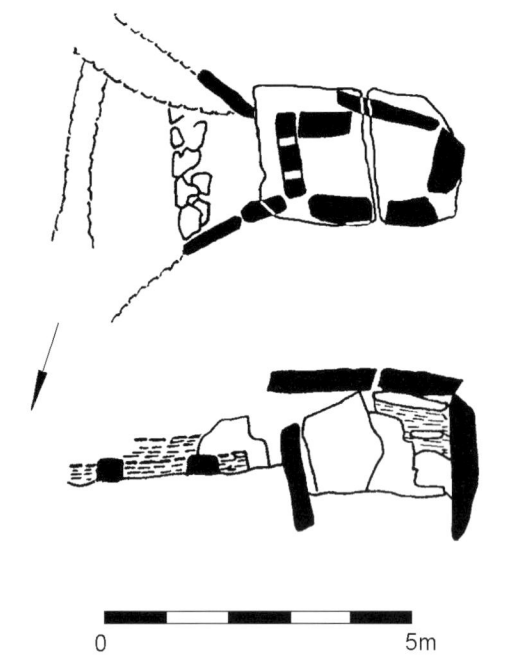

Figure 8.16 Plan and elevation of the chamber at Bryn yr Hen Bobl (after Lynch 1969b).

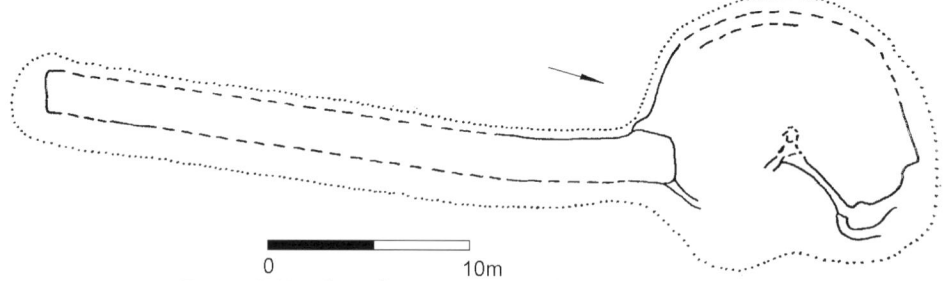

Figure 8.17 Plan of Bryn yr Hen Bobl (after Lynch 1969b).

beneath this site produced considerable quantities of pottery, scraps of human and animal bone and a large number of flint flakes, cores and arrowheads. Flakes of Graig Lwyd stone were also found as well as four polished stone axes (Lynch 1969a, 166). Other finds include a bone and a stone ball, shells and a stone with a pecked triangle (Hemp 1935).

Landscape setting: Today there are trees in most directions but the site would have had clear views out over the Menai Straits and to Snowdon beyond (Hemp 1935, 253). There would have been a more restricted view inland. It seems likely that entering the chamber there would have been wide-ranging views of the sea and the mountains to the left, while to the right there would have been a restricted view.

References: Gresham 1985; Hemp 1935; Lynch 1969b, 115–18; Lynch 1991, 83ff.

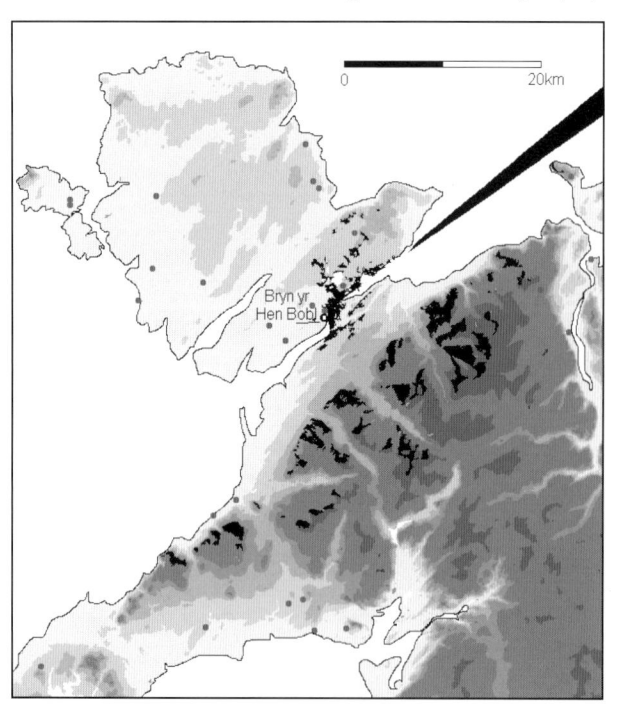

Figure 8.18 The viewshed of Bryn yr Hen Bobl. Reproduced by kind permission of Ordnance Survey. © Crown copyright NC/03/20516.

9. Plas Newydd (ANG 9) SH 520 697

Description: Set at 20m OD this monument is located in the gardens of Plas Newydd estate. The entire area has clearly been landscaped and therefore it is quite hard to ascertain the nature of the original topography. It may originally have been on the side of a gentle hill rising up from the Menai Straits. It is now located on a flattened lawn, but the wide and impressive views of the Menai Straits and the Snowdonia mountains are still clearly visible. Bryn yr Hen Bobl is located less than 1km to the south. The site itself is well preserved and consists of two chambers set side by side, the southern chamber much smaller in scale than that to the north. Both sites have a capstone resting on supports, although the capstone of the larger chamber may have shifted slightly (Grimes 1936, 131). It seems likely that the structure has also been altered in more recent years, as there are a large number of stones in the portal area which may not be original. There has even been the suggestion the whole structure is recent, although Lynch (1995, 17) believes that it is genuine by virtue of it being on Anglesey. The site has not been excavated.

Landscape setting: The landscape is partially obscured by trees to the west, but it appears that the landscape would have been reasonably restricted in this direction. There is certainly a restricted view to the north, before the view opens up to reveal wide and stunning views of the Menai Straits and the mountains behind. Snowdon itself is clearly visible. Standing at the portal to the largest chamber the view to the left looks out over the straits and mountains, while the view to the right is completely restricted.

Figure 8.19 Plan and elevation of Plas Newydd (after Lynch 1969b).

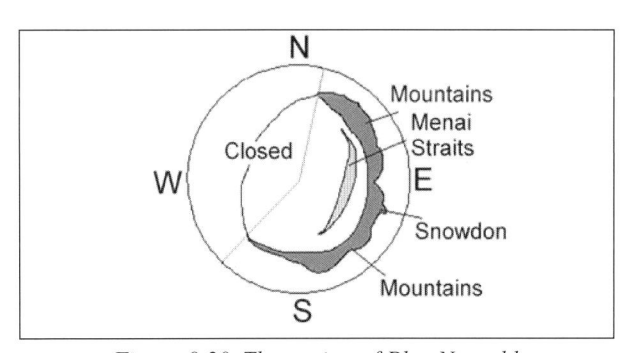

Figure 8.20 The setting of Plas Newydd.

References: Lynch 1969b, 122–3; Lynch 1991, 85–7; Lynch 1995, 16–17.

10. Ty Mawr (ANG 10) SH 539 722

Description: This site is located in a small field next to the A5025 at 85m OD on the edge of the town of Llanfair Pwllgwyngyll. It is set near to the summit of a gentle hill near to another outcrop. The site consists of a collapsed capstone and several fallen uprights. The smaller stone still upright is thought to be a sillstone like the one at Bodowyr. The site collapsed in the nineteenth century (Lynch 1995, 17) and has not been excavated.

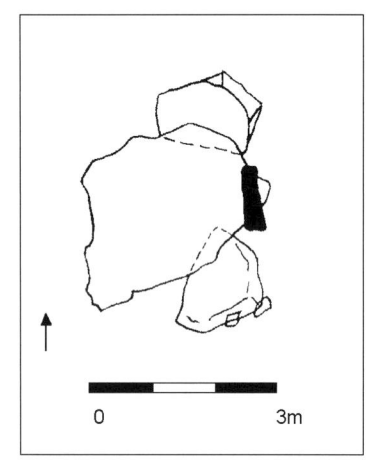

Figure 8.21 Plan of Ty Mawr (after Lynch 1969b).

Landscape setting: The landscape setting is quite impressive and like the other sites on the southern side of Anglesey has wide views out over the Snowdonia mountains. The view is obscured by hedges and the village of Llanfair Pwllgwyngyll to the west, but there is a restricted view to the north, partly filled by the nearby outcrop. There are wide views out over the mountains from the NE to the south. The northern mountains of the Lleyn peninsula are also visible to the SW.

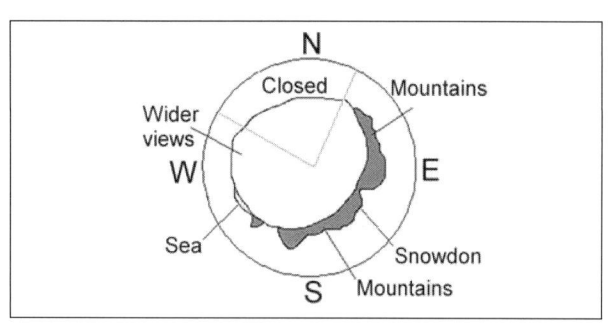

Figure 8.22 The setting of Ty Mawr.

References: Lynch 1969b, 117; Lynch 1991, 63–4; Lynch 1995, 17.

11. Hen Drefor (ANG 11) SH 551 773

Description: The site is set at 100m OD in a field and stands on a slight rise at the centre of the field. This site has been badly damaged and survives as a single upright with several large slabs lying in two piles. The standing stone seems to be a portal stone. The eastern chamber was still standing in 1802 when visited by an antiquary, but was 'thrown down' a few decades later (Lynch 1991, 70). The western stones seem to represent a fallen capstone and two supports. The site has been compared to Trefignath and Din Dryfol (Lynch 1991, 70). There are two different stone types in use in the monument, but the poor preservation means that little more can be said.

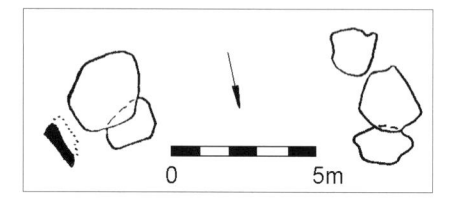

Figure 8.23 Plan of Hen Drefor (after Lynch 1969b).

Landscape setting: The site is positioned to have wide views of the Snowdon mountains and western Anglesey with a more restricted view to the north.

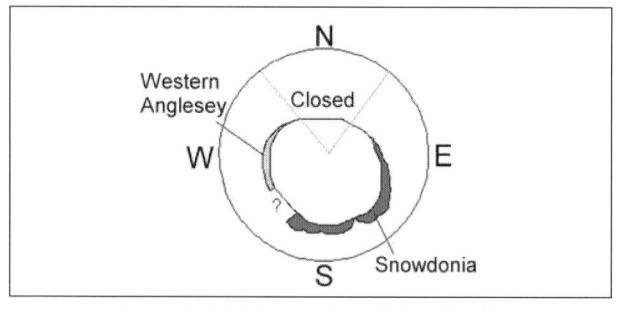

Figure 8.24 The setting of Hen Drefor.

References: Lynch 1969b, 115–6; Lynch 1991, 69–70; Lynch 1995, 17.

12. Glyn (ANG 12) SH 514 817

Description: This site is located at 75m OD on the outskirts of the town of Benllech. The site itself is situated in a hedge on the edge of a field. It is only 800m from Pant y Saer which is found to the NW. The monument survives as several uprights supporting a capstone. It seems that a slab of limestone was propped up to create a chamber area and the cavity beneath the chamber enlarged (Lynch 1969b, 121). Nothing was found in the chamber when it was emptied out by treasure-seekers in the nineteenth century.

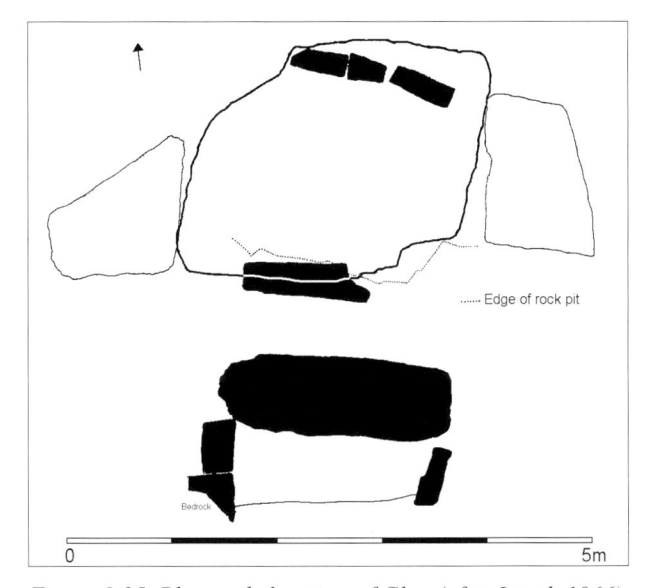

Figure 8.25 Plan and elevation of Glyn (after Lynch 1966).

Landscape setting: The site is surrounded by trees in most directions but half of the view is restricted by the gentle rise of the hill to the north while there are much wider views out to the south.

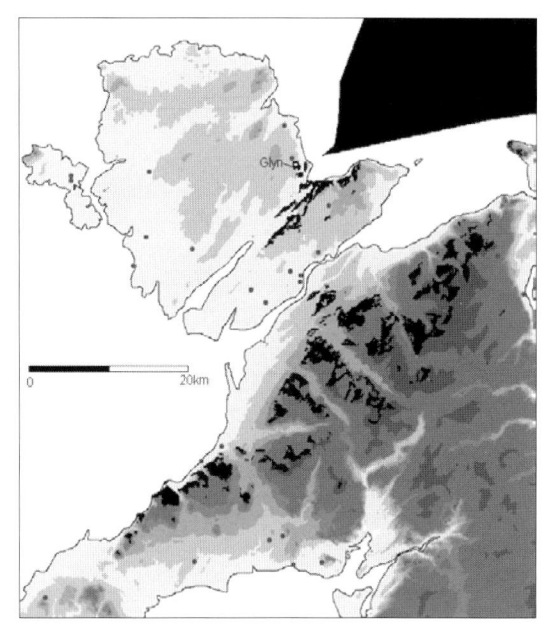

Figure 8.26 The viewshed of Glyn. Reproduced by kind permission of Ordnance Survey. © Crown copyright NC/03/20516.

References: Lynch 1969b, 121; Lynch 1991, 90–1.

13. Pant y Saer (ANG 13) SH 509 824

Description: This monument is located at 70m OD in poor quality land covered with gorse bushes on the edge of the town of Benllech. It is just over a kilometre from Red Wharf Bay which is a safe landing place for boats (Scott 1933). Structurally the site is poorly preserved as all the limestone slabs which make up the chamber are literally crumbling away. The capstone sits over two large uprights and a backslab and it is still possible to make out the shape of the cairn or platform. The site was excavated in 1875 and again in 1932. A roughly rectangular pit was cut into the limestone over which the chamber was constructed. A central passage ran from the chamber through to a circular forecourt which was surrounded by a broad, low wall (Scott 1933). The forecourt was cut through solid rock and much of the floor had disintegrated through burning. A peristalith surrounded a small mound. Previous excavations uncovered human and animal bone, pottery and sea shells in the chamber. Later excavations found more human bone, which represented a total of 54 people, including six children and nine full-term foetuses (Scott 1933, 207). Animal bone, pottery, arrowheads, quartz pebbles, charcoal and shells were also found in the chamber. Pottery, a scratched pebble, a portion of a human skull and animal bones were deposited at the entrance which was eventually blocked. There were other deposits found throughout the monument which included shale, a bone point, iron pyrites and a sandstone disk. At a later date a cist was set within the chamber, floored with sea shells and containing human remains including two skulls (Scott 1933, 188).

Landscape setting: The site has wide views of mountains and the sea to the NE and SE and a closed view to the NW. There are clear views of Great Orme Head (Scott 1933).

References: Scott 1933; Lynch 1969b, 118–20; Lynch 1991, 79–83; Lynch 1995, 18.

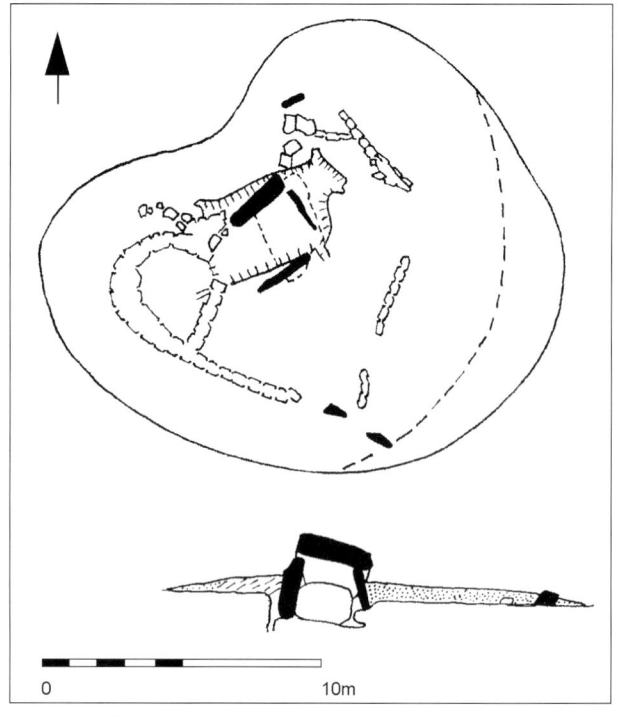

Figure 8.27 Plan and elevation of Pant y Saer (after Lynch 1969b).

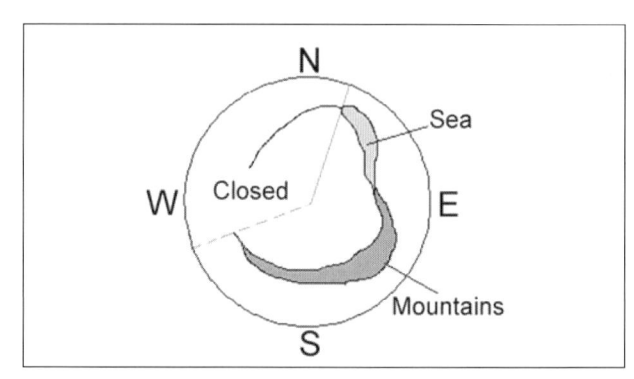

Figure 8.28 The setting of Pant y Saer.

14. Lligwy (ANG 14) SH 501 860

Description: This site is set at 60m OD on the edge of a field used for crops. The site is very well preserved and survives as an enormous capstone covering a series of supporters with the entrance to the east. It seems that the chamber itself was created by digging around an outcrop and putting supports underneath. The site has been excavated and produced considerable quantities of material including inhumations which appeared to be *in situ* when excavated (Baynes 1909). The chamber contained a layer of mussel shells over a layer of black earth mixed with bones, worked flint and pottery. Above this was a layer of paving followed by more black soil with human bones, flint and pottery (Baynes 1909, 224). This was covered with a layer of limpet shells. North of the chamber more deposits were found including human and animal bone, flint and a bone pin. Between 15 and 30 people are represented and the presence of Beaker and Grooved Ware suggests a late Neolithic date (Lynch 1995, 19) or at least late Neolithic activity. The monument is made from a really distinctive rock which is covered in grooves and hollows. The surface of the capstone has deep hollows which fill with water and the sides have deep grooves. The entire structure would have been below ground level in the Neolithic.

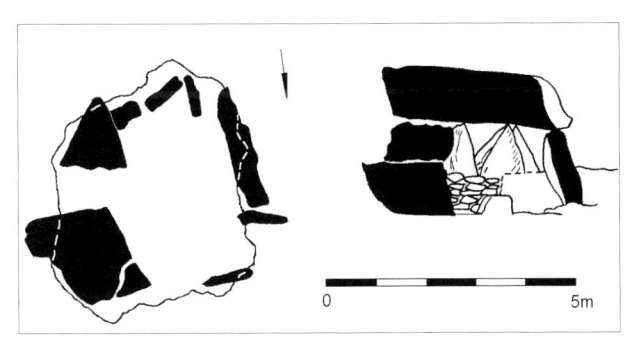

Figure 8.29 Plan and elevation of Lligwy (after Lynch 1969b).

Landscape setting: The site has quite impressive views of the landscape, although the view is blocked to the S and W by dense modern woodland. A very small portion of the view is restricted to the N, before wide views of the sea become visible. Would the Isle of Man and Cumbria have been visible from this site on a clear day? To the east Great Orme's Head and more distant headlands are visible, with Puffin Island in the foreground. The headland rises up to the mountains of Tan y Fran and Foel Fran, and more mountains are visible but the view becomes obscured by trees at this point. On exiting the tomb you would see out over the widest view to Great Orme's Head and distant headlands. This monument certainly would not have been very visible in the landscape, especially if it were in a landscape of outcrops and was below ground level. It certainly would not have been visible from Din Lligwy, A Roman settlement which has produced Neolithic artefacts, and it may have been the distinctive capstone which was the most noticeable and perhaps also most symbolic part of this site.

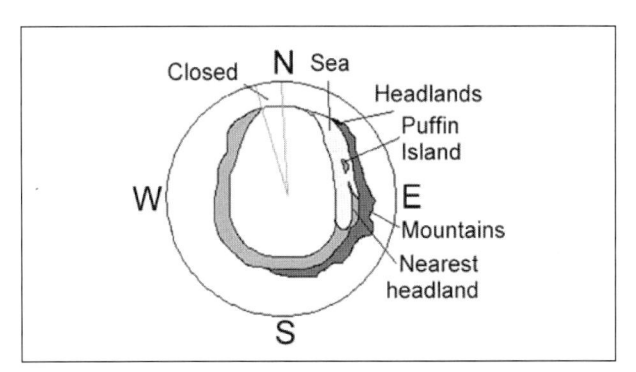

Figure 8.30 The setting of Lligwy.

References: Baynes 1909; Baynes 1932; Lynch 1969b, 119–21; Lynch 1991, 88–90; Lynch 1995, 18–19.

15. Trearddur (ANG 16) SH 259 800

Description: This site survives as a single large upright stone surrounded by a few cairn blocks and a prostrate slab on a domed outcrop on a field close to Trefignath. These remains seem to resemble the small western chamber at Trefignath (Smith and Lynch 1987, 19) and the location of the site is also similar to that of Trefignath (Smith and Lynch 1987).

Landscape setting: Located only 500m from Trefignath, this site is in much the same landscape setting as Trefignath, surrounded by outcrops and with clear views of Holyhead Mountain. Trees and the nearby aluminium works have obscured some of the views, but it is clear that Trefignath itself was visible from this site. There are also wide views of the Snowdonia mountains to the SE.

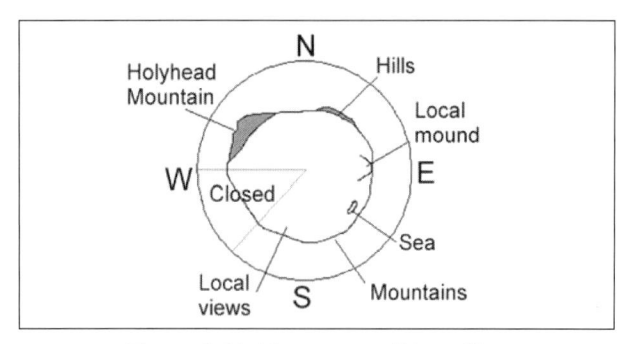

Figure 8.31 The setting of Trearddur.

Reference: Smith and Lynch 1987.

16. Perthiduon (ANG 17) SH 480 668

Description: This site survives as a single large capstone and a single collapsed upright in a small field surrounded by trees and hedges on the edge of Brynsiencyn village. The site is only 1km from the Menai Straits and Bodowyr is 2km to the north-west.

Landscape setting: Most of the surrounding landscape is hard to see today because the site is surrounded by tall hedges and trees, but there are clearly wide and impressive views of the Snowdonia mountains. The view is restricted from the SW round to the NE.

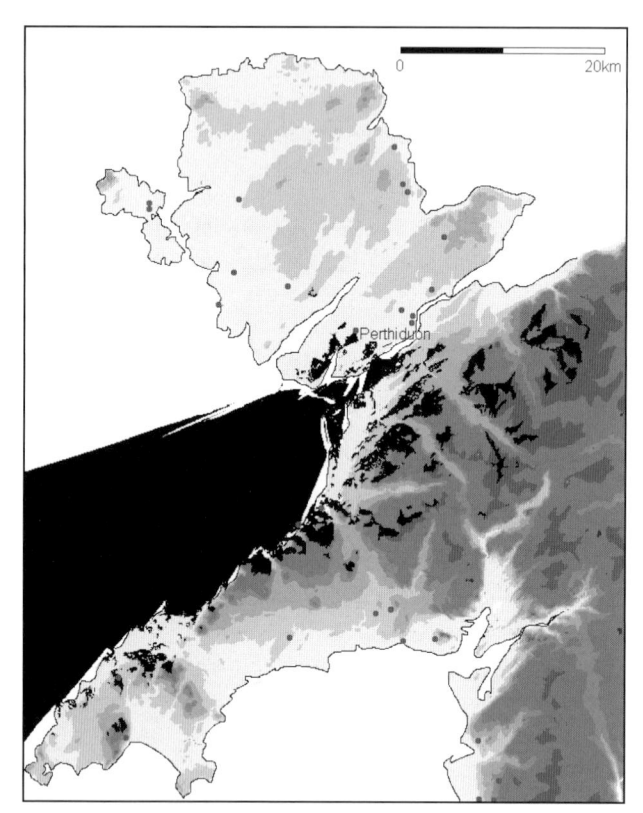

Figure 8.32 The viewshed of Perthiduon. Reproduced by kind permission of Ordnance Survey. © Crown copyright NC/03/20516.

Reference: Lynch 1969b, 299.

CAERNARVONSHIRE

17 Lletty'r Filiast
18 Maen y Bardd
19 Porth Llwyd
20 Sling
21 Penarth
22 Bachwen
23 Ystuim Cegid Isaf
24 Cefn Isaf
25 Cist Cerrig
26 Four Crosses
27 Mynydd Cefn Amwlch
28 Tan y Muriau
29 Cae Dyni

The following texts discuss the monuments of Caernarvonshire. Some of these also have more detailed information on individual sites and these are listed at the end of each entry where relevant.

Daniel 1950; Davies 1923; Grimes 1936; Leivers 1999; Lynch 1969a; Lynch 1969b; Lynch 1976; Lynch 1995; Lynch 2000a; Lynch 2000b; RCAHMW 1956; RCHAMW 1960; RCAHMW 1964.

17. Lletty'r Filiast (CRN 1) SH 772 829

Description: This monument is located at 140m OD in a marshy depression on a limestone headland (Lynch 1969b, 140). The site is in a completely transformed landscape. Today it stands at the end of a street in a small field only a short distance from the Great Orme copper mines. There are many outcrops around the area, but many of them have been exposed by mining from the Bronze Age onwards. Structurally, the monument survives as a collapsed chamber consisting of several uprights supporting a small broken capstone. A large mound is found behind the chamber which incorporates a natural rock outcrop.

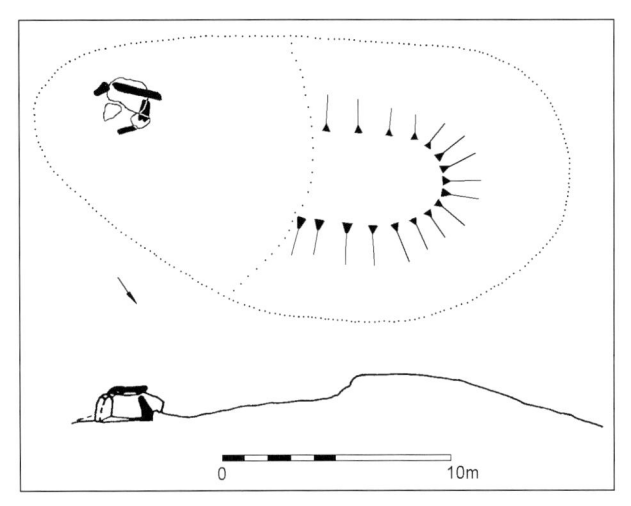

Figure 8.33 Plan and elevation of Lletty'r Filiast (after Lynch 1969b).

Landscape setting: Because of the massive alterations to the landscape, and all of the modern houses, it is rather hard to work out what the original landscape setting would have been. It seems, however, that there are two restricted views here, one to the N and the other to the SW. The view to the NW is of Great Orme's Head, while the view to the E looks out over the valley area to Llangernyw.

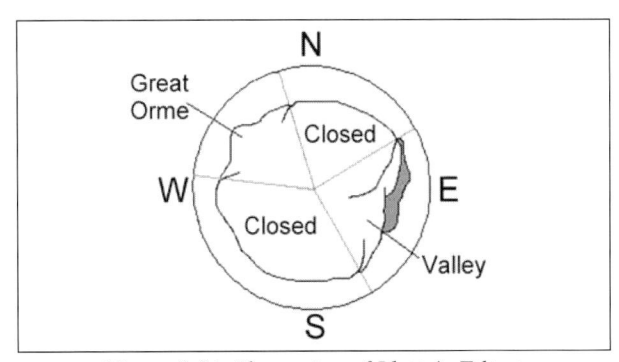

Figure 8.34 The setting of Lletty'r Filiast.

References: Lynch 1969b, 140; Lynch 1995, 19.

18. Maen y Bardd (CRN 3) SH 741 718

Description: Set at 330m OD next to the Roman road, this site is in an area of upland grazing and moorland. It is situated in a field boundary and is only 100m away from Roe Wen East. Its location is one of the highest in north Wales, comparable perhaps only with Carneddau Hengwm and it is one of the most difficult to reach. It is located in an area literally covered with outcrops on the upper reaches of a hill which rises up from the Afon Conwy to the SE. Structurally the site is quite well preserved, with a capstone supported by five uprights. The chamber area is quite small compared to many similar monuments in the area and uses local rock only.

Figure 8.35 Plan and elevation of Maen y Bardd (after Lynch 1969b).

Landscape setting: The landscape setting is impressive, with really clear views out over the River Conwy and mountains. The view from the W round to the NE is restricted by the hill on which the monument stands. To the NE a chunk of sea is visible and the Afon Conwy comes into view here also. The view from the S to the W is of mountains. Interestingly, the landscape setting is not quite as wide ranging as Roe Wen East just 100m away which also has views of the point where the Conwy reaches the sea and Great Orme's Head. Upon exiting the chamber the view to the left is of the Conwy valley and the view right is of mountains. It has been noted that the monument is located close to Bronze Age and Roman routes over the mountains to Penmaenmawr and the coast (Lynch 1969b, 141). The vicinity to the axe factory of Graig Lwyd has also been noted.

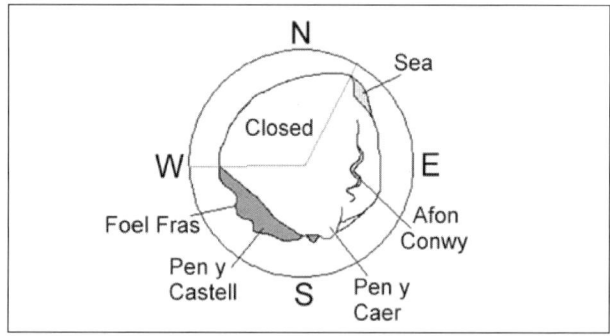

Figure 8.36 The setting of Maen y Bardd.

References: Lynch 1969b, 141–2; Lynch 1995, 19–20.

19. Porth Llwyd (CRN 4) SH 770 677

Description: This site is located at 10m OD in thick woodland in a boundary next to Dolgarrog works. The area has been considerably altered (Daniel 1950, 191) but two orthostats remain in position with the capstone now embedded on its end. These stones may once have formed a rectangular chamber.

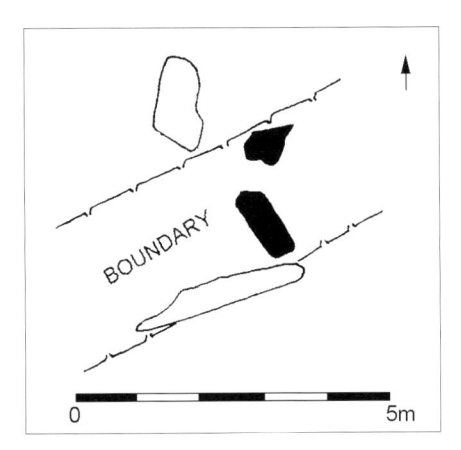

Figure 8.37 Plan of Porth Llwyd (after Lynch 1969b).

Landscape setting: Approximately half of the view is restricted as the site is close to the steep crags of Bont Newydd. The Afon Conwy is clearly visible to the east with small hills behind it. This view is very similar to all of the monuments which stand along the Conwy such as Hendre Waelod 7km to the north. The site also stands close to a tributary of the Conwy, the Afon Porth-Llwyd. Lynch classifies this site as the remains of a portal dolmen on the 'siting of the monument on the flood plain of the Conway, and close to the backs of a stream' (Lynch 1969b, 142).

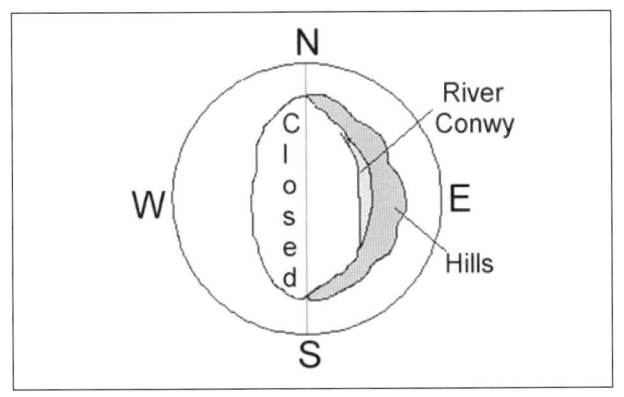

Figure 8.38 The setting of Porth Llwyd

Reference: Lynch 1969b, 142.

20. Sling (CRN 5) SH 605 669

Description: The site is positioned at 100m OD in an area strewn with outcrops and boulders and overgrown with thick, dense gorse bushes. The site is close to the road on the northern slopes of Moel y Ci. The site survives as a collapsed chamber with a large capstone supported by a small upright (Daniel 1950, 191).

Landscape setting: The view is out towards Ynys Mon to the north with a restricted view to the NE round to the NW. This means that there are no views of the Snowdonia mountain range, even though those hills are close by.

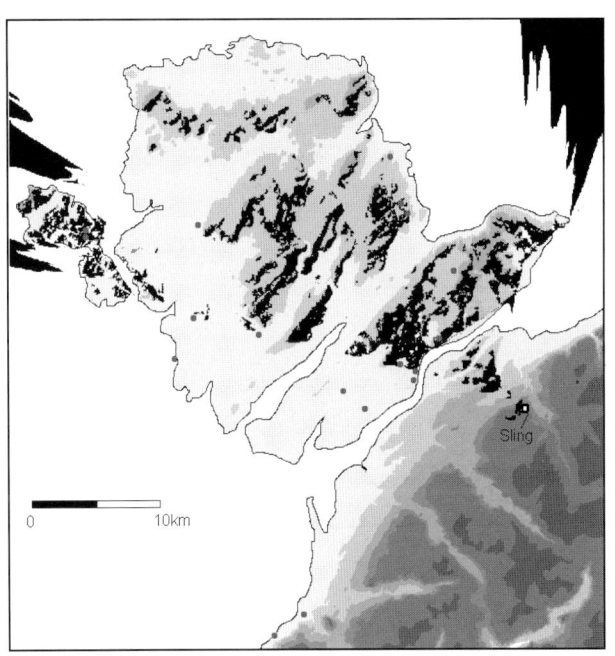

Figure 8.39 The viewshed of Sling. Reproduced by kind permission of Ordnance Survey. © Crown copyright NC/03/20516.

Reference: Lynch 1969b, 148.

21. Penarth (CRN 6) SH 430 511

Description: This site is located at 25m OD in a field in rich agricultural land on the northern side of the Lleyn peninsula. The monument is only a few hundred metres from the sea with the Afon Desach 200m to the north. The site of Bachwen is less than 3km to the SW. The capstone has been dislodged at this small monument which is now partly supported by three surviving orthostats. The capstone is characteristically chunky but is quite small in comparison with other sites.

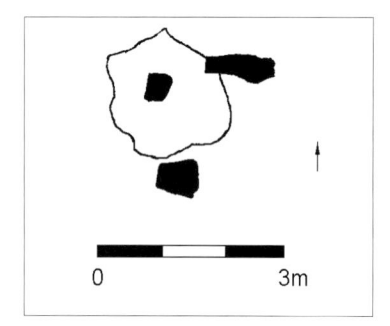

Figure 8.40 Plan of Penarth (after Lynch 1969b).

Landscape setting: Views of the sea are prominent at this site with Ynys Mon and Caergybi visible on the horizon. Yr Eifl and Garn Goch are also visible, the two prominent mountains of the Lleyn Peninsula. One of the most distinctive aspects of this site is that Snowdon is not visible. This is perhaps surprising since the Snowdon range is visible from almost all places in this stretch of coastline. Overall, this site is in a rather unspectacular setting. It is not highly visible in the landscape and would not have been visible from the coastline. There would have been a view of the sea as one entered the chamber, with a closed view and mountains of Lleyn to the left and the sea and Ynys Mon and Caergybi to the right.

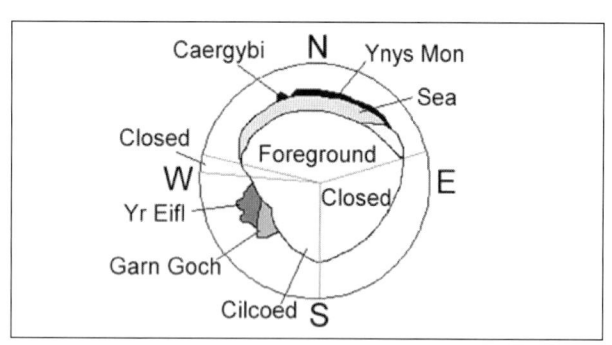

Figure 8.41 The setting of Penarth.

Reference: Lynch 1969b, 130.

22. Bachwen (CRN 7) SH 407 495

Description: Set at 25m OD in the middle of a field overlooking the sea, this site stands on the northern edge of the distinctive mountains of Bwlch Mawr and Gyrn Goch. The site is well preserved and survives as four uprights covered with a small capstone. The surface of the capstone at this monument is covered with cupmarks which has led to debate regarding their number and meaning (Lynch (1995) says there are 110). The site was excavated in the nineteenth century and the southern orthostat was restored last century. A paving of cobbles was found on the chamber floor and black material which may have been the remains of a fire (Hemp 1926).

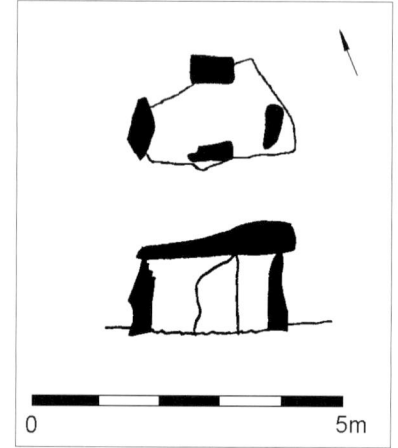

Figure 8.42 Plan and elevation of Bachwen (after Lynch 1969b).

Landscape setting: The site is located in rich agricultural land a few hundred metres from the coast and as such the sea can be seen and heard although the actual coastline itself is not visible. It is also perhaps surprising that there is no restricted view in any direction at this site. Instead there are stunning views of Yr Eifl, Blch Mawr (both on Lleyn) and Ynys Mon and Caergybi.

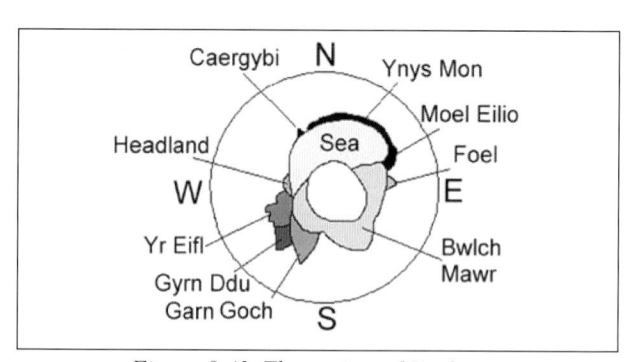

Figure 8.43 The setting of Bachwen.

References: Hemp 1926; Lynch 1969b, 130; Lynch 1995, 22.

23. Ystum Cegid Isaf (CRN 8) SH 499 413

Description: The site is found at 95m OD and is located in rich agricultural land. The site is only 1.5km from Cefn Isaf chambered tomb and 500m from the Afon Dwyfor, both of which are found to the west. The monument is located on a slight rise in relatively flat land and it appears and disappears from view as one approaches it. It is well preserved although presently incorporated into a field boundary. It consists of a number of uprights which support a large flat capstone. Other stones are visible to the north which seem to be the remains of a passage. However, it seems likely that the entire structure was rebuilt at some stage in the late nineteenth century, so the surviving remains may not be in their original positions (Daniel 1950, 192). Antiquaries described this site as a passage grave which has led to comparisons with Bryn Celli Ddu and Barclodiad y Gawres (Daniel 1950; Daniel and Powell 1949; Grimes 1936; 1965). More recently, Lynch (2002) suggested it may be a Cotswold-Severn outlier. There is also the possibility that other monuments may have been nearby and have since been destroyed (Daniel 1950, 192). The site has not been excavated.

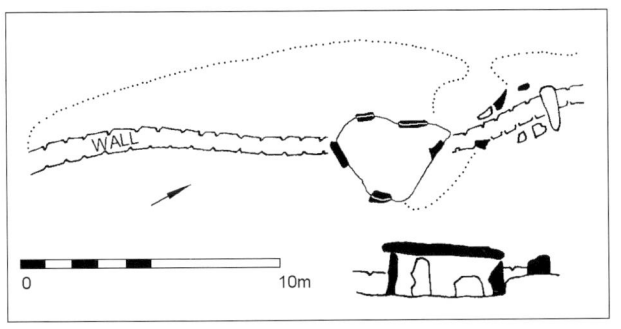

Figure 8.44 Plan and elevation of Ystuim Cegid Isaf (after Lynch 1969b).

Landscape setting: There is marshy land nearby and wide views in most directions. A number of mountains are visible on the horizon including Craig y Garn which is prominent and other mountains on the Lleyn peninsula. The setting of the site, therefore, is very different from the dolmens of north Wales. Parallels with passage graves are thus strengthened by its overall location and wide-ranging views in all directions, although its setting would not be unusual as a Cotswold-Severn monument.

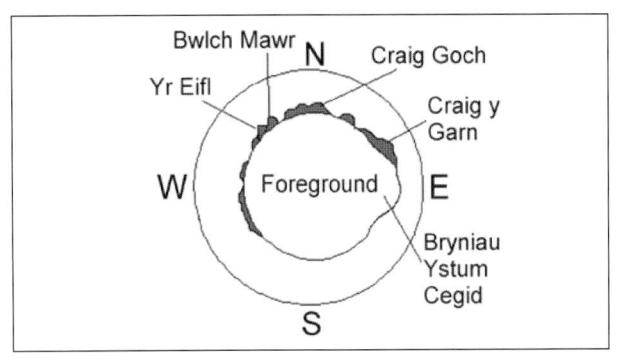

Figure 8.45 The setting of Ystum Cegid Isaf.

References: Lynch 1969b, 139; Lynch 2002.

24. Cefn Isaf (CRN 9) SH 484 409

Description: The site is located at 80m OD on marshy land between the Afon Dwyfor and the Afon Dwyfach rivers. The site is located in rich agricultural land on a flat piece of land which then gently rises up to the NE. The site is well-preserved consisting of four supports with a large capstone, although the south-eastern side has been completely destroyed (Lynch 1969b, 129). There is no trace of a cairn and the site has not been excavated.

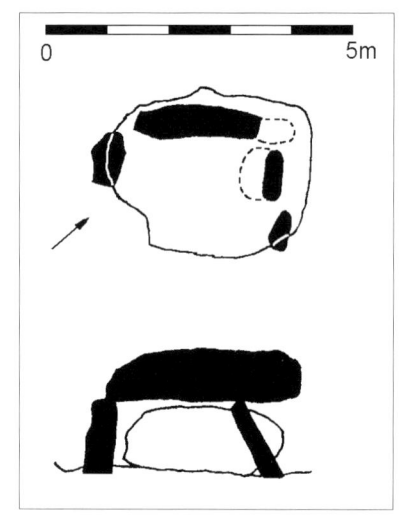

Figure 8.46 Plan and elevation of Cefn Isaf (after Lynch 1969b).

Landscape setting: The site is in a remarkably featureless landscape although a number of large stones in adjacent boundaries suggest that this area may once have had a number of outcrops. A stream runs right next to the monument. There are clear views of Moel Ddu and Mynydd Craig Goch and the mountains behind Dyffryn Ardudwy are visible. The mountains of the Lleyn peninsula would also have been visible. The monument would have been visible for a long distance if approaching from the sea.

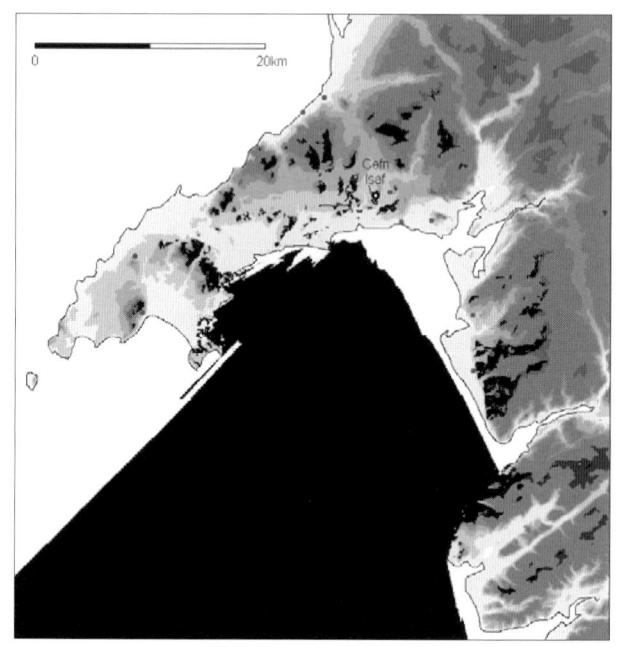

Figure 8.47 The viewshed of Cefn Isaf. Reproduced by kind permission of Ordnance Survey. © Crown copyright NC/03/20516.

Reference: Lynch 1969b, 129–30.

25. Cist Cerrig (CRN 10) SH 543 384

Description: This site is located at 60m OD on the lower slopes of Moel y Gest a few kilometres west of Porthmadog. The site is in a field with a number of outcrops nearby. This site survives as three large upright stones which have been interpreted as the remains of a portal dolmen, with the three stones representing the portal itself (Lynch 1969b, 129). If this is the case then this site would have been very substantial. Cairn material lies around the stones although there is no sign of the cairn beyond this. On a nearby outcrop there are a line of cupmarks (Hemp 1938).

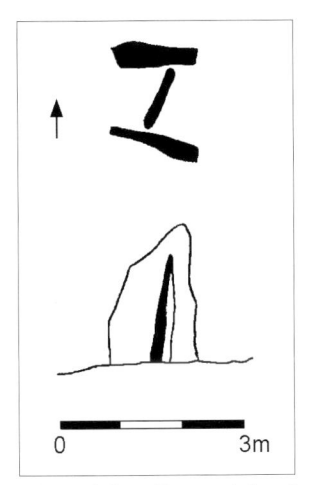

Figure 8.48 Plan of Cist Cerrig (after Lynch 1969b).

Landscape setting: There is higher and rougher ground to the NE while to the W there are views out over the sea and the Lleyn Peninsula. There are also wide views out over Moel y Gest which is visible from a number of sites in this area, and may have been of local significance. There is a restricted view to the east, blocked by the outcrop with the cupmarks. It is a view of the hills behind Dyffryn Ardudwy which is closed from view, suggesting that the builders were more focussed on the immediate landscape and monuments found on the Lleyn.

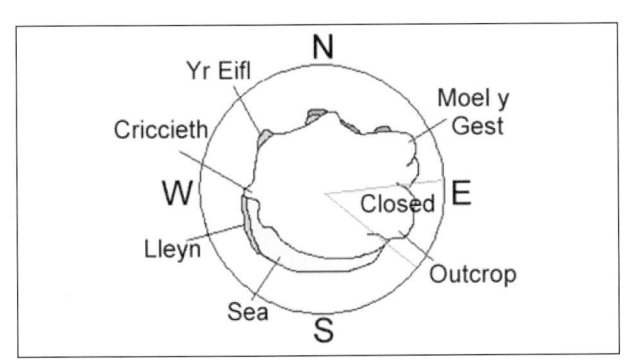

Figure 8.49 The setting of Cist Cerrig.

References: Hemp 1938, 140–1; Lynch 1969b, 129.

26. Four Crosses (CRN 11) SH 399 385

Description: Set at 60m OD a few hundred metres from the Afon Erch, this site is set in a field close to a boundary wall. There are lots of small stones in the surrounding walls and also larger boulders which may suggest that this area had once been covered with rocky outcrops. The monument presently consists of three uprights which support the capstone and a fourth slab. The site was reconstructed in 1936 when two stones were re-erected and a third straightened (Daniel 1937). The plan and elevation is based on the site before it was rebuilt.

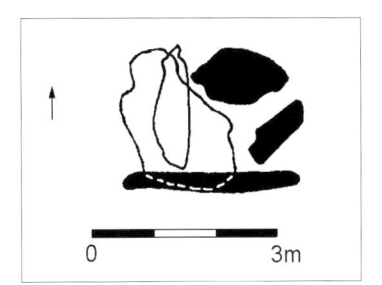

Figure 8.50 Plan and elevation of Four Crosses (after Lynch 1969b).

Landscape setting: 'The ridge on which the tomb is situated provides one of the best routes across the Lleyn peninsula' (Lynch 1969b, 129). There are really wide-ranging views of mountains from the north to the east, including Snowdonia, the hills behind Dyffryn Ardudwy and the sea. There are also quite wide views of the Lleyn peninsula but a more restricted view to the NW.

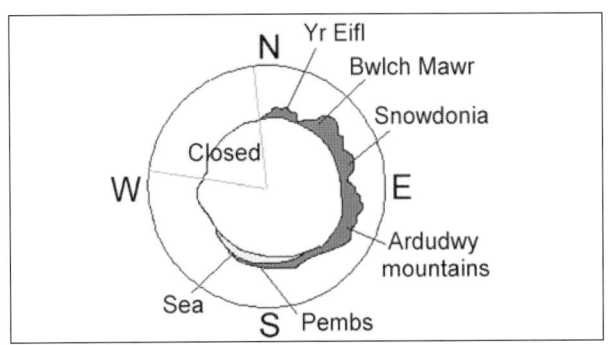

Figure 8.51 The setting of Four Crosses.

References: Daniel 1937; Lynch 1969b, 129.

27. Mynydd Cefn Amwlch (CRN 12) SH 230 346

Description: This site is found at 100m OD on the northern side of Mynydd Cefnamwlch hill. The site is in the middle of a field and the chamber comprises three orthostats supporting a capstone. A second large slab may be the remains of a second chamber. The original shape of the chamber and its cairn are uncertain (Lynch 1995, 24).

Figure 8.52 Plan and elevation of Mynydd Cefn Amwlch (after Lynch 1969b).

Landscape setting: This site is set on the side of Mynydd Cefnamwlch hill which restricts the view from the S to the N. There are spectacular wide ranging views of the mountains of the Lleyn peninsula and out to Ynys Mon and the sea is also visible to the NE.

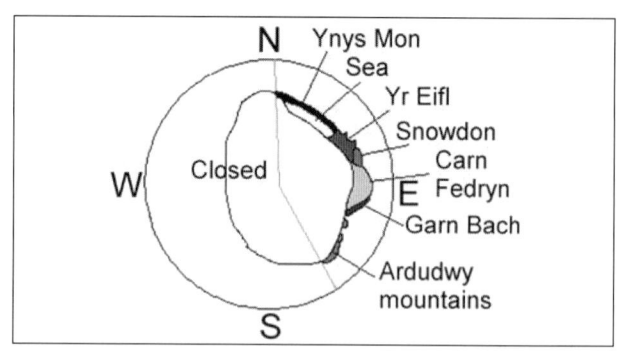

Figure 8.53 The setting of Mynydd Cefn Amwlch.

References: Lynch 1969b, 131; Lynch 1995, 24.

28. Tan y Muriau (CRN 13) SH 238 288

Description: Set at 125m OD on the lower slopes of Mynydd Rhiw, this site is set in bracken in an area surrounded by good agricultural land. It is a few hundred metres from the sea and beach at Porth Neigwl. The monument survives as a large chamber to the NW which consists of four uprights supporting a large capstone. At present this chamber is half-buried in a wall and very overgrown in the summer. The three stones buried in the wall can be considered a low closed portal (Lynch 1969b, 133). Further down the slope is another smaller chamber consisting of two uprights and a thin capstone. Considerable cairn material survives to the SE of this second chamber. The remains of a possible third chamber can be seen amongst the cairn (Daniel 1950, 193). Lynch (1969b; 1995) suggests that this may be a multi-phase monument, with the first phase being the large portal dolmen at the northern end which subsequently had another chamber and additional cairn added. This suggestion is supported by the multi-phase construction sequence found at Dyffryn Ardudwy. The site has not been excavated.

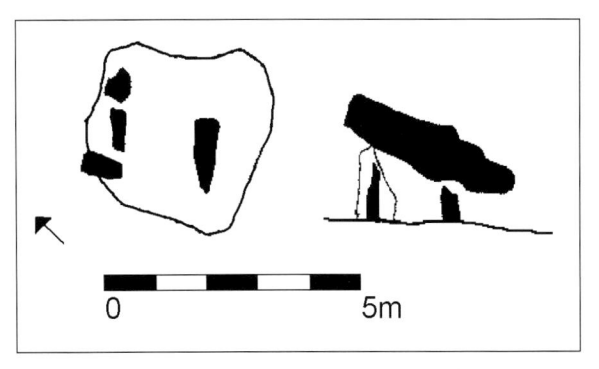

Figure 8.55 Plan and elevation of the main chamber at Tan y Muriau (after Lynch 1969b).

Landscape setting: Half the view is restricted from roughly the S to the N, while there are wide ranging views of the Snowdon range, the mountains behind Dyffryn Ardudwy, Cader Idris and out to Pembrokeshire and the Preselis. The beach at Hell's Mouth is clearly visible as is the sea.

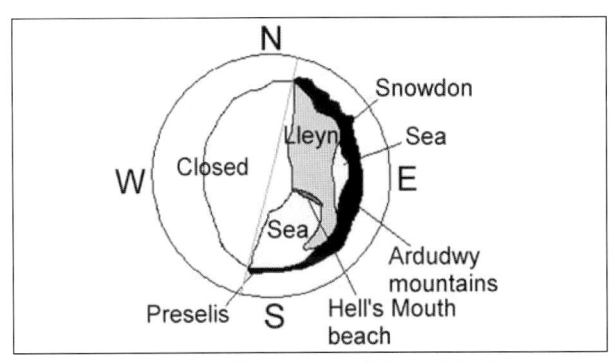

Figure 8.56 The setting of Tan y Muriau.

References: Lynch 1969b, 132–3; Lynch 1995, 25.

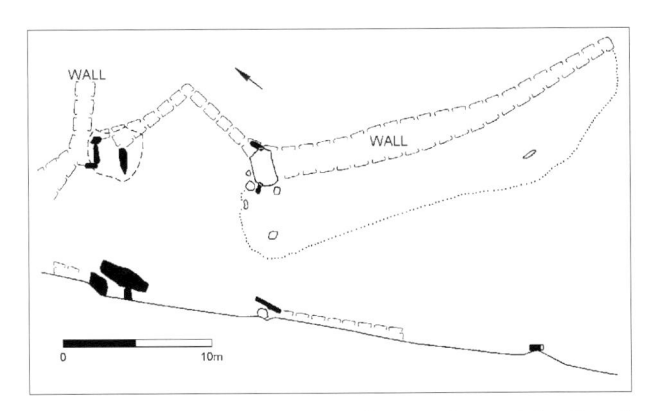

Figure 8.54 Plan and elevation of Tan y Muriau (after Lynch 1995).

29. Cae Dyni (CRN 14) SH 511 382

Description: This site is positioned in a field a few hundred metres from the coast on the western edge of the town of Criccieth. It is positioned on a small rise in an area of outcrops and is quite hard to spot from any distance. The site consists of a capstone and several other rather ambiguous slabs. Other large stones survive in the area. This site is now considered to be a large Bronze Age cist (Lynch 1969b, 306), although the site has been so badly damaged that we cannot rule out the possibility that it is Neolithic in date.

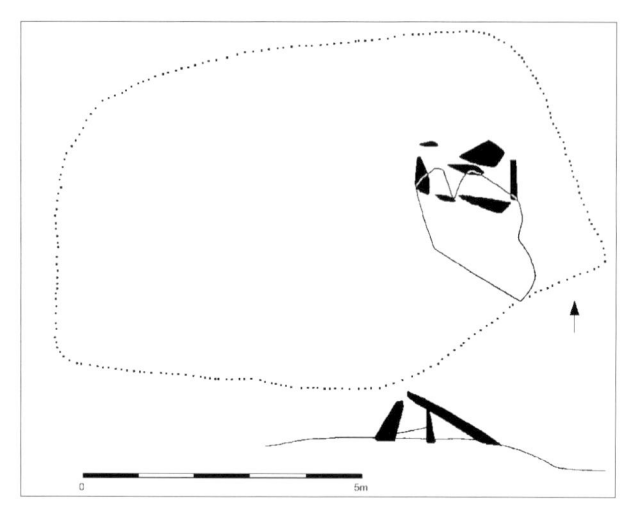

Figure 8.57 Plan and elevation of Cae Dyni (after RCAHMW 1960).

Landscape setting: The most distinctive landscape features visible from the site are the outcrop on which Criccieth Castle now stands and the Lleyn Peninsula behind. There are also clear views of the mountains around Dyffryn Ardudwy and it seems likely that it would be possible to see all the way to Pembrokeshire on a clear day. Moel y Gest is also prominent on the skyline between two more restricted views.

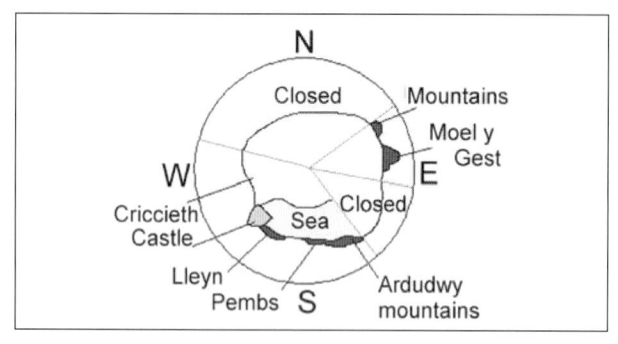

Figure 8.58 The setting of Cae Dyni.

Reference: Lynch 1969b, 306.

MERIONETHSHIRE AND DENBIGHSHIRE

30 Gwern Einon
31 Bron y Foel Isaf
32 Dyffryn Ardudwy
33 Cors y Gedol
34 Carnedd Hengwm North
35 Carnedd Hengwm South
36 Tan y Coed
37 Branas Uchaf
38 Hendre Waelod
39 Tyddyn Bleiddyn
40 Capel Garmon
41 Maen Pebyll

The following texts discuss the monuments of Merionethshire and Denbighshire. Some of these also have more detailed information on individual sites and these are listed at the end of each entry where relevant. Bowen and Gresham 1967; Daniel 1950; Davies 1929; Grimes 1936; Hemp 1952; Leivers 1999; Lynch 1969a; Lynch 1969b; Lynch 1976; Lynch 1995; Lynch 2000a; Lynch 2000b; Powell 1973.

30. Gwern Einon (MER 1) SH 587 286

Description: Positioned at 100m OD, this site stands on a gentle hill which runs down to the sea at Llanfair. The site is located in good quality grazing land next to a deserted farmhouse. There are many small outcrops in the area but it seems that the area has been altered by field clearance. The site is presently incorporated into a wall and it is clear that the site has been altered over time; one of the sidestones has been moved (Lynch 1996, 194) and the capstone may not be in its original position (Bowen and Gresham 1967, 17). Five uprights create a chamber area which support a sloping capstone. There is little evidence of a surrounding cairn, although this is likely to have been used to build the walls which surround the site (Lynch 1969b, 125). The site has not been excavated.

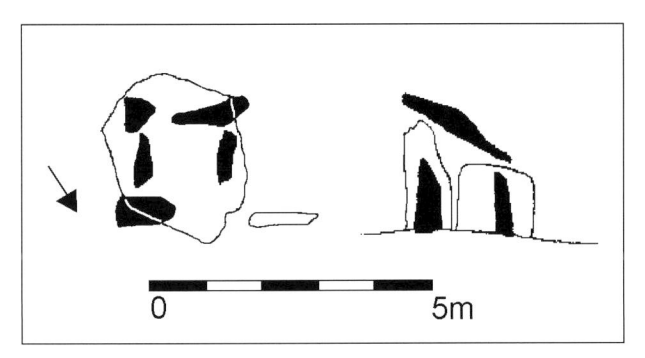

Figure 8.59 Plan and elevation of Gwern Einon (after Lynch 1969b).

Landscape setting: The monument has clear views out to the Lleyn Peninsula and the sea. There is a more restricted view to the NW. The mountains of Ardudwy are visible to the NE and SE. Penarth Hill is prominent to the E. Going directly towards the portal stones the sea is visible behind the portal stones. Standing right at the entrance to the chamber the view to the left is out to sea while the view to the right is the most restricted view. This seems to create opposing views of the landscape. Turning away from the monument one looks directly at Penarth Hill with mountains either side. This seems to mark out the axis of the monument.

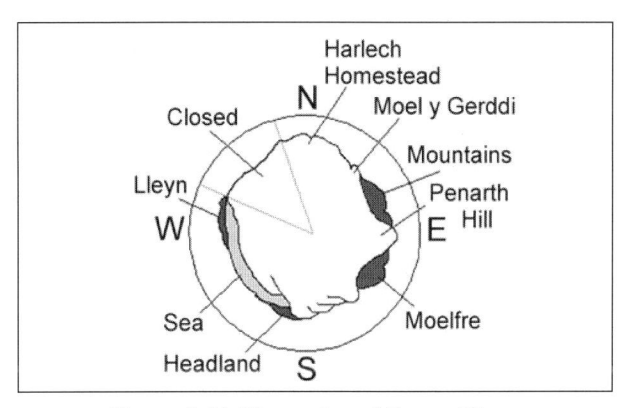

Figure 8.60 The setting of Gwern Einon.

References: Bowen and Gresham 1967, 15–17; Lynch 1969b, 125.

31. Bron y Foel Isaf (MER 2) SH 608 247

Description: Set at 195m OD on the lower slopes of Moelfre, this monument is embedded within a wall on the edge of a field. It is located in an area used for grazing sheep and there are many stone walls in the vicinity making it hard to ascertain the nature of the topography. There are a number of outcrops visible in the fields, however, as well as a number of clearance cairns, which suggests that the area may have been rocky in the past. Only three stones and the displaced capstone make up the much ruined chamber although there are the remains of a cairn or platform still visible.

Landscape setting: The site has clear views out to the Lleyn Peninsula and the sea and it is possible to see part of the Snowdon range to the N. The views to the east are dominated by Moelfre, while the views E to S are restricted.

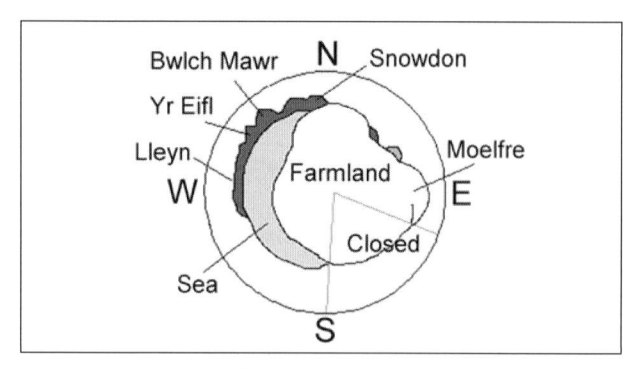

Figure 8.62 The setting of Bron y Foel Isaf.

References: Bowen and Gresham 1967, 21; Lynch 1969b, 125–6; Lynch 1995, 28–9.

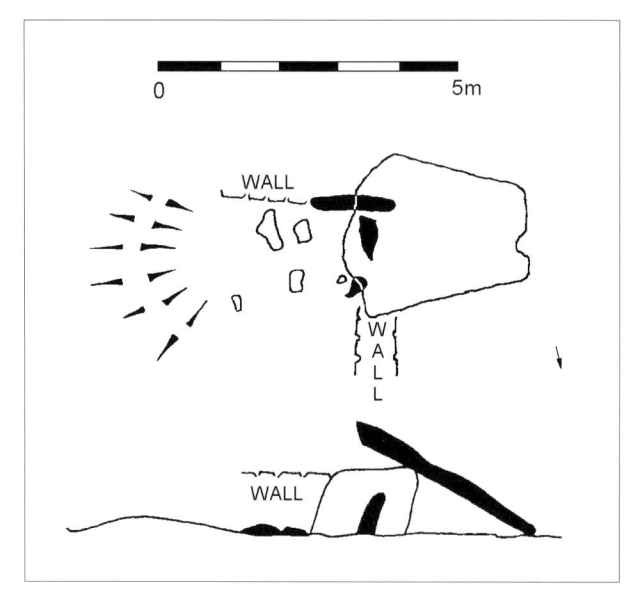

Figure 8.61 Plan and elevation of Bron y Foel Isaf (after Lynch 1969b).

32. Dyffryn Ardudwy (MER 3) SH 588 229

Description: Set at 40m on the lower slopes of Moelfre this site is on the outskirts of the village from which it takes its name. The site is located on a gentle slope enclosed on all sides by a wall and woodland. The site has been excavated and restored and substantial remains exist at the site. The smaller western chamber consists of six uprights which support a capstone, while the eastern chamber includes a modern column to support the larger capstone. Both chambers are enclosed within a long cairn or platform and it is possible to see the shape and size of the original small oval cairn around the western chamber. The site was excavated in 1960 (Powell 1973) and revealed that the monument was built in at least two phases. First a small megalithic chamber was built, surrounded by a small oval cairn. A pit in front of the portal contained portions of several Neolithic vessels. Second a large chamber was built to the west and a long cairn which incorporated the entire monument constructed. Pottery from the eastern chamber represented several Neolithic and Bronze Age vessels. The eastern chamber had a portico with a depression which contained dark-brown earth with a few small abraded sherds of plain ware. The small amount of surviving tomb deposit consisted of fine dark earth and a small concentration of cremated bone which represents a single individual. There were also two broken Mynydd Rhiw shale pendants (Powell 1973, 18). Seven flints were found among the cairn stones and a broken flint arrowhead at the eastern end of the cairn (Powell 1973, 30).

Landscape setting: Half of the view is restricted by the hill on which the cairn stands. The views from the S to the W are out over the sea, with the Lleyn Peninsula visible from the W to the N. The sea is visible behind both chambers when one is standing in the forecourt and may have been nearer to the site that it is today (Bowen and Gresham 1967, 17). Standing at the portal stones of the earliest chamber the view to the left is out over the sea, while that the right is the sea with the Lleyn Peninsula.

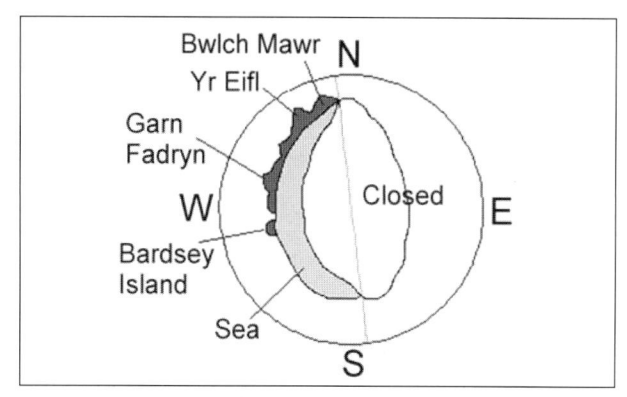

Figure 8.64 The setting of Dyffryn Ardudwy.

References: Bowen and Gresham 1967; Lynch 1969b, 149–55; Lynch 1995, 27–8; Powell 1963; Powell 1973; Yates 1989.

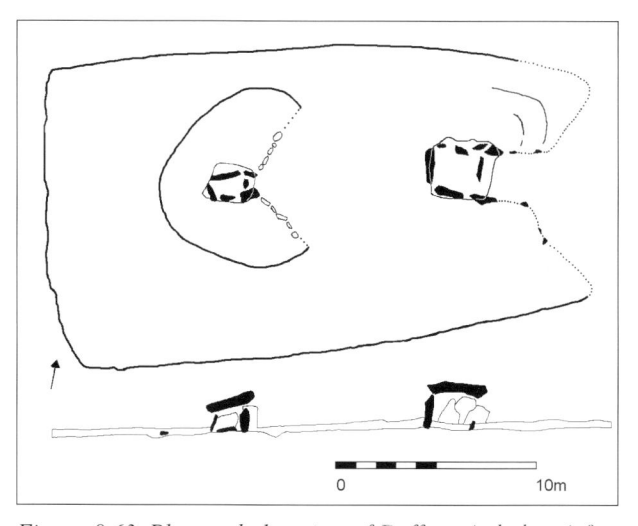

Figure 8.63 Plan and elevation of Dyffryn Ardudwy (after Lynch 1969b).

33. Cors y Gedol (MER 4) SH 603 228

Description: This site is found at 170m OD on the lower slopes of Moelfre. The site is located in open grazing land in an area with many outcrops. The site is only a short distance from the Afon Ysgethin. There are chambered tombs to the N (Bron y Foel Isaf 2km away), W (Dyffryn Ardudwy 1.5km away) and S (Carnedd Hengwm North and South 2.5km away). The monument is badly damaged and survives as two small uprights and a displaced capstone. A cairn is still clearly visible to the W.

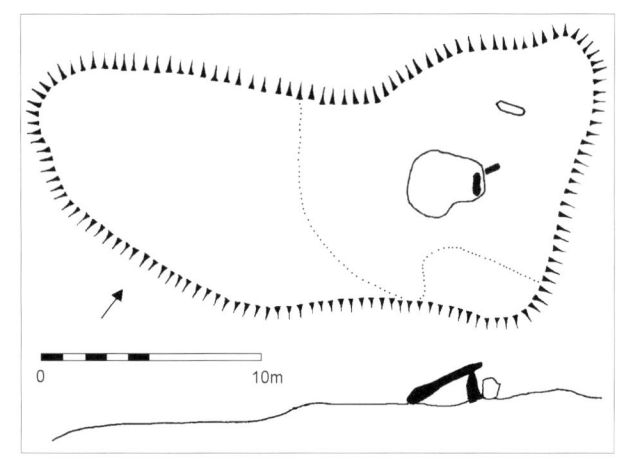

Figure 8.65 Plan and elevation of Cors y Gedol (after Lynch 1969b).

Landscape setting: This monument has clear views of all the local mountains including Moelfre and Craig y Grut. To the S the Ceredigion coast and Pembrokeshire are visible on a clear day, with the Preselis just discernible on the horizon. There are also clear views of the sea and the Lleyn Peninsula with a restricted view to the N.

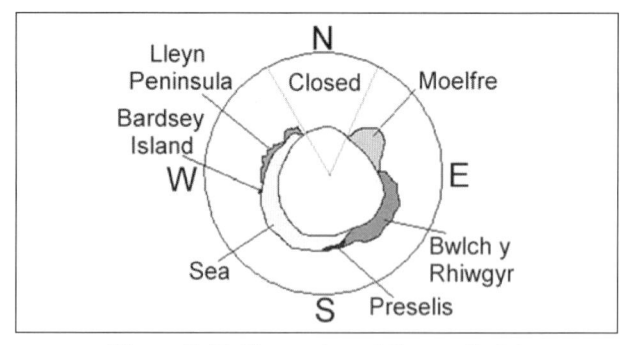

Figure 8.66 The setting of Cors y Gedol.

References: Bowen and Gresham 1967, 19–20; Lynch 1969b, 128–9; Lynch 1995, 29.

34. Carnedd Hengwm North (MER 5) SH 614 205

Description: This site is set at 270m OD on the side of Craig y Grut only a short distance from Carnedd Hengwm South. These sites are two of the most difficult sites to reach in north Wales although they stand in a landscape which has seen considerable activity over the millennia (see Lynch 1996, 172). A few hundred metres to the east of the site is a Bronze Age landscape consisting of a ring cairn as well as a settlement enclosure and round huts. To the NW is the hillfort of Pen y Dinas and further down the stream valley are a series of medieval houses and field walls. Both cairns are only a short distance from a stream and a deserted farm. In the seventeenth and eighteenth centuries the cairns stood close to a main road which ran through Bwlch y Rhiwgyr (Lynch 1996, 29). Carnedd Hengwm North survives as a denuded cairn with two laterally opposed chambers to the E and a large capstone to the W. A central depression has also been interpreted as a chamber. The laterally opposed chambers and the short section of drystone walling have led authors to suggest that this may be a Cotswold-Severn style monument (Lynch 1969b, 137). The site has been substantially altered over the years but never excavated.

Landscape setting: There are clear views of the Lleyn Peninsula and the sea to the W and NW. Moelfre is visible to the N and Craig y Grut is a dominating presence to the E. Only a very small portion of the view is restricted and Pembrokeshire is visible on the skyline to the SSW. The two lateral chambers or cists are placed at right angles to the main axis of Carnedd Hengwm North, and are aligned on Moelfre in one direction and Carnedd Hengwm South in the other direction.

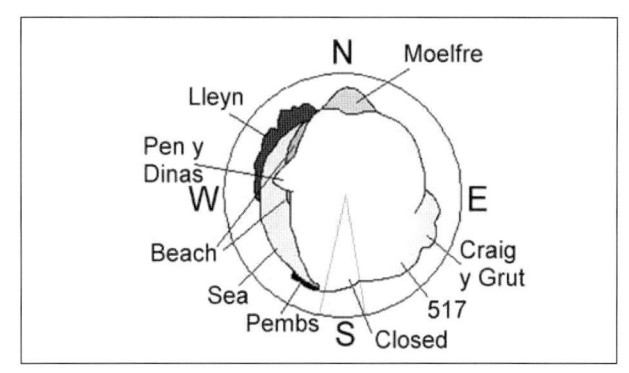

Figure 8.68 The setting of Carnedd Hengwm North.

References: Bowen and Gresham 1967, 10–14; Crawford 1920; Hemp 1936; Lynch 1969b, 137–8; Lynch 1995, 29–30.

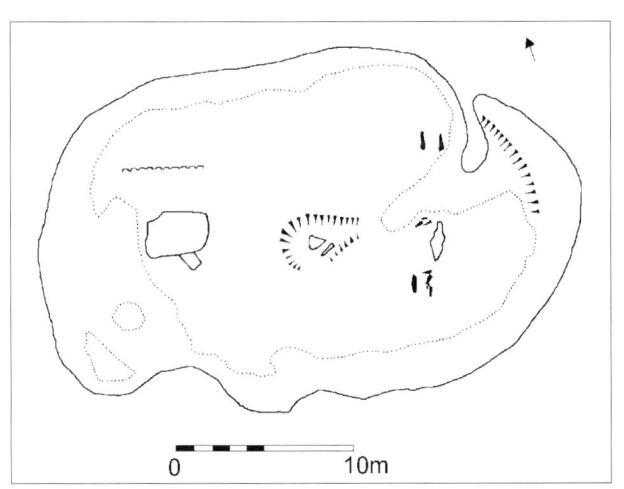

Figure 8.67 Plan of Carnedd Hengwm North (after Lynch 1969b).

35. Carnedd Hengwm South (MER 6) SH 614 205

Description: Set only a short distance from Carnedd Hengwm North, this monument is located in upland grazing. The site is so high above the modern coast that very little of the beach can actually be seen, although the sea is clearly visible. This site is larger than the cairn to the north, and is presently divided by a large stone wall. In the centre of the cairn is a small drystone walled chamber and at the western end of the cairn are a row of stones which may represent the edge of the cairn. Lynch suggests that this chamber may be linked to the Cotswold-Severn tradition (1996, 30). To the east of the wall are the remains of what would once have been a very large and impressive portal dolmen. One of the portal stones and the blocking stone are still standing, but the other stones have collapsed. A report from the eighteenth century claimed the chamber had two overlapping capstones (Lynch 1996, 30). A considerable quantity of cairn material survives also.

Landscape setting: There are virtually identical views of the surrounding landscape from this site which include views of Lleyn and the sea. Moelfre and Craig y Grut are both visible. Only a very small portion of the view is restricted and Pembrokeshire is visible on the skyline to the SSW. Carnedd Hengwm North is visible to the NNW.

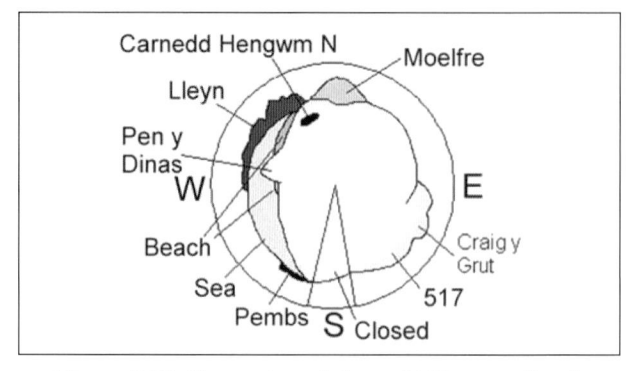

Figure 8.70 The setting of Carnedd Hengwm South.

References: Bowen and Gresham 1967, 10–14; Crawford 1920; Hemp 1936; Lynch 1969b, 138–9; Lynch 1995, 29–30.

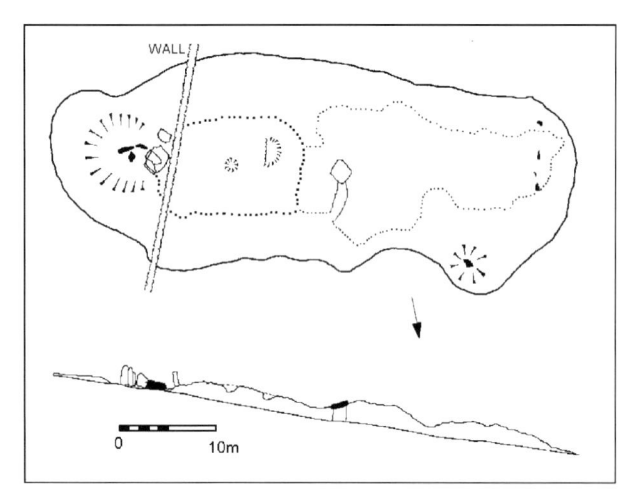

Figure 8.69 Plan and elevation of Carnedd Hengwm South (after Lynch 1969b).

36. Tan y Coed (MER 7) SJ 048 396

Description: This monument is located at 150m OD on the edge of a field with a farm track cutting through the eastern side. It is close to a modern road and is only a short distance from the River Dee. This site and Branas Uchaf exist in isolation in this inland part of north Wales, but both are in good quality agricultural areas set back from the river. The site survives as a grassy mound with a large laminated capstone visible at the top and a single upright underneath. It has not been excavated.

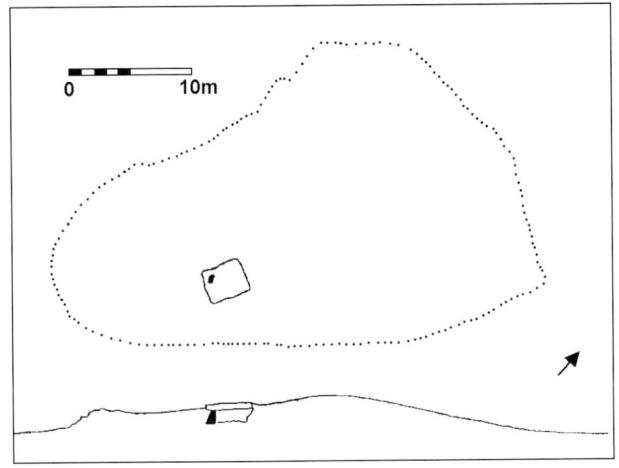

Figure 8.71 Plan and elevation of Tan y Coed (after Lynch 1969b).

Landscape setting: There are no really distinctive landscape features nearby, with views of the river and gentle hills behind. There is a restricted view to the E. The axis of the cairn seems to follow the axis of the river, and it seems likely that this site was positioned in relation to the river and movement along it. Lynch suggests that this was a route over the Berwyns in prehistory (1969b, 147).

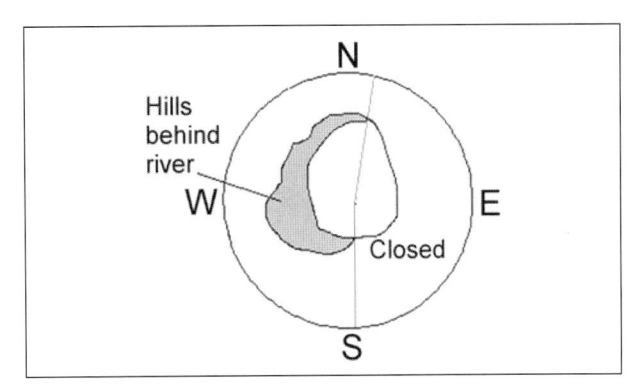

Figure 8.72 The setting of Tan y Coed.

References: Bowen and Gresham 1967, 31; Hemp 1952; Lynch 1969b, 147.

37. Branas Uchaf (MER 8) SJ 011 376

Description: Set at 150m OD alongside the River Dee, this site stands in the middle of a field. There is a dismantled railway just to the south of the site which has substantially altered the landscape in that direction. The river is currently not visible to the south, but it is difficult to know whether this would have been the case in the Neolithic. The site survives as a grassy mound with a number of visible uprights although the site is so badly damaged that its authenticity has been doubted (Lynch 1969b).

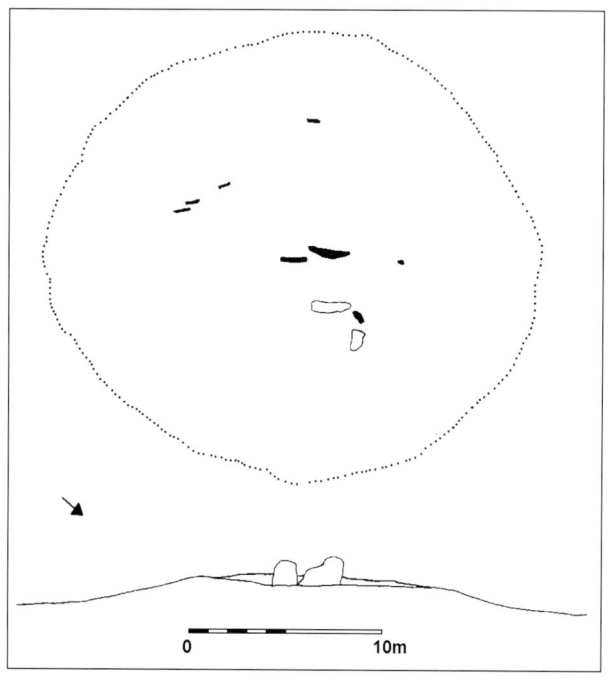

Figure 8.73 Plan and elevation of Branas Uchaf (after Lynch 1969b).

Landscape setting: Just like Tan y Coed, located a few kilometres away, it is located in an unimpressive landscape with few distinctive features. Instead its location is perhaps more likely to reflect a relationship with the river. This was clearly an important routeway in the past, illustrated by the presence of a number of mottes nearby. The landscape setting is primarily of the immediate landscape. Views from the SW to the NE are restricted, while the rest of the view looks out over nearby hills.

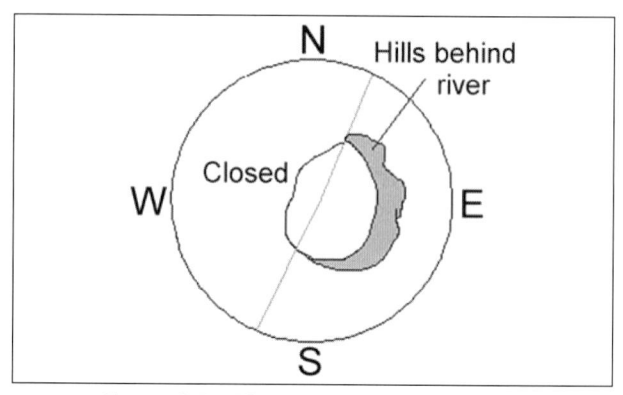

Figure 8.74 The setting of Branas Uchaf.

References: Bowen and Gresham 1967, 30; Burnham 1995, 12–13; Hemp 1952.

38. Hendre Waelod (DEN 1) SH 793 748

Description: Located at 20m OD in rich agricultural land, this site is located on the edge of a small patch of trees on the side of a hill rising up from the Afon Conwy. It stands on a hummock and there are other knolls in the area but none as large or distinctive as the one that the monument is on. The monument itself is well preserved and consists of a large capstone which seems to have collapsed, although several uprights are still in place, all of which are presently set within a fence. The portal stones now stand above the low chamber area as the forecourt area has filled up with soil. It seems unlikely that the capstone was ever supported by these portals, although there is the possibility that another capstone existed (Lynch 1969b, 141). A long cairn is also still visible (Lynch 1996, 21).

Landscape setting: The landscape setting of this site is quite stunning. The view from the NE round to the S is restricted by the hill on which the monument stands. There are really clear views of the Afon Conwy framed by mountains to the SW. You cannot actually see the sea but the point where the river would soon meet the sea near Llandudno Junction. The focus here is clearly the river and the monument is set a little way up from this important pass. The monument would not have been very visible from the river itself although it sits on quite a prominent and unusually shaped hill which would have been visible from the river. To reach the portal stones the monument would have to be approached from uphill, coming down on to the chamber.

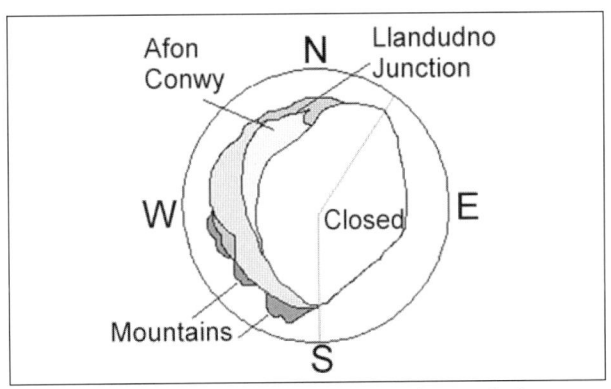

Figure 8.76 The setting of Hendre Waelod.

References: Lynch 1969b, 140–1; Lynch 1995, 20–1.

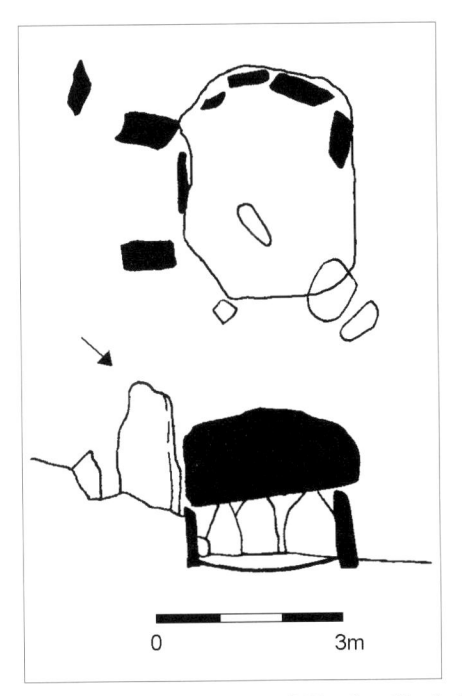

Figure 8.75 Plan and elevation of Hendre Waelod (after Lynch 1969b).

136   *Vicki Cummings*

39. Tyddyn Bleiddyn (DEN 2) SJ 008 724

Description: Set at 120m OD, this monument is located in a small field. It is positioned just over half a kilometre from the Afon Elwy and stands on the side of the gentle hill of Cefn Meiriadog. The site survives as a chamber set within a long cairn. The northern chamber was excavated in 1869 and in 1871 another chamber was found to the S but nothing survives of this today apart from a hollow in the cairn. It is reported that the chamber was filled with sand and that human bones were found in the cairn (Davies 1929, 64). The chamber itself was said to contain human skulls, teeth and bone representing at least 12 people. The second chamber contained more human remains, the jaw of a roebuck, remains of a goat, a broken flint and round quartz pebbles. The passage of this chamber contained dog and pig remains (Davies 1929, 64). It has been suggested that this site may be similar to Capel Garmon (Lynch 1969b, 145).

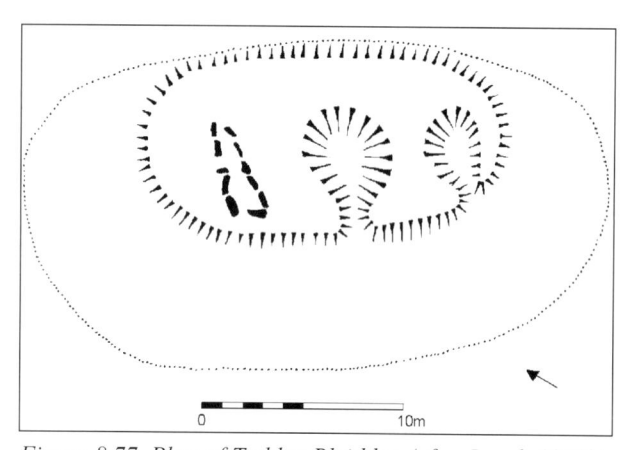

Figure 8.77 Plan of Tyddyn Bleiddyn (after Lynch 1969b).

Landscape setting: There is a restricted view from the NW to the SE, with wider views from the SE to the NW looking out over the river valley. However, there are no long distance views in any direction, with the focus on the local topography.

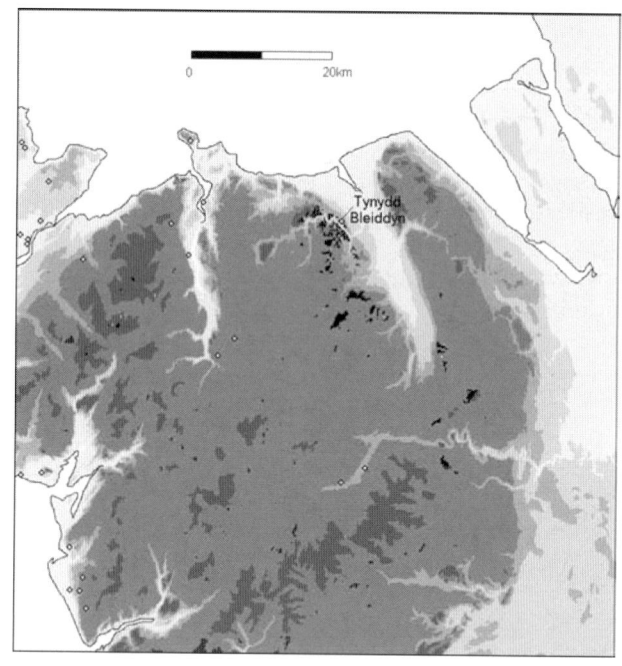

Figure 8.78 The viewshed of Tyddyn Bleiddyn. Reproduced by kind permission of Ordnance Survey. © Crown copyright NC/03/20516.

Reference: Lynch 1969b, 145.

40. Capel Garmon (DEN 3) SH 818 544

Description: Set at 240m OD, the site is in agricultural land with marshy ground just to the W of the site. It is set in a landscape filled with rocky outcrops and knolls and is only 1km from the Afon Conwy. The site is well preserved although it has been restored over the years. The shape of the cairn is marked out on the ground, and the passage and chambers survive. Only the western chamber has a capstone, and it can now be entered from the W, although this was not an original feature. The site was excavated in 1925. However, the site had been cleared out previously so little material culture survived. A flint flake and some pottery were found (Hemp 1927, 24). More recently a smaller excavation revealed pre-cairn activity and a skull fragment (Yates and Jones 1991). The site quite clearly has parallels with the Cotswold-Severn tradition of monument building (Lynch 1969b).

Landscape setting: The site is positioned in a quite hidden location in a landscape of knolls and outcrops. Three-quarters of the view is restricted by the surrounding hills, while the remaining quarter has views of the Snowdon range. The site is only 1km from the Afon Conwy yet the river is not visible. Instead the monument is tucked away out of sight.

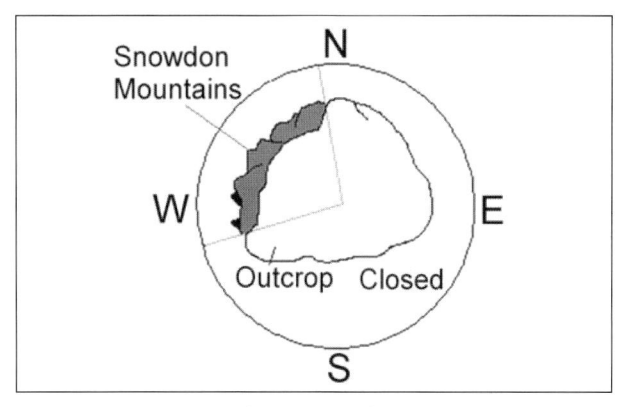

Figure 8.80 The setting of Capel Garmon.

References: Hemp 1927; Lynch 1969b, 143–5; Lynch 1995, 21–2; Yates 1996; Yates and Jones 1991.

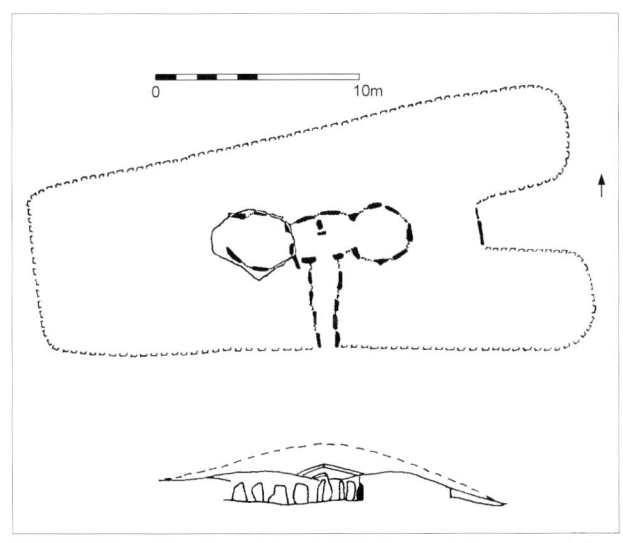

Figure 8.79 Plan and elevation of Capel Garmon (after Lynch 1969b).

41. Maen Pebyll (DEN 4) SH 844 566

Description: This site is located at 350m OD on the lower slopes of Moel Seisiog a few kilometres to the east of the Afon Conwy. The site is set in a field close to a stream. It survives as four large stones and what might be the remains of a cairn. Earlier writers described the site as a Cotswold-Severn outlier. However, later writers such as Lynch do not consider the remains to be Neolithic in date (Lynch 1969b, 146). The remains are so poorly preserved only excavation could resolve this question.

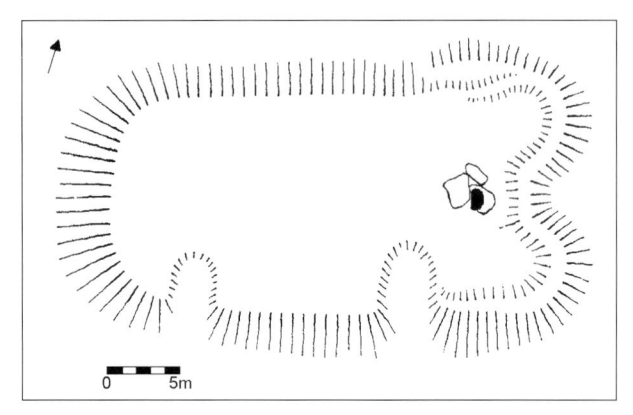

Figure 8.81 Plan of Maen Pebyll (after Grimes 1936).

Landscape setting: About half of the view is restricted while the other half has wide-ranging views of the mountains to the W. This is a wider view of the landscape than the nearby Capel Garmon monument.

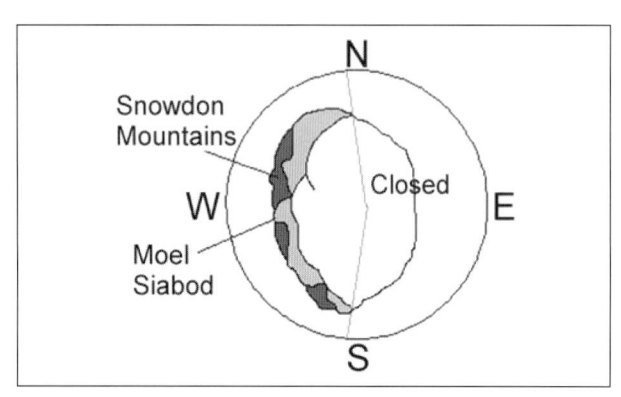

Figure 8.82 The setting of Maen Pebyll.

References: Hemp 1923; Lynch 1969, 145–6.

PEMBROKESHIRE

42 Llech y Dribedd
43 Trellyffaint
44 Carreg Coetan
45 Cerrig y Gof
46 Pentre Ifan
47 Mountain
48 Bedd yr Afanc
49 Eithbed
50 Colston
51 Garn Turne
52 Parc y Llyn
53 Carn Wen
54 Parc y Cromlech
55 Carn Wnda
56 Garn Gilfach
57 Ffynnondruidion
58 Ffyst Samson
59 Carreg Samson
60 Trewalter Llwyd
61 Treffynnon
62 White House
63 St Elvies
64 Carn Llidi
65 Coetan Arthur
66 Hanging Stone
67 Devils' Quoit
68 King's Quoit

The following texts discuss the monuments of Pembrokeshire. Some of these also have more detailed information on individual sites and these are listed at the end of each entry where relevant. Barker 1992; Children and Nash 1997; Cummings 2001; Daniel 1950; Grimes 1936; Lynch 1972; Lynch 2000a Rees 1992; Tilley 1994.

42. Llech y Dribedd (PEM 1) SN 101 432

Description: Set at 185m OD on the western side of a gentle hill, this site is one of the most impressive monuments in SW Wales. It is located in the Nevern Valley, only 2km away from the chambered tomb of Trellyffaint. Surrounded on all sides by fields, the site itself is positioned in a flat, uncultivated field. The monument consists of three standing uprights and a large capstone. A fourth upright has collapsed, but it was recorded as standing in the seventeenth century (Barker 1992, 18). There is no sign of a cairn, although Lynch has claimed that one once existed at the site (1972, 78). A trench was dug 10m to the N of the chamber in 1977 by Dyfed Archaeological Trust, but no prehistoric finds or features were found.

Figure 8.83 Plan and elevation of Llech y Dribedd (after Barker 1992).

Landscape setting: The view is restricted from the NW round to the E, although it is possible to just see the sea over the hillslope to the NNW. From E to NW, the view opens up and looks out over the Nevern Valley. In the distance, the Mynydd Preseli are clearly visible. Carn Meini can be seen to the SE, and Carn Ingli dominates the view to the SSW. To the W, Dinas Head is visible with Fishguard Bay, a portion of sea, and a small tip of St David's Head. Pentre Ifan can clearly be seen to the S as well as the Carnedd Meibion Owen outcrops behind it. This setting is very similar to the site of Trellyffaint only 2km away. Children and Nash point out (1997, 55) that even though the monument is only a kilometre from the coast, the site focuses instead on the valley area beneath. Tilley (1994) and Children and Nash (1997) both suggest that the relationship with Carn Ingli may be significant. The distant views of both Carn Meini and St David's Head may also have been important.

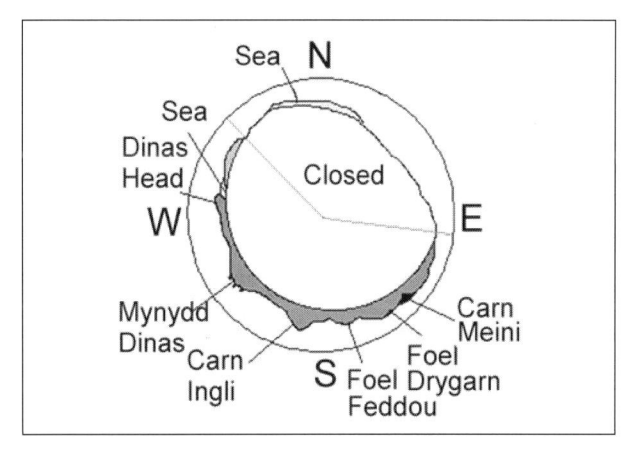

Figure 8.84 The setting of Llech y Dribedd.

References: Barker 1992, 17–18; Lynch 1972; Rees 1992, 18–9.

140 Vicki Cummings

43. Trellyffaint (PEM 2) SN 082 425

Description: Positioned at 140m OD on the southern side of a gentle hill, this site is set in agricultural land in the Nevern Valley. The site is positioned roughly between two streams, which flow into the Afon Nyfer, the river which reaches the sea by Carreg Coetan. Llech y Dribedd is located 1km to the NE. The larger main chamber consists of four stones which support a capstone. The outer surface of the capstone is covered with cupmarks. There has been some speculation as to the status of these cupmarks, and opinion is split as to whether they are real or natural. It may be of relevance that the other cupmarked stone in Pembrokeshire, also believed to be the capstone of a chambered tomb, is only 3km away to the SE (the site of Trefael: SN 103 403). The height of the chamber area was, until recently, much greater, but the capstone has slipped and broken off (Barker 1992, 18). Barker also suggests that originally another capstone would have existed at the site, covering the two portal stones. An additional chamber can be found to the N of the main chamber, which may be another chamber, perhaps a later addition or possibly even a cist. It seems possible that a small cairn or platform once covered both chambers.

Landscape setting: The view from the W round to the E is entirely restricted by the hill on which the monument stands. From the E round to the W the Nevern Valley is visible, with the Mynydd Preseli in the background. Carn Meini is visible to the S, and Carn Ingli to the SSW. Pentre Ifan is visible to the SSE. To the WSW Fishguard Harbour is just visible behind Dinas Head, and the hills stretching off towards St David's Head are visible before the view is restricted once again. The landscape setting of this site is similar to Llech y Dribedd. The appearance of the landscape is split into two, with half of the view wide-ranging and the other half completely restricted.

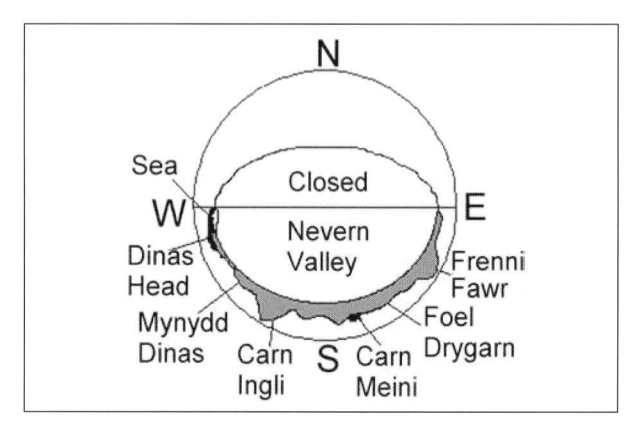

Figure 8.86 The setting of Trellyffaint.

References: Barker 1992, 18–19; Lynch 1972; Rees 1992, 17–8.

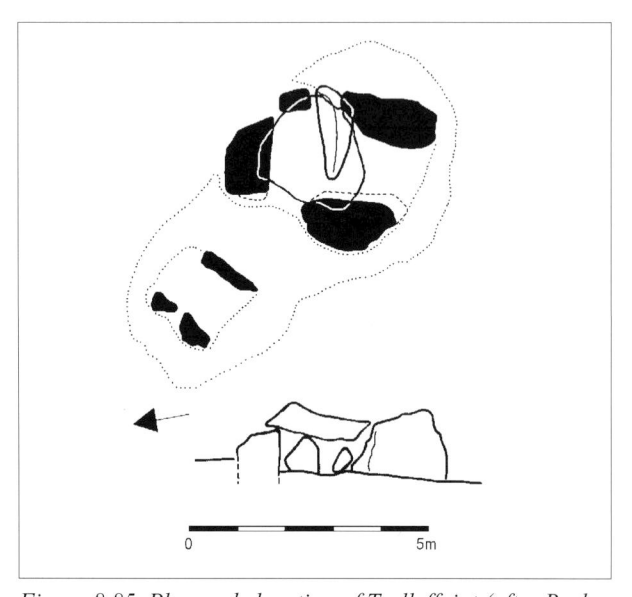

Figure 8.85 Plan and elevation of Trellyffaint (after Barker 1992).

44. Carreg Coetan (PEM 3) SN 060 393

Description: Set at 10m OD, this is the lowest lying monument in Pembrokeshire. The site is now in a small fenced off area at the end of a residential street. It is located only a short distance from the point where the Afon Nyfer meets the sea a few metres from Newport Sands, in the inter-tidal zone. The site lies only 2km to the N of Carn Ingli and the site of Cerrig y Gof lies 2km to the W. The monument consists of a large capstone and four uprights, of which two support the capstone. This monument has been excavated and revealed no evidence for further stoneholes. This was surprising as Lynch believed that this was a classic portal dolmen with a closing slab and that a stone was missing from the W (Lynch 1972, 69–70). Excavations by Sian Rees in 1979/1980 did show that the chamber area would have been considerably taller than it is at present, as the supporting stones stand more than 2m high. There was rather tentative evidence of a circular cairn which may have been the remains of a ring cairn (Barker 1992, 20). Four radiocarbon dates of around 3500 BC were taken from the chamber and cairn area. From the disturbed chamber floor small amounts of powdery cremated bone as well as two small sherds of corded Beaker and three sherds of possible Grooved Ware were found. On the unsealed old ground surface were two patches of cremated human bone and a ware similar to that found at Clegyr Boia. Under the re-deposited subsoil were more cremations and a fourth type of pottery. The pottery here was 'reminiscent of Abingdon Ware' (Lynch 1984, 108).

Landscape setting: This site is surrounded by both houses and a hedge, which means that the landscape cannot be seen in some directions. It is clear, however, that the sea would have been visible to the NW, along with Dinas Head. Carn Ingli is clearly visible to the S. GIS viewshed analysis shows that the Mynydd Preseli would not have been visible but that the site of Trellyffaint may have been visible on the horizon to the NE.

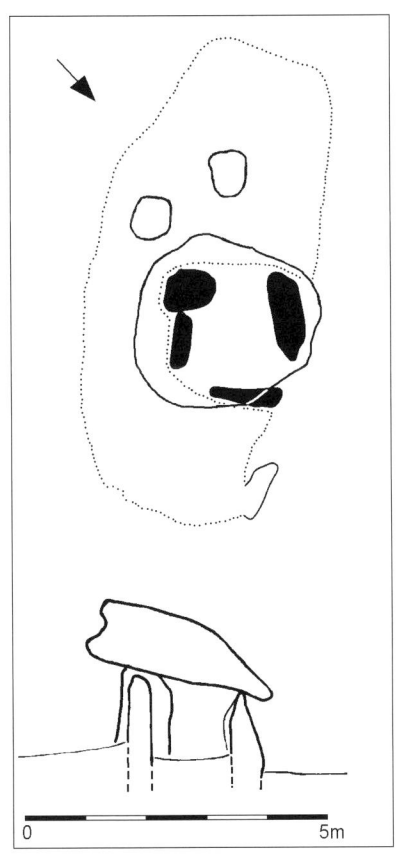

Figure 8.87 Plan and elevation of Carreg Coetan (after Barker 1992).

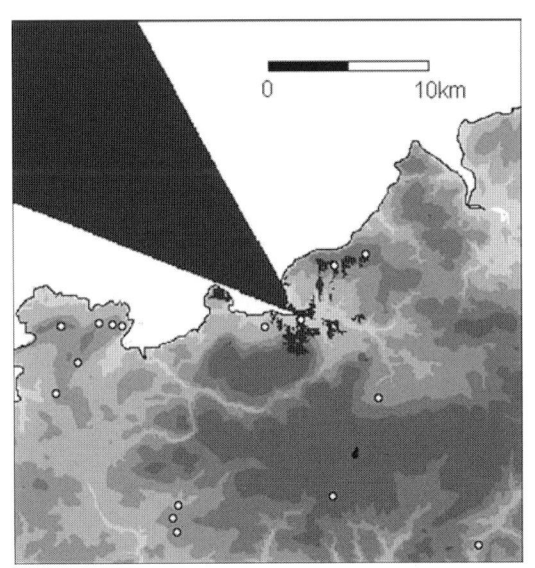

Figure 8.88 The viewshed from Carreg Coetan. Reproduced by kind permission of Ordnance Survey. © Crown copyright NC/03/20516.

References: Barker 1992, 19–20; Lynch 1972; Rees 1992, 15–6.

45. Cerrig y Gof (PEM 4)   SM 037 389

Description: Situated at 50m OD, this site is located in agricultural land close to a landscape filled with Bronze Age remains. It is positioned next to a stream which runs from Carn Ingli 2km to the S to the sea at Newport Bay. The site is only 2km from Carreg Coetan in Newport. The site itself consists of five chambers set within a circle and is unparalleled in Pembrokeshire, although it has been compared to Mull Hill on the Isle of Man. It is quite well preserved, and four of the chambers have capstones, two of which are still *in situ*. The remaining chambers survive as side stones. The best preserved chamber is to the E, where the entrance would have been to the SSW through a low portal. The five chambers set within a cairn were excavated in 1810 by Fenton (Barker 1992, 21). He discovered layers of charcoal, pottery, bone and sea pebbles. The proximity of Bronze Age hut circles and Carn Ingli, which may have been a Bronze Age fort, has led to suggestions that Cerrig y Gof is Bronze Age in date (Children and Nash 117, 46). This site is certainly quite different from other sites in the immediate area as it is the only one with multiple chambers set in such a configuration.

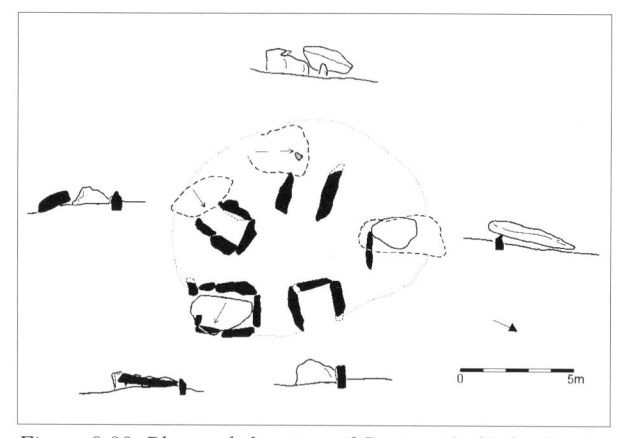

Figure 8.89 Plan and elevation of Cerrig y Gof (after Barker 1992).

Landscape setting: The landscape is obscured by dense evergreens from the N to the S, so it is difficult to make out the landscape setting in full. To the N the view is downhill towards agricultural land and the sea. It is not possible to see the beach below. To the NE there seems to be a restricted view downhill. Trees block the view to the E. To the ESE is Carn Ingli which looks like a single large outcrop from this direction. To the SE is a nearer hill with highly visible rocky outcrops. To the S are hills and to the SSW a hill with a prominent outcrop. SW-W are near hills (probably about 300m). Dinas Head promontory is highly visible to the WNW-NE and the white cliffs are visually dominating. Needle Point is also visible, with the sea directly to the N. It is possible to hear water from this site, but it is from a stream, not from the sea.

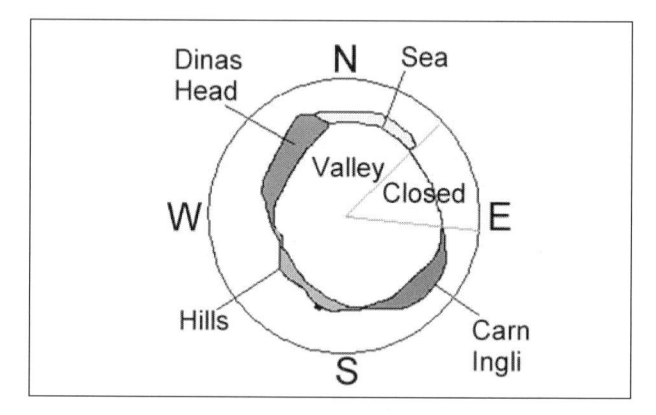

Figure 8.90 The setting of Cerrig y Gof.

References: Barker 1992, 21–2; Lynch 1972; Rees 1992, 16–17.

46. Pentre Ifan (PEM 5) SN 099 370

Description: Set at 150m OD, this is one of the most impressive monuments in Wales. The site itself is in guardianship but is surrounded by pasture in all directions. It is just over a kilometre from the Afon Nyfer and a kilometre from the outcrops of Carnedd Meibion Owen. The site has been well documented over the years as well as being excavated twice (Grimes 1948; 1960). Today, most of the façade along with the capstone survive intact and it is possible to see the extent of the long cairn or platform in many places. Excavation revealed that the entire chamber area was undercut by a large pit and there was evidence of activity in the forecourt and to the E of the chamber. A slab was once upright to the E and a fire had been built at its base. Charcoal was also found. The portal entrance had been blocked. In 1603, Owen claimed that four slabs enclosed the chamber area to the E and W. However, excavation found stone holes only to the western side of the chamber. Debate has since raged about the original form and construction sequence of the site. The excavator believed that the monument was a single phase construction, but this has since been contested. Lynch (1972, 71) believes that the monument was built in two phases. She claims that the chamber and forecourt were constructed first along with a small square cairn. A later phase saw the addition of the façade and the lengthening of the cairn. Barker (1992) agrees that the monument was constructed in two phases but suggests that the first phase saw the construction of the chamber and the façade. The blocking portal stone, he claims, was a false entrance with entry gained through the eastern side. He suggests that the second phase was simply the construction of the cairn over the monument.

Finds from the excavation included a few flint flakes and four sherds from the neck of a carinated bowl, all from the chamber. The pottery was similar to that found at Dyffryn Ardudwy (Lynch 1969, 167). In the forecourt, a flint arrowhead and a few fragments of pottery were also found. To the E of the chamber charcoal and flint flakes were found.

Landscape setting: The view from the E round to the S is restricted by the hill on which the monument stands. As the view opens out, the Preselis can be seen in the distance. The four outcrops on the top of Carnedd Meibion-Owen are particularly prominent to the SW. Carn Ingli can be clearly seen to the W. To the NW, the view drops down to Dinas Head and the sea, before the hills encircling the Nevern Valley obscure the view. The valley area containing the Afon Nyfer stretches out to the N and NE, before the view is closed down to the E. Llech y Dribedd is visible, skylined on the horizon to the N. Thus a quarter of the view is restricted, while roughly a quarter of the view is very wide-ranging, looking out to sea. Rocky outcrops are very prominent on the horizon, and lie scattered around the immediate area, and Carn Ingli is prominent to the W. Standing in the façade, the view to the left looks out to the sea, while the view to the right is inland, looking out over the Nevern Valley. This is also the axis on which the long cairn is placed. The Mynydd Preselis are also clearly visible to the SSW when standing in the façade. However, from further down the cairn, the Preselis are no longer visible. This suggests that the chamber and façade may have been carefully located in the landscape so that these mountains were visible.

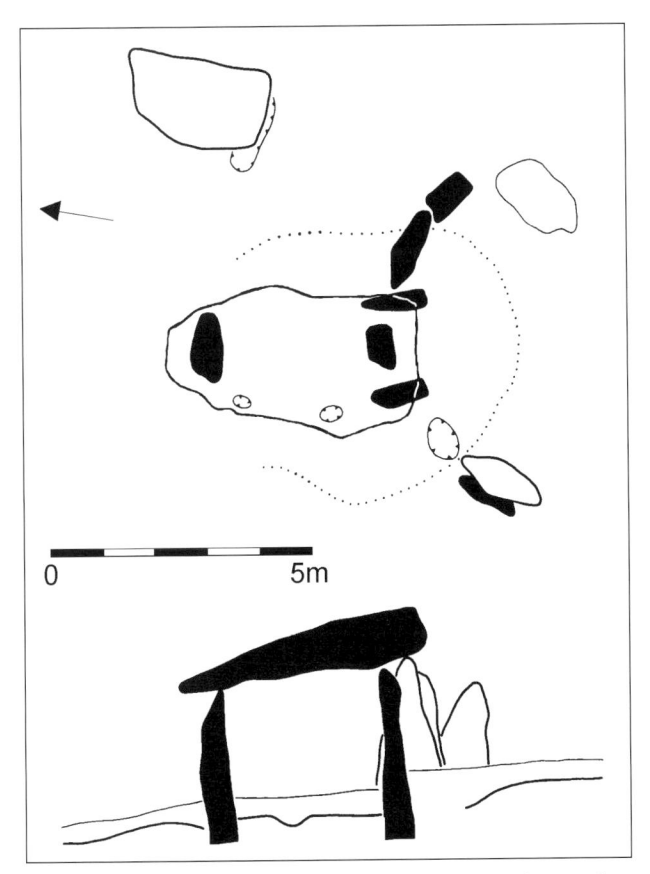

Figure 8.91 Plan and elevation of Pentre Ifan (after Barker 1992).

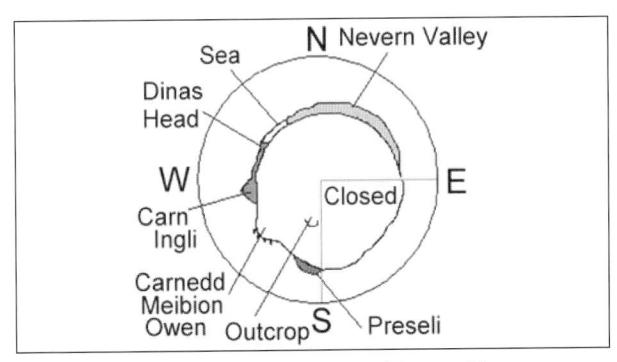

Figure 8.92 The setting of Pentre Ifan.

References: Barker 1992, 23–6; Grimes 1948; Lynch 1972; Murphy 1999; Rees 1992, 14–15; Tilley 1994, 105–7.

47. Mountain (PEM 6) SN 166 329

Description: Set at 250m OD on the western edge of the Mynydd Preseli, this site is positioned at the source of the Eastern Cleddau. It is set on the southern side of the Preselis between Foel Drygarn and Maes y Garn. It is currently in a field boundary in agricultural land. A number of prostrate supports survive, along with a large capstone plus some natural stones. This site would once have been a large and impressive monument, but it is now in a poor state of repair. Only one slab seems to survive *in situ* and it currently supports the collapsed capstone. The boundary wall which surrounds most of the site may have been constructed using cairn material from the site and a roughly circular mound is visible around the slabs.

Landscape setting: The view from the NNW to the NNE is restricted looking up at the immediate hillslope. To the NE there is a gentle rise to the summit of Crug yr Hwch, followed by Crugiau Dwy and Foel Dyrch to the S. To the SSW a small chunk of a distant hill is visible. The W looks to Carn Sarn, and then to the NNW Foel Drygarn can be found with two Bronze Age cairns on its summit. The landscape setting is quite similar to many monuments in this area, with a closed view in one direction and a view of a more distant rocky outcrops and a valley area in another. Although the spectacular form of Carn Meini is nearby, it is not visible from this site. The landscape is basically halved, with half of the view wide-ranging and the other half much more restricted. The site is also positioned at the head of a valley and the source of the River Cleddau, and this may have been one of the most important factors for deciding the precise location of the monument.

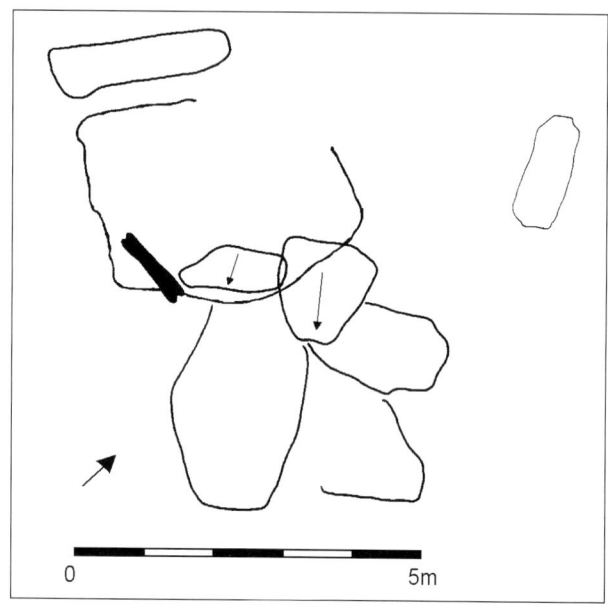

Figure 8.93 Plan of Mountain (after Barker 1992).

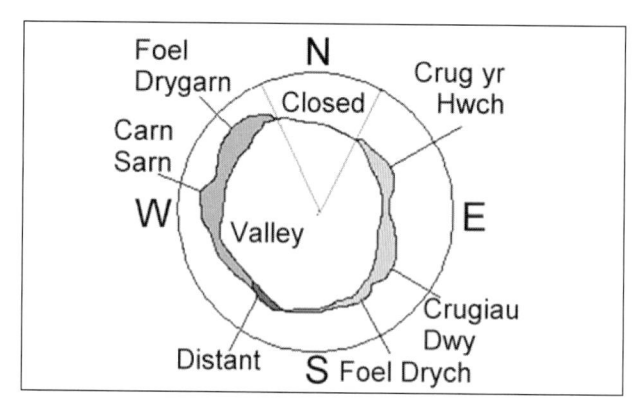

Figure 8.94 The setting of Mountain.

References: Barker 1992, 26; Lynch 1972.

48. Bedd yr Afanc (PEM 27) SN 108 346

Description: Set at 140m OD, this site is now in marshy ground surrounded by small streams. The site is right on the northern edge of the Mynydd Preseli, in between two large streams which run down from the mountains. The site stands at the centre of an upland valley area on a small knoll in an area of open moorland covered with gorse. This monument consists of 22 small orthostats, most of which seem to be in their original positions. The site was excavated by Grimes (1939) who concluded that the site was a gallery grave, originally covered with a cairn. There were no finds. The site survives much as Grimes left it, with the remains of a small cairn still clearly visible. The stones themselves run ENE – WSW, aligned on the axis of the valley.

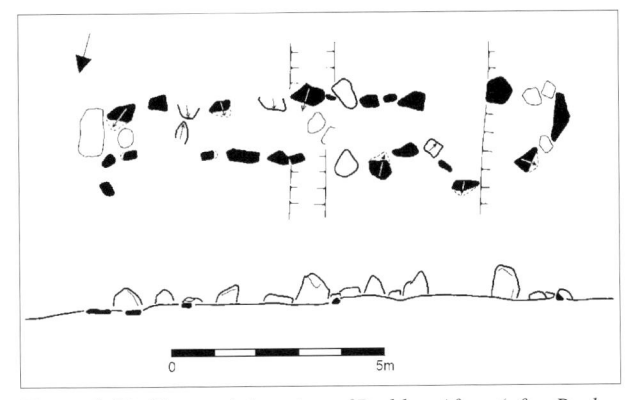

Figure 8.95 Plan and elevation of Bedd yr Afanc (after Barker 1992).

Landscape setting: There are quite wide-ranging views in all directions apart from to the NE where the view is slightly restricted. This view looks uphill, but it is possible to see hills in the background from most places in the chamber. The view from here round to the SW is wide-ranging, looking at the Preseli mountains. The view from the SW round to the NE is still quite wide-ranging, but is of closer, smaller hills. The rocky outcrops of Carnedd Meibion-Owen to the NW are those visible on the skyline at Pentre Ifan. Looking N, the view is of more immediate hills, the valley and river and a settlement area. This site is clearly in a very different location from the other chambered tombs in the area which are usually located in pasture, with part of the view restricted by a hillslope. Only the stone circle of Gors Fawr is located in a similar location and in rough moorland. Since the structural design of this monument is unique in Wales, as is its location, this site might be thought of as much more typically Bronze Age.

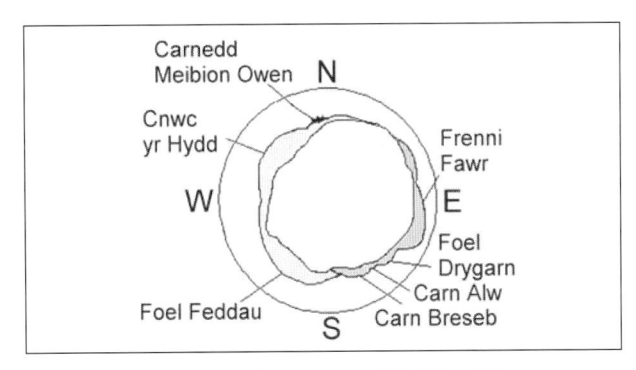

Figure 8.96 The setting of Bedd yr Afanc.

References: Barker 1992, 39–40; Grimes 1939a Lynch 1972; Rees 1992, 19–20.

49. Eithbed (PEM 31) SN 080 286

Description: Located at 250m OD, these monuments are set on the side of a gentle hill on the southern side of the Preselis. The sites themselves are found in a field used for grazing, close to and, in parts, in a field boundary. To the S and W are a number of standing stones suggesting that this entire landscape may once have been significant. The architectural remains are poorly preserved; Barker records the recent removal of the megalithic remains (1992, 52).

Landscape setting: The view from the WNW round to the ENE is restricted by the immediate hillslope. This effectively means that the Preselis cannot be seen from the site. The domed hill of Mynydd Bach is visible to the E and then the view widens out to look over southern Pembrokeshire and the valleys to the S. The location of this site is not dissimilar to that of Mountain. Both are located on the southern side of the Preselis but neither have views of these mountains. These are also two of the highest monuments in Pembrokeshire.

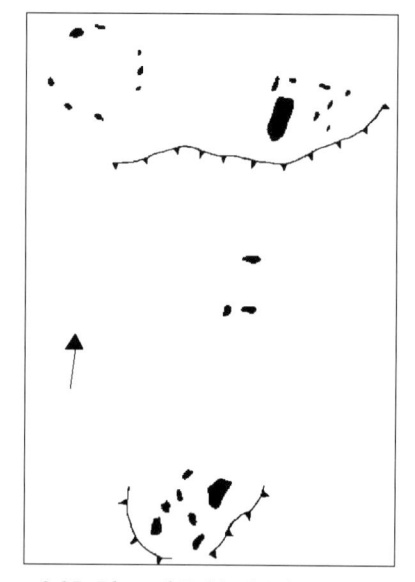

Figure 8.97 Plan of Eithbed (after Barker 1992).

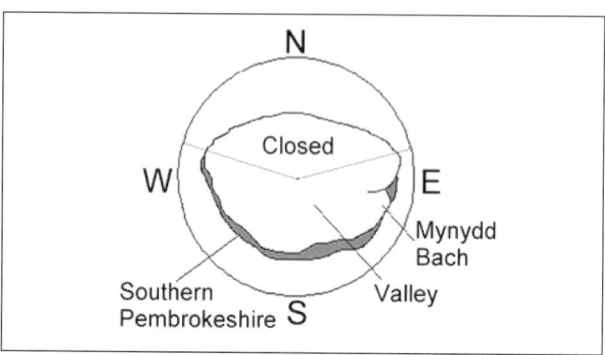

Figure 8.98 The setting of Eithbed.

Reference: Barker 1992, 51–2.

50. Colston (PEM 10) SM 983 281

Description: This site is set at 100m OD in a hedge which separates a field from the road. The site is positioned on the NW side of a gentle hill and overlooks the point where the Afon Anghof and the Afon Glan-Rhyd meet to form the Western Cleddau. The monuments of Garn Turne and Parc y Llyn can be found within 2km of the site. Structurally this is one of the worst preserved monuments in Pembrokeshire. The capstone and several uprights are clearly visible although the site is embedded in a thick field boundary, which has covered most of the remains. The part of the monument that remains visible is used by cattle as a shelter which has disturbed the ground around the chamber considerably. An early Royal Commission report suggests that there are two chambers at this site and it has been proposed that a long cairn covered the site (Barker 1992, 28).

Landscape setting: Since the site is embedded in a large hedge, most of the view is obscured from view. However, it does appear that the view is restricted from the E round to the W. The view from the W round to the E looks down at the valley area below, towards the start of the Western Cleddau river and to the hills beyond. This site is considerably smaller than its neighbour, Garn Turne, although it does seem to have a similar structure and be in a similar landscape setting. This site also seems to be positioned close to the start of the Western Cleddau. There is also a chambered tomb positioned at the source of the Eastern Cleddau, suggesting that these were highly significant natural features.

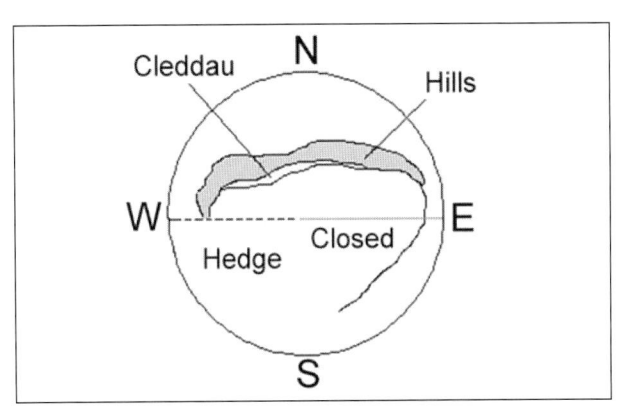

Figure 8.100 The setting of Colston.

Reference: Barker 1992, 28.

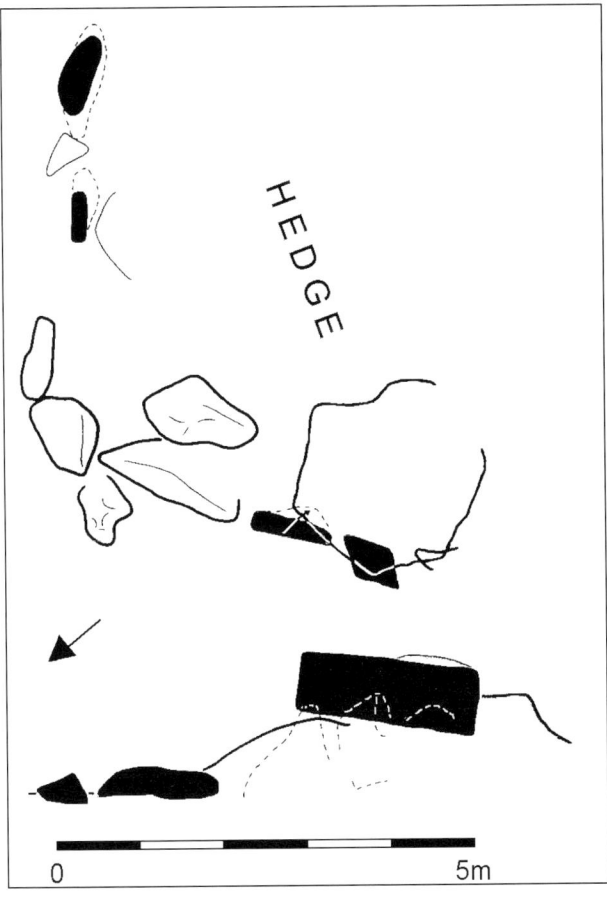

Figure 8.99 Plan and elevation of Colston (after Barker 1992).

148   *Vicki Cummings*

51. Garn Turne (PEM 11) SM 979 273

Description: This site is set at 135m OD in an area of rough grassland. The whole area is covered with rocks and small outcrops, although most of the surrounding area is farmland. Two other monuments can be found nearby, Colston to the N and Parc y Llyn to the S. The site is set on the SW side of a hill rising up to the rocky summit of Garn Turne. This site is one of the largest and most impressive sites in Pembrokeshire. It survives as an enormous collapsed capstone with an orthostatic façade. Barker believes that the capstone was never raised from the ground to form a portal tomb as it is too large (1992, 29), but the stones which lie around the chamber suggest otherwise. Some authors suggest that a long cairn may also have existed at the site (Rees 1992, 27). Some of the stones which make the façade are clearly natural slabs which have been carefully incorporated into the structure by the monument builders. A large natural sandstone slab is visible in the centre of the façade area.

Landscape setting: The view is closed from the N round to the SE by the hill on which the monument stands. A whole range of hills is visible to the NE just a little higher up the hill or standing on the capstone. From the forecourt area, however, these are totally obscured. The rest of the view from the SE round to the N looks out over rich agricultural land and the valley containing Wolf's Castle. Prominent on the skyline are the outcrops of Poll Carn and Maiden Castle to the SSW, Carn Llidi to the W and Penberry to the WNW. The monument seems to have been placed very precisely in the landscape. The dominant rocky outcrops of Poll Carn and Maiden Castle are skylined behind the capstone when standing in the forecourt. Furthermore, Carn Llidi and Penberry can just be seen on the horizon. The view to the NE looking out towards the Preseli mountains is also specifically closed off from view. It seems that the monument has been fitted into the landscape so that all of these landscape features are either visible or invisible. Like other monuments in this area, this site is positioned so that it has rocky outcrops, Poll Carn and Maiden Castle, visible on the distant horizon.

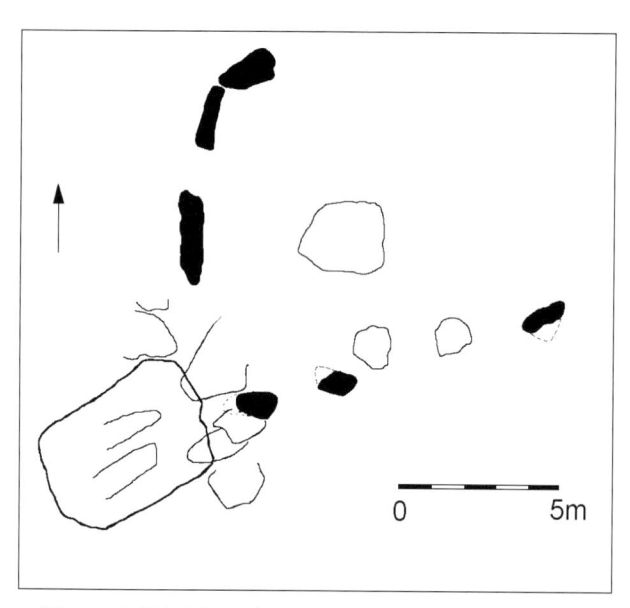

Figure 8.101 Plan of Garn Turne (after Barker 1992).

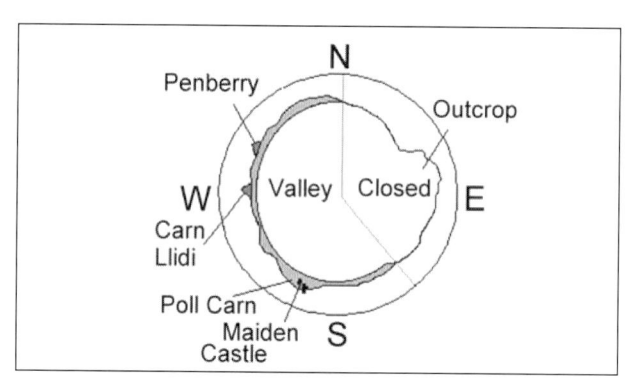

Figure 8.102 The setting of Garn Turne.

References: Barker 1992, 28–31; Rees 1992, 27.

52. Parc y Llyn (PEM 12) SM 982 266

Description: Set at 130m OD in the corner of a field, this site is set on the NW side of a gentle hill. The site is not far from a spring which flows down to the Western Cleddau at Wolf's Castle. The site is located within 2km of two other chambered tombs, Garn Turne and Colston. The site survives as a capstone and four uprights with what may be the remains of a cairn or platform. Deeply buried within the nearby field boundary are the remains of a possible second chamber.

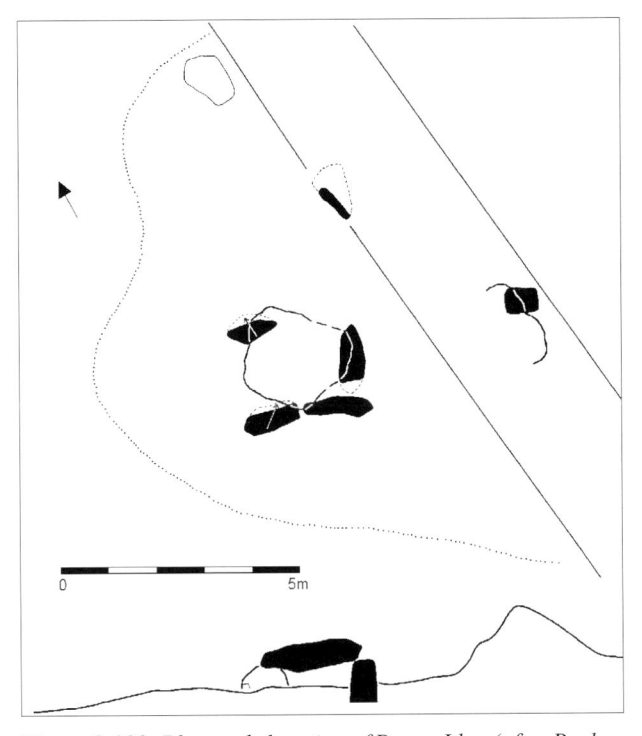

Figure 8.103 Plan and elevation of Parc y Llyn (after Barker 1992).

Landscape setting: The view from just past E round to the W is restricted by the hill on which the site stands. The view then opens up and looks out over the valley area to the W and agricultural land to the N. The prominent feature of Poll Carn can clearly be seen on the side of the Great Treffgarne Mountain to the WNW, and Mynydd Castlebythe, and the Preselis can be seen to the NE. Garn Turne would be visible to the NNW, although it is presently blocked from view by trees. Therefore the view to the N is open and wide-ranging, while that to the S is closed and restricted. This site is positioned in the landscape in a similar way to Garn Turne, which looks out over the Great Treffgarne Mountain and its prominent outcrops. Like Colston, it also looks over a valley area containing a stream which flows into the Cleddau.

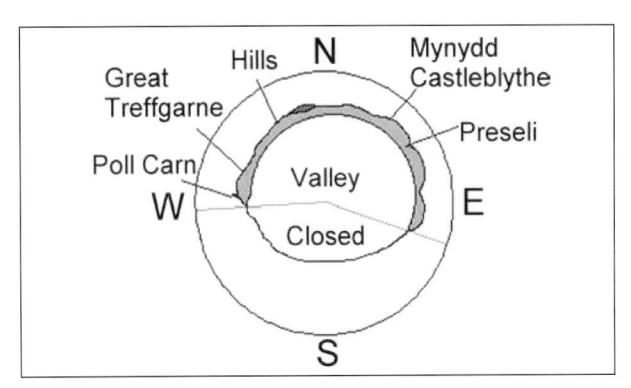

Figure 8.104 The setting of Parc y Llyn.

Reference: Barker 1992, 30–2.

53. Carn Wen (PEM 7–9) SM 948 391

Description: Situated at around 110m OD, these monuments are set on a hillside rising up from Fishguard Harbour. Although the hillside is quite steep, the tombs themselves are set on a flat area of land, next to a housing estate. Behind the monuments are rocky outcrops which run across the length of the hillside roughly N-S. The monuments themselves are situated in an area of rough, overgrown common land. The site consists of three chambers in a line. It was suggested that all three chambers were set within small round barrows (Daniel 1950, 200), but today there is no evidence to support this. Two other chambers may also have existed at the site, but have since been destroyed (Barker 1992, 27). The northern chamber consists of a single upright and a capstone. The second chamber has a much larger capstone than the northern chamber and several *in situ* uprights. The southern chamber is the largest of the three chambers although the large capstone is displaced to the N. There is also another large upright, apparently *in situ* a short distance from the capstone. It is quite sizeable, over 1.5m tall and may once have supported the capstone. Other uprights are still visible under the collapsed capstone.

Landscape setting: The view from the S round to the N is entirely restricted by a view of the nearby outcrops. From the N round to the S, the view is presently obscured by the row of houses, but the view would have been of the sea around Fishguard Bay and the harbour. To the NE, Cemaes Head is visible, with Dinas Head prominent to the ENE. The three outcrops on the top of Mynydd Dinas are also clearly visible, with Carn Ingli poking out behind this massif to the ESE. To the SE, the harbour and the town of Fishguard are clearly visible. These sites certainly seem to have been placed in a prominent position within the landscape. The rocky outcrops against which the tombs are placed would have been visible from the other side of the harbour (they are now obscured by houses) and Tilley suggests that these outcrops were dominant focal points within the wider landscape (1994, 99). The outcrops are also rather distinctive when examined at close range. Large natural hollows are present over many of the slabs. A large natural crevice can also be found amongst the outcrops, which creates an enclosed space much like those of the chambers.

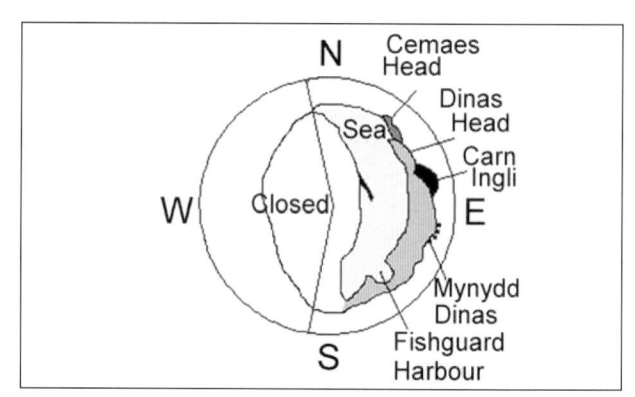

Figure 8.106 The setting of Carn Wen.

References: Barker 1992, 27–8; Rees 1992, 20–1.

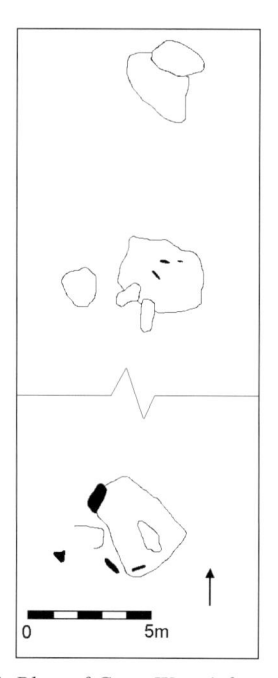

Figure 8.105 Plan of Carn Wen (after Barker 1992).

54. Parc y Cromlech/Penrhiw (PEM 14) SM 942 391

Description: This site is located at 140m OD on agricultural land on the SW side of a gentle hill. The landscape around the monument is fairly flat and featureless with no distinctive features visible, although there is a rocky outcrop to the W. Garn Wen is located only 0.5km to the E, and Carn Wnda 1km to the W. The site itself consists of three large uprights which support a large capstone. The capstone was replaced recently, and the remains of a cairn or platform can still be seen at the site (Barker 1992, 32).

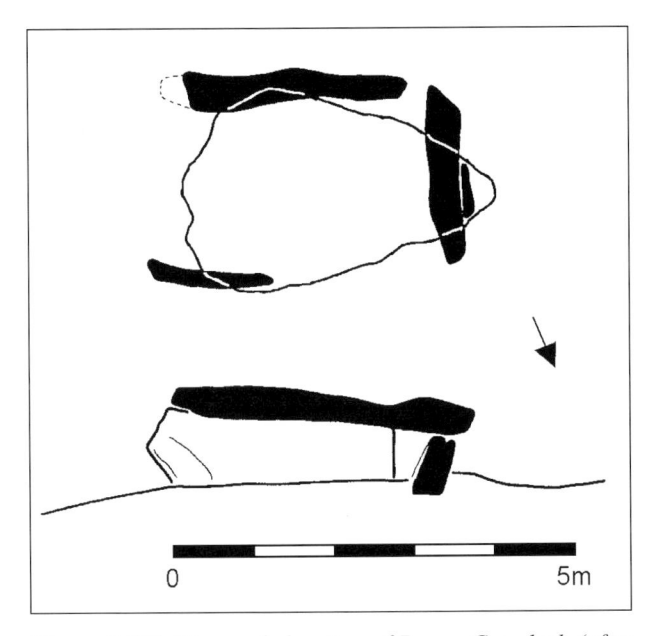

Figure 8.107 Plan and elevation of Parc y Cromlech (after Barker 1992).

Landscape setting: The site is currently surrounded by trees which encircle the nearby farmhouse and some of the field boundaries but it is still possible to make out the surrounding landscape. The view from the WSW round to almost the N is closed by the gentle rise of the hill on which the monument stands. From here round to the E, there is a wide view of the sea. To the ENE Camaes Head and then Dinas Head are visible. To the ESE, Fishguard Harbour is visible with Carn Ingli in the distance. The three distinctive outcrops on Mynydd Dinas are also clearly visible. The view from the SE round to the SW is of distant hills. The outcrop which has the monument of Ffyst Samson near its summit is also visible from this site, to the SW. One of the most distinctive elements of this site is its wide-ranging views of the landscape, particularly of the sea and Carn Ingli.

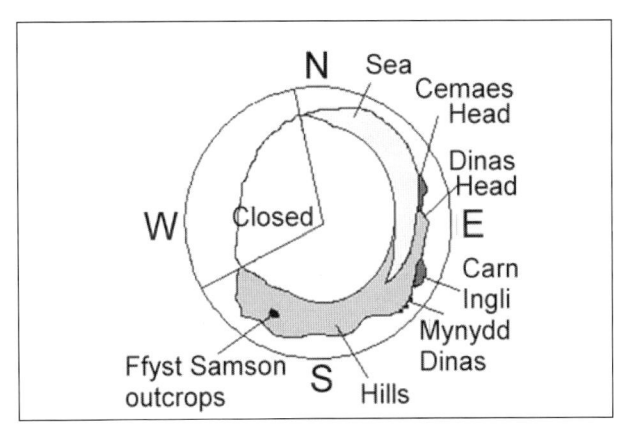

Figure 8.108 The setting of Parc y Cromlech.

Reference: Barker 1992, 32.

152   *Vicki Cummings*

55. Carn Wnda (PEM 13) SM 933 392

Description: Located at around 150m OD only a few metres from the large outcrop from which the site takes its name, this site stands in a small flat area on the western slopes of a hill which leads to the outcrop. Three other chambered tombs can be found within 2km of this site. Although the site itself is in rough open land, it overlooks an area of agricultural land, as well as the modern settlement of Ty Isaf and Llanwnda. Although this site consists of only two stones, a capstone and supporting slab, it is a large and impressive structure. Dry stone walling exists on either side of the supporting stone, which creates a substantial inner chamber. The site was examined in the nineteenth century by Fenton (1848, 284) who found a small urn containing cremated bone, which might suggest a late Neolithic/early Bronze Age date or at least use in this period. Tilley suggests that monuments of this type may have been recalling caves and rock shelters of the Mesolithic in their construction, while the outcrops key the monument into the wider landscape (1994, 96–9).

Landscape setting: The view from just beyond N round to the SSW is entirely restricted by the rocky outcrop against which the monument stands. To the SW St David's Head is prominent on the horizon and it may be no coincidence that St David's Head has a chambered tomb on it. A small stretch of sea with two islands can also be seen beyond the headland. Garn Gilfach is visible in the more immediate landscape to the W, with another outcrop, that of Garn Fawr just behind it. The views from here to the N are of the sea and agricultural land in the foreground. Strumble Head can clearly be seen.. This monument is also placed in an area with a large number natural features which resemble built monuments (Cummings 2002a).

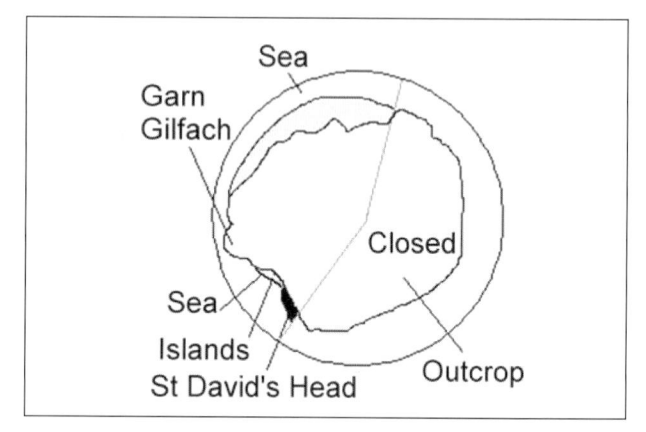

Figure 8.110 The setting of Carn Wnda.

References: Barker 1992, 32; Fenton 1848; Rees 1992, 21–2.

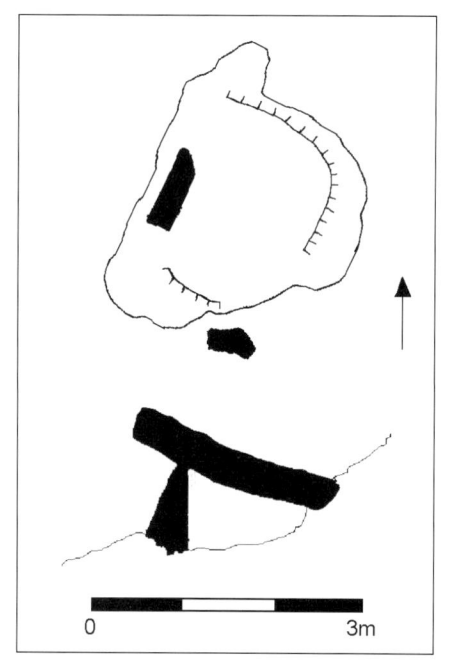

Figure 8.109 Plan and elevation of Carn Wnda (after Barker 1992).

56. Garn Gilfach (PEM 15) SM 909 390

Description: This site is positioned at 170m OD on the southern side of Garngilfach Hill, which rises up from agricultural land. The site is just beneath the summit of rocky outcrops next to an old stone wall. The site is in rough land covered with thick gorse and brambles. The site is the most westerly of a row of monuments across this area of land. To the E the monuments of Carn Wnda, Parc y Cromlech and Carn Wen can be found. This site survives as a large capstone with several supports. The site has never formally been excavated, but antiquaries found charcoal, pottery and a flint (Barker 1992, 33). The capstone is only just above ground level and it backs directly on to the large outcrop behind it. It is possible that a large pit underneath the monument may have acted as a chamber area; it is unlikely that this was ever covered with a cairn.

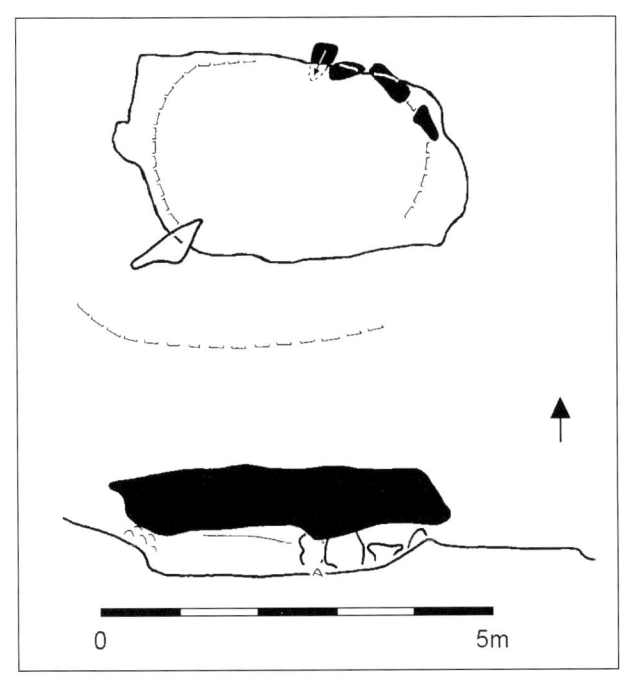

Figure 8.111 Plan and elevation of Garn Gilfach (after Barker 1992).

Landscape setting: More than half of the view is obscured by the rocky outcrops against which the monument stands. From the E round to the SW the view is more open. The immediate view is of agricultural land. To the E, Mynydd Dinas can be seen, as well as the Preselis in the distance. Round to the SSW, St David's Head can clearly be seen, along with a small chunk of the sea. This view is then obscured by the more immediate coastline. The site is set within in an area literally covered with natural features which resemble monuments. Antiquaries, in fact, could not tell the difference between the natural and artificial monuments (see Barker 1992, 32; Cummings 2002a).

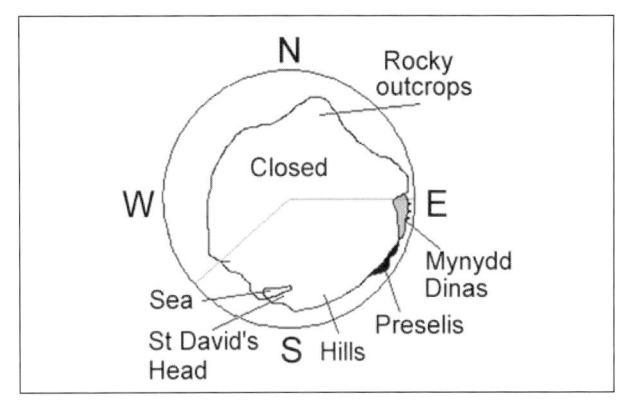

Figure 8.112 The setting of Garn Gilfach.

Reference: Barker 1992, 32–3.

57. Ffynnondruidion (PEM 28) SM 920 368

Description: Set at 115m OD on the SE side of a gentle hill, this site would have stood on relatively flat ground in an area of rocky outcrops although this is in an area of agricultural land. Four other chambered monuments can be found to the N, and Ffyst Samson is only 2km away to the SW. The site was destroyed by the tenant farmer in 1830, who apparently leveled the site, unearthing a stone axe of quartz diorite and an adze. Later accounts claimed that the capstone and two uprights still survived at the site (Barker 1992, 50). Although many large stones lie around the area, nothing survives which now resembles a monument.

Landscape setting: The view from the WNW round to the NE is effectively closed by the hill on which the site once stood. To the NE, the sea and a peninsula can be seen, around the Fishguard area. The three outcrops on top of Mynydd Dinas can clearly be seen. The view then opens up to look at the valley area framed by hills in the distance.

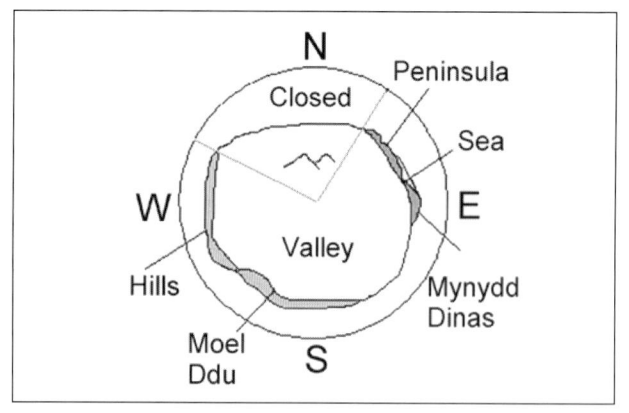

Figure 8.113 The setting of Ffynnondruidion.

Reference: Barker 1992, 50–1.

58. Ffyst Samson/Trellysycoed (PEM 16) SM 906 349

Description: Set at 130m OD, this site is positioned on the western side of Trellys y Coed hill, below the prominent outcrops of Carn Llys. It is on a flat area of land amongst thick gorse, overlooking rich agricultural land. Carreg Samson is located 2.5 km to the NW. The site survives as two uprights supporting a capstone with the remains of a low cairn or platform.

Landscape setting: The view from the NE round to the SE is closed, but there are two small areas where more distant hills are visible on the horizon. From the SE round to the SW the view is of agricultural land rising to hills. To the SW, St David's Head is prominent on the horizon, and the sea becomes visible. The sea and the coastline are then visible round to the NW. From the NW, a series of dramatic rocky outcrops are visible including Garn Gilfach.

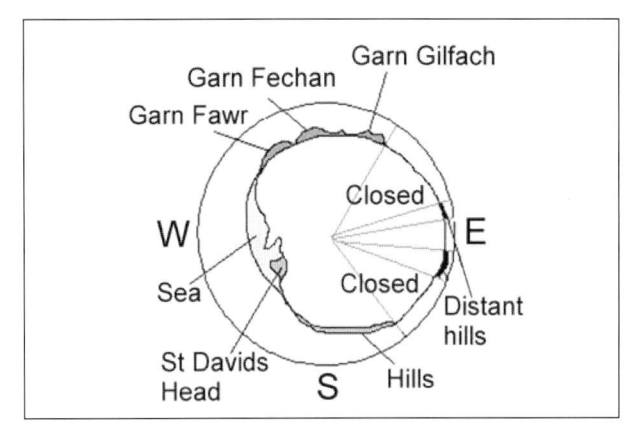

Figure 8.115 The setting of Ffyst Samson.

References: Barker 1992, 33–4; Rees 1992, 22.

Figure 8.114 Plan and elevation of Ffyst Samson (after Barker 1992).

59. Carreg Samson/Longhouse (PEM 18) SM 848 335

Description: This site is set at 40m OD on the eastern side of a gentle hill. It is located in agricultural land less than 1km from the village and harbour of Abercastle. The site stands at the head of a natural creek and several springs can be found nearby. The monument presently consists of six large uprights and a capstone. The site has been excavated (Lynch 1975) and this revealed that another upright had once existed, in the gap to the NNE. Dry stone walling may also have existed between the uprights. The entire structure was built over a large pit, which may have been created in order to extract the capstone. There is also evidence of a passage, at least 2m in length and this can be seen on the plan and elevation as three stone holes to the NW. Lynch suggested that a cairn once covered the monument (1975, 16), but there is no surviving evidence of this. There were relatively few finds from the site, although it appears that the site had been disturbed before excavation. A few pieces of flint were found in the chamber, including a finely worked microlith. A red deer tooth was also found in the fill in the chamber along with a quantity of sherds, all from the same pot. Lynch suggests that the chamber originally contained a single large bowl standing on the floor to the E of the entrance (1975, 23). This pot is from an early Neolithic bowl tradition.

Landscape setting: The view from the SW round to the NW is closed by the immediate hillslope. Due to the presence of a wall, it is difficult to estimate, but an outcrop may just be visible to the WNW. From the NW, the sea becomes visible, with Strumble Head appearing to the NNE followed by a series of prominent outcrops. At a closer distance, a series of peninsulas are visible, including a large area of land (Ynys y Castell) which has a large sea cave in it. Abercastle Harbour, however, cannot be seen. To the E, a very prominent outcrop is visible just over 1km away, with the distant Mynydd Preseli framed behind. The rest of the view is fairly unspectacular, simply looking over more immediate hills. The site seems to be positioned in relation to a number of landscape features. The harbour at Abercastle is one of the few safe landing ports in the area. The sea cave in the harbour is also quite distinctive. The monument is also positioned near to several small Mesolithic sites (this may explain the inclusion of a microlith in the chamber) as well as natural springs. The site is also positioned near to, although not next to, two large and distinctive outcrops, a relationship which is repeated at monuments throughout Pembrokeshire. Two monuments are visible from this site, Trewalter Llwyd to the SE and Ffyst Samson to the ENE. The outcrop of Garn Gilfach is also visible although the monument itself is not.

Figure 8.116 Plan and elevation of Carreg Samson (after Barker 1992).

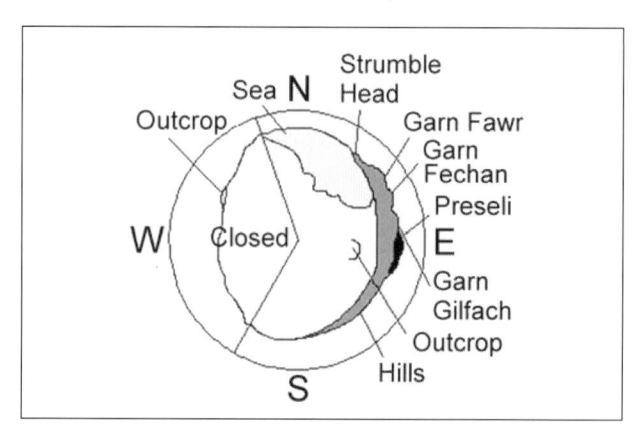

Figure 8.117 The setting of Carreg Samson.

References: Barker 1992, 34; Lynch 1975; Rees 1992, 23.

60. Trewalter Llwyd (PEM 17) SM 868 318

Description: This site is located at 105m OD on the western side of a gentle hill which rises up to the village of Mathry. The site is positioned in a field boundary surrounded by agricultural land. The Western Cleddau can be found less than a kilometre to the S and Carreg Samson is only 2.5km to the NW. The site consists of a massive capstone and a single upright. The capstone is buried deep within a hedge, and it is likely that more structural remains survive. A passage may once have existed at the site (Lynch 1975, 25).

Landscape setting: There is a restricted view from the NE round to the SW looking up-slope at agricultural land. To the SW, hills appear in the distance and continue to the W where the sea becomes visible. The sea and a series of peninsulas are visible from the W round to just past N. Carreg Samson is visible to the NW. To the NNE the distant band of outcrops becomes visible, of which Garn Gilfach outcrop is particularly prominent. This site would once have been a very impressive and large monument, comparable perhaps to Llech y Dribedd or Carreg Samson (Children and Nash 1997, 62). This monument has a clear view of the stream valley which leads to Carreg Samson as well as the monument itself. A basic landscape division seems to be working here, with half of the view restricted and facing inland, while half the view is expansive, looking at the coast and out to sea.

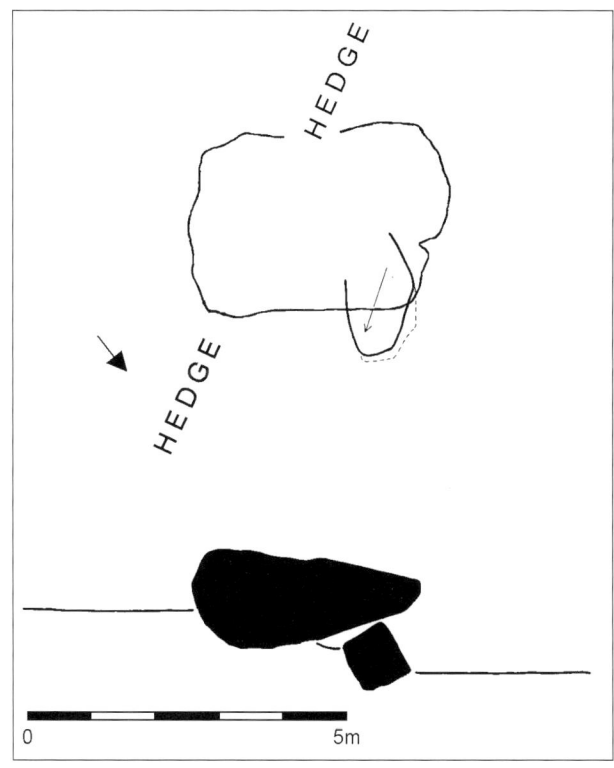

Figure 8.118 Plan and elevation of Trewalter Llwyd (after Barker 1992).

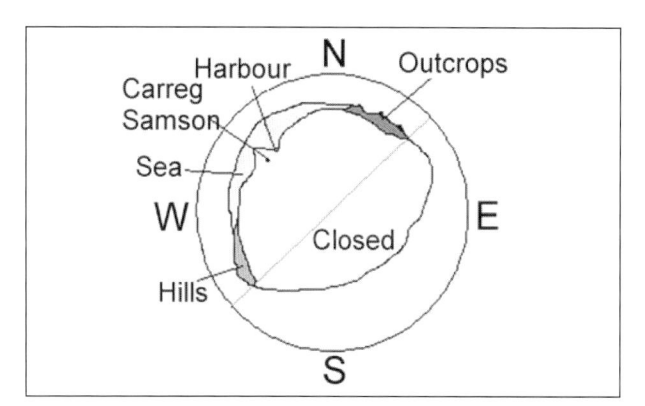

Figure 8.119 The setting of Trewalter Llwyd.

Reference: Barker 1992, 45.

61. Treffynnon (PEM 19) SM 853 287

Description: Set at 125m OD on the edge of a ploughed field, this site is surrounded by agricultural land on all sides. The site stands on the southern side of a gentle hill, which rises up to the N. The site consists of three uprights and a capstone which has been displaced.

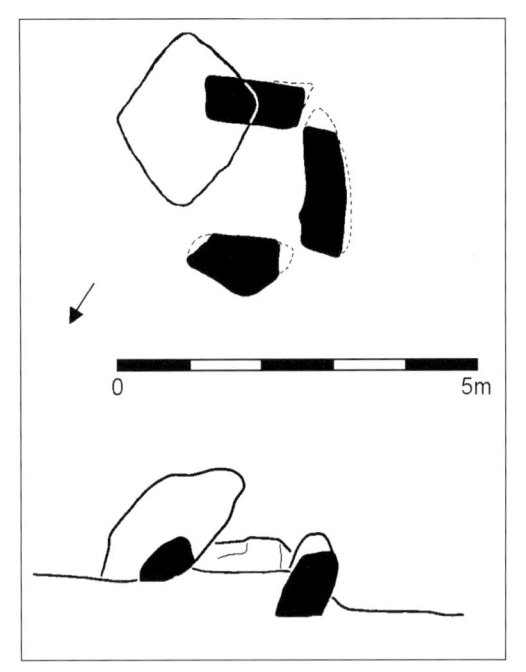

Figure 8.120 Plan and elevation of Treffynnon (after Barker 1992).

Landscape setting: The view from the NW round to the ENE is restricted by the hill on which the monument stands. For the rest of the view there are wide and expansive views out across the agricultural land surrounding the site. To the SE the Great Treffgarne Mountain and Plumbstone Mountain are visible. To the SSW, a small chunk of sea is visible with the next peninsula, Skomer and Skokholm Islands clearly visible on the horizon. Ramsey Island can also be seen to the SW. The dominating presence of Carn Llidi and Penberry can both be seen to the W and NW respectively, before the view is restricted again. The location of the site within the landscape is quite similar to other monuments, particularly White House only 3km away to the W. Like this site, Treffynnon has a small distant view of the sea with islands and the next peninsula visible. Rocky outcrops are located in the vicinity of this monument, and they are skylined. If the monument had been placed any further down the hill the view of the sea and the islands would be obscured.

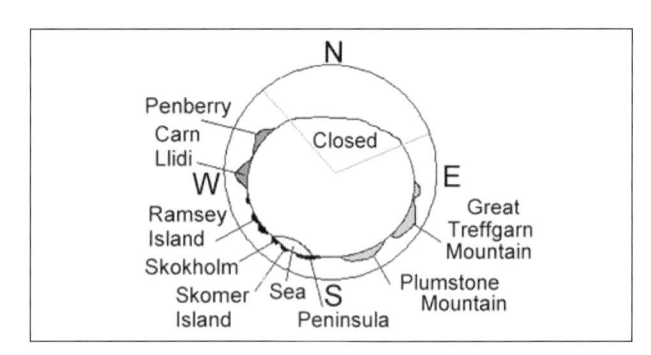

Figure 8.121 The setting of Treffynnon.

Reference: Barker 1992, 34.

62. White House/Tresewig (None) SM 826 284

Description: Set at 85m OD, this site is set in the middle of a field, surrounded on all sides by agricultural land. The site is positioned on the southern side of a gentle hill and a spring is located near to the site. It is only 3km from the site of Treffynon. The site survives in a rather poor condition, so much so that Barker (1992) classes it only as a probable site. Barker notes that the capstone (on its side) and a single side stone along with one portal stone are undisturbed. He suggests that the northern portal stone has been moved and that the other slabs are simply propped against the chamber but it is not clear whether these were ever part of the monument (Barker 1992, 48). In contrast, Children and Nash (1997, 84) claim that the chamber area is intact and undisturbed, with five surviving uprights. This monument would certainly have been very impressive when first built. All around and right up to the monument has been ploughed, so there is no sign of a cairn or mound. Most of the slabs are no longer earth-fast, or barely so. The capstone lies on its side in the chamber along with another large slab.

Landscape setting: The view from the NNE round to the NE is restricted by the hill on which in the site stands. The view round the rest of the circle looks out over the agricultural plain with hills in the distance. However, to the SSW, a small portion of the sea is visible, with the next peninsula and Skomer and Skokholm Islands visible. To the NW, the nearby outcrop of Carn Tregremaes is visible as well as Carn Llidi and Penberry in the distance. This site is placed near a prominent rocky outcrop, but not against it and this is a situation mirrored at sites like Pentre Ifan and Carreg Samson.

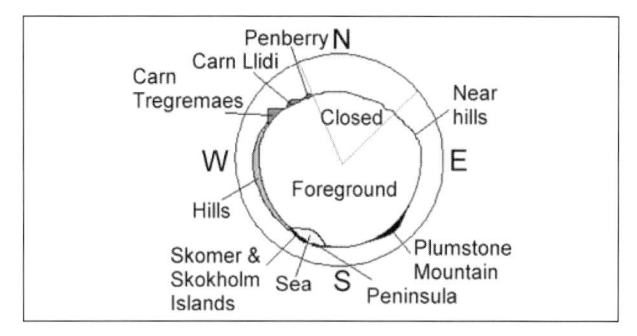

Figure 8.122 The setting of White House.

Reference: Barker 1992, 48.

63. St Elvies (PEM 20) SM 812 239

Description: This site is set at 60m OD on the northern side of a gentle hill which slopes up to the S, concealing the sea which is only 500m away. The site is now fenced off, but it is set in agricultural land above a stream gorge. The harbour at Solva is less than a kilometre away and a spring can be found 100m to the N. The site presently consists of two chambers, each with a displaced capstone and two upright supports. In the eighteenth century the tenant farmer 'blasted and carried off two legs of the eastern cromlech' (Barker 1992, 35). It is likely that the western chamber was also damaged by this farmer. The site was also excavated but without significant result (Grimes 1936a, 13). The two chambers are both in a quite poor state of preservation, but it is possible to see that they are quite different. The western chamber has a large igneous capstone with a natural cupmark on its upper surface. The chamber to the E is smaller than that to the W and the capstone is a different type of stone from that of the first chamber.

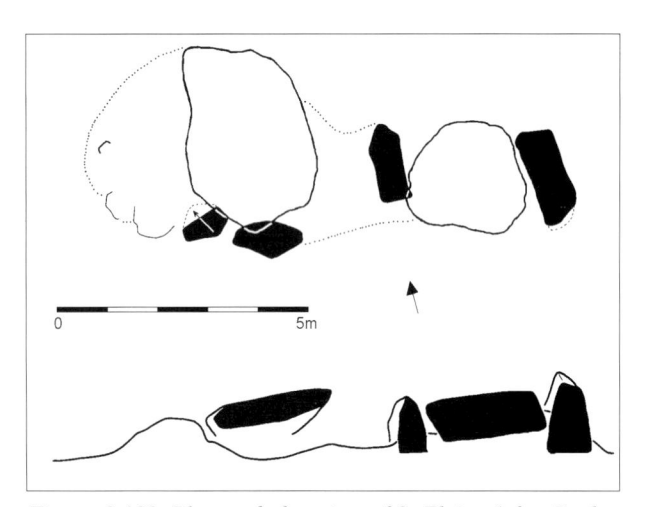

Figure 8.123 Plan and elevation of St Elvies (after Barker 1992).

Landscape setting: The landscape setting around this site is quite unspectacular. In fact, this site almost seems to have been located specifically so that few landscape features can be seen. The view from the NE round to the WSW is closed by the hill on which the monument stands. The view from the NW round to the NE is not very expansive, looking at slightly more distant inland hills and a small stream valley. Ramsey Island can just be seen when standing on top of the capstones. It has been noted that this site seems to have been purposefully concealed from the sea (Tilley 1994). However, although the sea cannot be seen, it can be clearly heard. This suggests that either the location of this monument in relation to the sea was not considered important, or it was located here because the builders deliberately chose to close off the view of the sea.

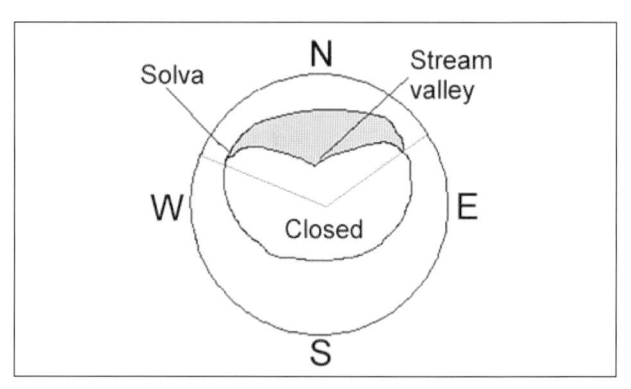

Figure 8.124 The setting of St Elvies.

References: Barker 1992, 35; Rees 1992, 26–7.

64. Carn Llidi (PEM 21 & 22) SM 735 279

Description: This site is set at 130m OD on the western side of Carn Llidi outcrop. The site is on marginal land, covered with gorse and bracken, near the aptly named Highwinds outcrop. A series of World War Two complexes surround the monument. To the N extensive (Bronze Age) field systems survive and the tomb of Coetan Arthur is located only 1km away on St David's Head. The site itself consists of two small, disturbed chambers set into the rocky outcrop of Carn Llidi. It is unlikely that a substantial mound ever existed at the site. The NW chamber consists of a capstone and two uprights. Other stones lie around the chamber, and these may have been dry stone walling. The smaller NE chamber consists of three uprights and a capstone which, although displaced, lies right up against the outcrop. A flake of stone removed from one of the supports was identified as ophitic dolerite (Houlder 1988, 253).

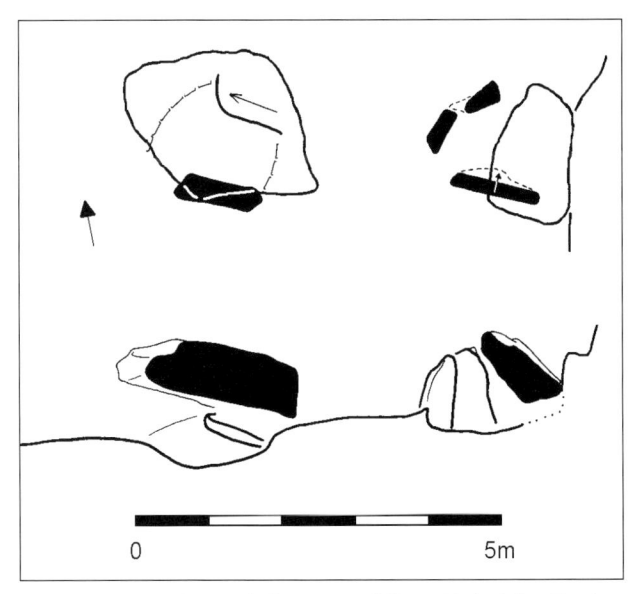

Figure 8.125 Plan and elevation of Carn Llidi (after Barker 1992).

Landscape setting: The view from the N to the S is totally restricted by the outcrops against which the monuments are placed. Visible to the S is the next peninsula along the coast, which terminates with Wooltack Point. Beyond this, Midland Island and Skomer Island are both visible in the distance with the more immediate coastline in the foreground. To the W, Whitesands Bay is visible with Ramsey Island in the distance. The Bishops and Clerks rocks can be seen dotted around the sea. St David's Head is visible to the WNW, and it is possible that Ireland is too in clear conditions. Coetan Arthur is visible to the NW. These two chambers are positioned in a similar way to other monuments in the area, directly against outcrops. The outcrops at Carn Llidi are certainly very visually spectacular and are visible from many places around Pembrokeshire.

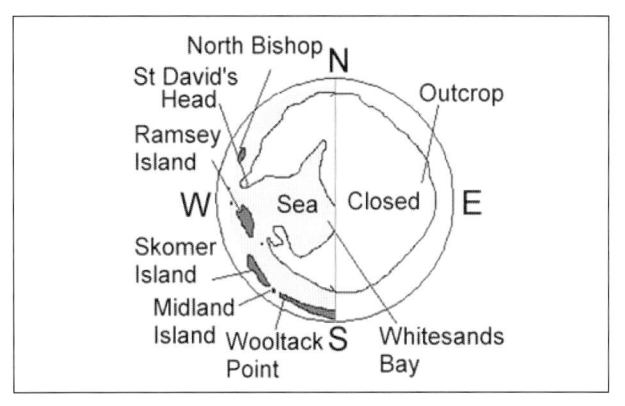

Figure 8.126 The setting of Carn Llidi.

References: Barker 1992, 35–6; Rees 1992, 25.

65. Coetan Arthur (PEM 23) SM 725 281

Description: This site is located on St David's Head in an area of rough grassland and rocky outcrops. It is set at 55m OD on the southern side of the headland as it rises up from the sea. It is positioned only 1km to the W of the double chambered monument of Carn Llidi. The site consists of a single upright and a capstone. It was excavated in 1898 but there were no finds. Daniel (1950) identified a passage to the W, but, if it ever existed, it no longer survives.

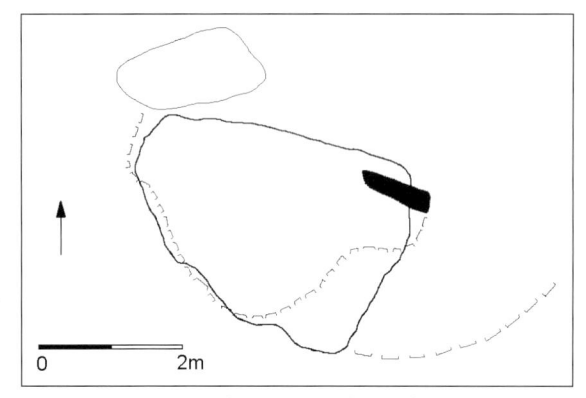

Figure 8.127 Plan of Coetan Arthur (after Barker 1992).

Landscape setting: The view is essentially half wide-ranging, half closed. From the SW round to the NNE, the view is restricted by the outcrops against which the monument stands and the immediate hillslope. However, it is possible to see the sea in the distance between the WNW and the NNW. The view opens up to the NE, where Carn Llidi is a dominant feature. A distant peninsula can be seen to the SE and Whitesands Bay can be seen to the SSE. Ramsey Island dominates the view to the SW, along with a number of smaller islands. A small part of St David's Head is visible before the view is restricted once again. Like Carn Llidi 1km away this site is placed up against a rocky outcrop. However, this outcrop is not as visually impressive as Carn Llidi, although the entire headland is quite visually distinctive. Like other monuments placed right up against outcrops, this site is very difficult to find. Approached from the SE, for example, the site blends in with the outcrops around it. Only approached from Whitesands Bay or Carn Llidi is the characteristic propped stone visible.

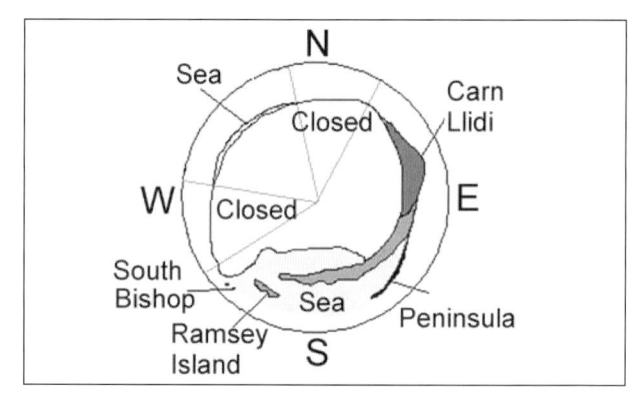

Figure 8.128 The setting of Coetan Arthur.

References: Barker 1992, 36; Baring-Gould, Burnard and Enys 1898; Rees 1992, 24.

66. Hanging Stone/Burton (PEM 24) SM 972 082

Description: Set at 75m OD on the southern side of a small hill, this site is in the corner of field, buried in thick bushes. Half of the monument has disappeared into the field boundary. The site is surrounded by agricultural land and is positioned 5km from where the Western and Eastern Cleddau rivers meet. As such, it overlooks the Pembroke Dock estuary and valley area. This site may be a double monument. A capstone supported by three uprights is clearly visible as well as a large stone embedded in the field boundary next to the chamber, which may be the capstone from another chamber. Grimes (1936a, 13) recorded a passage to the NE, but Barker is unconvinced (1992, 37). A mound or cairn may once have covered the whole monument.

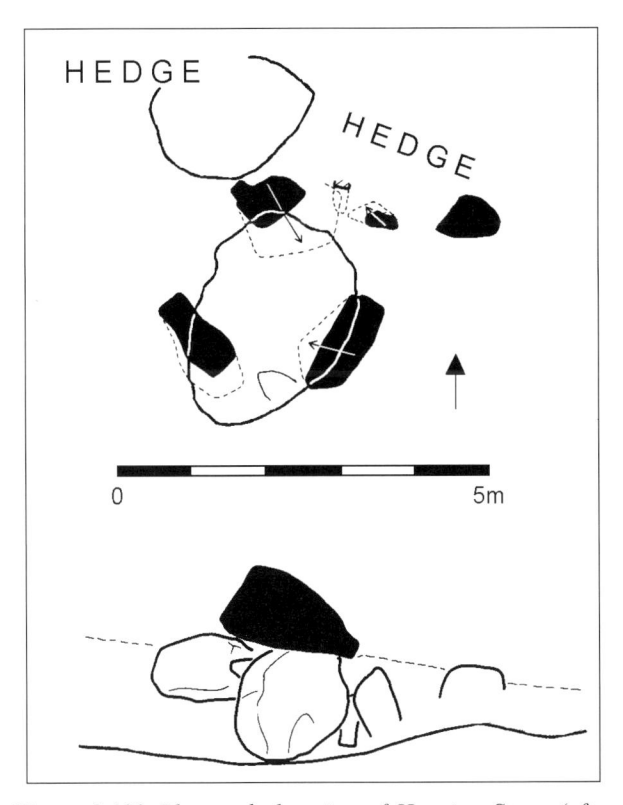

Figure 8.129 Plan and elevation of Hanging Stone (after Barker 1992).

Landscape setting: Half of the view is restricted, simply looking uphill. Only to the WNW is a nearby outcrop visible, located about 100m from the site. The more open view is not particularly spectacular, and it looks out over the estuary and valley area around Pembroke Dock. More distant hills can be seen in the distance. This site is many miles from another similar monument, but in many ways, it is not too different from its counterparts in the N of the county. It is located near but not next to a large outcrop (like Pentre Ifan for example). Structurally, it is quite similar to Carreg Samson, with the suggested presence of a passage strengthening that possibility. It is noticeable that this site is in a rather unspectacular landscape setting, although the southern half of Pembrokeshire is not nearly as hilly as the N. This site does not seem to look at any particularly remarkable features apart from the outcrop 100m away. It is in a quite similar location to sites such as Pentre Ifan, however as it looks down on a valley. The estuary near Pembroke Dock would also have been a resource as well as a landing place.

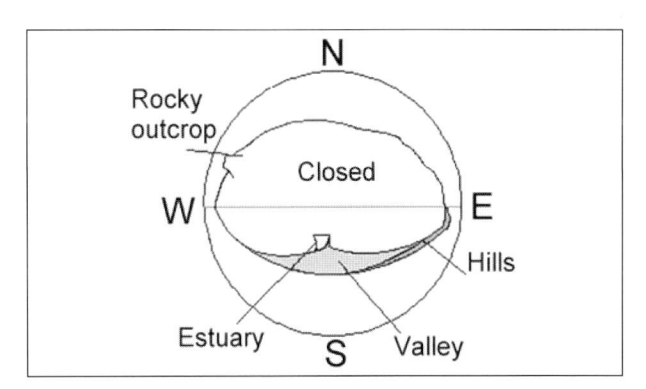

Figure 8.130 The setting of Hanging Stone.

References: Barker 1992, 36–7; Rees 1992, 28.

67. Devil's Quoit (PEM 25) SM 887 008

Description: Situated at 60m OD, this site is set in a field on the sand dunes of Broomhill Burrows. The immediate area is agricultural land and there are several springs nearby. To the S are dunes and to the N an oil refinery. The site is set in a large hollow and consists of a large capstone and two standing uprights. A mound or cairn may once have existed here (Barker 1992, 38).

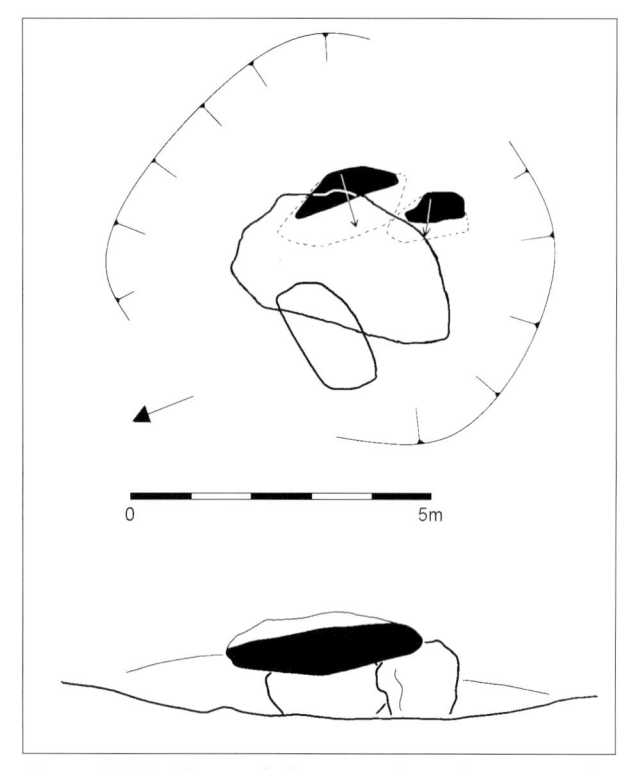

Figure 8.131 Plan and elevation of Devil's Quoit (after Barker 1992).

Landscape setting: The site currently stands on sand dunes and there is the possibility that the landscape was considerably different in the Neolithic. The view from the ENE round to the WSW is restricted by the rise of the hill on which the monument stands. To the W a small portion of the sea is visible. This is then restricted from view by the dunes, but it is possible this view would have been more open in the Neolithic. Hills are visible on the horizon with the water around Milford Haven visible in the foreground. In the distance, Carn Llidi can just be seen on the horizon. The Mynydd Preseli are also visible on the horizon to the NE before the view is restricted again.

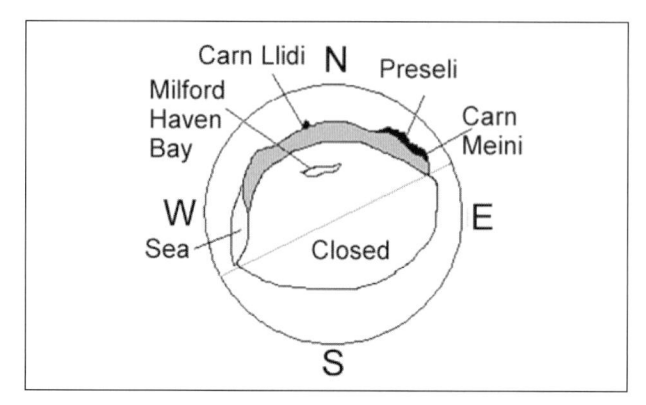

Figure 8.132 The setting of the Devil's Quoit.

References: Barker 1992, 38; Rees 1992, 29.

68. King's Quoit (PEM 26) SS 060 973

Description: Set at 30m OD on the Pembrokeshire coastal path, this site overlooks Manorbier Bay to the NE. It is set into the hillside which is now covered with rough grass and bracken. The site is located near several large blowholes as well as a spring which flows into the sea. This site stands in relative isolation, especially compared to northern Pembrokeshire. The nearest monument is 14km away to the NW. The site is set up against natural outcrops. This left antiquaries unsure whether this was a genuine chambered tomb or a natural formation (Barker 1992, 38). The site consists of a large capstone and three uprights. The capstone is very large and earth-fast to the S. It is supported by two of the uprights to create quite a large internal chamber area. There are also large slabs set behind the capstone. These are natural but create a flat façade at the back of the monument.

Landscape setting: Just over half of the landscape is restricted by the cliffs against which the monument stands. The view out to the W is of the sea with a distant peninsula. It is possible to clearly make out both Barafundle Bay and Freshwater East beaches. To the NW, the next peninsula is visible. To the NE, just before the view becomes restricted, Manorbier Beach and Manorbier Castle are visible. The structure of this site is not unlike that of the Devils Quoit 19km to the W and may represent a local variation of a broader monument type. The site is positioned with quite dramatic landscape views. The location of the site on the edge of the cliff means that there is a spectacular view out to sea as well as the next peninsulas along and back at Manorbier beach. This may have been an important harbour in the Neolithic as it is a very sheltered area of the coast. This monument is also located near a number of very dramatic natural features. There are several blowholes and natural crevices created by the erosion of weaker strata in the rock. Several of these are covered by land bridges so that they appear to be inland.

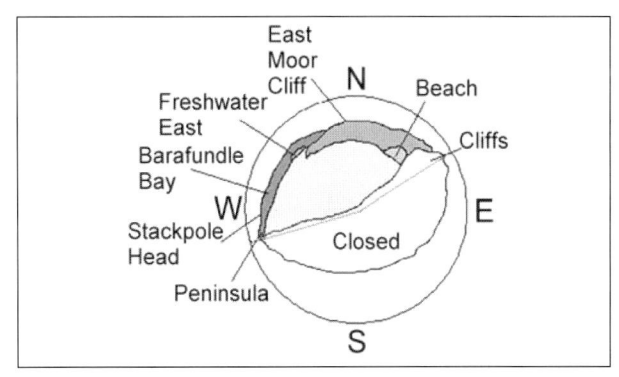

Figure 8.134 The setting of The King's Quoit.

References: Barker 1992, 38–9; Rees 1992, 30.

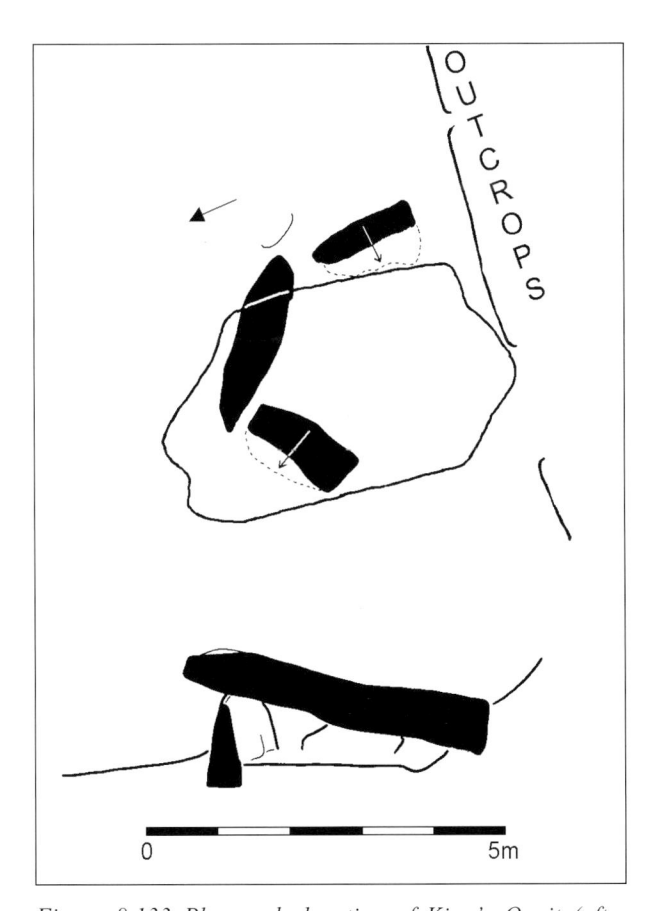

Figure 8.133 Plan and elevation of King's Quoit (after Barker 1992).

CARMARTHENSHIRE

69 Gwal y Filiast
70 Morfa Bychan
71 Twlc y Filiast
72 Mynydd Llangynderyn
73 Gelli
74 Cerrig Llwydion

The following texts discuss the monuments of Carmarthenshire. Some of these also have more detailed information on individual sites and these are listed at the end of each entry where relevant. Barker 1992; Children and Nash 1997; Daniel 1950; Grimes 1936; Lynch 2000a; Rees 1992; Tilley 1994.

69. Gwal y Filiast (CAM 1) SN 171 256

Description: Set at 100m OD on the western side of a gentle hill this site is positioned right next to the Afon Taf only a few kilometres from the edge of the Mynydd Preseli. The site is presently set on a slope in a clearing in woodland. The site consists of six uprights and a large capstone. It is likely that the entrance once existed as an additional upright was once recorded to the SW (Barker 1992, 9).

Figure 8.135 Plan and elevation of Gwal y Filiast (after Barker 1992).

Landscape setting: The site is presently surrounded by trees and it is difficult to make out the surrounding landscape. However, it is clear that about half the view would be closed, as the site stands on the side of a hill, while half the view would be more open and expansive, looking down over a river terrace (although the river itself cannot be seen) and towards hills beyond.

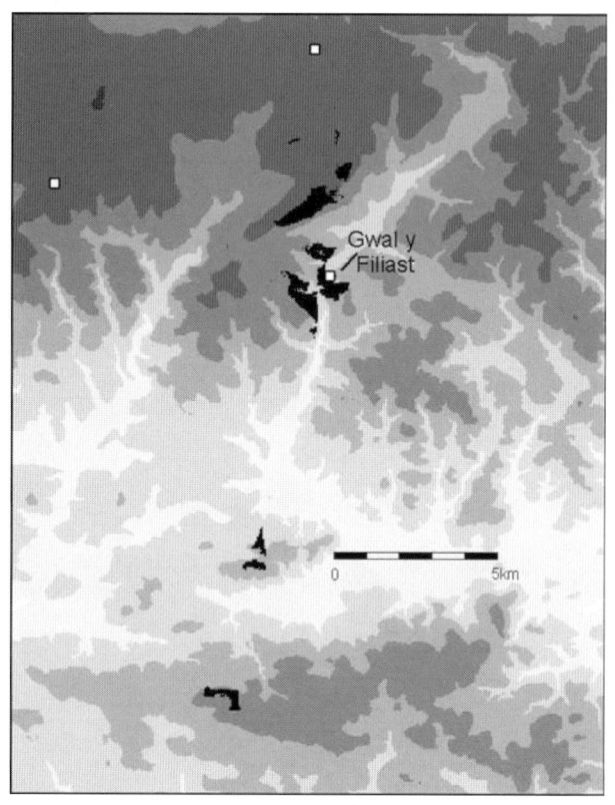

Figure 8.136 The viewshed from Gwal y Filiast. Reproduced by kind permission of Ordnance Survey. © Crown copyright NC/03/20516.

References: Barker 1992, 8–9; Rees 1992, 31–2; Tilley 1994, 109–10.

70. Morfa Bychan A, B, C and D (CAM 2–5) SN 222 075

Description: Set between 70 and 110m OD off the coastal path, these four monuments are located in the Morfa Bychan cemetery on the cliff edge of Ragwen Point. They are situated between Pendine Sands and Marros Sands next to a ridge of outcrops. The entire area is covered with outcrops and loose boulders in rough land covered with bracken. This is one of only two monument groups in south-west Wales, the other being the Garn Wen monuments in Pembrokeshire. Here, four (three definite and one possible) chambers survive. The monuments are quite different from those found elsewhere in the region, which suggest a later (possibly Bronze Age?) date, although one chamber (D) has elements that are similar to some of the small outcrop sites in Pembrokeshire. This site consists of a large capstone with at least 10 uprights as well as what appears to be a passage. It may have been surrounded by a cairn. It was discovered and excavated in

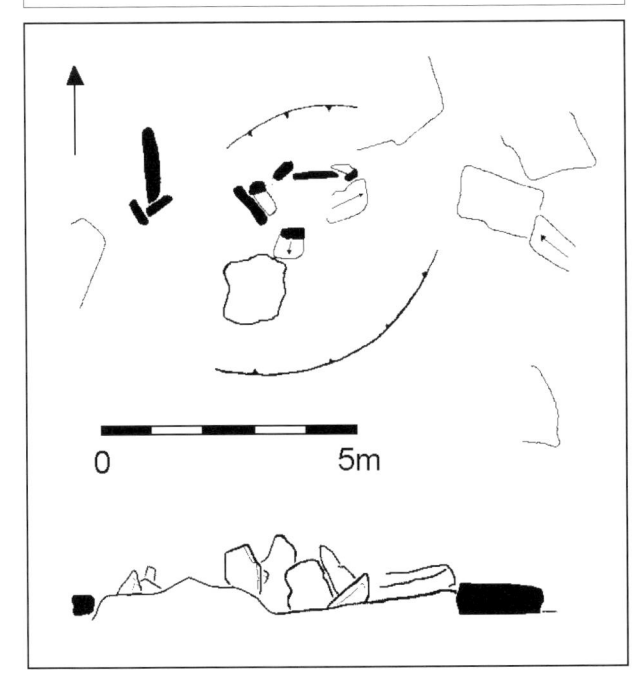

Figure 8.137 Plan and elevation of Morfa Bychan A and B (after Barker 1992).

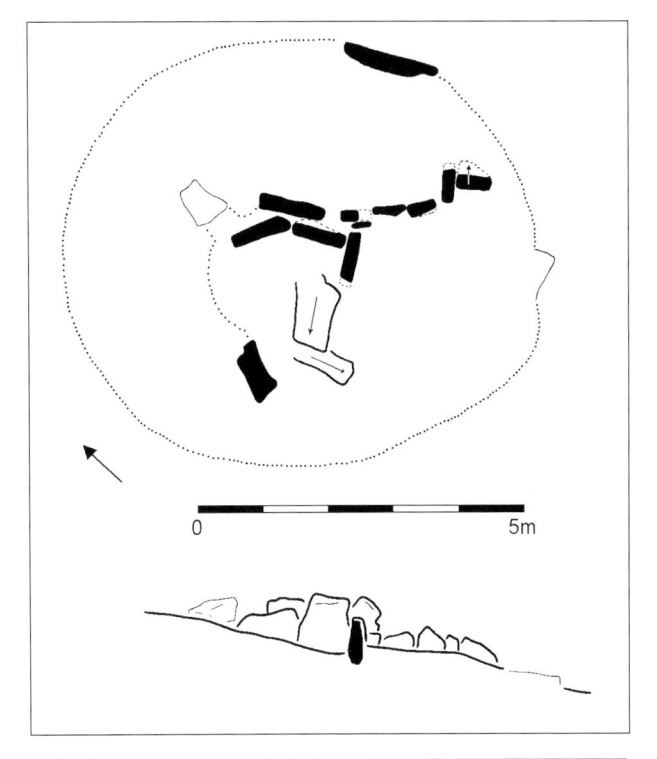

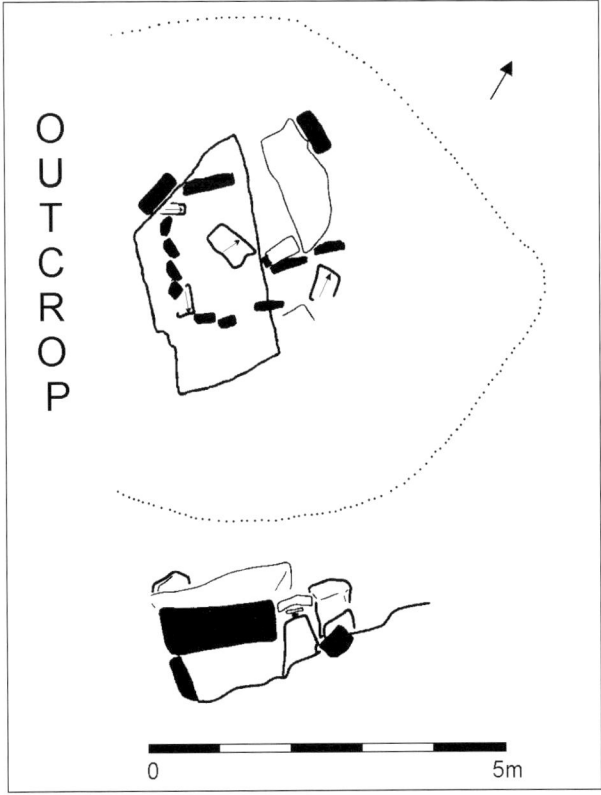

Figure 8.138 Plan and elevation of Morfa Bychan C and D (after Barker 1992).

1910 (Barker 1992, 13), but there were no finds. Morfa Bychan A consists of nine uprights and a displaced capstone and was excavated in 1910 when the stones were restored to their original positions. The excavation revealed a sequence of layers, including what appeared to be paving, and few human bones and 11 pieces of flint were found (Ward 1918). The chamber is surrounded by a cairn and Barker (1992, 11) suggests that an additional chamber may have been added to the SW. Morfa Bychan B is not in such good repair as A. It was also excavated in 1910 which revealed that the chamber had already been disturbed. Only three pieces of flint were found. As at A, it appears that a second chamber has been built into the cairn. Morfa Bychan C is only a 'possible'. It appears to be a ruinous chambered monument, with the SW side mostly destroyed.

Landscape setting: The view from the W round to the NE is restricted by the hillside on which the monuments stand. To the E, the sea can clearly be seen as well as the Gower in the distance, Pendine Sands a few kilometres away and Gilman Point, the next headland along, in the foreground. The high hills of the Gower can be see to the SE and then there is an expanse of sea. The next peninsula to the W is clearly visible on the horizon as well as Caldey Island to the SW before the view becomes restricted once again. The landscape setting of these sites is quite remarkable. The views are wide-ranging in one direction, looking towards the Gower as well as looking to the nearby coastline and beaches. This is a rather unusual setting for a monument, particularly compared to the Pembrokeshire monuments. The other very noticeable element of these monuments is their position right up against the outcrops along the edge of Ragwen Point. The outcrops may have been symbolic in their own right, as there are many natural monuments here as well as cupmarked rocks (natural) and interesting natural formations. The monuments literally blend into the surrounding outcrops which makes them difficult to locate.

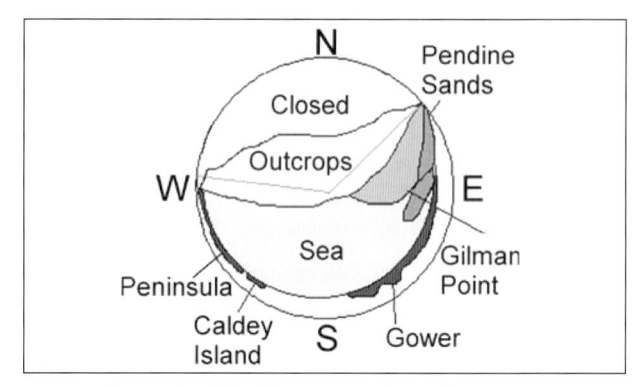

Figure 8.139 The setting of Morfa Bychan.

References: Barker 1992, 10–13, 41; Rees 1992, 30–1; Tilley 1994, 94–7.

71. Twlc y Filiast (CAM 6) SN 338 161

Description: This monument is located at 100m OD in the village of Llangynog. It is located next to a stream which flows S to meet the Afon Taf where it reaches the sea. The site stands above the brook in a small steep-sided valley (Savory 1956, 300). The site is extremely overgrown and survives as three upright slabs and a collapsed capstone which still rests on the uprights. The site was excavated in 1953 and revealed a small outer chamber with the remains of a cremation deposit under it to the S of the main chamber itself. The inner and outer chambers were defined by a sill of smaller stones and the whole chamber may have been reached through a forecourt (Savory 1956, 301). The entire monument stood within a long cairn or platform which was poorly defined in most areas. In fact the entire monument had been badly damaged in recent times and there were only two finds from the site, a flint scraper and an 'axe-amulet' of igneous rock (Savory 1956, 304). Barker (1992, 14) suggests that some of the stones identified as archaeological by Savory may in fact be natural.

Landscape setting: The site is surrounded by extremely dense vegetation in all directions and thus it is difficult to see the landscape. There would have been views uphill to the hill on which the monument sits.

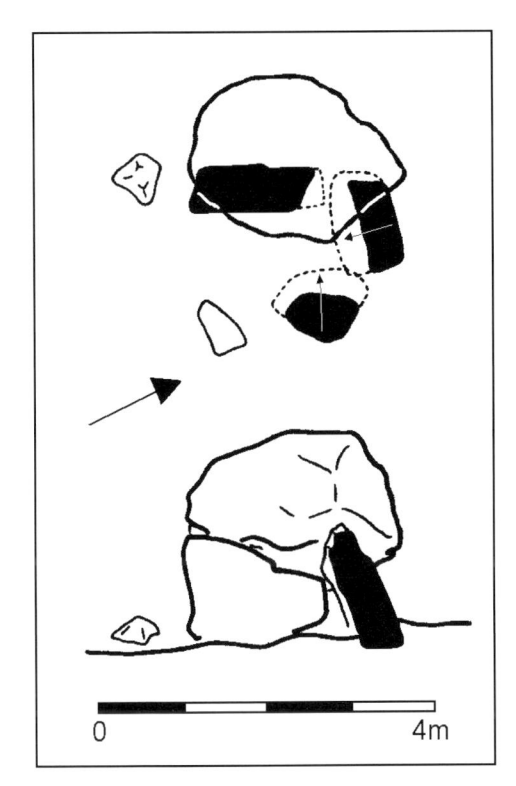

Figure 8.140 Plan and elevation of chamber at Twlc y Filiast (after Barker 1992).

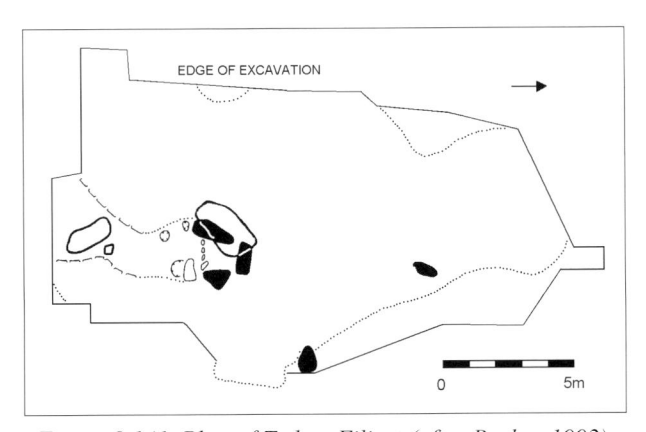

Figure 8.141 Plan of Twlc y Filiast (after Barker 1992).

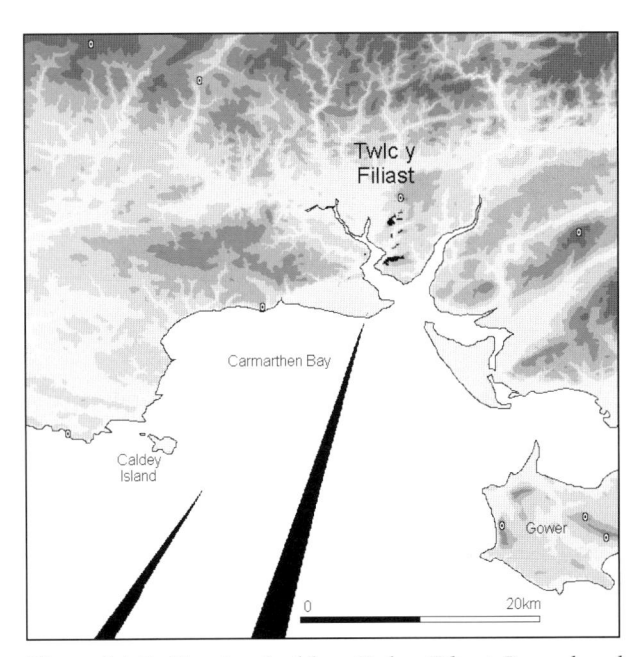

Figure 8.142 The viewshed from Twlc y Filiast. Reproduced by kind permission of Ordnance Survey. © Crown copyright NC/03/20516.

References: Barker 1992, 13–14; Rees 1992, 32–3; Savory 1956.

170   *Vicki Cummings*

72. Mynydd Llangynderyn (CAM 7&8) SN 485 133

Description: The two monuments are set at 245m OD and stand up against the limestone ridge of Mynydd Llangynderyn. The sites are known as Bwrdd Arthur and Gwal y Filiast and are located in a rich Bronze Age landscape of cairns, ring-cairns, standing stones and enclosures (Ward 1976). Both of the chambers are quite badly damaged and the entire area is also covered with natural slabs.

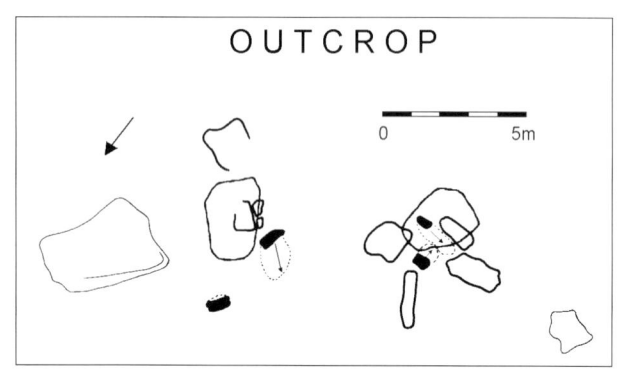

Figure 8.143 Plan of Mynydd Llangynderyn (after Barker 1992).

Landscape setting: The monuments are set right up against a natural outcrop which restricts the view in that direction. In most other directions there are views of the immediate landscape around the monuments, looking at Mynydd Llangynderyn ridge. However, to the NNE and ENE there are two wider views looking out over the landscape to more distant ridges.

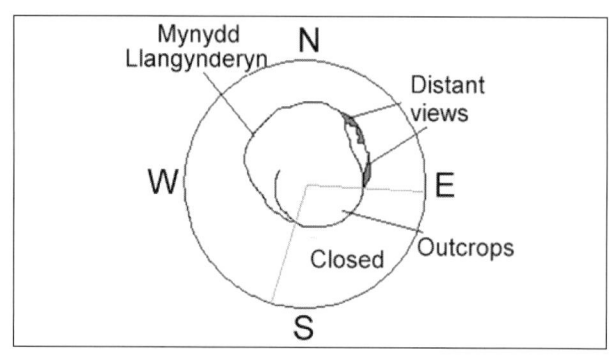

Figure 8.144 The setting of Mynydd Llangynderyn.

References: Barker 1992, 14–15; Rees 1992, 47; Ward 1976.

73. Gelli (CAM 9) SN 770 458

Description: This site is located at 180m OD and is located next to a track in a marshy field. The site is positioned only a short distance from the Afon Tywi in an area covered in natural outcrops. It survives as a grassy mound with a few stones and a large slab visible at the top of the mound.

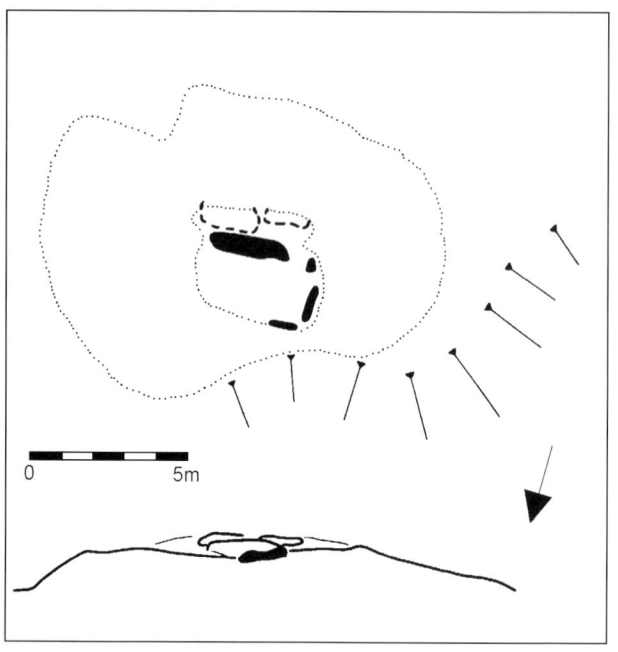

Figure 8.145 Plan and elevation of Gelli (after Barker 1992).

Landscape setting: The landscape setting is quite unusual for a chambered monument. There are views in all directions of the hills that surround the Tywi. The view to the E is more wide-ranging than the others, looking at hills which mark out the path of the river. At present trees block out the view of the river, but it can be heard very clearly.

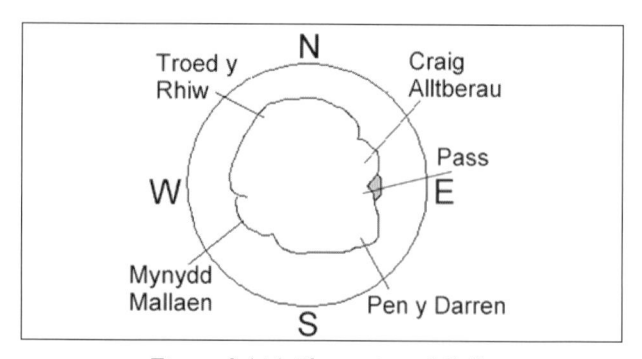

Figure 8.146 The setting of Gelli.

Reference: Barker 1992, 15.

74. Cerrig Llwydion (None) SN 374 326

Description: This site is found at 250m OD in farmland in inland Carmarthenshire and is presently embedded within a hedge and wall which obscure much of the monument. The multiple chambers can be made out, however, and there is also a large depression to the E of the chamber.

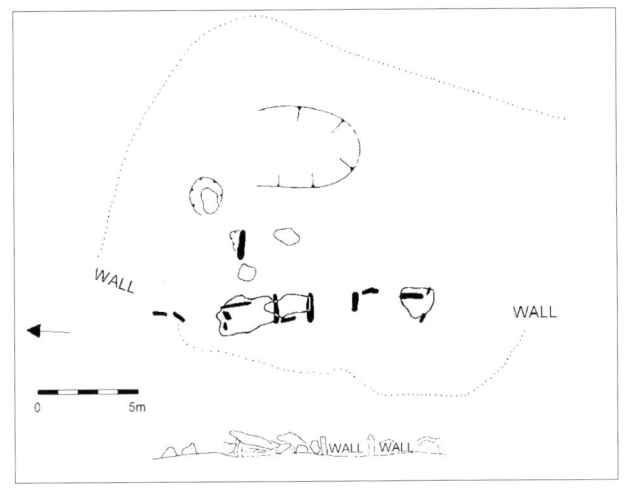

Figure 8.147 Plan and elevation of Cerrig Llwydion (after Barker 1992).

Landscape setting: The landscape setting of this monument is unremarkable but rather unusual. Set above the Afon Duad, but not in sight of the river, the site is on the summit of the domed hill of Cerrig Llwydion. There are two wide-ranging views visible from the hill, to the N and the SSE, but otherwise the views are of the immediate landscape.

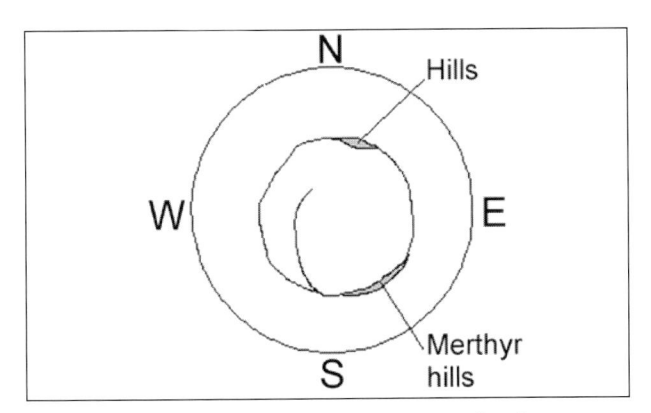

Figure 8.148 The setting of Cerrig Llwydion.

Reference: Barker 1992, 16–17.

GOWER

75 Sweyne's Howe North
76 Sweyne's Howe South
77 Arthur's Stone
78 Parc le Breos Cwm
79 Penmaen Burrows
80 Nicholaston

The following texts discuss the monuments of Gower. Some of these also have more detailed information on individual sites and these are listed at the end of each entry where relevant. Corcoran 1969; Daniel 1950; Darvill 1982; Fox 1937; Grimes 1936; Lynch 2000a; RCAHMW 1976; Whittle 1992.

75. Sweyne's Howe North   (GLA 1) SS 421 898

Description: Located at 140m OD on Rhossili Down, this monument stands on the side of a steep hill covered with outcrops a short distance from Sweyne's Howe South. The monument is set within a broader ritual landscape which consists of a number of Bronze Age cairns and mounds. The site itself consists of three uprights, two of which are still standing and support the displaced capstone. A cairn survives around the chamber. The site has never been excavated but is generally categorised as a portal dolmen (e.g. Corcoran 1969, 17).

Landscape setting: The site has wide views from the N round to the S, with views of the hills to the E and the coastline. What is perhaps the most surprising is that the views from the S to the N are completely restricted by the side of the hill on which the site stands. This effectively means that views of Rhossili Bay and southern Carmarthenshire and Pembrokeshire are blocked from sight. Thus the landscape setting of this site contrasts sharply with the Bronze Age cairns in the area which are all positioned along the summit of Rhossili and therefore have very expansive views to the W.

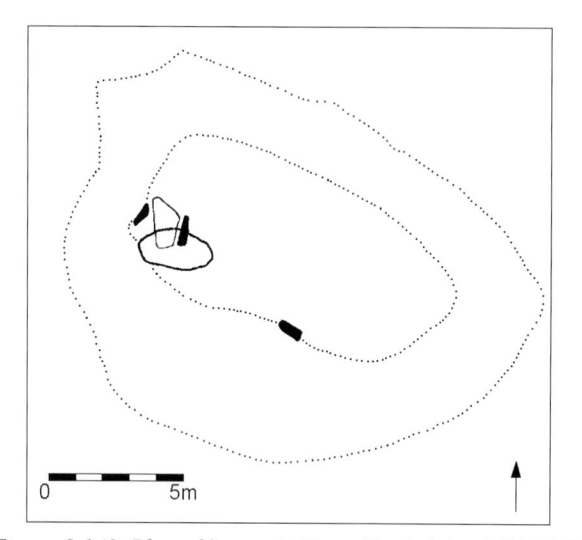

Figure 8.149 Plan of Sweyne's Howe North (after RCAHMW 1976).

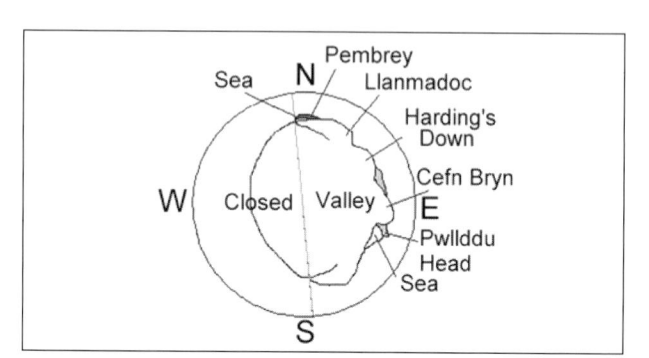

Figure 8.150 The setting of Sweyne's Howe North.

Reference: RCAHMW 1976, 30.

76. Sweyne's Howe South (GLA 2) SS 421 899

Description: This monument is located at 140m OD on Rhossili Down, on the side of a steep hill covered with outcrops a short distance from Sweyne's Howe North. This site consists of a number of upright and collapsed slabs which are hard to distinguish from natural outcrops in the area. The structural remains at this site are so ambiguous that the site can only be classified as a possible chambered monument which is generally considered to be similar to the northern cairn.

Landscape setting: As at Sweyne's Howe North, the wide-ranging views from the site are to the E with the view completely restricted from the S to the N. One can see a small part of the Carmarthenshire coastline to the N, and Sweyne's Howe North is skylined here also. Llanmadoc Hill, Harding's Down and Cefn Bryn are all visible from the N to the E and then there is a view of the coastline with Pwlldu Head particularly striking. Although it is not possible to see the Rhossili Bay and beach, one can quite clearly hear the surf.

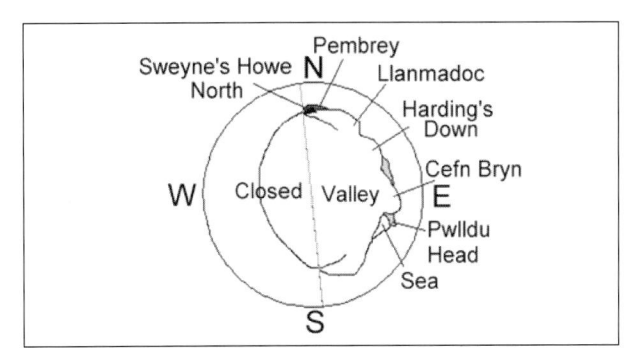

Figure 8.152 The setting of Sweyne's Howe South.

Reference: RCAHMW 1976, 30.

Figure 8.151 Plan of Sweyne's Howe South (after RCAHMW 1976).

77. Arthur's Stone/Maen Ceti (GLA 3) SS 491 906

Description: Set on the side of Cefn Bryn at 140m OD, this site is in an exposed location in open moorland. The site stands in a hollow with wide views out to the N. A Bronze Age cairn is only a few hundred metres to the W and the chambered tomb of Nicholaston is 2.5km to the SE. The site survives as an enormous capstone still supported by four of the uprights. A total of ten stones are still upright which form two main chambers, with several collapsed stones nearby. Approximately a quarter of the capstone has split off the main stone and lies in pieces to the west of the main capstone, perhaps a result of frost action (RCAHMW 1976, 31). The entire structure stands in a hollow with the remains of a cairn in it, and it seems likely that the chamber by was created by digging out the large capstone and propping it up from beneath. The site has never been excavated and over the years considerable doubt has been cast over the status of this site, and whether or not it is Neolithic in date. Parallels have been drawn between this site and Lligwy in north Wales (RCAHMW 1976, 26), both of which have subterranean chambers covered by massive capstones.

Landscape setting: The site is positioned on the side of a hill which effectively means that the view is restricted in this direction (ESE to SW). The hills of Rhossili Down are visible to the W as is Llanmadoc Hill, both prominent landforms on the Gower. The Preselis are visible to the NW as is the Black Mountain to the NE. The inter-tidal zone between the sea and the Afon Llwchwr is visible from the NW to the NNE. The monument can be seen from many locations to the N, skylined on the side of Cefn Bryn. In fact it is this prominent setting in the landscape which sets it apart from the other monuments on the Gower, in particular Parc le Breos Cwm 5km to the E which is in a very secluded location.

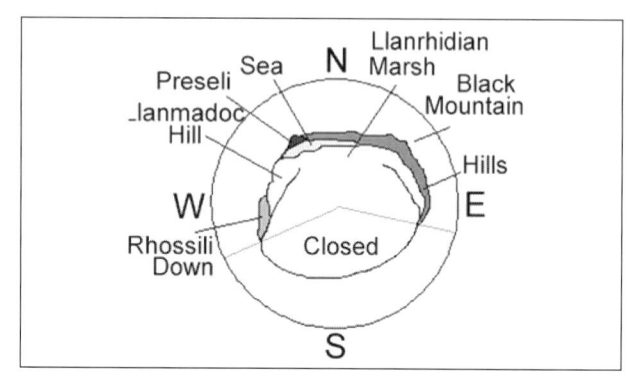

Figure 8.154 The setting of Arthur's Stone.

References: RCAHMW 1976, 32–3; Whittle 1992, 12.

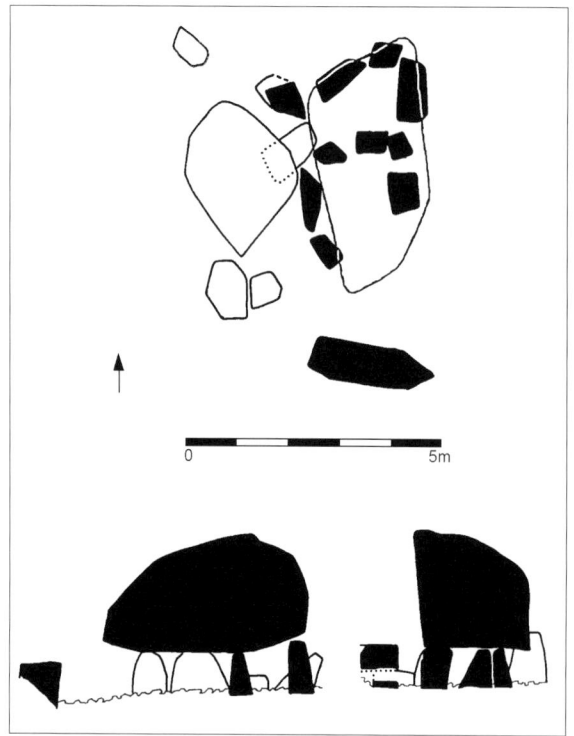

Figure 8.153 Plan and elevation of Arthur's Stone (after RCAHMW 1976).

78. Parc le Breos Cwm (GLA 4) SS537 898

Description: This monument is located at 15m OD on the floor of a limestone gorge cut by a stream which leads to Oxwich Bay to the S. The site is surrounded on all sides by the limestone outcrops, and Cathole Cave is a short distance to the N. The site is extremely well preserved and is considered an outlier of the Cotswold-Severn transepted long cairn tradition. It was excavated in 1869 and again in 1960–1 when the site was consolidated. The excavations of the site have recently been reconsidered and published (Whittle and Wysocki 1998). A total of 40 individuals were recovered as well as cremation deposits. Domesticated and wild animal bones were also found as well as 32 knapped flint pieces and the pot sherds (Whittle and Wysocki 1998). A series of radiocarbon dates suggest that the monument was built around 3800–3500 BC. There was also evidence of late Neolithic or Beaker use of the site. Stable isotope analysis of the bone demonstrated that the people buried there had not eaten marine foods (Whittle and Wysocki 1998, 166).

Landscape setting: The unusual landscape location of this site has frequently been noted. Its setting in a confined valley means that there are restricted views in all directions, and this type of location for a chambered tomb is unparalleled in Britain (see discussion in main text). It may be significant, however, that Cathole Cave, with earlier deposits, is located only a short distance from the site.

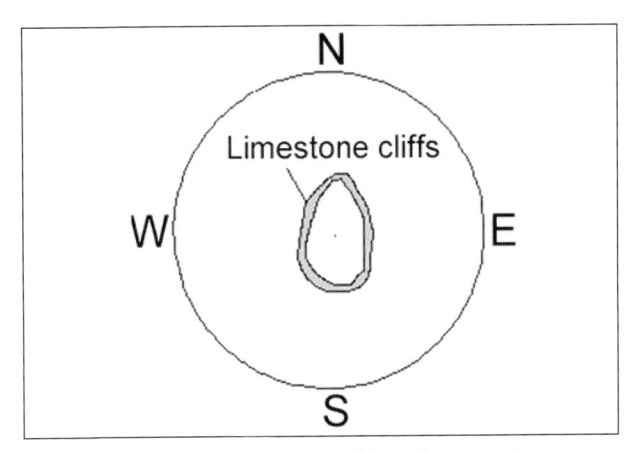

Figure 8.156 The setting of Parc le Breos Cwm.

References: Daniel 1937; RCAHMW 1976, 34–5; Whittle 1992, 9–10; Whittle and Wysocki 1998, 139–82.

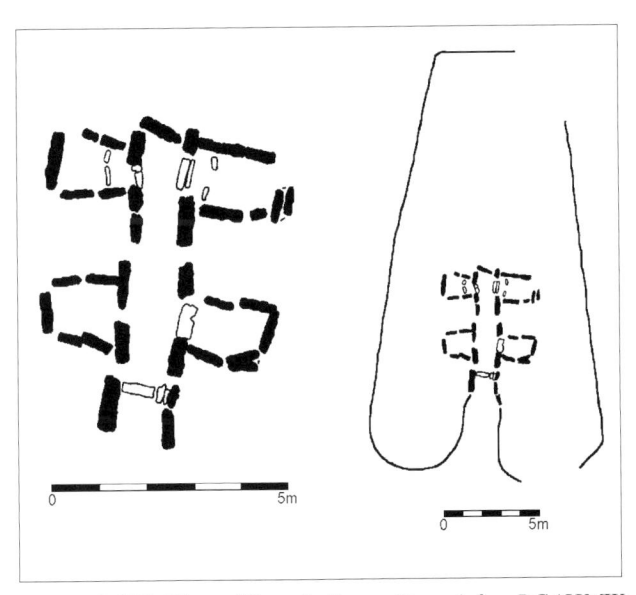

Figure 8.155 Plan of Parc le Breos Cwm (after RCAHMW 1976).

79. Penmaen Burrows (GLA 5) SS 532 882

Description: Set at 45m OD, this site is located amongst the sand dunes off Threecliff Bay. The site is set at the point where the stream which flows next to Parc le Breos Cwm reaches the sea. Parc le Breos itself is located 4km to the NNE. This site is also generally considered to be a Cotswold-Severn monument, although it is not as well preserved as Parc le Breos. It survives as a series of uprights with a displaced capstone which appears to mark out a passage area and side chambers. There is no evidence of a cairn at present. The site has not been properly excavated but there were minor investigations in 1860 and 1881 which recovered bone. Deposits were cleared out down to the original ground level in 1893 (RCAHMW 1976, 32).

Landscape setting: The site is set amongst sand dunes and much of the view is restricted by these. It seems unlikely that these were present in the Neolithic and as such there may have been much wider views out over the coast and the sea. It is clear that the views from the W to the E would be of the nearby hills of Cefn Bryn and Pennard Burrows.

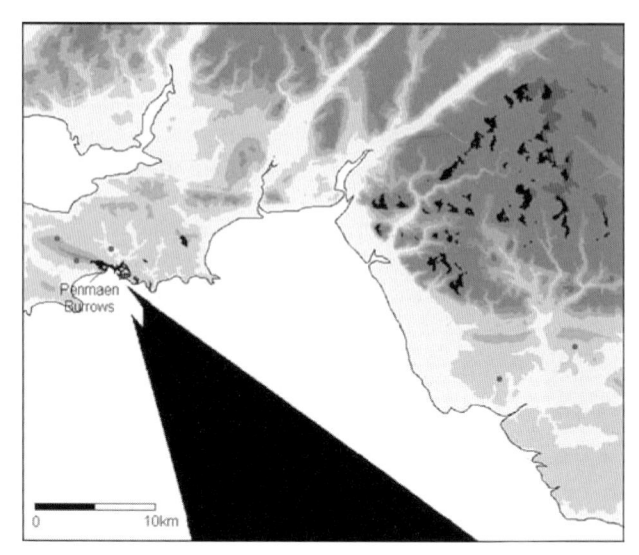

Figure 8.158 The viewshed from Penmaen Burrows. Reproduced by kind permission of Ordnance Survey. © Crown copyright NC/03/20516.

Reference: RCAHMW 1976, 32–4.

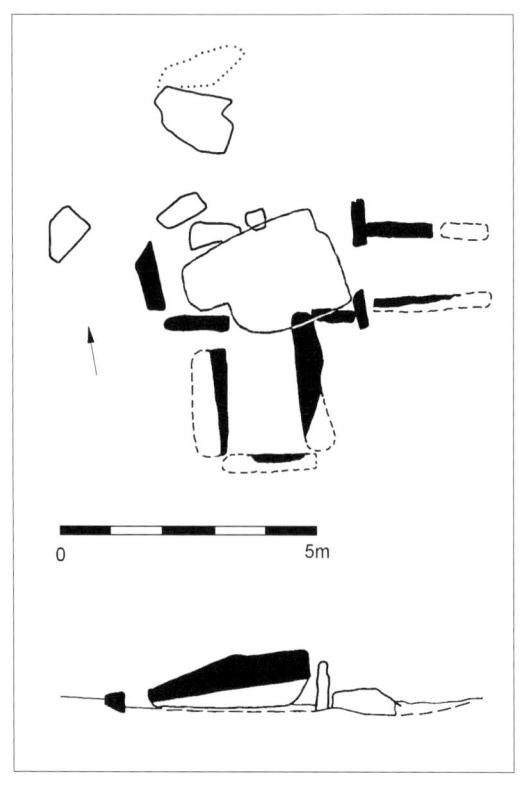

Figure 8.157 Plan and elevation of Penmaen Burrows (after RCAHMW 1976).

80. Nicholaston (GLA 11)   SS 508 888

Description: This site is at 100m OD and is located in scrubland on the side of the hill of Cefn Bryn. The site is presently overgrown and survives as a roofed chamber. The site was excavated in 1939 and revealed a long pear-shaped cairn. This covered a single chamber with two capstones. The only find was charcoal.

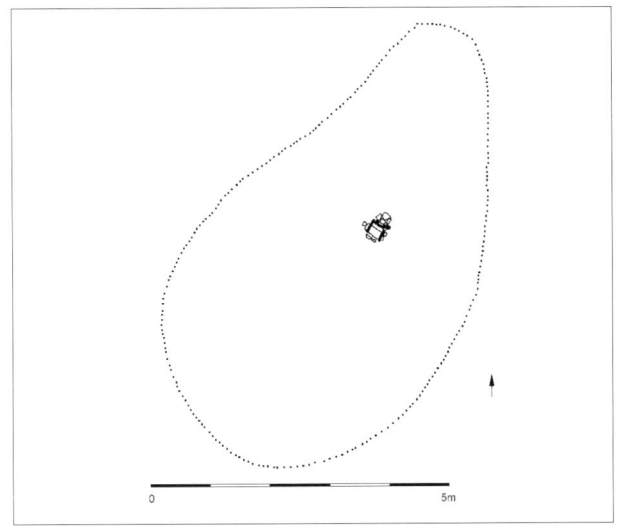

Figure 8.159 Plan of Nicholaston (after RCAHMW 1976).

Landscape setting: The view from the W round to the E is restricted by the hill on which the monument stands. From the E round to the W there are wider views out over Oxwich Bay and Oxwich Point.

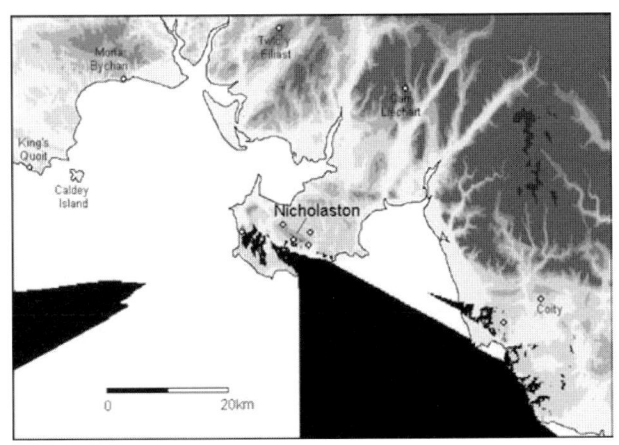

Figure 8.160 The viewshed of Nicholaston. Reproduced by kind permission of Ordnance Survey. © Crown copyright NC/03/20516.

References: RCAHMW 1976, 32–3; Williams 1940.

GLAMORGAN

81   Tythegeston
82   Coity
83   Pentyrch/Cae yr Arfau
84   Tinkinswood
85   St Lythans
86   Carn Llechart

The following texts discuss the monuments of Glamorgan. Some of these also have more detailed information on individual sites and these are listed at the end of each entry where relevant. Corcoran 1969; Daniel 1950; Darvill 1982; Grimes 1936; Lynch 2000; RCAHMW 1976; Whittle 1992.

81. Tythegeston (GLA 6) SS 864 793

Description: Located at 80m OD on a domed hill a few kilometres W of Bridgend, this site stands at the edge of a ploughed field next to a small wood. There is a small quarry a few metres to the E of the site. The monument is approximately 1km to the N of Merthyr Mawr Warren and the Coity chamber is 7.5km away to the ENE. The site survives as a large overgrown grassy mound which covers cairn material (RCAHMW 1976, 36). The capstone and a single upright are visible at the top of the mound.

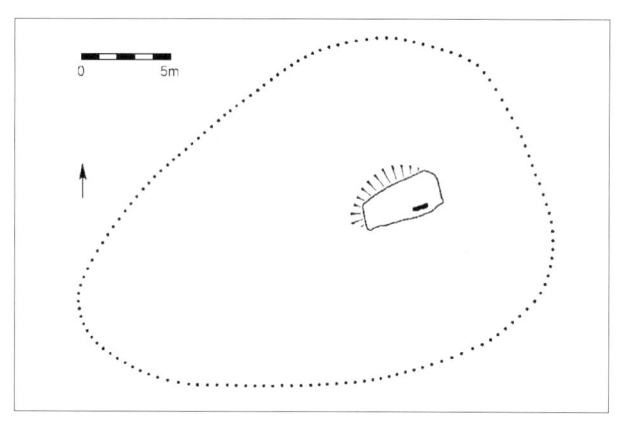

Figure 8.161 Plan of Tythegeston (after RCAHMW 1976).

Landscape setting: The site stands near the summit of a hill and thus commands wide views in most directions, although the views to the S are presently obscured by dense woodland. To the SW the sea is visible with the Somerset hills beyond. There are views of a local hill to the west, and wider views out over the Rhondda hills to the N and E. The monument seems to be orientated so that there are much wider views to one side (NW) than the other.

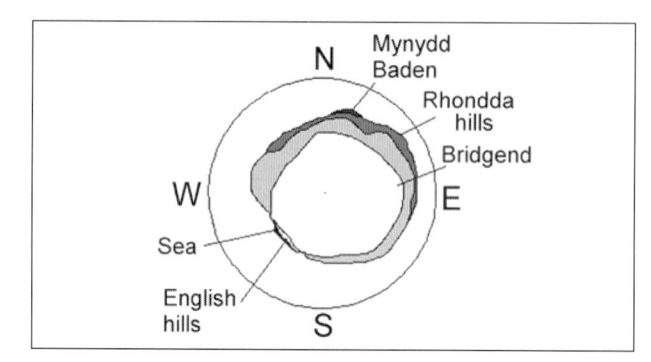

Figure 8.162 The setting of Tythegeston.

Reference: RCAHMW 1976, 36–7.

82. Coity (GLA 7) SS 927 819

Description: This site stands at 70m OD in a field just outside Bridgend. The site has been described as the remains of a portal dolmen (Corcoran 1969, 20). It consists of a capstone supported by collapsed uprights. A large amount of cairn material can be found in the nearby wall.

Landscape setting: There is a restricted view from the N round to the S. There are views up to Cefn Hirgoed to the N and out towards Colwinston to the SSE. Although only a few miles from Tythegeston, the two sites are not intervisible.

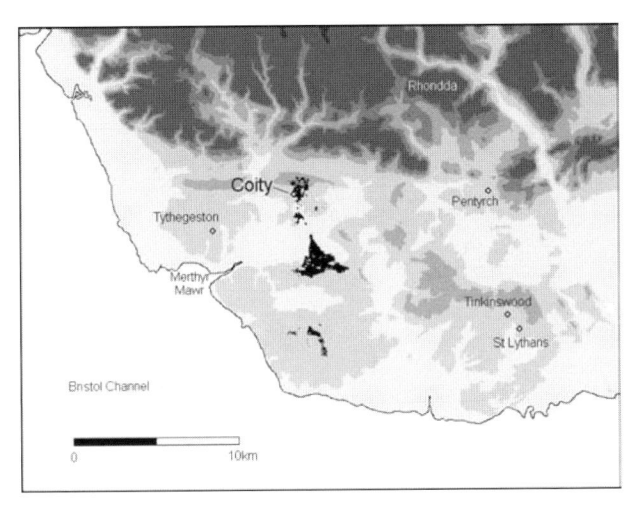

Figure 8.163 The viewshed from Coity. Reproduced by kind permission of Ordnance Survey. © Crown copyright NC/03/20516.

Reference: RCAHMW 1976, 36.

83. Pentyrch/Cae yr Arfau (GLA 8) SS 077 821

Description: This site stands at 75m OD up against a stone wall in a flower bed in a front garden. The site consists of two upright slabs which support a capstone. Several large stones were removed before 1875 and a mound that was visible to the S of the site was also levelled (RCAHMW 1976, 37).

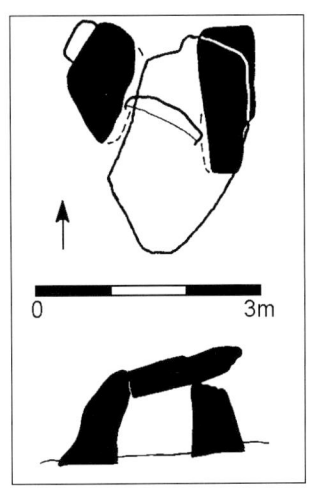

Figure 8.164 Plan and elevation of Pentyrch/Cae yr Arfau (after RCAHMW 1976).

Landscape setting: At present, the views are obscured in most directions by houses and trees. It is clear that there is a restricted view to the E, and much wider views out to the W. The Ely River runs to the W and S of the site and Tinkinswood is only 9km to the S.

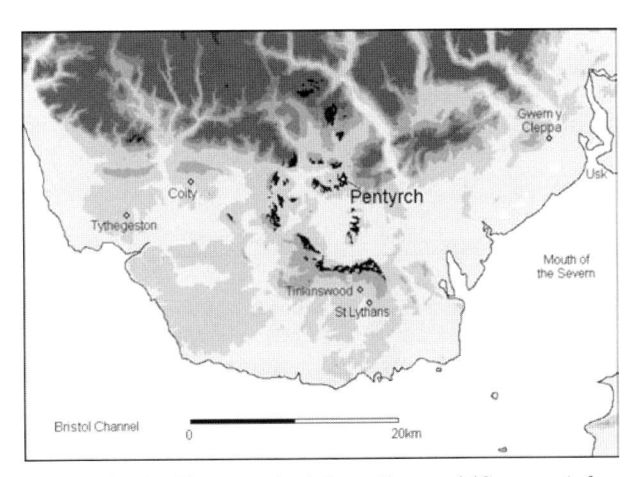

Figure 8.165 The viewshed from Pentyrch/Cae yr Arfau. Reproduced by kind permission of Ordnance Survey. © Crown copyright NC/03/20516.

Reference: RCAHMW 1976, 37–9.

84. Tinkinswood (GLA 9) ST 092 733

Description: Set at 75m OD, this site stands in an enclosure at the corner of a field next to a small wood. St Lythans is just over 1km away to the SE. The site is well preserved and has been restored. It consists of an enormous capstone supported by a number of original uprights and a modern pillar which define a rectangular chamber. The chamber is enclosed within a long cairn and some of the original drystone walling survives. The reconstructed drystone walling is all in herring-bone style. The site was excavated in 1914 (Ward 1915; 1916). A number of parallel rows of upright stones were found within the body of the cairn as well as a walled pit which contained animal bones. The forecourt area had originally been paved and Neolithic pottery was found scattered on the surface. The entrance to the chamber was originally along a small passage to the NE of the forecourt and under the gap in one of the slabs. A blocking stone was found in the forecourt which may have acted as a door to the chamber, and the entire forecourt has been filled in with small stones. The southern side of the chamber itself had been destroyed before the excavations, and the chamber deposits had been disturbed. However, 920 pieces of human bone were recovered representing at least 50 people (RCAHMW 1976, 37). All the bone was disarticulated and represented men, women and children. Other finds included flint implements, bone pins and pottery including undecorated ware and Beaker. There is evidence of quarrying to the S of the monument, which is of unknown date, and there may be other destroyed monuments nearby also (RCAHMW 1976, 40).

Landscape setting: The site is located in a fairly unimpressive landscape setting. There are views of rolling hills to the NW and S, and a restricted view to the NE. The site seems to be intervisible with St Lythans a kilometre down the road, although this cannot be seen on the ground at present as the site is surrounded by trees. The focus is very much on the immediate landscape, and the gentle undulating ground around the monument.

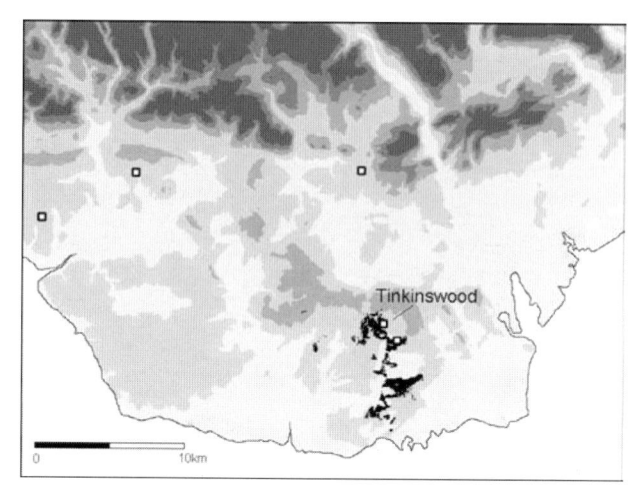

Figure 8.167 The viewshed from Tinkinswood. Reproduced by kind permission of Ordnance Survey. © Crown copyright NC/03/20516.

References: RCAHMW 1976, 36–8; Ward 1915; Ward 1916; Whittle 1992, 10–11.

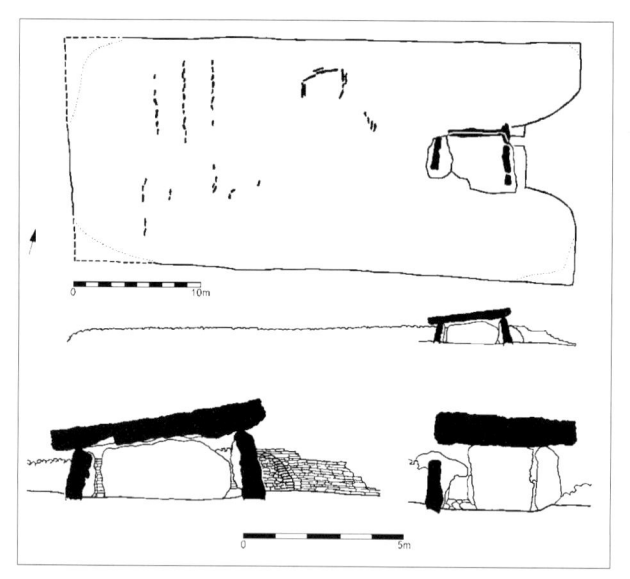

Figure 8.166 Plan and elevations of Tinkinswood (after Ward 1915).

85. St Lythans/Maes y Felin (GLA 10) ST 101 723

Description: Set at 70m OD on a rise in a field, this site is located in quite a commanding position in the landscape. The site consists of three large uprights which support a capstone. All the slabs are of mudstone and are striking in appearance; the western slab has a hole in it. There are the remains of a long mound to the west of the chamber which has led to suggestion that this site might be similar to Tinkinswood (RCAHMW 1976, 39). The site has not been excavated but human remains and pottery were found in 1875 when the interior of the chamber was cleared out.

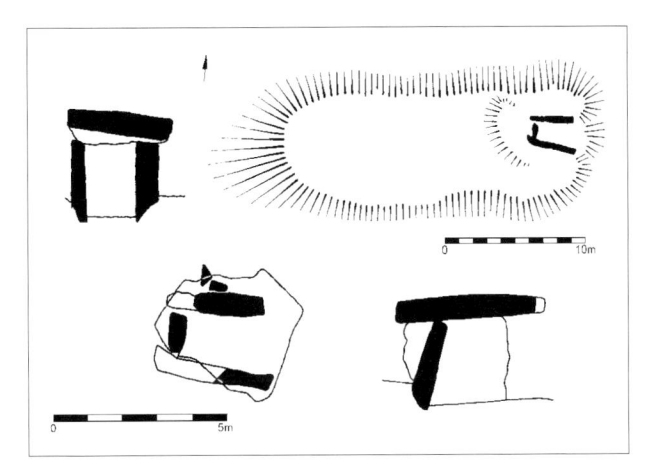

Figure 8.168 Plan and elevation of St Lythans (after RCAHMW 1976).

Landscape setting: The site is not positioned at the highest point of the hillside on which it stands so there is a restricted view to the E. In other directions it is possible to see more distant hills. The cairn itself is set along the axis of the hillside. There are more open views behind the chamber as you enter, with the restricted view visible upon exiting. There are wider views from this monument than from Tinkinswood just down the road.

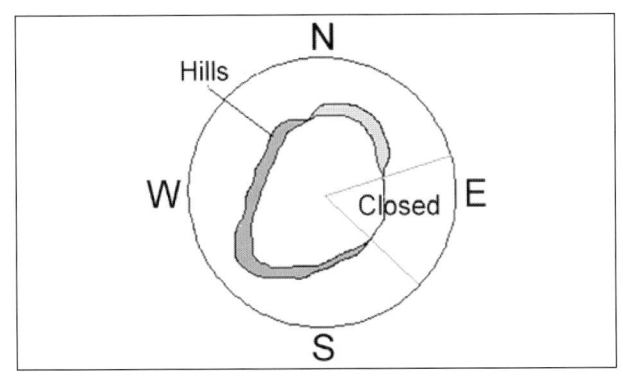

Figure 8.169 The setting of St Lythans.

References: RCAHMW 1976, 39; Whittle 1992, 11–12.

86. Carn Llechart SN 698 063

Description: Set at 280m OD in open moorland, this site is close to the Bronze Age stone circle and cist of the same name. The site stands in an upland location, in an area covered with rocky outcrops. The remains are ambiguous, confused by the presence of several large natural slabs. There appear to be three supporting stones surviving and a displaced capstone.

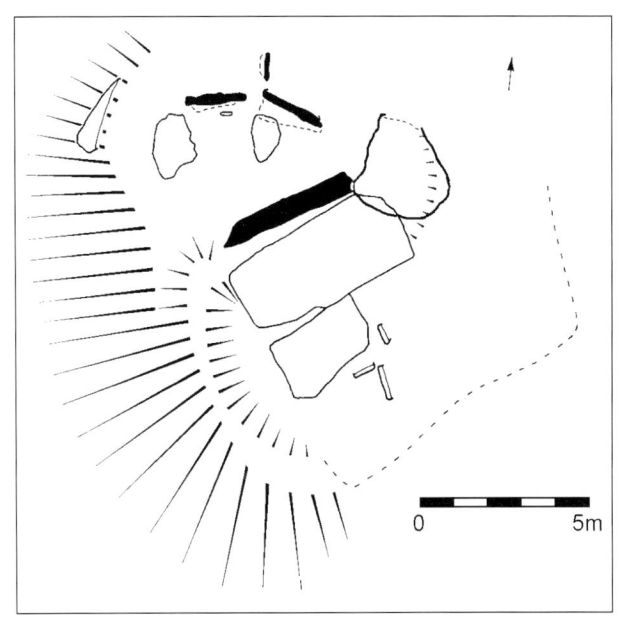

Figure 8.170 Plan of Carn Llechart (after RCAHMW 1976).

Landscape setting: The landscape setting of this site is rather unusual for a chambered monument, with obvious parallels to the nearby stone circle. This may suggest a later date for this monument. There is a restricted view to the N and E; this is the hill on which the stone circle stands and it is just visible on the horizon. The rest of the setting has views out over the uplands, and no lower-lying valley areas are visible.

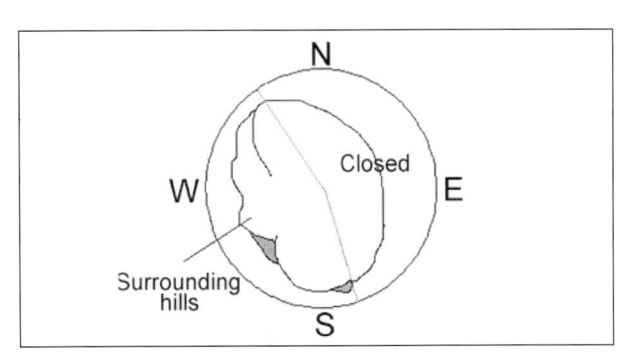

Figure 8.171 The setting of Carn Llechart.

Reference: RCAHMW 1976, 32–3.

MONMOUTHSHIRE

87 Gwern y Cleppa
88 Gaer Llwyd
89 Heston Brake
90 Thornwell Farm

The following texts discuss the monuments of Monmouthshire. Some of these also have more detailed information on individual sites and these are listed at the end of each entry where relevant. Bagnall-Oakeley and Bagnall-Oakeley 1889; Children and Nash 1996; Corcoran 1969; Daniel 1950; Darvill 1982; Grimes 1936; Whittle 1992.

87. Gwern y Cleppa (MON 1) ST 276 851

Description: Set at 85m OD, this site stands in a field only a short distance from the M4. The area has been substantially altered by the cutting for the M4 and there are also a series of quarry pits in the field. The site is located on the side of a hill and a stream runs near the site to the W. The site has been badly damaged and survives as a number of upright and recumbent stones. It is difficult to assess the form that the monument would originally have taken, although it has been suggested that it may have been a terminally chambered long cairn (Corcoran 1969, 21).

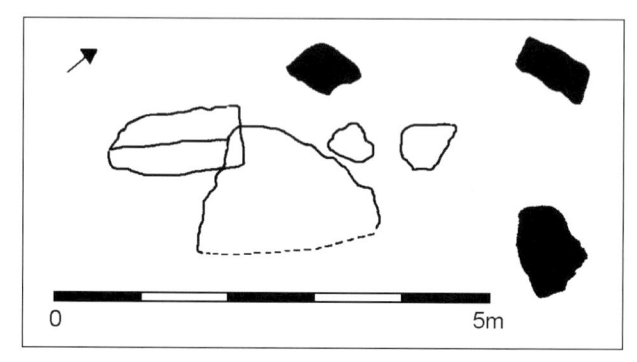

Figure 8.172 Plan of Gwern y Cleppa (after Bagnall-Oakeley and Bagnall-Oakeley 1889).

Landscape setting: 'Facing the Bristol Channel, with a glorious expanse of hill and vale stretching out for many miles beyond it, the situation of this burial place is grand in the extreme...' (Bagnall-Oakeley and Bagnell-Oakeley 1889, 11). The landscape setting of this site is very similar to Heston Brake 20km to the E with wide views of the Severn. There are also wide views to the SW towards Cardiff.

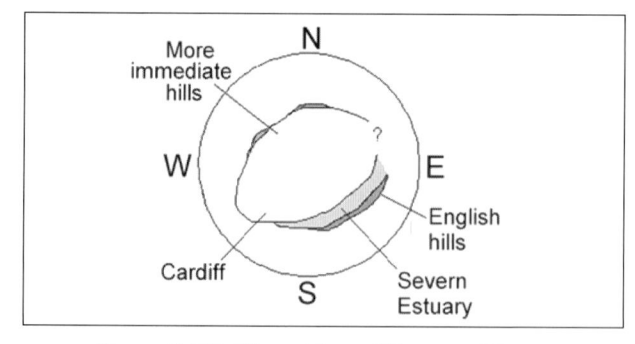

Figure 8.173 The setting of Gwern y Cleppa.

References: Bagnall-Oakeley and Bagnall-Oakeley 1889, 11–12; Children and Nash 1996, 31–2.

88. Gaer Llwyd (MON 2) ST 448 968

Description: This site is located at 190m OD in the corner of a field next to a road. The site is only a short distance from two streams which run down to the Severn either side of Heston Brake. Although the site is in a field, another outcrop can be seen nearby suggesting that this area may once have been in a rocky area. The site itself consists of five uprights which partly support the capstone. The capstone is large but has fallen off the uprights and has split. Two other stones lie around the chamber and seem to be collapsed uprights. It is clear, however, that this would once have been an impressive monument.

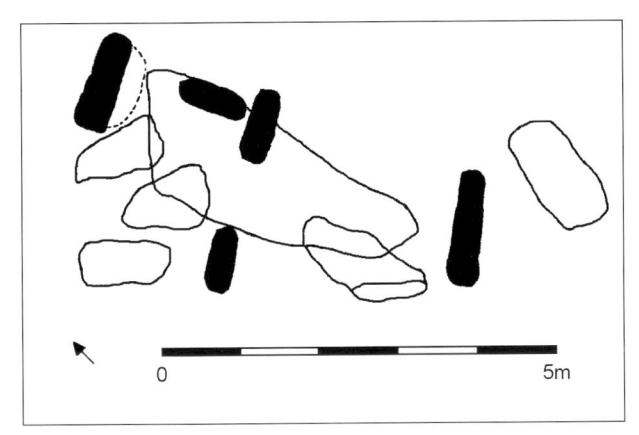

Figure 8.174 Plan of Gaer Llwyd (after Bagnall-Oakeley and Bagnall-Oakeley 1889).

Landscape setting: The site is presently surrounded by houses and a hedge which obscures the view. There is clearly a restricted view to the NE and wider views to the W.

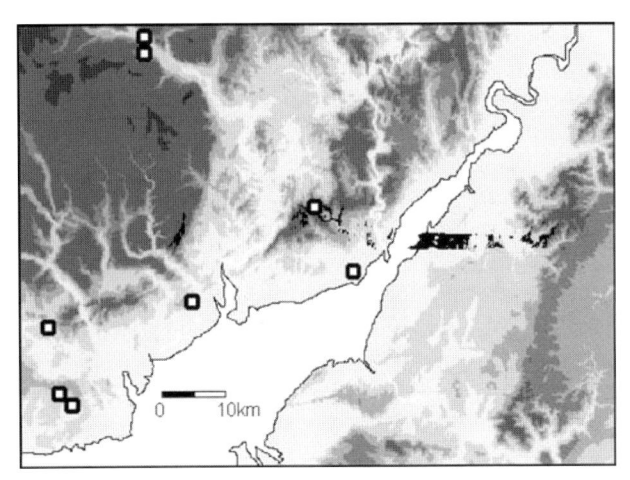

Figure 8.175 The viewshed from Gaer Llwyd. Reproduced by kind permission of Ordnance Survey. © Crown copyright NC/03/20516.

References: Bagnall-Oakeley and Bagnall-Oakeley 1889, 10; Children and Nash 1996, 33–4.

89. Heston Brake (MON 3) ST 505 887

Description: Set at 40m OD on top of a small hill in a field, this site is located close to the village of Portskewett less than a kilometre from the River Severn. The site survives as two distinctive entrance stones and a number of stones which make up an elongated chamber. This chamber stands at the eastern end of a poorly defined long cairn which is orientated E-W. The site was excavated in 1888 and parts of a human skull, broken bones, bones from an 'ox' and two smooth stones were found (Bagnall-Oakeley and Bagnall-Oakeley 1889, 19). The chamber itself is made from water-worn stones which may have come from the River Severn (Bagnall-Oakeley and Bagnall-Oakeley 1889, 19). It is also of interest that the two entrance stones are different lithologies, one a smooth sandstone and the other a rougher conglomerate.

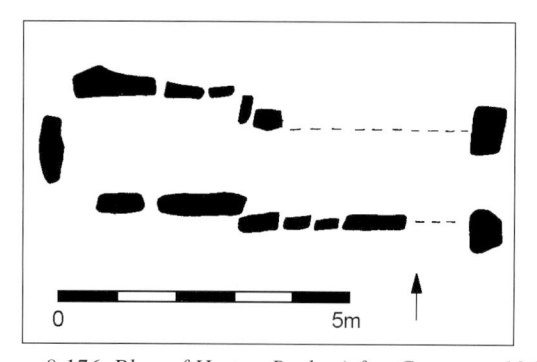

Figure 8.176 Plan of Heston Brake (after Corcoran 1969).

Landscape setting: The landscape setting of this monument is quite stunning with almost 180° of the view dominated by views of the Severn River and estuary and the English hills beyond. None of the views are restricted although there are closer hills visible to the NW. The site can clearly be seen from a distance and is skylined as you approach it along the modern road. The site is also visible from the railway line which runs along the River Severn between Caldicot and Chepstow. The landscape setting of this site is remarkably similar to that at Gwern y Cleppa.

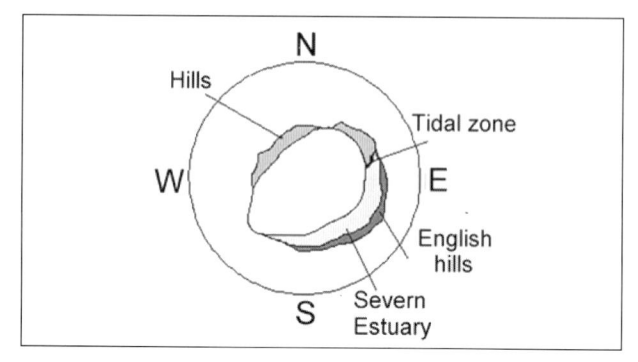

Figure 8.177 The setting of Heston Brake.

References: Bagnall-Oakeley and Bagnall-Oakeley 1889, 18–19; Children and Nash 1996, 35–7; Corcoran 1969, 45.

90. Thornwell Farm ST 539 917

Description: This site was excavated in 1990–1. The remains of a chambered tomb were found containing the remains of four adults and two children as well as early Neolithic pottery and flint tools (Children and Nash 1996, 38). The human bone was both articulated and disarticulated and some was burnt suggesting a range of different burial practices. A large quantity of bones from birds of prey were also found (Children and Nash 1996, 39).

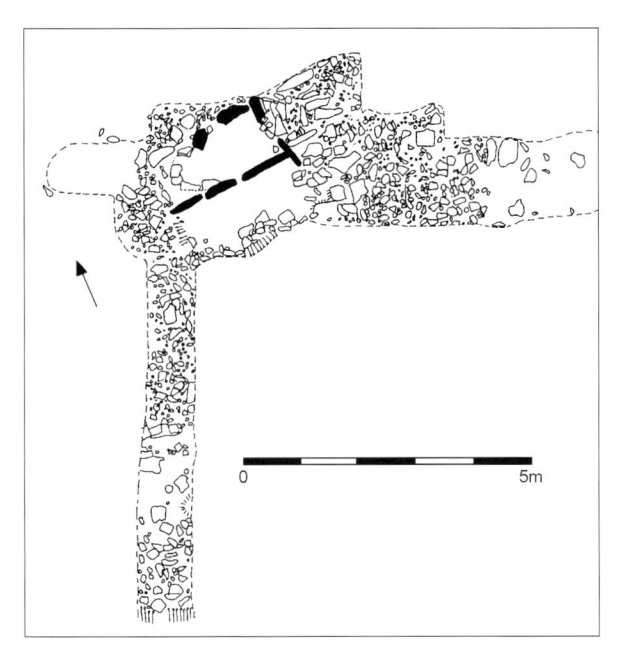

Figure 8.178 Plan of Thornwell Farm (after Children and Nash 1996).

Landscape setting: The site is presently situated close to a housing estate, so many of the views are obscured. However, there is still a clear view down to the River Severn and across to the Somerset Hills.

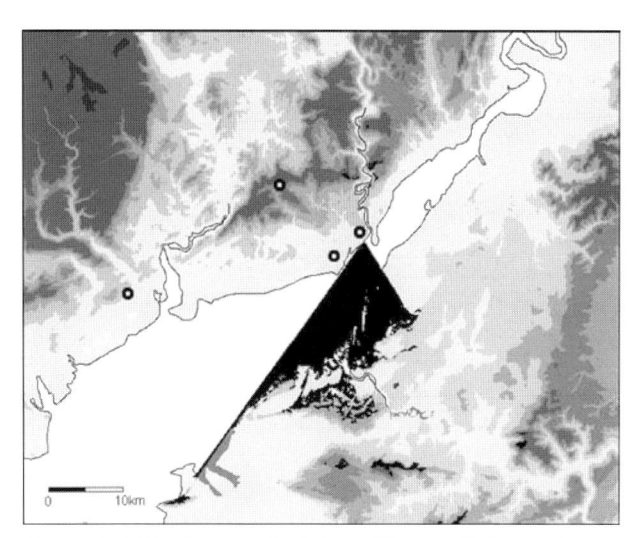

Figure 8.179 The viewshed from Thornwell Farm. Reproduced by kind permission of Ordnance Survey. © Crown copyright NC/03/20516.

Reference: Children and Nash 1996, 38–40.

BLACK MOUNTAINS

91 Pen-y-wyrlod, Llanigon
92 Little Lodge
93 Ffostyll North
94 Ffostyll South
95 Ty Isaf
96 Ty Illtyd
97 Gwernvale
98 Pipton
99 Mynydd Troed
100 Garn Goch
101 Penywyrlod, Talgarth
102 Clyro
103 Arthur's Stone
104 Cross Lodge

The following texts discuss the monuments of the Black Mountains. Some of these also have more detailed information on individual sites and these are listed at the end of each entry where relevant. Britnell and Savory 1984; Burnham 1995; Corcoran 1969; Cummings, Jones and Watson 2002; Daniel 1950; Darvill 1982; Fleming 1999; Grimes 1936a; Grimes 1936b; Lynch 2000a; Nash 1997; Olding 2000; RCAHMW 1997; Tilley 1994; Wysocki and Whittle 2000.

91. Pen-y-wyrlod, Llanigon (BRE 1) SO 225 399

Description: This monument is located at 250m OD on the side of a hill in rough pasture. The landscape to the S of the site has been altered by quarrying (RCAHMW 1997, 60). The site survives as four large sandstone orthostats which create a rectangular chamber. Two other upright stones are found to the W of the main chamber and these seem to be the remains of a second chamber. All the orthostats are set in a turfed mound. The site was partially excavated in the early 1920s and produced the remains of at least 20 people. However, there may have been more than one phase at the site and it is not clear how many of these bones come from the primary deposits (RCAHMW 1997, 61). Pottery, flint and animal bone were also found (Morgan and Marshall 1921). The shape of the mound led Corcoran to suggest that it may have been constructed in two separate phases (Corcoran 1969, 43).

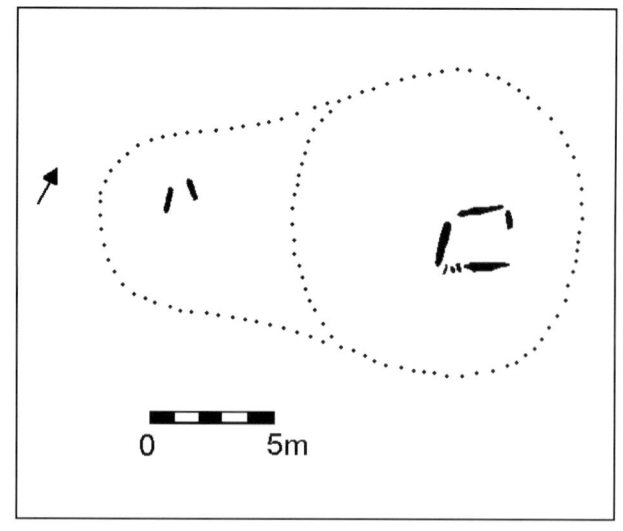

Figure 8.180 Plan of Pen-y-wyrlod, Llanigon (after Corcoran 1969).

Landscape setting: There a restricted view to the S of this monument, with views looking up the hill on which the site stands. To the W there are wide views out over the Wye Valley and the River Wye is visible to the NW. Behind the valley are higher mountains. The more immediate hills of Mouse Castle and Cusop Hill are visible to the NE. Most of the Black Mountains are actually blocked from view and this includes Hay Bluff which is behind a rise in the hill.

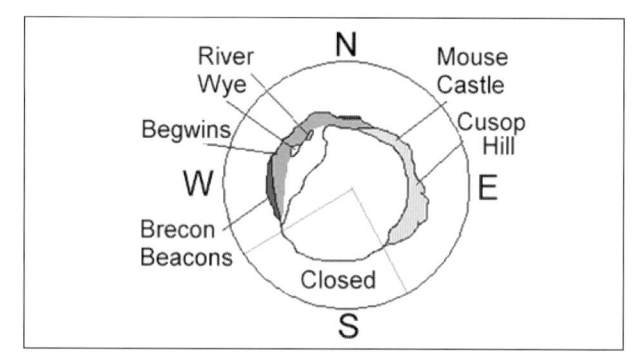

Figure 8.181 The setting of Penywyrlod.

References: Burnham 1995, 13; Corcoran 1969, 43; Morgan and Marshall 1921; RCAHMW 1997, 60–2.

92. Little Lodge (BRE 2) SO 182 380

Description: Located at 130m OD this site is set in a field just above a stream which runs to the River Wye. The site is located on the lower slopes of a hill which has a tumulus set on its summit. The site survives as a number of quite sizeable uprights set within a mound. The site was excavated in the 1920s and revealed a large chamber set at the centre of the mound. A pair of smaller chambers were also found to the S (Vulliamy 1929). The main chamber contained a number of human bones which represent at least eight individuals. Charcoal, red deer, sheep and cattle bones were also found. The smaller southern chambers produced only one flint flake (RCAHMW 1997).

Landscape setting: The view to the N is restricted, looking up at the hill on which the monument is set. There are wider views out to the SW, looking out to the Black Mountains scarp. A local hill is dominant to the SW before there are wider views of the Wye Valley to the W.

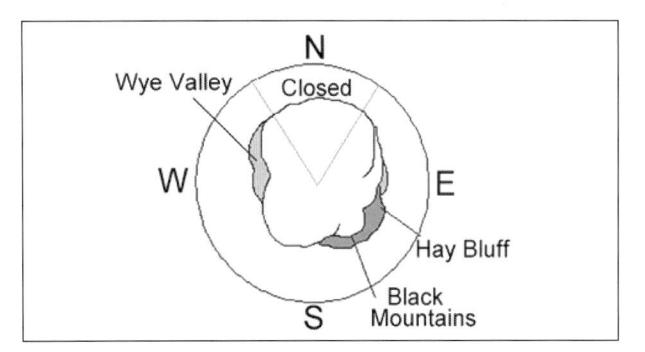

Figure 8.183 The setting of Little Lodge.

References: RCAHMW 1997, 51–3; Vulliamy 1929.

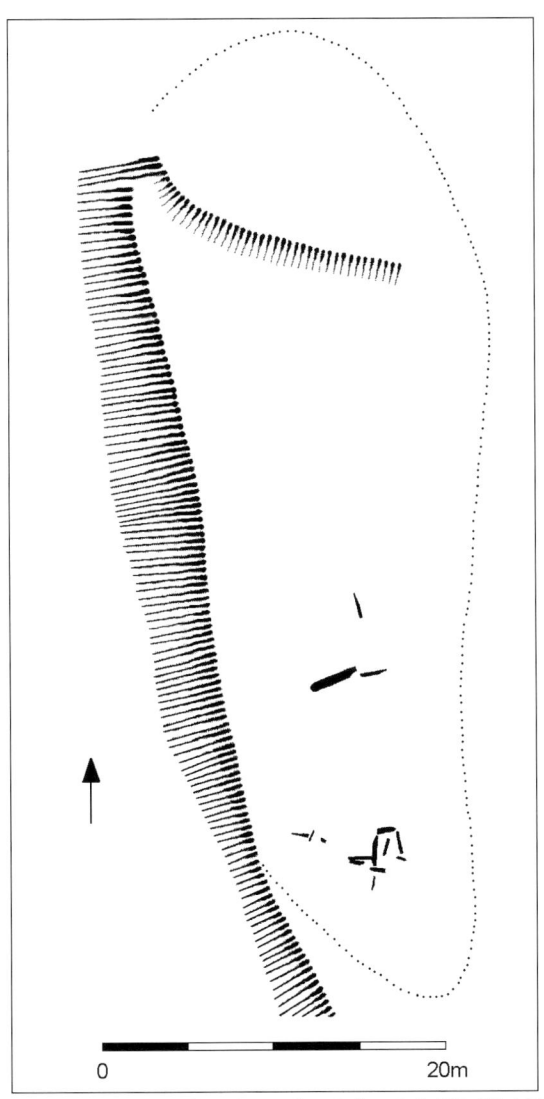

Figure 8.182 Plan of Little Lodge (after RCAHMW 1997).

93. Ffostyll North (BRE 3) S179 350

Description: Located at 310m OD this site is in the centre of a small field only a short distance from Ffostyll South. Set on the south-eastern side of a hill this site is very much on the edge of the Black Mountains. The site survives as a large mound with 5 upright slabs defining the eastern chamber. A number of other large slabs lie on the mound. The site has been excavated (Vulliamy 1923), although the eastern chamber had been emptied before excavation. A central chamber was revealed which contained the bones of six or seven individuals as well as horse, dog, ox and pig remains, flint flakes and pottery. Another chamber to the W was also uncovered which contained the remains of four people, animal bones and a flint flake (Vulliamy 1923). Corcoran (1969, 43) suggests that the cairn may be multi-phase, and that the northern and eastern chambers may originally have been in their own smaller cairns.

Landscape setting: The view is restricted from the NW round almost to the E, although the Wye Hills are just visible to the NNW. The rest of the view has wide vistas of the Black Mountains and the Brecon Beacons. Twmpa is visible to the E, and Mynydd Troed is prominent to the S. Pen y Fan can clearly be seen to the SW. The position of the monument means that there is a restricted view to one side of the monument and a wide-ranging view to the other.

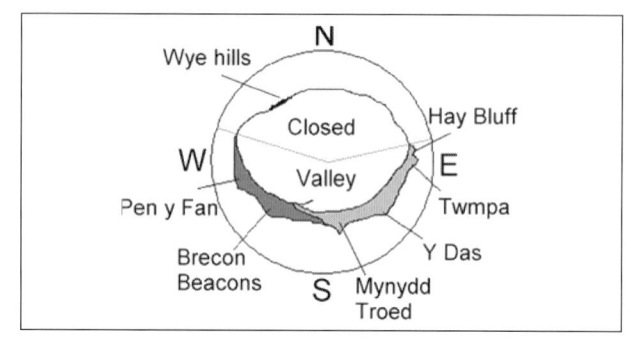

Figure 8.185 The setting of Ffostyll North.

References: Corcoran 1969, 43; RCAHMW 1997, 43–6; Tilley 1994, 134; Vulliamy 1923.

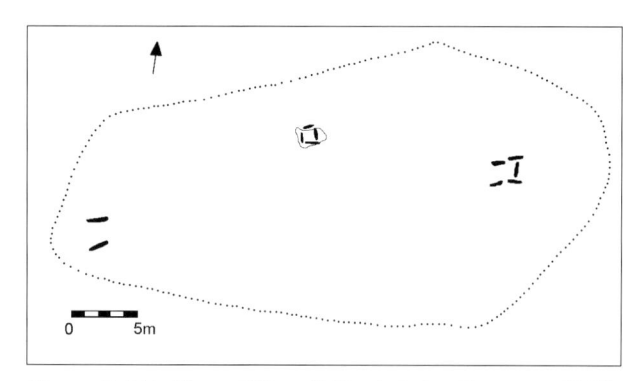

Figure 8.184 Plan of Ffostyll North (after Corcoran 1969).

94. Ffostyll South (BRE 4) SO 179 349

Description: Set at 310m OD, this site lies a few metres downslope from Ffostyll North. A number of sandstone slabs survive in the northern part of the cairn which make up the remains of a chamber. Before the monument was excavated, it is claimed that this site produced a number of human bones (RCAHMW 1997, 41). Two layers of bone were found in the chamber. The upper layer contained human and animal bone, while the lower layer consisted of a large quantity of human bone with animal bone. In the body of the mound were additional burials, which included a child cremation, as well as animal bone, pottery and flint (RCAHMW 1997, 41). At least nine people were represented from the bone evidence which includes both the inhumations and cremations (Vulliamy 1921).

Landscape setting: Although the two monuments are only 50m apart, the view from Ffostyll South is different from the monument to the N. Since it is set lower down the hillside, more of the view is restricted, from the WSW to the ESE. Ffostyll North is visible on the horizon to the NE. There are wide views of the Black Mountains and Beacons from this site as at Ffostyll North.

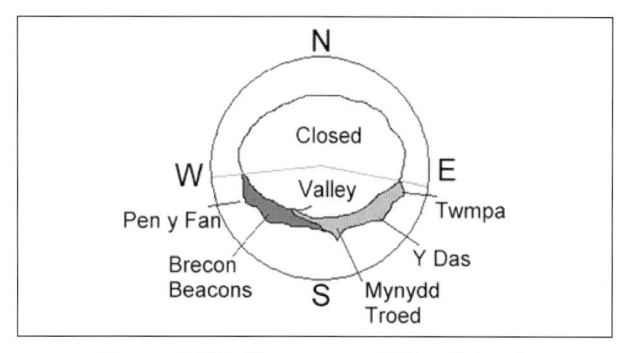

Figure 8.187 The setting of Ffostyll South.

References: Corcoran 1969, 45; RCAHMW 1997, 41–2; Tilley 1994, 134; Vulliamy 1921; Vulliamy 1923.

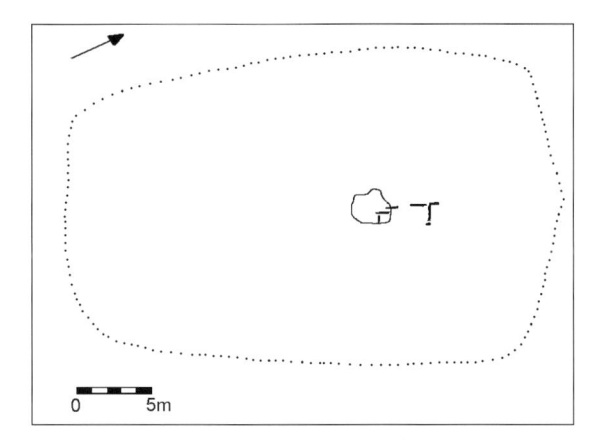

Figure 8.186 Plan of Ffostyll South (after Corcoran 1969).

95. Ty Isaf (BRE 5) SO 182 291

Description: Set at 265m OD in the valley between Mynydd Troed and Pen Trumau, this site is set between two streams which form the River Rhiangoll. The monument is located in the middle of a small field in a farm. It is in poor condition, and very little is visible on the surface: only a few of the larger slabs of the chambers. The rear cist is the most visible structural part of the monument. The site has been excavated (Grimes 1939) and revealed a wedge-shaped cairn with extra-revetment. A false portal was found to the N of the site. A pair of chambers were found with passages to the E and W respectively. The western chamber contained the remains of at least 17 people, as well as leaf-shaped arrowheads, a complete stone axe, a bone pin and pottery. This chamber also had evidence of Beaker re-use. The eastern chamber contained the remains of only one individual, although there were two burials in the passage and a small green sandstone disk. Pottery was also found in this chamber. Excavation also revealed a double-walled rotunda containing a large transepted chamber. This contained the remains of nine people and pottery. Finally, a fourth chamber was found to the S of the cairn which was badly damaged but contained cremated bone and a Bronze Age urn. Animal bones were also recovered from the site and included the remains of ox, sheep or goat, pig and dog (Grimes 1939, 130). The excavator believed that this was a single-phase construction. However, Corcoran suggests that the cairn may be multi-phase. He suggests that the rotunda was inserted at a later date, although the possibility that the rotunda was the first phase is also considered (Corcoran 1969, 94).

Landscape setting: This monument is located to have quite restricted views in most directions. The nearby hill of Mynydd Troed is visible to the SW, and this is the closest view at the site. To the NW Castell Dinas is prominent and then the Black Mountains themselves are visible including Pen Trumau almost directly E and Pen Allt-Mawr directly S. To the E the landscape drops down steeply to the Rhiangoll streams. Mynydd Troed monument is only 2km away but is on the other side of Mynydd Troed itself and so is not visible.

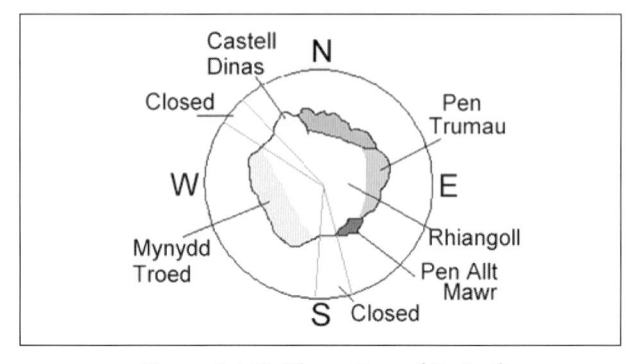

Figure 8.189 The setting of Ty Isaf.

References: Corcoran 1969, 84–90; Grimes 1939; RCAHMW 1997, 36–8.

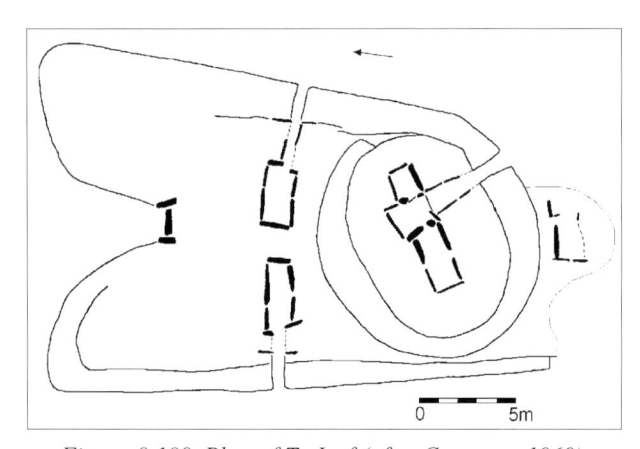

Figure 8.188 Plan of Ty Isaf (after Corcoran 1969).

96. Ty Illtyd (BRE 6) SO 098 264

Description: This site is located at 320m OD and is the most westerly of the Black Mountains group. The site is positioned on the side of Ty Elltud hill above the River Usk. The monument is set in the middle of a field. It is well preserved and consists of a chamber with capstone set in a long mound. The site has never been excavated although the chamber seems to have been cleared out in antiquity, and the cairn has also been quarried (RCAHMW 1997, 31). An interesting feature of this monument are the inscriptions on the stones. There are many crosses, and it is claimed, two possible inscribed dates, 1311 or 1312 and 1510. It is possible that this tomb was a place of pilgrimage in the medieval period or a hermit's dwelling (Burnham 1995, 14).

Landscape setting: There are really spectacular views of both the Black Mountains and the Brecon Beacons from this monument. To the N there is a restricted view with Mynydd Troed distinctive to the NE. To the SW the two peaks of Pen y Fan and Fan y Big are visible with the Usk Valley in the foreground. The River Usk is also clearly visible. The axis of the monument means that the Black Mountains are visible to one side, opposed by the Brecon Beacons the other.

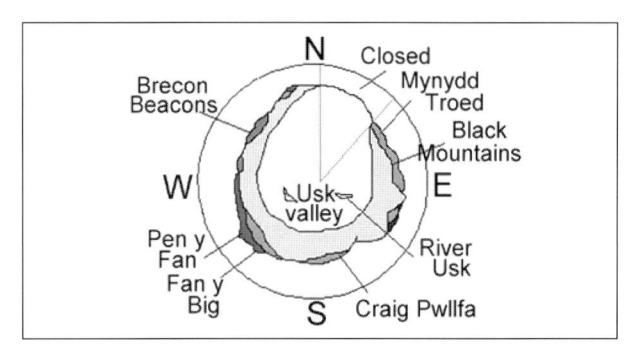

Figure 8.191 The setting of Ty Illtyd.

References: Burnham 1995, 13–14; Corcoran 1969, 66; RCAHMW 1997, 31–4.

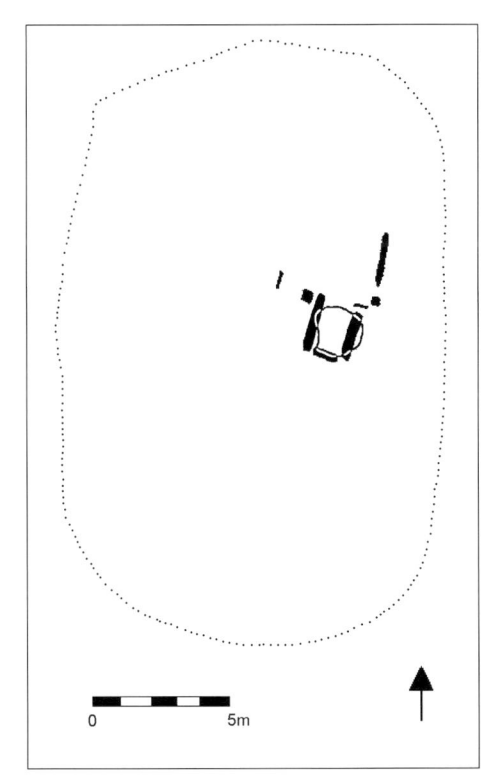

Figure 8.190 Plan of Ty Illtyd (after Corcoran 1969).

97. Gwernvale (BRE 7) SO 211 192

Description: Positioned at 75m OD, this site is located in a grass verge next to the A40. The site stands above the River Usk on the edge of Crickhowell. The cairn is no longer visible, but is marked out by concrete posts. Part of the cairn lies under the road. Only the large stones of the southern chamber now survive on the ground. The site has been excavated (Britnell and Savory 1984) and has added a wealth of information to our knowledge of this site. The monument itself had been damaged over the years, with the SE chamber emptied out by antiquaries in 1804 (they found charcoal and bones). The excavation revealed an additional three chambers, two opposite one another to the SW and NE, and a further chamber to the W which was mostly destroyed. These four chambers were set within a trapezoidal long cairn with a false portal. The remains of at least three individuals were recovered as well as pottery, an arrowhead fragment and a flint core. After about 600 years of use, the passages were blocked and the outer revetment was pulled down (Britnell and Savory 1984). The excavation of Gwernvale also revealed pre-cairn activity. This included both Palaeolithic and Mesolithic flint assemblages and the remains of Neolithic activity dating to around 3900 BC (Britnell and Savory 1984, 152). The traces of two rectangular buildings were found as well as lithics, quern fragments, pot sherds and charred organic remains. However, these may well be the remains of mortuary practices as domestic activity, and this suggestion is supported by the fact that two parallel rows of six post-holes in the forecourt are found on the same axis as the stone monument.

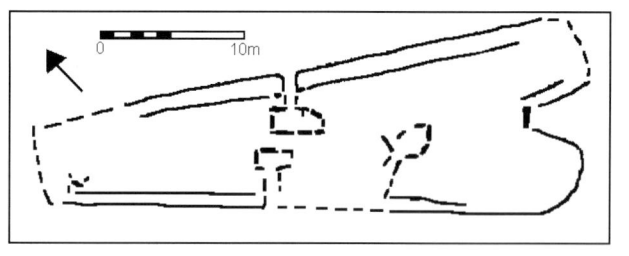

Figure 8.192 Plan of Gwernvale (after Britnell and Savory 1984).

Landscape setting: Only a small portion of the landscape is a restricted view with most views being wide and expansive looking out over the Usk Valley with mountains behind. To the W distant hills and mountains are visible including Graig and Cerrig Calch. The distinctive form of Table Mountain can also be seen to the N.

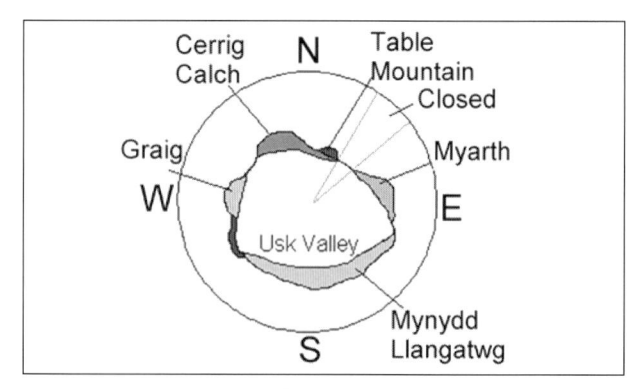

Figure 8.193 The setting of Gwernvale.

References: Britnell and Savory 1984; Burnham 1995, 15–16; RCAHMW 1997, 56–60.

98. Pipton (BRE 8) SO 160 373

Description: Set at 150m OD, this site is on the eastern side of a gentle hill. The site overlooks the Afon Llynfi to the E and the River Wye to the N. The site is located in a field and Little Lodge is only 2km to the NE, and the Ffostyll cairns 3km to the SE. The site is poorly preserved and at present consists of two stones, one of which is only just above the level of the turf. Several trees are growing on the denuded cairn, and there are the remains of other tree stumps. The site was excavated in 1949 (Savory 1956) and revealed a wedge-shaped cairn with extra-revetment. The cairn had a false portal and two chambers. The first of the chambers was an enclosed cist, which would only have been accessible by removing the capstone. This chamber contained seven discrete heaps of human bone, which represent at least nine individuals (Wysocki and Whittle 2000). The second chamber was divided into three compartments and contained a ritual pit as well as human bone, animal bone, flint, hazelnuts and decayed organic objects (Savory 1956). There was also evidence of internal revetment walls as at Ty Isaf. There is the suggestion that this site may also be a multi-phase construction (Corcoran 1969, 87).

Landscape setting: Almost a third of the view is restricted, looking up the hill on which the monument stands. The view then opens up to look out over the Wye Valley to the N with hills beyond. There are clear views of the Black Mountains scarp and Hay Bluff and Twmpa are particularly prominent. Mynydd Troed is just visible before the landscape becomes more restricted by the immediate topography. The wider views to the E are quite different to the restricted views to the SW, and this ties in with the overall axis of the monument.

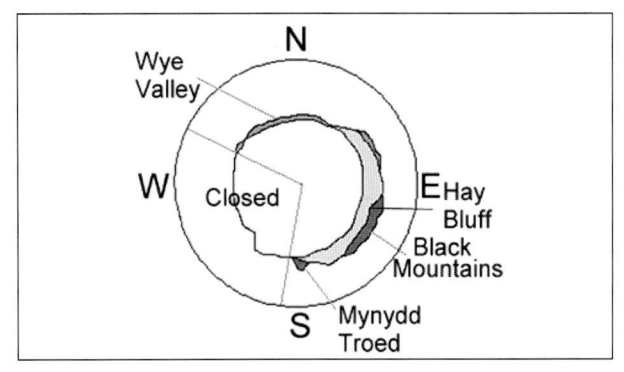

Figure 8.195 The setting of Pipton.

References: Corcoran 1969, 65–6; Savory 1956; RCAHMW 1997, 48–51.

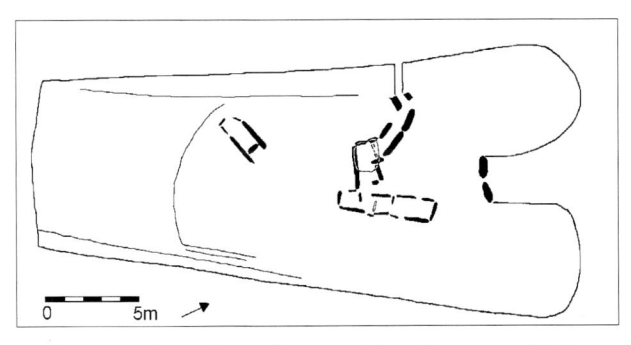

Figure 8.194 Plan of Pipton (after Corcoran 1969).

99. Mynydd Troed (BRE 10) SO 162 284

Description: This site is positioned at 350m OD and is positioned on the lower western slopes of Mynydd Troed. The monument is in open unenclosed moorland and is only a few hundred metres from a stream which runs down the hillside to form the Afon Rhiangoll. The site survives as a large grassy hillock with a few slabs just visible above the turf-line. Two small trenches have been excavated on the edge of the mound (Crampton and Webley 1966), but the one definite and two possible chambers have not been touched. These excavations demonstrated that the landscape had been heath and open woodland when the monument was constructed. The surface vegetation had been burnt before the cairn was built. The excavation also produced flint flakes and pottery.

Landscape setting: The landscape seems to be divided quite neatly into two halves with the two mountains of Mynydd Troed itself, on which the monument stands, visible to the N and Cockit Hill visible to the S. Directly to the E the hill of Pen Allt Mawr is visible, while opposing that to the W is Llangorse Lake, the valley around Llangorse and the Brecon Beacons.

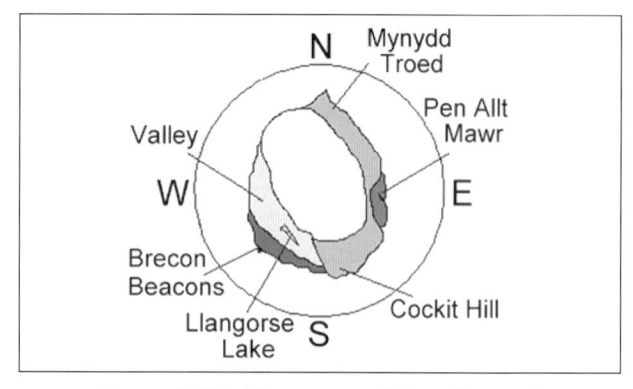

Figure 8.197 The setting of Mynydd Troed.

References: Burnham 1995, 14–15; Crampton and Webley 1966; RCAHMW 1997.

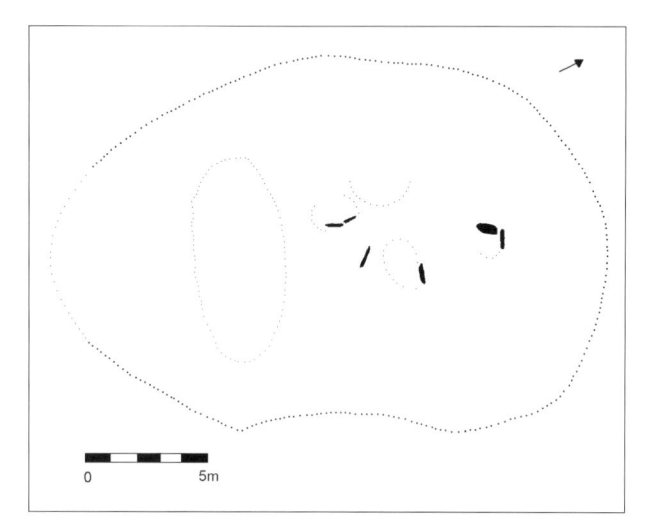

Figure 8.196 Plan of Mynydd Troed (after Grimes 1936).

100. Garn Goch (BRE 12) SO 212 177

Description: Set at 85m OD, this site is located in a public park in Llangattock. The site now stands between the River Usk to the N and the Monmouthshire and Brecon Canal to the S. Gwernvale is only 1.5km to the N. The site survives as a large grassy mound with a large slab near the top. The site has not been excavated, but when it was discovered in 1847 it is claimed that a cist or cromlech was uncovered which contained human remains (RCAHMW 1997, 54).

Landscape setting: There are wide-ranging views in all directions as the site is set just above the River Usk. Table Mountain and Sugar Loaf Mountain are particularly distinctive on the horizon with their flat-topped profiles, and Mynydd Llangatwg is also prominent to the S.

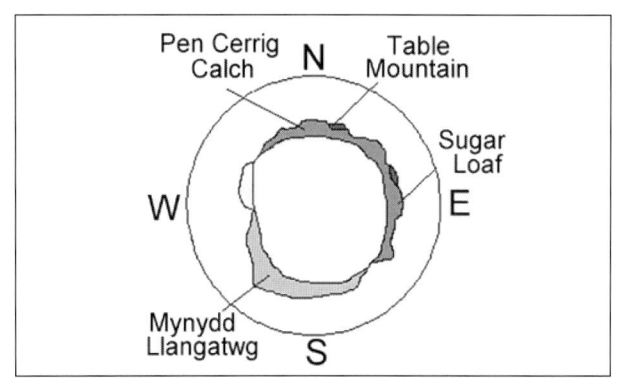

Figure 8.199 The setting of Garn Goch.

References: Burnham 1995, 17; RCAHMW 1997, 54–6.

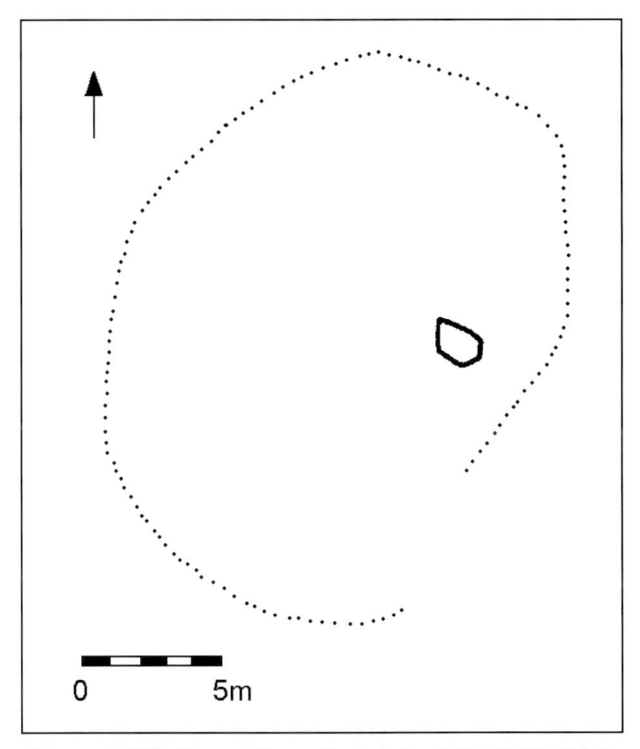

Figure 8.198 Plan of Garn Goch (after RCAHMW 1997).

101. Penywyrlod, Talgarth SO 150 316

Description: This site is located at 255m OD in an enclosure in a field. The Afon Llynfi is 1km from the site to the W, and the monuments of Ffostyll, Ty Isaf and Mynydd Troed are all within 5km of the site, to the NE, SE and S respectively. The site is reasonably well-preserved, although there is a large chunk of the cairn missing to the SE, destroyed by quarrying. It is possible to see some of the chambers, and the cairn itself is enormous. The site was discovered in 1972 and the disturbed areas only have been excavated. One chamber has been found to the SW and three to the NE, all of which were damaged before excavation. They are set within a reveted cairn with a false portal and produced disarticulated human and animal bone, a flint knife, pottery and a possible bone flute (Britnell and Savory 1984). It seems likely that more chambers survive intact.

Landscape setting: There are spectacular views of the surrounding landscape from this site. The Brecon Beacons are visible to the W and it is possible to see the peak of Pen y Fan. There are wide views out to the Wye Valley and beyond to the NW. The hill of Parkwood is visible to the NNE and this has the two Ffostyll cairns on it (4.5km away). To the E and S the Black Mountains are visible, with Hay Bluff, Y Das, Y Grib and Mynydd Troed particularly dominant. To the SW there is a restricted view. The façade itself seems to be aligned on the gap between the mountains of Y Grib and Mynydd Troed.

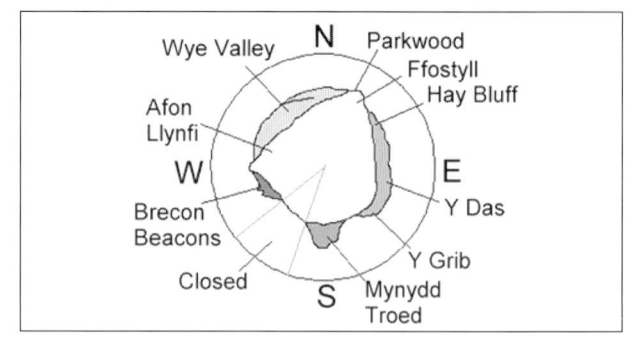

Figure 8.201 The setting of Penywyrlod, Talgarth.

References: Britnell and Savory 1984; RCAHMW 1997, 38–40; Savory 1973.

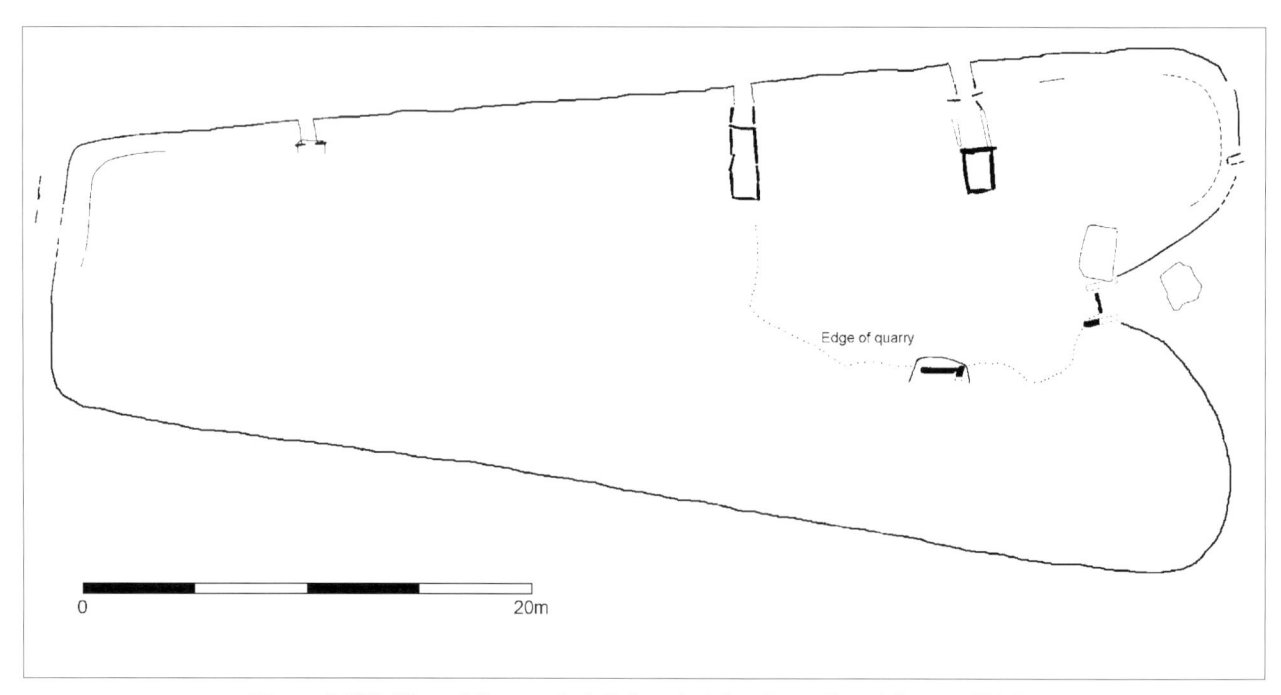

Figure 8.200 Plan of Penywyrlod, Talgarth (after Britnell and Savory 1984).

102. Clyro SO 212 431

Description: This site is positioned at 60m OD in a field close to Court Farm. Positioned on the lower slopes of Clyro Hill, the site is on the edge of a terrace which drops steeply to the SE. The site overlooks the Wye Valley and river. The site survives as a grassy mound with six reasonably sizeable stones visible near the surface. The site has never been excavated and was only recognised in 1973 (RCAHMW 1997, 63), but the area has produced many flints and a stone axe.

Landscape setting: Approximately half of the view from this site is of the immediate landscape including Clyro Hill. The other half is much more wide-ranging with clear views out over the Wye Valley. To the E Mouse Castle is visible, with the peaks of the Black Mountains dominant from the SE to the SW. Mynydd Troed is visible to the WSW and a small part of the Brecon Beacons is just visible before the view becomes more restricted. The landscape setting also ties in with the axis of the monument, with a restricted view to one side of the cairn and wide open views to the other.

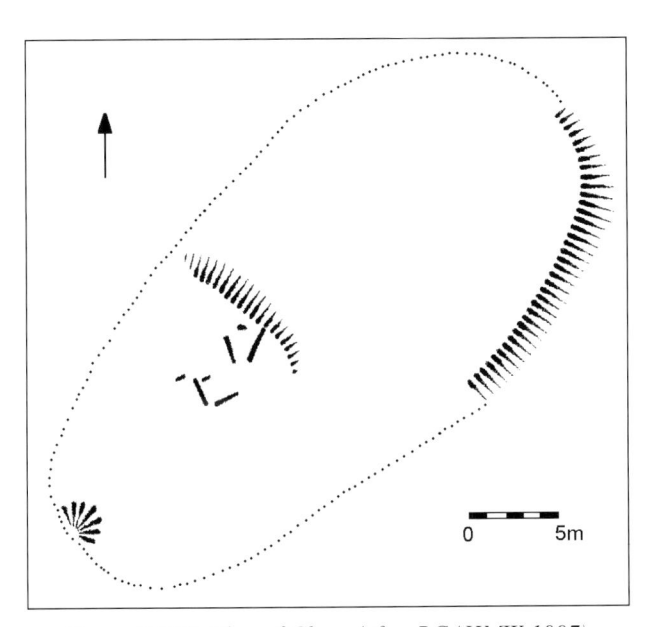

Figure 8.202 Plan of Clyro (after RCAHMW 1997).

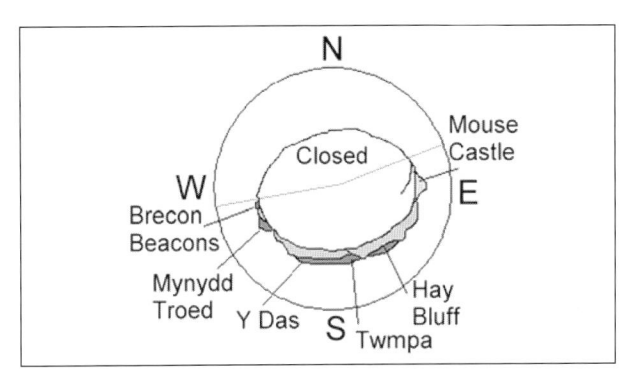

Figure 8.203 The setting of Clyro.

Reference: RCAHMW 1997, 63–4.

198 *Vicki Cummings*

103. Arthur's Stone (HRF 1) SO 319 431

Description: Set at 270m OD on the southern side of Bredwardine Hill, the site is presently in a small fenced enclosure next to a small road. The site is well preserved and consists of a large chamber covered with two capstones. The stones of the passage are also clearly visible, as are the large stones behind the main chamber area.

Landscape setting: The view from the N to the NE is restricted and cuts off a view of the Wye Valley. Instead there are wide views out over the Golden Valley to the S. Dorstone Hill is visible to the E which has Neolithic settlement activity (Olding 2000, 12). Particularly prominent on the horizon are Graig Syfyrddin, Mynydd Merddin, Ysgyrydd Fawr and Hay Bluff. Clyro Hill is just visible before the view becomes more restricted.

Figure 8.204 Plan of Arthur's Stone (after Grimes 1936).

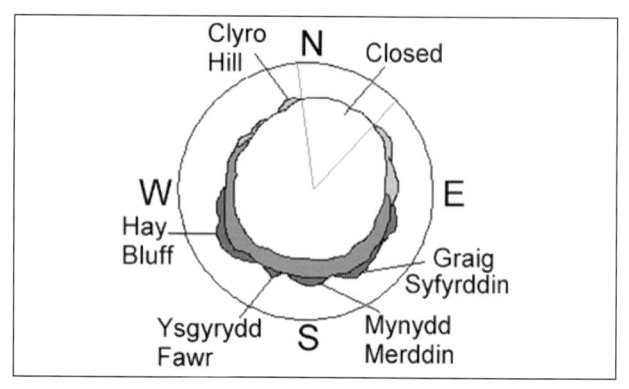

Figure 8.205 The setting of Arthur's Stone.

References: Hemp 1935; Tilley 1994, 140.

104. Cross Lodge (HRF 4) SO 323 417

Description: Set at 170m OD on the side of a gentle hill, this site is located in farmland, set within its own enclosure in a field. The site is only 2km from the River Wye, but it looks out over the Golden Valley to the SW. The River Dore runs beneath the monument to the SW, and Arthur's Stone is only 2km to the NW. The site survives as a large grassy mound with several large trees growing out of it. The site has never been excavated.

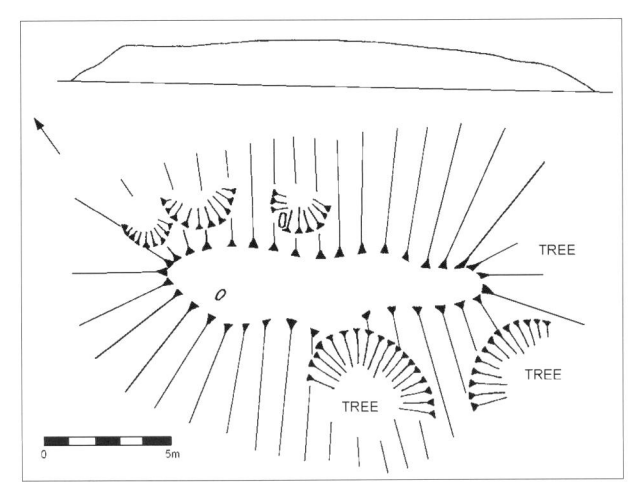

Figure 8.206 Plan and elevation of Cross Lodge (after Olding 2000).

Landscape setting: The view from this site can be divided into two halves. From the WNW to the ESE the view looks up to hill on which the monument stands (Woodbury Hill) thus creating a more restricted view. The rest of the view looks out over the Dore Valley with the Black Mountains scarp visible behind. Dorstone Hill is visible before the view becomes more enclosed, and this is the hill with Neolithic activity on it (Olding 2000, 12). This division of the landscape into two halves fits in with the axis of the long cairn, which effectively means that there are more expansive views to one side of the monument, and more restricted views to the other.

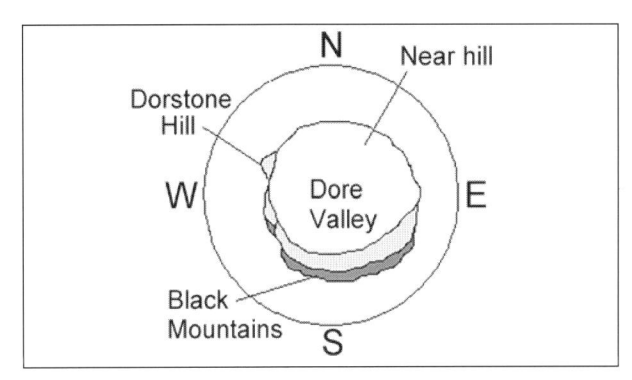

Figure 8.207 The setting of Cross Lodge.

Reference: Nash 1997, 24–5.

Colour plate 1 The summit of Carn Meini, Preselis, south-west Wales

Colour plate 2 Carreg Coetan with the Afon Nyfer visible to the left

Colour plate 3 One of the chambers at Mynydd Llangynderyn, Carmarthenshire, which stands against outcrops

Colour plate 4 Carreg Samson, south-west Wales

Colour plate 5 Pentre Ifan, south-west Wales

Colour plate 6 The distinctive summit of Carn Llidi on St. David's peninsula, south-west Wales

Colour plate 7 Snowdonia, as seen from Bodowyr

Colour plate 8 Plas Newydd with Snowdonia in the distance

Colour plate 9 Bryn Celli Ddu, with the large outcrop visible to the left of the monument

Colour plate 10 The Black Mountain escarpment

Colour plate 11 Parc le Breos Cwm, Gower

Colour plate 12 St Lythans, near Cardiff

Colour plate 13 The view of Carn Ingli through trees in the summer

Colour plate 14 The view of Carn Ingli through trees in the winter

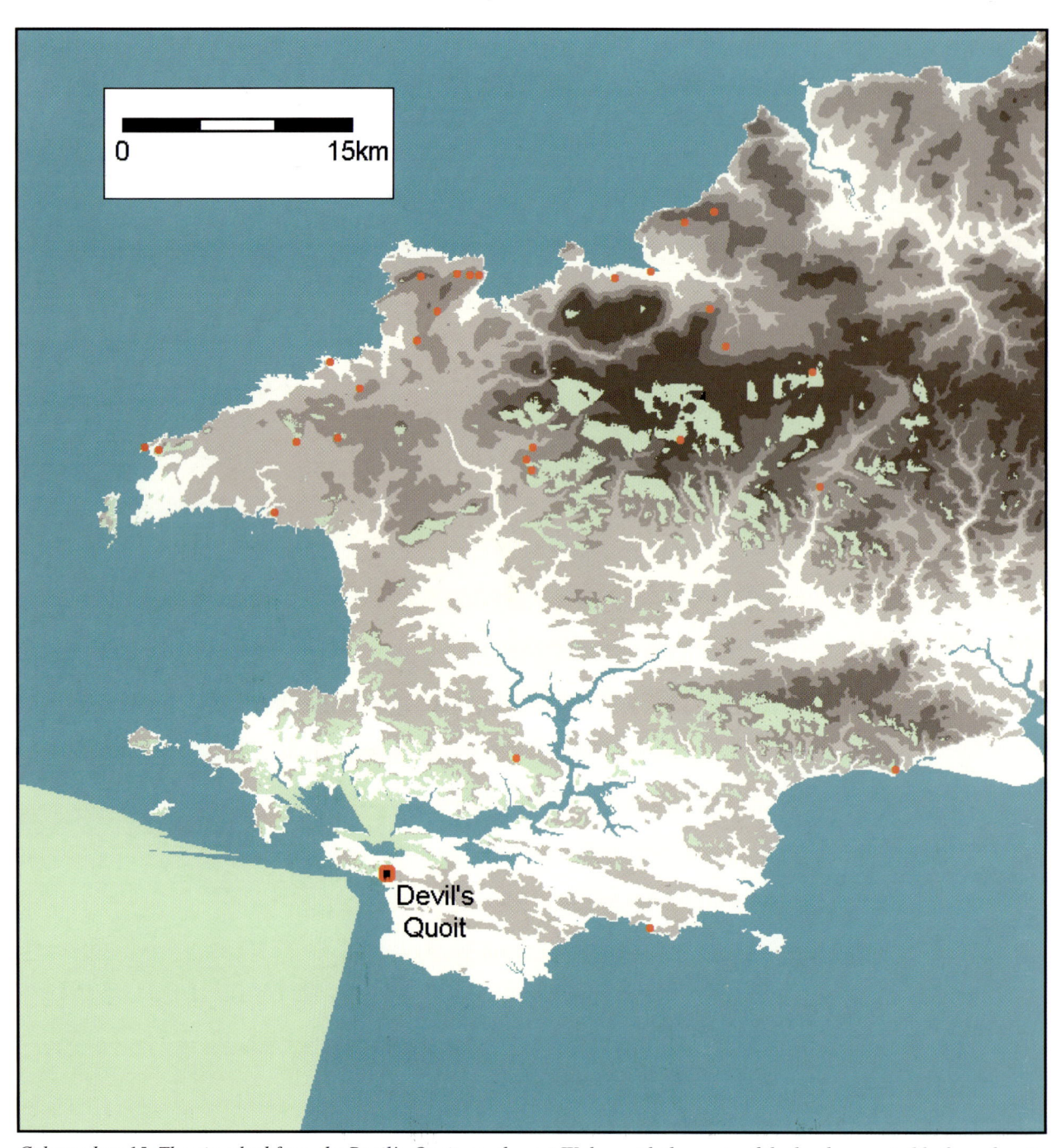

Colour plate 15 The viewshed from the Devil's Quoit, south-west Wales, with the parts of the landscape visible from the site in green